Cypriot Nationalisms in Context

Thekla Kyritsi · Nikos Christofis
Editors

Cypriot Nationalisms in Context

History, Identity and Politics

Editors
Thekla Kyritsi
Political Science and History
Panteion University of Social
and Political Sciences
Athens, Greece

Nikos Christofis
Center for Turkish Studies and School
of History and Civilization
Shaanxi Normal University
Xi'an, China

ISBN 978-3-319-97803-1   ISBN 978-3-319-97804-8   (eBook)
https://doi.org/10.1007/978-3-319-97804-8

Library of Congress Control Number: 2018950734

This Palgrave Macmillan imprint is published by the registered company Springer Nature Switzerland AG
The registered company address is: Gewerbestrasse 11, 6330 Cham, Switzerland

ACKNOWLEDGEMENTS

The present volume derives from a conference organized in Nicosia, Cyprus, under the title *The Emergence and Development of Nationalisms in Cyprus*. The conference—held on April 27, 2013—was organized by Petros Nikolaou and Thekla Kyritsi together with the Association for Historical Dialogue and Research. The idea of the present volume was originally developed by Nikolaou and Kyritsi. However, the final outcome does not resemble much the initial idea, as is almost always the case with such endeavors, where a lot of time is needed to bring the project to fruition and other obligations inevitably intervene. Nevertheless, Petros Nikolaou's contribution to the idea and the first stages of the project was crucial and we would like to thank him for that. Without him this project would not be possible.

In addition, we would like to express our appreciation to the late Rolandos Katsiaounis (1954–2014), one of the most prolific historians of Cyprus, who participated in the initial conference and warmly encouraged the organizers to collect its material for publication. Although he will never see the final outcome of the book, his presence through his work is palpable.

We would also like to thank all the contributors to this volume for their impeccable collaboration throughout the different stages of the project as well as the Historical Labour Museum of the Pancyprian Federation of Labour (PEO) for providing the copyright permission to reproduce the image on the cover of the book. Thanks also go to the PROMITHEAS Research Institute for the picture of

Rolandos Katsiaounis (Fig. 12.1) and to all the people at Palgrave and the reviewers of the chapters.

Nikos Christofis would like to thank his partner in life, Liana, for her continuous support (and patience) throughout the writing and editing process of this volume. Thekla Kyritsi would like to thank her husband, Giorgos, and her parents, Kriti and Pambis, for each of them has been an endless source of warm encouragement throughout the making of this project. She'd also like to deeply thank Savvas for his continuous feedback and support.

As a collective volume dealing with controversial and highly political issues, this book includes different and often contradictory views on the Cyprus issue. Without necessarily agreeing with every position, the editors have included all perspectives and opinions, as expressed by each individual author. Finally, the editors would like to note that both editors contributed equally in the preparation of the volume, as well as in the introduction of the book.

CONTENTS

Part IV   The Local and the Global

NOTES ON CONTRIBUTORS

Alexios Alecou is teaching History at the University of Cyprus and has been a Fellow at the Institute of Commonwealth Studies of University of London. He is the author of the books *Communism and Nationalism in Postwar Cyprus* (Palgrave Macmillan, 2016) and *1948: The Greek Civil War and Cyprus* (Power Publishers, 2012). Current work includes the study of post-war Greece and Cyprus, contemporary political history and British colonialism.

Mustafa Çıraklı is the deputy director of the Near East Institute at Near East University. He completed his doctoral studies in Politics at Lancaster University (UK). During this time, he taught on various undergraduate and postgraduate courses at Lancaster University and the University of Manchester on comparative politics, IR theory and European studies. His primary areas of interest lie in the fields of identity, immigration and citizenship. His more recent work is on unrecognized states and kin-states in international relations which has grown out of his work on local responses toward patron-states and their role in constructing counter-hegemonic/hybrid identities.

Nikos Christofis is an Assistant Professor at the Center for Turkish Studies and at the School of History and Civilization at Shaanxi Normal University, Xi'an, China. He has published extensively in peer-reviewed journals and edited volumes in Greek, Turkish, English and Spanish. He is the author of Turkey in the Long Sixties: *The Left and the*

Radicalization of the Student Movement and edited, and contributed to, *Cyprus, the Left and (Post)Colonialism* (both in Greek). He is a member of the editorial board of the journal *New Middle Eastern Studies*.

Maria Ioannou is a Lecturer at the University College Groningen, in the Netherlands. Prior to her appointment, she was a postdoctoral researcher at the University of Cyprus and a Senior Researcher at the inter-communal NGO 'SeeD' in Cyprus. Her research interests fall in the area of Conflict Resolution more broadly, and intergroup contact and prejudice reduction more specifically.

Dimitris Kalantzopoulos completed his Ph.D. in History at King's College London (Department of History and Centre for Hellenic Studies) in 2015. His thesis was titled *Competing Political Spaces in Colonial Cyprus, 1931–1950*.

Sossie Kasbarian is Senior Lecturer (Associate Professor) in Comparative Politics at the University of Stirling. Her research interests and publications broadly span diaspora studies; contemporary Middle East politics and society; nationalism and ethnicity; transnational political activism; refugee and migration studies. She is co-editor of the journal *Diaspora—A Journal of Transnational Studies*.

Angelos P. Kassianos is a postdoctoral Research Associate in the UCL, Department of Applied Health Research. He studied in Panteion University of Social and Political Sciences in Athens and obtained his Ph.D. in Health Psychology from the University of Surrey in the UK.

Yiannos Katsourides is the Director of the Prometheus Research Institute and teaches political Science at the University of Cyprus. His research interests include Cyprus and Greek politics, radical left and extreme right political parties and political participation. He is the author of three books: *The History of the Communist Party in Cyprus* (I.B. Tauris, 2014); *The Radical Left in Government: The Cases of SYRIZA and AKEL* (Palgrave Macmillan, 2016); *The Greek Cypriot Nationalist Right in the Era of British Colonialism* (Springer, 2017). His articles have appeared in *West European Politics, South European Society and Politics,* and in the *Journal of European Integration,* among others.

Şevki Kıralp was born in 1986 in Famagusta, Cyprus. He is an Assistant Professor of Political Science, having studied Modern Greek Language and Literature at Ankara University. He completed his Masters and

Doctoral degrees in Politics and International Relations at Keele University. He now teaches Politics and History at Near East University in Nicosia, Cyprus. His ongoing research covers the Cyprus question, Cypriot history and politics, Turkish history and politics, ethnic conflicts, and nationalism. He is also on the editorial board of the Turkish Cypriot journal *Gaile*.

Thekla Kyritsi is a Ph.D. candidate in Political Science and History at Panteion University of Social and Political Sciences in Athens, Greece. She has an interdisciplinary backgound of studies on history, social sciences, political theory and gender issues, and she has published academic chapters dealing with women's history in relation to gender, nationality and political ideology in Cyprus. She is a founding member of the Cypriot NGO Center for Gender Equality and History, where she currently works as a researcher.

Iliya Marovich-Old currently works at Flinders University in South Australia. After working in the Law early in his career he returned to his interest in History. He has researched and written about British Imperialism focusing on the Mediterranean and the Levant in the twentieth century. He completed his Ph.D. at Flinders University in 2016. His thesis is titled *Challenges to British Imperial Hegemony in the Mediterranean, 1919–1940*.

Petros Nikolaou is a Ph.D. candidate at the Turkish and Middle Eastern Studies Department, University of Cyprus. His dissertation topic is *Class, Nationalism and Intercommunal Relations in Cyprus, 1878–1954*.

Meltem Onurkan-Samani is an Assistant Professor of History at the European University of Lefke. She is currently the special adviser of the Turkish Cypriot leader Mustafa Akıncı on political affairs and history. She is a former co-president of the Association for Historical Dialogue and Research, Cyprus. Among her research interests are the impact of colonial policies on (political) culture of the (Turkish) Cypriots, the development of Turkish Cypriot nationalism, the role of history education and textbooks in Turkish Cypriot politics. She holds a B.Sc. and a Ph.D. in History, respectively, from the Middle East Technical University and Hacettepe University, Turkey.

Eugenia Palieraki received her Ph.D. from the Sorbonne (Paris) and she is associate professor in Latin American Studies at the University of

Cergy-Pontoise. Her current research focuses on political connections and the circulation of revolutionary ideas, practices and activism between Latin America and the Mediterranean. She is the co-editor of two volumes and four journal issues published in the UK, Chile, Argentina, and France. Her monograph *¡La revolución ya viene! El MIR chileno en los años 1960* was published by LOM Ediciones in Chile in 2014.

Andrekos Varnava FRHistS, is Associate Professor at the University of Flinders, Australia and Honorary Professor at De Montfort University, Leicester. He is the author of two books in the Studies in Imperialism Series of Manchester University Press: *Serving the Empire in the Great War: The Cypriot Mule Corps, Imperial Loyalty and Silenced Memory* (2017) and *British Imperialism in Cyprus, 1878–1915: The Inconsequential Possession* (2009; paperback, 2012) and has edited/co-edited six volumes. He has published articles in *English Historical Review, The Historical Journal, Historical Research, War in History, Itinerario, Britain and the World* and *First World War Studies*.

ABBREVIATIONS

AAPSO	Afro-Asian Peoples' Solidarity Organization
AKEL	[Ανορθωτικό Κόμμα Εργαζόμενου Λαού] The Progressive Party of the Working People
AKP	[Adalet ve Kalkınma Partisi] Justice and Development Party
CTP	[Cumhuriyetçi Türk Partisi] Republican Turkish Party (northern Cyprus)
DIKO	[Δημοκρατικό Κόμμα] Democratic Party (Cyprus)
DP	[Demokrat Parti] Democratic Party (northern Cyprus)
EAKX	[Εθνικόν Αγροτικόν Κόμμα Χιτών] National Agrarian Party of Chites
EAM	[Εθνικό Απελευθερωτικό Μέτωπο] National Liberation Front
EDA	[Ενιαία Δημοκρατική Αριστερά] United Democratic Left
EDEK	[Ενιαία Δημοκρατική Ένωση Κέντρου] United Democratic Union of Center
ELAM	[Εθνικό Λαϊκό Μέτωπο] National People's Front
ELAS	[Ελληνικός Λαϊκός Απελευθερωτικός Στρατός] The Greek People's Liberation Army
Enosis	Union with Greece
EOKA	[Εθνική Οργάνωσις Κυπρίων Αγωνιστών] National Organization of Cypriot Fighters
Evkaf	Muslim charitable endowment
GD	[Χρυσή Αυγή] Golden Dawn

KKE	[Κομμουνιστικό Κόμμα Ελλάδας] Communist Party of Greece
KKK or CPC	[Κομμουνιστικό Κόμμα Κύπρου] Communist Party of Cyprus
Kurtuluş Savaşı	Turkish War of Independence
NAM	Non-Aligned Movement
National Party of Chites	Εθνικό Κόμμα Χιτών ("X")
NATO	North Atlantic Treaty Organization
NGO	Non-Governmental Organization
PAK	[Πανελλήνιο Απελευθερωτικό Κίνημα] Panhellenic Liberation Movement
PASOK	[Πανελλήνιο Σοσιαλιστικό Κίνημα] Panhellenic Socialist Movement
PEO	[Παγκύπρια Εργατική Ομοσπονδία] Pancyprian Federation of Labour
PIO	[Γραφείο Τύπου και Πληροφοριών] Press and Information Office
SEK	[Συνομοσπονδία Εργαζομένων Κύπρου] Cyprus Workers' Confederation
Taksim	Partition
TİP	[Türkiye İşçi Partisi] Workers' Party of Turkey
TKP	[Toplumcu Kurtuluş Partisi] Communal Salvation Party (northern Cyprus)
TKP	[Türkiye Komünist Partisi] Communist Party of Turkey
TMT	[Türk Mukavement Teşkilatı] The Turkish Resistance Organization (Cyprus)
UBP	[Ulusal Birlik Partisi] National Unity Party (northern Cyprus)
UN	The United Nations

LIST OF FIGURES

CHAPTER 1

Introduction: Cypriot Nationalism(s) in Context

Nikos Christofis and Thekla Kyritsi

The word "nation" stems from the Latin verb *nasci*, "to be born," initially coined to define a group of people native to the same area. The word has assumed various meanings throughout the centuries: Once referring to students coming from the same region or country, it later acquired a new sense as a designation of the social elite representing any political or spiritual authority in the medieval arrangement (Dieckhoff and Jaffrelot 2005, p. 2). By the sixteenth century—largely as a result of political liberalization in England—its meaning had crystallized, coming to be identified with "the people," thereby elevating the latter as the new bearer of sovereignty, a concept that is, of course, closely linked with the state. As Dieckhoff and Jaffrelot (2005, p. 2) suggest "sovereignty became embodied in a state which had acquired the profile of a centralized apparatus." Thus, from the state as a political entity ruled by

N. Christofis (✉)
Center for Turkish Studies and College of History and Civilization,
Shaanxi Normal University, Xi'an, China

T. Kyritsi
Political Science and History, Panteion University of Social and Political Sciences,
Athens, Greece

© The Author(s) 2018   1
T. Kyritsi and N. Christofis (eds.), *Cypriot Nationalisms in Context*,
https://doi.org/10.1007/978-3-319-97804-8_1

the monarch, or the state as *being* the monarch—reflected in the famous quote *L'etat, c'est moi* which is attributed to the French king Louis XIV—we passed to *L'etat, c'est le peuple*, namely to the nation as *being*— and ruled by—its people.

This led many theorists to argue in favor of the idea of nationalism (like sovereignty) as a quintessentially modern phenomenon. Kedourie (1960), for example, argued that nationalism is "a doctrine invented in Europe at the beginning of the nineteenth century" (p. 9), while Gellner (1983) asserted that it was a necessary political doctrine that appeared in the modern world after the industrial revolution because political units were organized along nationalist principles, suggesting that "the political and the national unit should be congruent" (p. 1). Hobsbawm (1990) supplements Gellner's views with an understanding of nationalism as a tendency to collective identification, which is con- comitant with the state's extending reach (p. 9). This collective iden- tification for Anderson (2006) is depicted in the widely used notion of *imagined community*. In other words, we could agree, at least as a starting base, with the following definition, suggested by Antony Marx (2003, p. 6):

> Nationalism… [is] a collective sentiment or identity, bounding and bind- ing together those individuals who share a sense of large-scale political sol- idarity aimed at creating, legitimizing or challenging states. [And] as such, nationalism is perceived or justified by a sense of historical commonality which coheres a population within a territory and which demarcates those who belong and those who are not.

Nationalism, broadly conceived, has penetrated and interacted with a whole array of different ideologies and political attitudes, ranging across the political spectrum, including some segments of the Left. For example, many historians have observed that, in its initial stages, nationalism was associated with liberal movements (such as the French nationalism linked to the French Revolution) but through time it was "increasingly taken up by conservative and reactionary politicians" (Heywood 2007, p. 145). Similarly, one can talk of liberal nationalism as well as left-wing nationalism or anti-colonial nationalism et cetera (e.g., Nimni 1994; Christofis and Palieraki in this volume).

Relevant to that last point, and Cyprus for that matter, is the contribution made by anti-colonial scholars and Marxist ideas. For example, the leftist and anti-colonial intellectual Aimé Césaire (2000), although he removed himself from association with the USSR, made reference to Marxism and the role that socialism could play in the liberation of colonized people: "It is a new society that we must create... For some examples showing that this is possible, we can look to the Soviet Union" (p. 11). For Césaire—as for many leftists—the oppressed people under the term proletariat remained "the only class that still has a universal mission, because it suffers in its flesh from all the wrongs of history, from all the universal wrongs" (p. 24). A few years later, the Marxist philosopher and revolutionary, Frantz Fanon (1963) argued that "The Third World must not be content to define itself in relation to values which preceded it" (p. 55), namely the capitalist and the socialist system. For Fanon, the underdeveloped countries "which made use of the savage competition between the two systems in order to win their national liberation, must, however, refuse to get involved in such rivalry" (p. 55).

Fanon's analysis was quite revealing in many respects for the case of Cyprus, when he argued that "the colonialist bourgeoisie frantically seeks contact with the colonized elite" (p. 9), referring to the colonial powers' attempts to maintain control of the colonies through control of the "independent" governments. For Fanon, the process of decolonization as a response to colonialism was part of the struggle that the colonized faced to become free. He advocated that decolonization unified the people "by the radical decision to remove [it] from heterogeneity, and by unifying it on a national, sometimes a racial bias" (p. 30). Indeed, decolonization brought with it the rise of nationalism, which would rally anti-colonial movements and solidify cultural identity, and in doing so it would exclude other groups. This is apparent in the case of Cyprus where anti-colonial forces within the Greek Cypriot majority brought nationalism forward while "a Greek national identity missed out those who identified themselves as Turkish or as other minorities living within the two major ethnic groups" (Papastavrou 2012, p. 97).

It becomes evident that nationalism has proved to be one of the most powerful forces in the modern world (Hutchinson and Smith 1994, p. 3). As is well known, it has come to permeate, in various degrees, almost all aspects of daily life, from politics to economics and social relations. Nationalism is, however, not static; it therefore makes no sense to talk about a single nationalism; rather we must give credence to the existence of multiple nationalisms. Beyond the different forms of nationalisms based on internal characteristics and their relationships with other identities or affiliations—e.g., liberal/conservative/socialist/feminist nationalism—different distinctions between nationalisms have been suggested by scholars according to criteria such as their characteristics and their place in the history or the geography of the world. For example, some scholars have advanced a distinction between *formal/informal* (Eriksen 1993) and *official/unofficial* nationalism (Özkırımlı 2002). While official nationalism ought to be understood as a process imposed from above—involving bureaucracy and state institutions to structure and support it, becoming thus part of the official ideology that seeks to homogenize and discipline society (Katsourides, Kalantzopoulos, Christofis in this volume)—unofficial nationalism refers to more sentimental and reactionary values closely related to daily life. Of course, the two forms inevitably form a symbiotic relationship, even if at any given moment they are in harmony, overlap or are in competition with each other (Özkırımlı 708–709; also, Öztan 2015, p. 75). Another distinction, which is quite evident in some of the chapters in this volume (e.g., this chapter and Kıralp), is Smith's (1991) distinction between "civic" and "ethnic" nationalism. The former refers to a specific nationalism putting emphasis on common civic or political belonging and shared territory, while the latter refers to a national identity stressing common ethnicity, culture, and traditions—characteristics which could also be linked with "liberal" and "conservative" nationalism, respectively.

This brings us to the geography of nationalism and the distinction between Western/non-Western nationalisms. Although there is a distinct and recognizable continuity with nineteenth-century European forms and ideologies, there have been at the same time inevitable mutations, as nationalism has adapted to or been reconstructed by cultures with different traditions from the West. In this scheme, the dichotomy between colonizers and colonized nationalisms is quite relevant. It can be argued, as Krishna (1999) pointed out, that "the metaphor of nation as journey, as something that is ever in the making but never quite reached [is] central to nationalisms everywhere" (p. 17). In the non-Western space, however, this is a process which "[s]ecures the legitimacy of the postcolonial state by centering its historical role in the pursuit of certain desired futures. [And] it undergirds the legitimacy of the state by securing for it both time and space." Yet, one must bear in mind that this never-ending journey in subaltern, non-Western spaces shares commonalities with that of Western nation-states even as there are also significant differences. While in the latter, "the endless deferment is on the question of extending the idea of community to a global space," in the "space called the postcolony, the endless deferment is on the question of achieving national unity itself" (Krishna 1999, p. 18).[1]

The tendency therefore to locate nationalism on the "periphery" and to overlook the nationalism of Western nation-states has also been criticized on legitimate grounds. In other words, the sense that "those in established nations at the center of things are led to see nationalism as the property of others, not of 'us'" (Billig 2008, p. 5; Papadakis et al. 2006; also Christofis in this volume) is a false sense, resembling Orwell's (1953) observation—quite familiar to the Cypriot public—that "the nationalist not only does not disapprove of atrocities committed by his [or her] own side, but he [or she] has a remarkable capacity for not even hearing about them."

Following the end of World War II, the experience of decolonization, coupled with general developments in the social sciences, saw an intensive and prolific period of research on nationalism (Connor 1984; Young 2001; Özkırımlı 2010). There is no doubt that nationalism has attracted growing attention from scholars in a range of disciplines—sociology, anthropology, history, politics, even literature, and philosophy. This rich scientific work, some of which is mentioned above, has formed a core of theoretical approaches that have informed case studies on specific nationalisms. Although there is a booming literature on nationalism in general, and on Cyprus in particular (Christofis 2018), scientific research that looks at the phenomenon of nationalism in Cyprus in an interdisciplinary way and from the perspective of global developments remains underresearched (see also Trimikliniotis and Bozkurt 2012; Karakatsanis and Papadogiannis 2017). The present volume is an attempt in that direction, one that seeks to qualify the heterogeneity of nationalism in the Cypriot context.

NATIONALISMS AND THE CYPRUS QUESTION[2]: PAST AND PRESENT

Cyprus is an ethnically mixed island in the Eastern Mediterranean (see Figs. 1.1 and 1.2). Its central geostrategic position in the Mediterranean basin has made the island a target of outside conquest over the centuries:

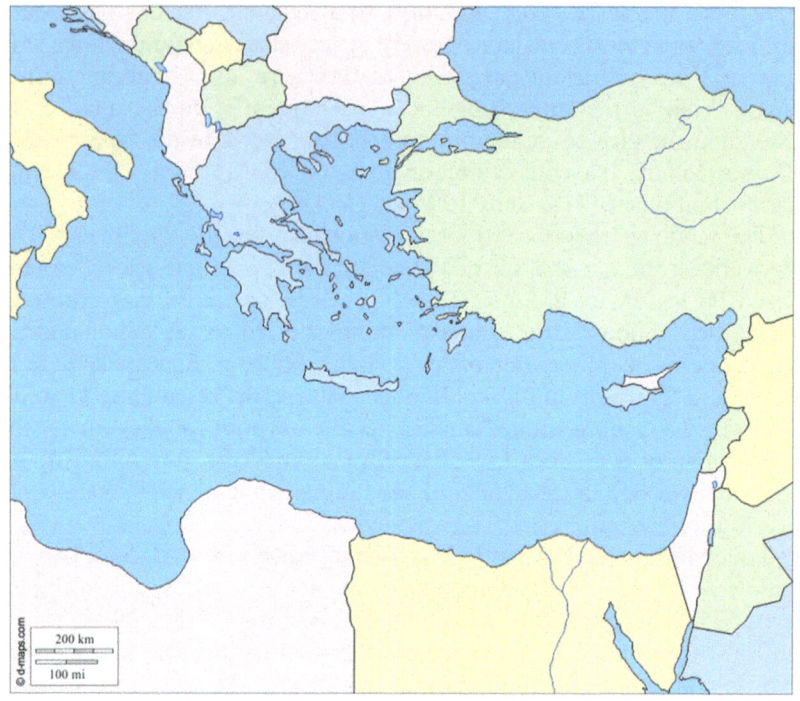

Fig. 1.1 Eastern Mediterranean Sea (*Source* http://d-maps.com/carte. php?num_car=33798&lang=en)

the Assyrians, Persians, Hellenes and Romans in ancient times, through to Byzantine, Lusignan, Venetian, and Ottoman rule across the medieval, premodern, and modern period; and, finally, the British from the nineteenth century. In its modern form, the Cyprus Question can be defined and analyzed "as a confrontation between two nationalisms on Cyprus, namely Greek Cypriot and Turkish Cypriot nationalism, which were forms of Greek nationalism and Turkish nationalism" (Carpentier 2017, p. 237). In that respect, the Ottoman rule of the island, especially the nineteenth century, as well as the British colonial administration of the island shaped the modern and contemporary history of Cyprus.

After three centuries of Ottoman rule (1571–1878), Cyprus became part of the British Empire in 1878. That year should be considered as a milestone in the process of transition from traditional social structures

Fig. 1.2 Map of Cyprus (*Source* http://d-maps.com/carte.php?num_car= 58294&lang=en)

to what is called modernity. As in other regions of the world, Cypriot modernity involved economic capitalism (Katsourides 2014); a modern system of transportation and technology (Varnava 2009); the development of the print world, mass media, and mass education (Katsiaounis 1996); along with the emergence of new ideas and movements, such as nationalism, socialism (Katsourides 2014; Alecou 2016), and feminism (Kyritsi in this volume).

However, modernity has not been experienced the same way everywhere in the world. In Cyprus, the legacy of the Ottoman Empire would shape the Cypriot experience of modernity itself (Anagnostopoulou 2015). The nineteenth-century Ottoman Empire was defined by a specific form of multi-culturalism, the *millet* system, which saw the subjects of the Empire categorized based on their confession or ethnoreligious community (*millet*). Each *millet* was internally autonomous, under the guidance of its respective religious authorities. When the British conducted the first census of the island, in 1881, this reality would be reflected in the multi-communality of the Cypriot population. According to the census, in a population of 186,173 people (Colonial Office 1881), the largest community were the

Orthodox Christians—the *millet-iRum* in Ottoman parlance—who made up 73.9% of the population. The second largest was the Muslim community, being 24.4% of the people. The rest—1.7%—belonged in other communities; more particularly, 0.7% of the population were Roman Catholics, then came the Maronites (0.4%) and the Protestants (0.4%). Moreover, there were 0.1% identified as Armenians or Copts and finally a small number of Jews and Gypsies (Colonial Office 1881).

In the scheme of the *millet* system, the representative of the Orthodox community of Cyprus was the Archbishop of the autocephalous Orthodox Church of Cyprus while the *kadı* (judge) and the *müftü* (interpreter of the Sharia law) made up the religious leadership of the local Muslim community (Aymes 2014). However, the arrival of the British in 1878 came at a moment when the Ottoman *millet* system had already begun to rupture under the influence of modern nation-states. The Greek War of Independence and the official recognition of the newly founded Greek state in 1830 played a central role in this process which in the case of the Greek Cypriot community would soon feed a desire for *enosis* (i.e., union with Greece). By the end of the nineteenth century, a small body of educated individuals within the Orthodox majority of the island had begun to think of their community in terms of ethnic identity.

That said, nationalism "was not… a constant feature in this Mediterranean isle's history, nor did it emerge as an axis of tension in a sudden instant" (Altay 2005, p. 11). Members of the literate minority—including teachers, lawyers, small business owners, as well as educated clerics—were the first to be affected by the ideology of Greek nationalism in Cyprus. This identity which was at first embraced by a small group of educated elites, such as the Greek immigrant teacher, politician, and journalist, Nikolaos Katalanos (Katsiaounis 1996, pp. 215–223), would gradually spread to the lower strata (Sakellaropoulos 2017) by the 1930s and 1940s.

The British arrival in Cyprus disclosed—and in a way, accelerated—the formation of the preconditions for nationalism to become a mass movement. Immediately upon their arrival, the British introduced a quasi-representative body, the Legislative Council—although its representativeness was undermined by the fact that even at the beginning of the twentieth century fewer than one in 10 people on the island were eligible to vote, due to age, property and gender-based exclusions (Protopapas 2012, p. 49). This, however, became the first time that Cypriots were engaged in a process of modern elections and politics. At the same time, immediately after the arrival of the British in 1878 the first Greek newspaper circulated on the island. By 1890, seven Greek-language newspapers existed, reaching approximately 3000 subscribers while 450 books had been published (Bryant 2004, p. 33).

In the same year, the sole Turkish language weekly, *Saded*, had only 64 subscribers (Bryant 2004, p. 33; also, An 1997). Like Turkish nationalism, the Turkish language press developed after the Greek. Nevertheless, after 1908 the Young Turk movement who had begun to act in the Ottoman Empire affected Cyprus. A number of Young Turks—exiled from the Ottoman Empire due to their opposition to the sultan's regime—arrived in Cyprus in the early 1890s and contributed to the publication of the Turkish newspapers *Zaman* and *Kıbrıs* (Bryant 2004, p. 34). During this period—and especially after the Young Turk Revolution of 1908 in the Ottoman Empire—a patriotic identity of "Ottomanism" started to affect the literate intellectuals among the Muslim Cypriots (Altay and Hatay 2009; Altay 2005).

The foundation of the Republic of Turkey by Mustafa Kemal (later Atatürk) in 1923 and his circle provided the conditions for the development of a Turkish Cypriot nationalism. The Kemalist modernization project, with its emphasis on secularism, republicanism, and nationalism, had a strong appeal for the Turkish Cypriots—or Muslim Cypriots as they were labeled at the time (Carpentier 2017, p. 244). In Cyprus, the Muslim Turks were redefined as Turks in the 1930s (Kızılyürek 2005), and other reforms, such as the Latin alphabet and Western forms of dress, were enacted almost simultaneously with those in Kemalist Turkey. Indeed, as Altay (2005) rightly pointed out, "the rise of Turkish nationalism on the island had become appreciable by the time of the October Revolt in 1931" (p. 442; also, Carpentier 2017).

Meanwhile, up until the 1920s, the Greek Cypriot alliance with the Greek state soon led all segments of Cypriot society to espouse *enosis*, except for the Communist Party of Cyprus (CPC) established in 1926 (Leventis 2002; Katsourides 2014). In that respect, during the twentieth century, the Greek Orthodox Church, the oldest institution in Cyprus, would be a key factor in the gradual development of a Greek national identity and an ethnic Greek nationalism, stressing ethnicity, tradition and cultural roots. The demand for *enosis*, however, did not constitute a threat to British rule during this period, and the same held true for Turkish Cypriots (Kızılyürek 2002). The nationalist sentiments of the Greek Cypriots were rather sporadic and carefully kept within the framework of cooperation with the colonial ruler and the friendship between Greece and Britain. From the late nineteenth century to the 1920s, nationalist opposition was rather mild and was thus generally tolerated by the colonial powers. Cypriot national demands did not go beyond resolutions and verbal claims, and remained strictly within the framework of legality (Faustmann 1999, p. 22).

However, in 1931, a nationalist Greek Cypriot Revolt was met with a harsh reaction from the British administration and a despotic crackdown against any expression of national sentiment for the remainder of the decade (Rappas 2014). Nevertheless, by the 1940s both Greek and Turkish nationalisms had crystallized and come to dominate their respective communities on the island. Following World War II, the Greek Cypriots felt that freedom and self-government was their due. In a Church-run referendum held between January 15–22, 1950, no less than 95.73% of the entire Greek Cypriot community recorded their votes in favor of independence (Loizides 2007, p. 175). The conflicting nature of the Cyprus Question can be traced to the 1950s, when the armed struggle against British rule unfolded alongside inter-communal violence among the two largest communities living on the island, Greek Cypriots and Turkish Cypriots, amid rising waves of nationalism (Yüksek and Carpentier 2018, p. 6). In the context of a growing nationalism and dissatisfaction with British rule, right-wing Greek nationalists formed the National Organization of Cypriot Fighters (*Εθνική Οργάνωσις Κυπρίων Αγωνιστών*, EOKA) in 1955, which conducted a guerrilla insurgency with the aim of ending the British rule in Cyprus and achieving *enosis* (Alimi et al. 2015, pp. 98–128). While Greek Cypriots strove for *enosis*, Turkish Cypriots, who initially opted for the continuation of British rule, demanded taksim—the partition of the island into two separate territories (Bahcheli 1990; Papadakis et al. 2006, pp. 2–4).

This gave nationalists, along with the political Right and the Church, a leading role in the anti-colonial movement, which during the 1940s was threatened by the growing anti-colonial forces of the Left and a vibrant labor movement—with the popularization of trade unions and the establishment of the new leftist Progressive Party of the Working People (*Ανορθωτικό Κόμμα Εργαζόμενου Λαού*, AKEL). Emerging in 1941, AKEL rapidly gained massive support as the legal umbrella party of the Left; in contrast to the low membership of the illegal and strictly communist CPC which had existed since 1926.

Drawing symbols from the "national center" of Greece, EOKA initially planned to initiate its actions on the anniversary of the 1821 Greek revolution, on 25 March 1955, also a major Orthodox religious holiday (Loizides 2007, p. 176; Papadakis 1999, p. 25). In addition, the leadership of EOKA, with Georgios Grivas at its head—known for his ultra-nationalist and anti-communist tactics and ideas during the Greek Civil War (1946–1949)—not only excluded the Turkish Cypriots and the Leftists from its lines but soon turned against them (Pollis 1979; Drousiotis 1998; Michael 2016).

On the nationalist front, a few years after the establishment of EOKA, in 1958, Turkish nationalists formed the Turkish Resistance Organization (*Türk Mukavemet Teşkilatı*, TMT), which would play a significant role in the following decades. In the meantime, Cyprus gained its independence in 1960 as the Republic of Cyprus, which was recognized as an independent state of 600,000 people, 80% of whom were Greek Cypriots and 18% Turkish Cypriots (Papadakis et al. 2006, p. 2). Independence was accompanied with particular conditions. These included retention, by Britain, of specific zones/areas of the island to be used as military bases and recognition of Greece, Turkey, and Britain, as the "guarantor" powers holding the right to take action to "re-establish the current state of affairs in Cyprus" if the latter was in jeopardy.

The relatively peaceful coexistence between the two communities of the island would not last for long. Following a constitutional crisis in 1963, a new wave of inter-communal violent conflicts re-emerged, and rejuvenating, if at all forgotten, the old demands for *enosis* and *taksim*. Beyond the human casualties—which this time impacted more the Turkish Cypriots in terms of casualties (Papadakis et al. 2006, p. 2), considering that one-fifth of them were gradually displaced during 1963–1967 (Patrick 1976)—the conflicts also resulted in the first geographical division between the two communities in some areas of the island, where the Turkish Cypriots were secluded in enclaves, or purely Turkish villages (Bryant 2004, p. 3). Since this time, the United Nations has maintained a continuous presence on the island.

In 1974, a *coup d'état* against the Cypriot government occurred—initiated by the military junta in Greece and supported by the Greek Cypriot ultra-nationalist paramilitary organization, EOKA B. This is considered the climax of confrontations between the competing groups within the

Greek Cypriot community. The coup was swiftly followed by a Turkish invasion of the island, on 16 August 1974, Turkey's pretext being the protection of the Turkish Cypriots, which it was pursuing as a guarantor power; a right vested in Ankara by the London–Zurich Agreements of 1959. The Turkish invasion saw more than 200000 people turning into refugees and internally displaced, 6000 killed and approximately 1500 missing (Kovras 2017, p. 159). This time, the Greek Cypriots were more affected in quantitative terms and almost one-third of them were displaced (Loizos 1981; Papadakis et al. 2006, p. 3). Moreover, the invasion forced the de facto division of the whole island into two parts; Greek Cypriots fled to the south and Turkish Cypriots moved to the north while Turkish forces occupied the northern part of Cyprus—some 36.2% of Cypriot territory.

Since 1974 Cyprus has remained divided in two: one part covering the southern part of the island, controlled by the internationally recognized Republic of Cyprus. The northern part declared itself unilaterally the "Turkish Republic of Northern Cyprus" in 1983, but is recognized only by Turkey. Even as the de facto partition continues, the two communities continue to be in reunification talks to solve the issue on the grounds of a bizonal, bicommunal federation. This should allow one central Cyprus government but two autonomous—more or less—zones/states. In the meantime, the bipolarity of this whole historical scheme has forced the smaller ethnic groups of Cyprus to in effect "choose" one or the other side; indeed, the 1960 Constitution recognized only two national communities—Greek and Turkish Cypriots—and minorities such as the Maronites, Armenians and Latins were seen as religious communities and were asked to choose which of the two national communities they wished to join (Kasbarian, this volume). Overall, the assumption of homogeneity regarding each "pole" has left little space for visible multi-culturalism and diversity, and continued to undermine other forms of identity beyond ethnicity.

THE SCOPE OF THE VOLUME

If there is a theoretical assumption that holds the chapters of this volume together, it would be the historical approach to nationalism, namely the view that the world of nations, ethnic identity, and national ideology are neither *eternal*, nor *ahistorical* or *primordial* but are rather socially constructed and function within particular historical and social contexts. Another premise of this volume is that Cyprus, as a place that was, and still is, marked by the collision of opposed nationalisms—that is, Greek and Turkish—constitutes a fertile ground for examining the history, the dynamics and the dialectics of nationalism.

The volume is a collection of chapters by authors of different perspectives and academic fields. Taking Cypriot nationalisms as its case study, it examines moments of nationalism; as a form of identity, as a form of ideology and as a form of politics. While the scope of the book is mainly empirical, in the sense that it does not aspire to discuss a universal definition or theory of nationalism, it draws heavily on the hypothesis that the case of Cyprus can illustrate general theories of nationalism and can be an interesting case to evaluate their central postulates.

Without following a strict chronological order, nor an order of "importance," that is, without suggesting that the particular subjects are the (only) key events or perspectives that have shaped the culture of nationalism in Cyprus, the chapters presented in the book examine specific moments in the development of nationalisms on the island. The goal is for this diversity to present a range of perspectives on the broader canvas of the Cypriot experience, presented in a comparative and interdisciplinary framework that underscores nationalism's relationship with other forms of identities and loyalties, such as religion, class, gender, and political orientation. The readers of the book will notice that "nationalism" is given its plural form in the title, not only to stress the existence of the opposing nationalisms (Greek, Turkish) that continue to shape Cyprus, but also because of the non-static nature of the phenomenon and the existence of internal distinctions.

PART I: EARLY AGENTS OF NATIONALISM

The first part of the volume examines early expressions of nationalism in Cyprus. In a global context, this historical period corresponds to phases A and B in the famous schema suggested by Miroslav Hroch (2012) regarding the historical phases of nationalist movements. According to Hroch, there are three phases in such movements: phase A refers to an initial period in which "activists [are] above all devoted to scholarly enquiry into and dissemination of an awareness of the linguistic, cultural, social and sometimes historical attributes of the non-dominant group— but without, on the whole, pressing specifically national demands to remedy deficits" (2012, p. 81). Phase B includes "a new range of activists" who "[seek] to win over as many of their ethnic group as possible to the project of creating a future nation, by patriotic agitation to 'awaken' national consciousness among them" (2012, p. 81). Finally, phase C refers to the formation of a mass national liberation movement.

The first chapter of the volume, by Yiannos Katsourides, emphasizes the social groups and institutions which consisted the first agents of Greek nationalism in Cyprus during the rise of Greek Cypriot Nationalism in the early twentieth century. Katsourides' contribution can be used also as a general introduction to the early agents of nationalism in Cyprus. Katsourides examines how an educated body of individuals, along with institutions such as the Church, the schools and the press, systematically promoted the new nationalist ideas. The second chapter, authored by Petros Nikolaou, unfolds the moments in which the relationship between the Greek Cypriots, as the *national self,* and the Turks or Turkish Cypriots as the *national other* was constructed. This is achieved through a detailed examination of an early agent of nationalism in Cyprus, that is, the Greek-language newspapers established between 1878 and 1914.

However, as Rebecca Bryant (2004) observes "there is no real contradiction between defining one's group in opposition to a constructive Other, and getting along with those others when in contact with them" (p. 2). The contradiction emerges in our case when "in modern representative politics claiming rights entails defining oneself as a certain type of person—a citizen—with claims on a particular state. It is there that the theoretical articulation of experience—namely, ideology—comes into play and divides." This process in the first years of the British rule in Cyprus was expressed by the Legislative Council, which was the body that the British administration introduced to supposedly represent the Cypriot communities.

The Legislative Council was the first institution resembling Western structures of representation in Cyprus, although it was characterized by limited authority and extremely limited representation. This is the subject of the third chapter of the volume, by Meltem Onurkan-Samani, who explores the role of this Council in the transition from religious to national identity and from traditional to modern sociopolitical structures. From 1882 to 1931, especially, the Council affected and expressed early nationalist sentiments as well as ethnic division and the competition between the two communities in the framework of a modern colonial Cyprus.

The final chapter of this part, penned by Thekla Kyritsi, examines the role of women in the first steps of the nationalist ideology in Cyprus. The analysis focuses on the strong attachment between the first feminists and the early national sentiments. Although the dominant narrative has considered the agents of nationalism to have been male—with women either completely neglected or understood as secondary agents—Kyritsi shows how (a category of) women played an important and distinctive role as agents of nationalism in Cyprus. These women were not simply handmaidens of their male nationalist counterparts but were themselves agents, experiencing nationalism as consistent with their interests and aspirations and expressing their national identities in that context. This offers insights into the way less privileged groups of the population experienced national identity, and the reasons that led them to become so extremely loyal to the new nationalist ideas.

PART II: MOMENTS OF A MASS MOVEMENT

The second part of the volume is also historical and examines nationalism in Cyprus as a mass movement. In Hroch's scheme, it corresponds to the third phase of nationalism, the era when nationalism acquires mass support. Part II moves chronologically forward from the 1940s, when nationalism in Cyprus became a dominant and popular ideology, to the aftermath of the Turkish invasion of 1974. This was a period when nationalism became a truly popular and political movement and gained militant supporters urging political demands on the future of the island. This part of the book allows the reader to become familiar with the historical process which led to the violent conflicts between the Greek and the Turkish Cypriots.

Dimitris Kalantzopoulos opens this part with his examination of the role of the political Right and the political Left in the development of Greek Cypriot nationalism during the 1940s. He focuses particularly on the Orthodox Church, which represented the political Right, and AKEL, which acted for the political Left. Within this context, Kalantzopoulos claims that the political discourse of the Left came to be increasingly nationalist, leading to the adoption of the politics of *enosis* by the party and, gradually, to the recognition of the Church as the national leader of the community. The second chapter of this part, by Alexios Alecou, examines the nationalism of the far-right, and the way the Greek far-right nationalist organization, named "X," affected the Greek Cypriot nationalists during the 1940s. At this point nationalism is pure politics with demands that move beyond Cyprus "belonging" to Greece, to who should be considered a "real" Greek and how "the nation" should be governed.

The next chapter, by Şevki Kıralp, examines two attempts at "reunification" of the island. The first refers to the period between 1968 and 1974 and the attempts made by the leader of the Greek Cypriots, Archbishop Makarios III. The second refers to the period between 1996 and 2004 and the Turkish Cypriot initiative of the platform *Bu Memleket Bizim* (This Country is Ours). Examining the two reunification attempts within a comparative framework and drawing on the fact that no attempt to reunite Cyprus could achieve unless supported by both communities, Kıralp demonstrates the role of ethnic nationalism as a key factor inhibiting the island's reunification.

PART III: NATIONAL IDENTITY AND THE DEVELOPMENT OF PREJUDICE

It is true that "Cypriotness" as a form of identity has appeared to have gained more ground in public opinion during the last decades (Mavratsas 1998). Bryant observed that approximately since the 1990s, there has indeed been "a growth of 'Cypriotness' defined against the Greeks of Greece and the Turks of Turkey" (Bryant 2004, p. 7). Nevertheless, she argued that this identity was not widely accepted before because—as her interviews with EOKA fighters showed—an independent Cyprus was for many, back then, "beyond the horizon of possibility."

A discussion on civic "Cyprus-centered" nationalism, in contrast to "ethnic" nationalism and Turkey and Greece as "motherlands," is also relevant to this part of the book. In the first chapter, Sossie Kasbarian discusses Cypriot nationality and the ways of "being Cypriot" through the Armenian Cypriot experience. The analysis allows the reader to reflect on the identity dichotomy, Greek/Turkish, and to assess the historic and symbolic role that minorities in Cyprus have played and can potentially play in a more inclusive Cypriot nation. The next chapter brings this issue to the discussion from the perspective of the Turkish Cypriot identity. Here, Mustafa Çıraklı examines the identity of Turkish Cypriots in the contemporary era, during the de facto partition of the island and the distinction between the Turks from Turkey, namely Turks who arrived in Cyprus after 1974 or later, either as settlers or as immigrants, and the Turkish Cypriots who were living on the island when partition was enshrined.

The volume then moves beyond history and sociology to the construction of national identity and ethnic prejudice from the perspective of human psychology. If history offers insights in regard to the development of nationalism in the modern and contemporary world, human psychology provides insights regarding the (pre)conditions which allow its emergence and development in human societies. In this context, Maria Ioannou and Angelos Kassianos examine the development of ethnic prejudice in Cypriot children through key concepts, such as category awareness, identification with categories, in-group preferences and out-group derogation.

Finally, this part of the volume concludes with a chapter concerning the historiography of Cyprus which—as much as everything else in Cyprus—has obviously been affected by the persistence of ethnic antagonism and community conflict. Although there is a growing literature of history-writing holding a critical perspective and aiming to question the dominant national(ist) narratives on Cyprus history, there is still a great deal to do toward a historiography that would overcome those narratives. In this context, Andrekos Varnava, examines the work of late Rolandos Katsiaounis, an authority in Cypriot historiography, in order to offer a critical analysis of his work, to shed light on his scholarly contribution, and—through a biographical narrative—to also offer insights on the evolution of Cypriot identity from the late Ottoman period to the present.

PART IV: THE LOCAL AND THE GLOBAL

The final part of the volume examines Cyprus and Cypriot nationalisms in a comparative and global context. Iliya Marovich-Old examines nationalism as resistance to British colonialism, comparing Cyprus with Malta from 1919 to 1940. In this framework, Marovich-Old compares two different nationalisms developed in the context of the British colonialism. Iliya's chapter is followed by the last two chapters of the book, which examine how Cyprus affected other regions of the globe. This is a novel contribution in the book, considering that Cyprus is usually seen as being influenced by the "outside" world rather than the other way around.

The central theme in the last two chapters of the book is, directly or indirectly, the national question (see also Kalantzopoulos in this volume), an issue that while imprinting a deep mark on the inter-war period, was almost forgotten during the Cold War owing to the bipolar ideological confrontation which was tearing the world in half (e.g., Dieckhoff and Jaffrelot 2005; Connor 1984). Nationalism, however, was not forgotten. The national liberation movements blended with socialism led to decolonization after World War II, but their specifically "national dimension was usually disguised behind a Marxist-leaning rhetoric and swamped in an internationalism of convenience" (Dieckhoff and Jaffrelot 2005, p. 1), reminding Anderson's (2006) remark that "[e]very successful revolution which succeeded has defined itself in national terms—the People's Republic of China, the Socialist Republic of Vietnam and so forth—and, in so doing, has grounded itself firmly in a territorial and social space inherited from the revolutionary past" (p. 2).

This becomes more than evident in the last two chapters of the book. The chapter by Nikos Christofis in particular focuses on how the Greek and the Turkish "Motherland" Left dealt with the Cyprus Question, an issue with national connotations that the Left did not deny. The chapter shows how the issue was integrated and instrumentalized into their practices and discourses, used as reference to prove both the Left's patriotism as well as its anti-imperialism during the 1950s and 1960s. Finally, Christofis attempts to identify whether the theoretical/ideological principles of Marxism, namely anti-imperialism and anti-colonialism, coincided with practical matters, especially, when the "nation" was a case in point.

Finally, Cyprus intersects with Greece and Latin America in Eugenia Palieraki's examination of how Cyprus became a major player in creating international links through its Non-Aligned and Third World policy, from the 1950s to the 1970s. Palieraki discusses how the Greek Left and Center-Left used Latin America in order to comprehend Cyprus' colonial situation and how, vice versa, the Greek Left made sense of the unfamiliar processes and realities of Latin America through the lens of the familiar to them Cypriot experience. This way, Palieraki suggests that Cypriot politics produced a dramatic change in the way the Greek parties and activists of the Left and Center-Left perceived both themselves and the world in which they acted.

NOTES

1. On the differences between "the East" and "the West", see Chatterjee (1993).
2. Although scholars tend to a variety of ways to describe the topic of Cyprus—e.g., "the Cyprus Issue", "the Cyprus Problem" and "the Cyprus Question"—the latter is the one adopted in the present volume.

REFERENCES

Alecou, A. (2016). *Communism and Nationalism in Postwar Cyprus, 1945–1955: Politics and Ideologies Under British Rule*. New York: Palgrave.

Alimi, E. Y., Demetriou, C., & Bosi, L. (2015). *The Dynamics of Radicalization: A Relational and Comparative Perspective*. New York: Oxford University Press.

Altay, A. (2005). *Nationalism Amongst the Turks of Cyprus: The First Wave*. Oulu: Oulu University Press.

Altay, N., & Hatay, M. (2009). Politics, Society and the Decline of Islam in Cyprus: From the Ottoman Era to the Twenty-First Century. *Middle Eastern Studies, 45*(6), 911–933.

An, A. C. (1997). *Kıbrıs'ta Türkçe Basılmış Kitapları Listesi, 1878–1997*. Ankara: K.K.T.C. Milli Eğitim, Kültür, Gençlik ve Spor Bakanlığı Yayınları.

Anagnostopoulou, S. (2015). Millet, Ethnicity, Colonial Community. Views of the Authoritarian Transition to Modernity, 19th–early 20th c. From the Ottoman to the British Empire. In M. N. Michael, T. Anastassiadis, & C. Verdeil (Eds.), *Religious Communities and Modern Statehood: The Ottoman and Post-Ottoman World at the Age of Nationalism and Colonialism*. Berlin: Klaus-Schwartz, 14–69.

Anderson, B. (2006). *Imagined Communities: Reflections on the Origin and Spread of Nationalism* (Rev. ed.). London and New York: Verso.

Aymes, M. (2014). *A Provincial History of the Ottoman Empire: Cyprus and the Eastern Mediterranean in the Nineteenth Century*. Abingdon: Routledge.

Bahcheli, T. (1990). *Greek-Turkish Relations Since 1955*. Boulder: Westview Press.

Billig, M. (2008). *Banal Nationalism*. London: Sage.

Bryant, R. (2004). *Imagining the Modern: The Cultures of Nationalism in Cyprus*. London and New York: I.B. Tauris.

Carpentier, N. (2017). *The Discursive-Material Knot: Cyprus in Conflict and Community Media Participation*. New York: Peter Lang.

Césaire, A. (2000). *Discourse on Colonialism* (J. Pinkham, Trans.). New York: Monthly Review Press.

Chatterjee, P. (1993). *The Nation and Its Fragments: Colonial and Postcolonial Histories*. Princeton, NJ: Princeton University Press.

Christofis, N. (2018). Politics and Nationalism in Cyprus. In P. James (Ed.), *Oxford Bibliographies in International Relations*. New York: Oxford University Press.

Colonial Office. (1881). *[C.-4624] Report on the Census of Cyprus, 1881*. London.

Connor, W. (1984). *The National Question in Marxist-Leninist Theory and Strategy*. Princeton, NJ: Princeton University Press.

Dieckhoff, A., & Jaffrelot, C. (Eds.). (2005). *Revisiting Nationalism: Theories and Processes*. New York: Palgrave.

Drousiotis, M. (1998). *ΕΟΚΑ: Η σκοτεινή όψη* [EOKA: The Dark Side]. Athens: Stachi.

Eriksen, T. H. (1993). Formal and Informal Nationalism. *Ethnic and Racial Studies, 16*(1), 1–25.

Fanon, F. (1963). *The Wretched of the Earth* (C. Farrington, Trans.). New York: Grove Press.

Faustmann, H. (1999). *Divide and Quit? The History of British Colonial Rule in Cyprus, 1878–1960*. Mannheim: Mateo.

Gellner, E. (1983). *Nations and Nationalism*. Oxford: Blackwell.

Heywood, A. (2007). *Political Ideologies: An Introduction*. Houndmills, Basingstoke, Hampshire, New York: Palgrave Macmillan.

Hobsbawm, E. (1990). *Nations and Nationalism Since 1780: Programme, Myth, Reality*. Cambridge: Cambridge University Press.

Hroch, M. (2012). From National Movement to the Fully-Formed Nation: The Nation-Building Process in Europe. In G. Balakrishnan (Ed.), *Mapping the Nation* (pp. 78–97). London and New York: Verso.

Hutchinson, J., & Smith, A. D. (Eds.). (1994). *Nationalism*. Oxford: Oxford University Press.

Karakatsanis, L., & Papadogiannis, N. (Eds.). (2017). *The Politics of Culture in Turkey, Greece & Cyprus: Performing the Left Since the Sixties*. London: Routledge.

Katsiaounis, R. (1996). *Labour, Society and Politics in Cyprus During the Second Half of the Nineteenth Century*. Nicosia: Cyprus Research Centre.

Katsourides, Y. (2014). *History of the Communist Party in Cyprus: Colonialism, Class and the Cypriot Left*. London: I.B. Tauris.

Kedourie, E. (1960). *Nationalism*. London: Hutchinson.

Kızılyürek, N. (2002). *Milliyetçilik Kıskacında Kıbrıs*. Istanbul: İletişim.

Kızılyürek, N. (2005). The Turkish Cypriot Community and Rethinking of Cyprus. In M. S. Michael & A. Tamis (Eds.), *Cyprus in the Modern World*. Thessaloniki: Vanias.

Krishna, S. (1999). *Postcolonial Insecurities: India, Sri Lanka, and the Question of Nationhood*. Minneapolis and London: University of Minnesota Press.

Kovras, I. (2017). *Grassroots Activism and the Evolution of Transitional Justice: The Families of the Disappeared*. Cambridge: Cambridge University Press.

Leventis, Y. (2002). *Cyprus: The Struggle for Self-Determination in the 1940s: Prelude to Deeper Crisis*. New York: Peter Lang.

Loizides, N. (2007). Ethnic Nationalism and Adaptation in Cyprus. *International Studies Perspectives, 8*(2), 172–189.

Loizos, P. (1981). *The Heart Grown Bitter: A Chronicle of Cypriot War Refugees*. Cambridge: Cambridge University Press.

Marx, A. (2003). *Faith in Nation: Exclusionary Origins of Nationalism.* Oxford and New York: Oxford University Press.

Mavratsas, K. (1998). *Όψεις του ελληνικού εθνικισμού στην Κύπρο: Ιδεολογικές αντιπαραθέσεις και η κοινωνική κατασκευή της ελληνοκυπριακής ταυτότητας 1974–1996* [Aspects of Greek Nationalism in Cyprus: Ideological Conflicts and the Social Construction of the Greek Cypriot Identity, 1974–1996]. Athens: Katarti.

Michael, M. (2016). *«Διμέτωπος ο αγών»: ΕΟΚΑ και Αριστερά την περίοδο 1955–1959* ["The struggle is on two fronts": EOKA and the Left during 1955–1959]. Limassol: Heterotopia.

Nimni, E. (1994). *Marxism and Nationalism.* London: Pluto Press.

Orwell, G. (1953 [1945]). *England Your England and Other Essays.* London: Secker & Warburg.

Özkırımlı, U. (2002). Türkiye'de Gayriresmi ve Popüler Milliyetçilik. In T. Bora (Ed.), *Modern Türkiye'de Siyasi Düşünce: Milliyetçilik* (pp. 706–717). İletişim: Istanbul.

Özkırımlı, U. (2010). *Theories of Nationalism: A Critical Introduction* (2nd ed.). New York: Palgrave.

Öztan, G. G. (2015). The Struggle for Hegemony Between Turkish Nationalisms in the Neoliberal Era. In İ. Akça, A. Bekmen, & B. A. Özden (Eds.), *Turkey Reframed: Constituting Neoliberal Hegemony* (pp. 75–91). London: Pluto Press.

Papadakis, Y. (1999). Enosis and Turkish Expansionism: Real Myths or Mythical Realities? In V. Calotychos (Ed.), *Cyprus and Its People: Nation, Identity, and Experience in an Unimaginable Community, 1955–1997.* Boulder: Westview Press.

Papadakis, Y., Peristianis, N., & Welz, G. (Eds.). (2006). *Divided Cyprus: Modernity, History, and an Island in Conflict.* Bloomington: Indiana University Press.

Papastavrou, S. (2012). Decolonising the Cypriot Woman: Moving Beyond the Rhetoric of the Cyprus Problem. *The Cyprus Review, 24*(2), 95–108.

Patrick, R. A. (1976). *Political Geography and the Cyprus Conflict: 1963–1971.* Department of Geography Publications Series No 4. Ontario: University of Waterloo.

Pollis, A. (1979). Colonialism and Neo-colonialism: Determinants of Ethnic Conflict in Cyprus. In P. Worsley and P. Kitromilides (Eds.), *Small States in the Modern World: The Conditions of Survival.* Nicosia: New Cyprus Association.

Protopapas, V. (2012). *Εκλογικήι στορία της Κύπρου: πολιτευτές, κόμματα και εκλογές στην Αγγλοκρατία, 1878–1960* [Electoral History of Cyprus: Politicians, Parties and Elections During the British Rule, 1878–1960]. Athens: Themelio.

Rappas, A. (2014). *Cyprus in the 1930s: British Colonial Rule and the Roots of the Cyprus Conflict.* London: I.B. Tauris.

Sakellaropoulos, S. (2017). *Ο Κυπριακός Κοινωνικός Σχηματισμός, 1191–2004* [The Social Formation of Cyprus, 1191–2004]. Athens: Topos.

Smith, A. D. (1991). *National Identity.* Reno: University of Nevada Press.

Trimikliniotis, N., & Bozkurt, U. (Eds.). (2012). *Beyond a Divided Cyprus: A State and Society in Transformation.* New York: Palgrave.

Varnava, A. (2009). *British Imperialism in Cyprus, 1878–1915: The Inconsequential Possession.* Manchester: Manchester University Press.

Young, R. (2001). *Postcolonialism: An Historical Introduction.* Oxford: Blackwell.

Yüksek, D., & Carpentier, N. (2018). Participatory Contact Zones and Conflict Transformation: The Participatory Intensities of the Cyprus Friendship Program. *Conjunctions: Transdisciplinary Journal of Cultural Participation, 5*(1), 1–21.

PART I

Early Agents of Nationalism

The Rise of Greek Cypriot Nationalism to Hegemony: Agency, Particularities, and Popularization

Yiannos Katsourides

INTRODUCTION

Scholars analyzing the appearance of modern societies and ideologies frequently focus on the concepts of tradition and modernity (Lekkas 1996, pp. 197–227), correctly identifying political, economic, social and cultural changes as the drivers of the transition. It must be acknowledged, however, that conditions and changes were/are not the same across the globe, and so there is not one single type of modernity (Hall and Gieben 2003, pp. 27–28). In colonized countries, it was the colonizers who defined the course of modernization. Moreover, in colonized countries the political context was more charged and more complex, involving issues of national emancipation and identity and the legitimacy of political institutions (Macridis 1967, pp. 16–17). In such countries, too, ethnicity was more socially relevant than class; as a result, politics tended to develop along ethnic lines (Reilly 2006, p. 812). Cypriot

Y. Katsourides (✉)
University of Cyprus, Nicosia, Cyprus

25
T. Kyritsi and N. Christofis (eds.), *Cypriot Nationalisms in Context*,
https://doi.org/10.1007/978-3-319-97804-8_2

society transitioned into modernism at a time when nationalism was developing and was quickly becoming the defining feature of island politics.

Nationalism in Cyprus was largely the outcome of the *Megali Idea* (Great Idea) project that was gradually transmitted from the political elite and intelligentsia of Athens to the major centers of Hellenism outside Greece (Lekkas 1996, p. 106; Kitromilides 1979, pp. 152–157).[1] While there is no strong evidence of nationalism in Cyprus before the late phase of Ottoman rule (Kitromilides 1979, p. 157), since the early nineteenth century there had been some expressions of nationalism (Hill 1952, p. 496). It would be more accurate, therefore, to refer to a generally conceived national orientation of Greek Cypriot elites, which gradually acquired a more specific ideological content at the same time that its social bases steadily grew.

It was in the late nineteenth century, and under the rule of the British, that Greek Cypriots increasingly saw their destinies linked to the ancient Hellenic past of Cyprus and their future tied to its revival through unification with Greece (Kitromilides 1979). Nationalism became identified with the political demand for union with Greece (*enosis*). The normative basis of the Greek Cypriot demand for *enosis* and politicized forms of Greek Cypriot nationalism resulted from their strong reaction against British colonial rule and their cultural and historic affinity with Greece (Loizides 2007, p. 175). By the early twentieth-century Greek Cypriot nationalism had become a truly popular movement. Nationalism (and *enosis*) became the language of mass politics, made possible by the growth of primary education, powerful political agents that endorsed its doctrines and the spread of newspapers.

To better understand Greek Cypriot (nationalist) politics at the time but also beyond we must consider it in the context of the kind and type of nationalism experienced in Cyprus, as well as in the context of Greece/Greek nationalism and British colonialism. Heywood (2003) argues that all forms of nationalism address the issue of identity and is usually divided into two types: ethnocultural and civic/political (pp. 167–168). The former places primary emphasis on the regeneration of the nation as a distinctive civilization, while the latter sees it as a discreet political community. Whereas political nationalism is "rational" and may be principled, cultural nationalism is "mystical" in that it is based on a romantic belief in the nation as a unique historical and organic whole. Ethnocultural nationalism presents the nation mainly as a cultural community, stressing the significance of ethnic ties, while civic nationalism supports a civic version. In Western Europe, nationalism was a political movement that aimed to limit government power and ensure political rights. In contrast, in Eastern Europe and the Balkans, regions where political ideas were less developed and the social structure was "backward" in comparison to western Europe, nationalism was a cultural movement first (Katsourides 2017, pp. 4–5).

Greek Cypriot nationalism would be defined as ethnic/cultural—the type of nationalism that precedes establishment of the state and the development of capitalism (Mavratsas 2003, p. 63). Countries marked by this sort of nationalism lack the political independence of the nation, and so acquire a liberationist, secessionist character: the nation exists only as an ideology and a plan for implementation (Liakos 2005, p. 5). Greek Cypriot nationalism developed before the island's (light) industrialization[2] and not as its legacy, as happened in Western Europe and at a time when Cyprus was an occupied country. Because of the ethnic and liberationist nature of Greek Cypriot nationalism, it belongs to the category of anti-colonial nationalism, since it was inspired by opposition to colonialism and by the idea of national self-determination. At the same time, however, it was linked with the desire for social development, giving it both an economic and a political dimension—two characteristics of anti-colonial nationalism.

Greek Cypriot anti-colonial nationalism developed and grew strong for two main reasons. One was the island's close affinity geographically, historically and linguistically with Greece, which had not so long ago become an independent European state. Second was the Orthodox Church/religion—Cyprus was a deeply religious society where the Greek Orthodox Church inevitably played a political role (Holland 2014, p. 14). In the absence of a secular indigenous statehood, this traditional institution had a unique status among the Greek Cypriots and became a repository of nationality and moral authority, which in practice was to a greater or lesser extent also political and "national" authority. The Greek Orthodox Church soon became a force for nationalism (Fenech 2014, p. 28; see also next section).

While Greek Cypriot nationalism was primarily anti-colonial, it can also be classified by other criteria. For example, it shared several characteristics with the liberal as well as the conservative paradigm. Like liberal nationalism, Greek Cypriot nationalism pursued the notions of popular sovereignty and constitutional government; like conservative nationalism, it promised social cohesion and public order, while also offering identity and security in the framework of an organic unity (on the traits of the two nationalisms, see Heywood 2003, pp. 155–187). The agents of these various types of nationalism—and not only in Cyprus—were sectors of the bourgeoisie with conflicting interests and perceptions (Hobsbawm 1994).

All the above relate to the position each scholar takes with regard to the three main approaches/theories in the study of nationalism: primordialism, modernism/constructivism, and ethnosymbolism. "Primordialist" approaches portray national identity as historically embedded: nations are rooted in a common cultural heritage and language that may long predate statehood or the quest for independence, and are characterized by deep emotional attachments that resemble kinship ties (Heywood 2003, pp. 163–164). Smith (1986), for instance, highlighted the continuity between modern nations and premodern ethnic communities, which he called "ethnies." This implies that modern nations are essentially updated versions of immemorial ethnic communities.

Modernists/constructivists view the nation as an artificial construct, an "invented tradition" (Hobsbawm and Ranger 2015 [1983]), or an "imagined community" (Anderson 1983). Gellner (1983) emphasized the degree to which that nationalism is linked to modernization, and in particular to the process of industrialization. The argument here is that the nation is a by-product of eighteenth-century Europe as an ideological project of the modern state and/or powerful social groups. Consequently, nationalism is closely related to modern societies and the new social and economic forces. In this regard, it was nationalism that created nations and not the other way around. A third approach in the study of nationalism which emerged as a critique to modernism is ethnosymbolism. This approach stresses the importance of myths, symbols, and traditions in the formation and endurance of the modern nation-state (for example, Smith 1998).

In this chapter, I examine Greek Cypriot nationalism and more specifically its political manifestation (*enosis*) drawing mostly on the constructivist/modernist approach. However, some features of the ethnosymbolist theory are acknowledged as well, rendering my approach a bit hybrid; although leaning toward constructivism. Examination takes place on three interconnected levels: political agency; particularities and characteristics; and popularization. Political agency looks at the two most important agents of nationalism, the Cypriot Orthodox Church, and the rising bourgeoisie; together they comprised the new historic bloc in Cyprus, a term coined by Gramsci to point the leading political and social forces of each time. This historic bloc was often divided in terms of interests and opinions which were reflected on the particular characteristics of Greek Cypriot nationalism. Both the carriers of nationalism and its particular characteristics rendered Greek Cypriot nationalism a mass movement in a short period of time making nationalism and *enosis* hegemonic for the most part of the twentieth century. The examination also takes into consideration modernization and colonialism, thus enabling the reader to grasp the complex reality of Greek Cypriot nationalism.

Greek Cypriot nationalism was a complicated, multifaceted phenomenon that included opposing traits and dynamics: modernization and secularization yet attachment to traditional values; friendly predisposition toward the British but also anti-colonialism (see below), etcetera. These were the outcome of a long process of Cypriot modernization and the effects of colonization that blended together all these opposing characteristics.

NATIONALISM AND POLITICAL AGENCY

Under the British, political life was structured along the ethnic lines of the two main Cypriot communities. The already existing idea of their respective origin and history with Turkey or Greece facilitated promotion of competing nationalist projects (Loizides 2007, p. 174). The British capitalized on this, and in fact even institutionalized segregation of the different ethnic groups with, for example, separate electoral lists, separate polling stations and consequently separate political representation (Katsourides 2013). With their traditional "divide and conquer" stance, the British forced political life to be drawn along ethnic lines, purposely denying all tools and mechanisms that might unify the two Cypriot communities (Katsiaounis 1994). An example of this policy is found in the legislative procedures as these were introduced by the British.

The British established the Legislative Council in 1882, essentially a vestige Parliament with a limited mandate. The Council was in part elected and partially appointed and could be sidelined at any time the Governor faced difficulties in promoting the colonial policies. The structure of the Legislative Council was based on communal representation and the distribution of the seats was done in a way to offset the votes of the official (British) and the Turkish members, on the one hand, and Greek deputies, on the other (Katsourides 2013, pp. 507–508). The workings of the Council "... depended upon the exploitation of the racial cleavage between the Greeks and the Turks"[3] and had placed the two communities on a permanent tension and confrontation that marked the farther political development of the island. This segregation had destroyed any possibility of a common citizenship.

Empirical evidence reveals that socioeconomic changes, primarily capitalism, were responsible for the rise of nationalism in Europe; those espousing this ideology subsequently influenced and shaped each country's specific path. The social classes that supported this view were those most directly tied to social progress: commercial circles, part of the landowners and bankers, the educated middle class, industrialists and entrepreneurs (Hobsbawm 2002, p. 193). New petty bourgeois classes became the vehicles of national movements, with teachers, merchants, lawyers and doctors as the agents of the ideological preparation and initial mobilization of national movements (Liakos 2005, p. 22). We can see that it was those social forces seeking to improve and legitimize their own social and political positions that were responsible for the rise of nationalism (Lekkas 1996, p. 69). Nevertheless, we cannot ignore the fact that there were, and still are, connections between nationalism and traditional structures and culture which nationalists incorporate in their narrative: for example, language, religion, myths, etcetera (Mavratsas 2003, p. 57).

In Cyprus, the chief proponents of Greek nationalism were lawyers, journalists, the literati, university students, priests, and small businessmen. These groups formed the new hegemonic, historic bloc, which rose to prominence as a result of the legal and social changes effected by the British (Katsiaounis 1996, pp. 16–17). This, in turn, meant that the traditional ruling group of priests, merchants and money lenders could no longer dominate social and political life without the emerging bourgeoisie. The commercial bourgeoisie of Larnaca played the most important role in transmitting the first nationalist ideas in the last decades of the nineteenth century, in that it was they who formulated a specific political discourse based around the demand for *enosis*.[4] In addition to the merchant class in Larnaca and in Limassol, the educated graduates of the University of Athens played an important role in the diffusion of national ideas. These included lawyers, medical doctors, and professors/teachers, many of whom had been encouraged by the Greek consul in Cyprus to study in Athens (Kitromilides 1979, p. 161). The advent of newspapers and the many new religious/cultural associations inspired the young intellectuals in Larnaca and Limassol, who soon became intensely active, writing articles on matters of popular concern including politics (Katsiaounis 1996, p. 311). The members of this bourgeois class, with their economic power, university education, political discourse and social superiority, gradually assumed control of the island's political and social life. And their mantra was nationalism. Thus it was nationalism that enabled the rising Greek Cypriot bourgeoisie and the middle classes to claim an increased role in political life.

Key to the dissemination of nationalism in Cyprus was free masonry, an ideology that rejected the social distinctions on which the old aristocratic order was based. Freemasonry united the first nationalists through its network of lodges, which were nationalism's first organizational structures. The Cyprus masonic lodge Zenon, established in 1893 in Limassol by doctor I. Karageorgiades (Tornaritis 1948, p. 9), had many leading nationalist members including F. Zannetos, G. Frangoudes, C. Sozos, I. Economides, I. Kyriakides and T. Theodotou (Katsiaounis 1996, p. 182).

Also crucial to the spread of nationalism were Cypriot graduates of Greek universities, who returned to the island as the most enthusiastic supporters of *enosis*. This generation viewed *enosis* as liberation, not only from the Turks, but also from the British (Richter 2007, p. 115). Mainland Greek school teachers, who staffed the Cypriot schools before and after the British occupation, also played an important role in the national cause, especially Nikolaos Katalanos (Katsiaounis 1996, p. 210), who promoted *enosis* through a chain of nationalist clubs ("Love of the People") and newspaper articles. Moreover, prominent members of the bourgeoisie established and directed associations, reading rooms and clubs that promoted nationalism and *enosis*. For example, they hosted (political) speakers from Greece and held celebrations to mark the annual Pan-Cypriot games in honor of the Greek national holiday of 25 March, among other things (Katalanos 2003, pp. 259–260).

As I have detailed above, *enosis* at the beginning of the twentieth century was "the war cry of the classes which were outside the political system" (Katsiaounis 2004, p. 28). This reaffirms the contention that the nationalist cause was taken up by those desiring to upgrade and legitimize their social standing. Moreover, they recognized that they could most easily mobilize the masses with the call for *enosis*. The bourgeoisie led the movement for *enosis*, which was further strengthened when the Church joined the cause. The national movement under the dual leadership of these two agents and linked with economic demands, such as the abolition of the tribute tax and the demand for political rights and freedoms, mobilized the population en masse.

THE CHURCH AND NATIONALISM

The Orthodox Church did not endorse nationalism during the first years of British rule: The idea of "nation" was too modern for the Church, the embodiment of tradition (Mavratsas 2003, p. 66). However, once the British questioned the powers and privileges of the established powers—of which the Church was the main pillar—the Church changed course. When the colonial power tried to eradicate the Cypriot tradition of projecting religious interests onto the political level (whereby the Church represented Greek Cypriots politically), making changes aimed to weaken the Church and its officials on all levels (economy, politics, culture, etc.), the Church immediately fought back (Peristianis 1993, p. 251). The rising bourgeoisie also challenged the Church's established privileges in political representation and its enormous wealth.

Recognizing the imminent threat to its power and the rise of new popular forms of power, the Church began to involve itself in the political field, to the point that before long, the secular activities of the Church were devoted almost exclusively to politics and endorsing nationalism. The Church turned to nationalism both to re-establish its legitimacy and to integrate political demands into its domain of control (Mavratsas 2003, p. 66; Katsiaounis 1996, p. 237). The Church really had no choice but to adapt in face of the rising bourgeoisie and the British, and it chose to identify with the nation—a decision that was concretized as a result of politics involved in the Archbishopric Question (1900–1909) (see below).

When nationalist ideology first appeared in Cyprus, Greek Cypriot national identity was defined, above all, by religion, making it easy for the Church to present itself as the vehicle for the preservation of Hellenism in the country. In actual fact, most Greek Cypriots believed that religion was a defining criterion of nationalism, as Greek meant Orthodox—another reason for the Church's easy assumption of authority in the Unionist cause, and the reason why it was able to remain the Greek Cypriots' most important institution of continuity with the past. This stance also served the Church in its conflict with the British: incorporating nationalism and *enosis* into its political discourse and practice, it acquired new legitimacy. The higher clergy not only maintained their authority, but in fact even increased their influence over the faithful, putting themselves at the head of the Unionist movement (Richter 2007, p. 94).

The Church was closely tied to the bourgeois groups that endorsed nationalism, a connection that was strengthened by the British attacks on the Church as this action provided a rallying point for the bishops and the educated bourgeoisie (Katsiaounis 1995, p. 227). The relation was marked by mutual interaction: once the Church took on the nationalist cause (and especially the higher clergy), it influenced the character of Greek Cypriot nationalism and the bourgeois groups that had introduced it, while, at the same time, the bourgeois groups that supported nationalism and whose power increased after the British occupation tried (and to some extent achieved) to reduce the Church's influence and authority.

This ideological discourse, based on much compromise, came to be known as *ellinochristianismos*, a term that includes Christian identity within Greek nationalist ideology. *Ellinochristianismos* was a framework for mediating the differences (and opposition) between the Ancient Greek past (considered by the Church as idolatrous) and the Byzantine Middle Ages (the "glorious past" according to the Church, but not according to the modernizing adherents of the Enlightenment). In the new transitional narrative, the two periods (Antiquity, Byzantine Empire) were considered continuous, and part of the history and evolution of the Greek nation (Panayiotou 2006a, pp. 81–82). In political terms, the Church adopted *enosis* as an ideology in opposition to the British colonial state, but they also saw it as a cultural claim to being just as "civilized," or advanced, as the colonizing West.

The interaction between nationalism and religion was possible due to the very nature of nationalism. Nationalism as a political ideology has the great advantage that it can be "simultaneously interwoven with modernizing and traditional movements" (Lekkas 1996, p. 13) and its plasticity allows it to be equated with anthropological categories such as kinship (Anderson 1983, p. 15). Although it is a modern ideology, nationalism is idiosyncratic insofar as time, which is seen as homogenous and blank: this allows nationalism to mix modern elements with traditional. It is within this context that we must interpret "Helleno-Christian ideals" (*ellinochristianismos*).

PARTICULARITIES OF GREEK CYPRIOT NATIONALISM

The various groups composing the Greek Cypriot historic bloc often held conflicting interests and opinions, resulting in a nationalism that blended features of anti-colonialism, liberalism, and conservatism. These divergent interests were reflected in its demands as well. Tension and ambiguity were also due to certain other factors: the involvement of foreign powers, i.e., Greece, Turkey and Britain; the role of the Turkish Cypriots; the role and place of the Greek Cypriot Left, etc. All these together produced a number of particularities with regard to the character of Greek Cypriot nationalism: irredentism, millennialism, exclusionism, and moderation.

The first singularity of Greek nationalism in Cyprus was its irredentism. In Cyprus, a logical extension of the Great Idea was the political demand for the island's union with Greece. Greek Cypriot nationalism was irredentist as it did not aim at independence but at union with another state: the Greeks of Cyprus genuinely believed that they were part of the great Greek nation and that union with Greece was only natural.

A second characteristic of the Greek Cypriot national movement was millennialism. Although anti-colonial, it was actually quite millennialist insofar as it was assumed that all problems, especially in the socioeconomic sphere, would be solved only in "another life," after union—a tactic that downplayed the class inequalities and class struggle marking Greek Cypriot society (Anagnostopoulou 1999, p. 206). In this sense, it was also contradictory since, although it revealed a dislike of British colonialists and their power structures, it also legitimized the domestic political power structure of the Greek Cypriots that excluded the majority of the people (Panayiotou 2006b, p. 277).

A third peculiarity of Cypriot nationalism was exclusionism—and not only toward the Turkish Cypriots. The nationalist demand for *enosis* was socially progressive to the extent that it expressed the interests of the rising bourgeoisie as opposed to those of the landowners, the clergy, and the colonialist power. However, it did not have democratic ambitions in the sense of safeguarding human rights and political freedoms as in the French Revolution; nor was it concerned with the political rights of the peasants, who constituted the overwhelming majority of the population. The nationalists accorded little importance to the masses—especially considering their numbers. The Greek Cypriot ruling elite single-mindedly pursued their community's right to national self-determination, a demand that overshadowed the rights and needs of the individual.

The fourth singularity of the Greek Cypriot national movement concerns its moderate attitude toward the British. While Greek Cypriot nationalism supported the withdrawal of Cyprus from the British Empire, it was not anti-British; it always worked within the framework of "legality" and verbal representations. Nor were the nationalists anti-western, considering themselves as allies of the British Empire and potentially the local representatives of its world hegemony (Panayiotou 2012). Particularly illustrative of this reality was a 1919 letter promoting *enosis* sent by members of the Greek Cypriot mission to London: "We have complete and blind faith in the British Nation, its traditions and principles and its sense of justice" (*Eleftheria*, March 15, 1919, p. 3). In the same document, it was suggested that military and naval bases be ceded to Britain in exchange for the acceptance of *enosis*.

To fully understand the particularities of Greek Cypriot nationalism, we must consider the heterogeneity that characterized the nationalist bloc. Within this bloc, there were both conflicting goals and ideological differences, which produced intra-*enosis* antitheses (Katsourides 2013). This heterogeneity resulted because of ideological inconsistencies, as well as economic attachments, feelings of inferiority and foreign dependencies (Greece).

Holland (1999) argues that to understand the contradictions within the *enosis* movement, we need look no further than the Orthodox Church, which was key to the creation of a Greek national consciousness (pp. 24–25). The intermingling of religion and ethnicity led to an unusual and sometimes contradictory ideology because, theoretically, religion and nationalism are contradictory: religion justifies everything by appealing to a metaphysical force, while nationalism turns to secularism. And yet there is a historical relationship between the two forces, as evidenced by the key role religion plays in the creation of nations and their survival. At the same time, this role is incompatible with religion.[5] In this particular case, the contradiction lies in the fact that a potentially revolutionary ideology of modernity (i.e., nationalism) was adopted by the most conservative institution, which was not only excessively attached to tradition but also insisted on social immobility (Yiallourides 1993, p. 165). Holland (1999) suggests that the *enosist* demand was circumscribed by reaction and obscurantism precisely because of its link with the Church (p. 33).

Economics also was a factor in the conflict within the nationalist bloc. Cyprus was already marked by delayed development of a domestic bourgeoisie when the main industrial sectors (mines) passed onto foreign ownership, which prevented the Cypriot bourgeoisie from acquiring a "national," anti-imperialist character, as had occurred in other colonized countries. Instead, despite its political affiliation with Greece, a significant part of the bourgeoisie was linked primarily to English capital, while financial involvement with Greek capital was minimal (Katsiaounis 1996, p. 34).

Furthermore, most Cypriot political leaders, at least in the first period of British occupation, admired the English, going so far as to consider an Englishman's greeting to be a blessing, and the expression "he's an Englishman" a compliment.[6] Conflicting views regarding the means of the anti-colonial struggle created a division within the nationalist movement between moderates and intransigents (see Katsourides 2013; Georghallides 1997). The intransigents believed that most nationalist political leaders of this period had been led astray by the promises and rhetorical aphorisms of the English Liberals, requested *enosis* as a favor rather than demanding it as a right.[7] As a result, the Greek Cypriot nationalists had, for the most part, conceptualized political protest within a law-abiding context. Also contributing to the Greek Cypriot nationalists' moderate stance was the Church and important Nicosia politicians, who believed acquiescence to their foreign rulers was the best policy (Katsiaounis 1996, pp. 186–187; Georghallides 1979, pp. 82–83).

Another important factor was Greece's heavy dependency on Britain, translated as a policy of compliance with Britain (Katsiaounis 2000, p. 275).[8] Therefore, Greece prioritized other fronts for its irredentist claims, offering Cyprus sentimental rather than direct interest. In fact, it appears that during the Balkan Wars (1912–1913), the Greek government sent "fire-fighting" messages to the Cypriot politicians warning them against stirring up the unionist movement (Papapolyviou 1997, pp. 13, 248–249).

The leading Greek Cypriots at the time, taking Athens' dependence on London for granted, believed that *enosis* could be achieved within the framework of Anglo-Greek friendship; in the meantime, they were content to exist as a colony while working for constitutional and economic concessions. In the context of this peculiar conceptualization of the *enosis* demand, some Greek Cypriot leaders never broke entirely with the British but, in fact, participated in political and other institutions. This "strange" and unequal Greco-British cooperation saw even the most committed advocates of *enosis* accepting appointments on the Executive Council (Georghallides 1997, p. 84). After the October 1931 events, when both the Executive and Legislative Councils were abolished and replaced by the Advisory Body, the same thing occurred. The October 1931 events were a spontaneous anti-colonial revolt of the Greek Cypriots that was spearheaded by the nationalists. Although the context was initially set by economic grievances because of a British decision to enforce by an order in council taxes that were jointly disapproved by Greek and Turkish Cypriot parliamentarians on a rear expression of common stance, the revolt soon took a national character with the *enosis* slogan dominating. The revolt was very soon defeated and led to a period of repressive British rule known as Palmerocratia. Among those who accepted appointment to the Advisory Body and to the Executive Council over the years included such renowned nationalists as the Bishop Kyrillos of Kition, Christodoulos Sozos, Theofanis Theodotou, Spyros Araouzos and Antonis Triantafyllides. However, and despite these inherent contradictions, nationalism became hegemonic and *enosis* became a popular movement.

THE POPULARIZATION OF *ENOSIS*

Like all contemporary ideologies, Greek nationalism was very systematically promoted. Nationalism and *enosis* achieved a mass audience among the Greek population of the island utilizing certain social, political and cultural mechanisms. Such mechanisms as in many other cases beyond Cyprus, included schools, the mass media, institutionalized rituals and symbols (myths, flags, songs, etc.), national societies, books, journals and other institutional forms of political mobilization (Rokkan 1970, p. 61). The workings of such mechanisms were facilitated by the presence of certain "raw materials" that enabled the development of Greek Cypriot nationalism. The predominance of the Greek ethnic element provided the demographic and cultural infrastructure that allowed Greek nationalism to become established as the strongest political ideology in contemporary Cypriot history. Language, religion, common descent and the Greek antiquities that abound on Cyprus offered strong proof of the Cypriots' "Greekness"—a strong foundation upon which to build the national movement (Persianis 1978, p. 37). This led the former Governor of Cyprus, Roland Storrs, to write in his book *Orientations* (1945), "the Greekness of the Cypriots is in my view undoubted" (p. 469; see also Hill 1952, p. 441).

Hellenic nationalism successfully built on these elements in its early stages (especially before the British occupation), although the national movement lacked broad popular appeal: it was the Cypriots' illiteracy that prevented transmission of the nationalist ideology (Georghallides 1979, p. 81). Consequently, in its early years nationalism had neither a consistent political program nor a minimum level of support. Moreover, nationalism in Cyprus was initially quite an elitist movement (Richter 2007, p. 114). Nevertheless, although nationalists were few in number, they had a decisive influence because of their education and location in the larger towns, the centers of political power. Gradually, however, nationalism became more widely disseminated through newspapers, as well as through the reading rooms that were being established by leading political figures. Reading rooms were useful for the lectures they sponsored, as this meant ideas could be transmitted to an audience not necessarily literate (Katsiaounis 1996, p. 52).

Like all contemporary ideologies, Greek nationalism was very systematically promoted. A network of both local and external agents was mobilized to spread the irredentist ideology of the independent Greek state: "with the creation of associations to promote the education of the irredentists, and the sending of teachers and educational materials to the communities of the Greek periphery, Cyprus experienced the immediate consequences of these initiatives" (Kitromilides 1984, p. 12). The nationalists built their propaganda machine to function in relation to certain new developments in the economy and the society: a recent growth in literacy, expansion of the popular press, and the establishment of a postal service, road networks, new libraries, reading clubs and voluntary associations. The well-organized dissemination of the nationalist program and its adoption by the Church, allowed Greek nationalism to rapidly acquire a popular character. Key to this were public education and the advent of the print media, which were culturally unifying factors that became well established with the arrival of the British. In this way, ethnicity—traditionally a cultural category—gradually developed into a political agent.

In this context, two major historical events also played an important role toward the popularization of *enosis*. The Archbishopric question (1900–1909) and the Balkan Wars (1912–1913) rendered nationalism hegemonic and mass. The Archbishopric was the first major popular conflict in Cyprus: it was a fight for title of Archbishop of Cyprus, the highest authority of both the Church and the Greek Cypriots in this period. This conflict was also a battle between the traditionalists and the nationalists, and the catalyst for the nationalization and ideologization of the masses in Cyprus, as well as for the emersion and establishment of nationalist politics in Cyprus (see Katsourides 2017, Chapter 6; Michael 2005). The conflict concluded in a decisive victory for the nationalists and with the Church adopting a Greek nationalist policy. Nationalism had become the popular and dominant ideology ever since (Katsiaounis 1996, p. 228). The Balkan Wars (1912–1913) that followed solidified nationalist hegemony. Papapolyviou (1997) argues that it was the two Balkan Wars that shifted the balance in Cyprus–Greece relations decisively toward Athens, the "national center" (pp. 11–12). Not only did significant numbers of Greek Cypriot volunteer to participate, but they also organized numerous activities (e.g., fundraising) in support of the Greek state. These activities allowed the Greek Cypriots to express their feelings of "national solidarity" with the "motherland."

EDUCATION

It has been argued (Gellner 1983) that nations are constructed through a country's educational system. State leaders and political elites use education to promote a specific set of values and norms as well as for the national determination of their communities.[9] This presupposes a degree of literacy that did not exist in Cyprus at the period of transition to British rule; in fact, even as late as 1911, after 33 years of British occupation, more than seventy-three percent of the population could neither read nor write (Census 1911, p. 15). The development of education and the consequent rise in literacy levels were catalytic in molding a Greek national identity, as these enabled the national movement to grow from an elitist to a popular cause. Statistics reveal that by 1931 there was forty-five percent literacy (Census 1931, p. 16), and this was reflected in the growth and the spread of nationalist ideology (Kitromilides 1979, p. 160). The expansion of the network of primary and secondary schools first in the cities and later in the countryside opened up new audiences for Hellenic national values.

At the same time scholars credit nationalism with the development of the educational system, as universal education was part of the nationalist program from which it benefited (Persianis 1978, pp. 35–37). The British understood that education could potentially challenge their domination in Cyprus: as early as 1897 the first Governor, Wolsley, warned that the Greek schools could be transformed into "centers of Greek propaganda" (cited in Georghallides 1979, p. 47).

Although the British attempted to intervene in the education system on several occasions (Persianis 1978, pp. 64–65) they were largely unsuccessful. Cypriot politicians recognized the value of education, and also that of teachers as important political capital, and they strongly opposed any British interference in the education system. Teacher appointments, transfers, and salaries were the responsibility of the District Educational Councils, which were run by Cypriot politicians and the Church; to promote their careers teachers often offered services including electioneering (Georghallides 1979, p. 51; Storrs 1945, p. 500).[10] If we consider the important role of the teacher in the microcosm of the village—teachers were often the only educated person in the village—we can understand the political value in controlling them. Also, and more importantly, most primary and secondary school teachers were either mainland Greeks invited to work in Cyprus or Cypriots educated in Greece, and they tended to see themselves as missionaries of the Greek nation (Tzermias 2001, p. 88), operating on their own initiative to consciously promote the ideology of *enosis*. By virtue of his/her position in the village and in society, the teacher was at the heart of nationalist activities.

To conclude, although the British tried to intervene in the educational system, the *enosis* movement flourished, meaning that whole generations of Greek Cypriots were growing up in a system that was hostile to the British.

THE NEWSPAPERS

With the introduction of the press just three weeks after the arrival of the British, Cypriots were able to satisfy their growing interest in political issues. The newspapers were key to promote the Cypriot national consciousness (Ioannou 2007, p. 388), and most newspapers supported Greek nationalism and devoted considerable space to news about Greece. For most of the Greek Cypriot population, national identity developed in parallel with the dissemination of the written word (Katsiaounis 1995, p. 234).

Table 2.1 reveals how circulation levels of the Cypriot newspapers grew each year—which is highly indicative of Cypriots' growing interest in politics. Here we note the significance of "print capitalism to the spreading of nationalism" (Anderson 1983, pp. 46–47), meaning that

Table 2.1 Indicative circulation of Greek newspapers

Year	Number of issues	Number of newspapers issued	Number of magazines issued
1884	1200	3	–
1887	2400	4	–
1893	2990	6	–
1901	4630	7	1
1907	8500	12	–
1917	11,250	13	1
1922	14,650	14	2
1926	16,356	16	2
1931	12,600	9	2

Source Cyprus Blue Books 1883–1884; 1886–1887; 1892–1893; 1900–1901; 1908–1909; 1916–1917; 1922; 1926; 1931

the spread of nationalism was not due merely to the spread of the printed word, but owed much to the capitalist system which ensured the circulation and dissemination of printed material (see also Liakos 2005, p. 88).

It was prominent members of the Greek bourgeoisie who owned and edited the Greek nationalist newspapers, and it was nationalist-leaning clergymen, politicians, and intellectuals who filled their pages with essays and articles. The newspapers functioned as the public face and mouthpiece of Unionist demands and played a leading role in shaping public opinion to favor *enosis*. For example, an indicative formulation of the Unionist demand is revealed in the first issue of the newspaper *Kypriakos Fylax* (Cypriot Sentinel), whose editorial was entitled "The National Programme in Cyprus" and referred to the need for Hellenism in Cyprus to organize and plan for the aim of union with Mother Greece (8 April 1906, p. 1).

The Greek Cypriot newspapers regularly highlighted historical prophecies and legends in order to emphasize the continuity of the Greek community on the island with the Byzantine past and the ties with wider Hellenism, actions which Papapolyviou (1997) sets in the context of "preaching the Great Idea" (p. 78). They were also highly active in carrying out nationalist pursuits, for example fundraising for Greece when that country was at war. Thus it was with the help of the press that Cypriots—even those in the most isolated villages—began to understand that they were part of a broader whole. They began to identify with a common Greek national sentiment and with a political entity greater than the local environment of their village (Ioannou 2007, p. 389).

THE TRANSFORMATIVE POWER OF NATIONALISM

Nationalist ideology brought constant challenges and changes to Cypriot society. The Cypriot worldview ceased to be unitary and uncontested; it was a viewpoint that was no longer defined by religion and the Church; instead, it was a perspective open to multiple interpretations and conscious attempts to reshape it. At this time, nationalism began to cohere as a political position (i.e., *enosis*), particularly in the aftermath of the Archbishopric Question in 1909. The major socializing institutions, i.e., the education system, the press and the Church, worked together to promote *enosis*, while also working together to maintain their control over the lower strata. The nationalists belonged to a particular political generation for which *enosis* was a formative ideological experience.

The national movement was successful in linking the concept of Union to the identity of the Greek Cypriot. As Papapolyviou (1997) writes, "the press easily adopted accusations of 'national unworthiness'" (p. 49), belittling and ostracizing anyone who took a different stance (e.g., the communists). The Greek Cypriot bourgeoisie strategized, mobilized, and acted to convince the lower classes of the value of nationalism so that the movement would acquire a mass character and become a political force to be reckoned with. They succeeded, and so the popular strata took the stance maintained by the Greek ruling class, that is, the clergy and the urban bourgeoisie (Katsiaounis 2000, p. 21).

While it was the emerging bourgeoisie who first promoted Greek nationalism and *enosis*, it was when the Church joined the cause that the movement acquired real strength and momentum. After an initial period of adjustment to the new reality, the Cypriot Church was incorporated and, at the same time, it incorporated the *enosis* doctrine. Moreover, it became the most ardent promoter of *enosis*, and led the movement until Cyprus independence in 1960.

The early twentieth century (until the Asia Minor disaster of 1922) was characterized by the total dominance of intransigent forms of nationalism and of the idea of *enosis*. It was in this period that large-scale celebrations of national events took a prominent role in the way nationalist politics were performed. The object was to popularize *enosis* and communicate the fervor of the nationalist movement to a larger audience. Great stress was also placed on close and regular contact with the press whose engagement was crucial for the spread of nationalist ideas. The idea that the Greek nation was defined by a unique cultural individuality made manifest in its language, customs, religion, institutions and history, constituted the (Greek) nation as the new subject of history and subsumed the notion of individual and political freedoms beneath the superior ideal of national self-realization. This powerful tradition coexisted uneasily with ideals of liberal self-government.

NOTES

1. The main thrust of the Great Idea refers to the expansion of the national space (territorial, cultural and economic) into regions regarded as belonging 'by right' to the Greek nation.
2. The term light industrialization suggests that Cyprus never had a heavy industry sector apart from the mines that most of them are now abandoned; rather, Cypriot economy was primarily based throughout the twentieth century in small scale industries, craft industries and commerce, whereas after independence the service sector also grew heavily.
3. The National Archives, CO 883/8/3, X. 39518/29 Minute on the Cyprus Constitution by A. Dawe, 23 April 1929.
4. For the role of the commercial bourgeoisie of the two major coastal towns of Cyprus see Katsiaounis (1996) and Katsourides (2017).
5. On the relationship between nationalism and religion, see Hobsbawm (1994, pp. 99–105) and Lekkas (1996, pp. 178–193).
6. "Truth and reality", article by Achilleas Emilianides, secretary of the National Organization, *Eleftheria*, 11.3.1931, p. 1.
7. "Unorganized", *Eleftheria*, 20.5.1931, p. 1.
8. TNA, CO 67/228/39543 (Part 1), "Movement for union of Cyprus with Greece", No. 376, MacKillop (Athens) to Lord Cushenden, 1 October 1928. On the dependence of Greek foreign policy on Britain, see also Meynaud (2002, p. 60).
9. On the relationship between education and nationalism, see Hobsbawm (1994, p. 134); Lekkas (1996, p. 135).
10. "The non-transferability of teachers", *Eleftheria*, 13.4.1927, p. 1.

REFERENCES

Anagnostopoulou, S. (1999). Η Εκκλησία της Κύπρου και ο Εθναρχικός της Ρόλος: 1878–1960. Η «Θρησκευτικοποίηση» της «Κυπριακής» Πολιτικής Δράσης: Ένωση [The Cypriot Church and its National Role: 1878–1960. The Religiosity of Cypriot Political Activity: Enosis]. *Σύγχρονα Θέματα* [*Contemporary Issues*], 68–69–70, 198–227.
Anderson, B. (1983). *Imagined Communities: Reflections on the Origin and Spread of Nationalism*. London: Verso.

Census of Cyprus of 1911. (1912). London: Waterlow & Sons Ltd.

Census of Cyprus of 1931. (1932). London: F. S. Passingham, Government Printer.

Fenech, D. (2014). The Strangeness of Anglo-Maltese Relations. *Journal of Mediterranean Studies, 23*(1), 21–29.

Gellner, E. (1983). *Nations and Nationalism*. Ithaca: Cornell University Press.

Georghallides, G. (1997). *Ο Χαρακτήρας της Κυπριακής Πολιτικής, Οι Διχόνοιες των Κυπρίων και η Κρίση του 1931* [The Character of Cypriot Politics, the Divisions of the Cypriots and the Crisis of 1931]. Lectures of the Popular University, No. 5. Municipality of Nicosia Publications, pp. 81–95.

Georghallides, G. (1979). *A Political and Administrative History of Cyprus 1918–1926. With a Survey of the Foundations of British Rule.* Nicosia: Cyprus Research Center.

Hall, S., & Gieben, B. (Eds.). (2003). *The Emergence of Modernity. Economy, Society, Politics, Culture.* Athens: Savvalas [in Greek].

Heywood, A. (2003). *Political Ideologies*. Basingstoke: Palgrave Macmillan.

Hill, G. (1952). *A History of Cyprus* (Vol. IV). Cambridge: Cambridge University Press.

Hobsbawm, J. E. (1994). *Nations and Nationalism Since 1780: Programme, Myth, Reality.* Athens: Kardamitsa [in Greek].

Hobsbawm, J. E. (2002). *The Age of Revolution 1789–1848* (4th Ed.). Athens: Cultural Foundation of the National Bank [in Greek].

Hobsbawm, J. E., & Ranger, T. (2015 [1983]). *The Invention of Tradition.* Cambridge: Cambridge University Press.

Holland, R. (1999). *Britain and the Revolt in Cyprus.* Athens: Potamos [in Greek].

Holland, R. (2014). Cyprus and Malta: Two Colonial Experiences. *Journal of Mediterranean Studies, 23*(1), 9–20.

Ioannou, G. (2007). Κοινωνικοοικονομική Ανάπτυξη και Εθνικισμός: Εθνικισμός και Διαφήμιση στον Κυπριακό Τύπο, 1900–1931 [Socioeconomic Development and Nationalism: Nationalism and Advertisements in the Cypriot Press 1900–1931]. *Yearbook of Cypriot Scientific Research* (Nicosia), XXXIII, pp. 383–413.

Katalanos, N. (2003 [1914]). *Κυπριακόν Λεύκωμα Ο Ζήνων* [Cyprus Album Zenon], Nicosia.

Katsiaounis, R. (1994). Εκλέγειν και Εκλέγεσθαι στις Πρώτες Βουλευτικές Εκλογές της Αγγλοκρατίας, το 1883 [The Right to Vote and to Be Elected in the First Parliamentary Elections under British Rule in 1883]. *Yearbook of the Centre of Scientific Research* (Nicosia), XX, pp. 309–345.

Katsiaounis, R. (1995). Κοινωνική και Πολιτική Αλλαγή στην Κύπρο: 1878–1924 [Social and Political Change in Cyprus: 1878–1924]. *Yearbook of the Centre of Scientific Research* (Nicosia), XX, pp. 223–225.

Katsiaounis, R. (1996). *Labour, Society and Politics in Cyprus during the Second Half of the Nineteenth Century.* Nicosia: Cyprus Research Center.

Katsiaounis, R. (2000). Τα Πρώτα Βήματα της Επιτροπής Κυπριακής Αυτονομίας [The First Steps of Cyprus Autonomy Committee]. *Cyprus Research Centre Yearbook* (Nicosia), XXVI, pp. 263–287.

Katsiaounis, R. (2004). *Κοινωνικές, Εθνικές και Πολιτικές Αντιθέσεις στην Κύπρο την Περίοδο της Αγγλοκρατίας 1878–1950* [Social, National and Political Contradictions in Cyprus during the Period of British Rule 1878–1950]. Lectures of the Popular University, No. 16. Municipality of Nicosia Publications, pp. 19–43.

Katsourides, Y. (2013). Nationalism, Anti-colonialism and the Crystallisation of Greek Cypriot Nationalist Party Politics. *Common Wealth and Comparative Politics, 51*(4), 503–523.

Katsourides, Y. (2017). *The Greek Cypriot Nationalist Right in the Era of British Colonialism: Emergence, Mobilisation, Transformations of Right-Wing Party Politics*. Basel: Springer.

Kitromilides, P. (1979). The Dialectic of Intolerance: Ideological Dimensions of Ethnic Conflict. In P. Kitromilides & P. Worsley (Eds.), *Small States in the Modern World. The Conditions of Survival* (pp. 143–184). Nicosia: New Cyprus Association.

Kitromilides, P. (1984). Τα Συλλογικά Πεπρωμένα του Κυπριακού Ελληνισμού τον ΙΗ΄ και ΙΘ΄ Αιώνα [The Collective Fate of Cypriot Hellenism]. In *The Collective Fate of Cypriot Hellenism in the 18th and 19th Century: Findings and Prospects*. Lectures of the Popular University, No. 1. Municipality of Nicosia Publications, pp. 3–13.

Lekkas, P. (1996). *Η Εθνικιστική Ιδεολογία: Πέντε Υποθέσεις Εργασίας στην Ιστορική Κοινωνιολογία* [The Nationalist Ideology: Five Working Hypotheses in Historical Sociology] (2nd ed.). Athens: Katarti.

Liakos, A. (2005). *Πώς Στοχάστηκαν το Έθνος Αυτοί που Ήθελαν να Αλλάξουν τον Κόσμο;* [How Did Those Who Wanted to Change the World Imagine the Nation?]. Athens: Polis.

Loizides, N. (2007). Ethnic Nationalism and Adaptation in Cyprus. *International Studies Perspectives, 8*(2), 172–189.

Macridis, R. (1967). Introduction: The History, Functions, and Typology of Parties. In R. Macridis (Ed.), *Political Parties* (pp. 9–24). London: Harper and Row Publishers.

Mavratsas, C. (2003). *Εθνική Ομοψυχία και Πολιτική Ομοφωνία: Η Ατροφία της Ελληνοκυπριακής Κοινωνίας των Πολιτών στις Απαρχές του 21ου Αιώνα* [National Unity and Political Pluralism: The Atrophy of Greek Cypriot Civil Society at the Beginning of the 21st Century]. Athens: Katarti.

Meynaud, J. (2002). *Πολιτικές Δυνάμεις στην Ελλάδα, 1946–1965* [Political Forces in Greece 1946–1965] (Vol. I). Athens: Savvalas.

Michael, M. (2005). Το Αρχιεπισκοπικό Ζήτημα (1900–1910). Το Ιδεολογικό του Περιεχόμενο και η Ανάδειξη της Εκκλησίας της Κύπρου ως Εθνικής

Αρχής στο Βρετανικό Πλαίσιο Διοίκησης [The Archbishopric Question (1900–1910): Its Ideological Context and the Rise of the Church of Cyprus as a National Authority Within the British Context of Administration]. *Yearbook of the Cyprus Research Center* (Nicosia), XXXI, pp. 307–360.

Panayiotou, A. (2006a). Models of Compromise and Power Sharing in the Experience of Cypriot Modernity. *The Cyprus Review, 18*(2), 75–103.

Panayiotou, A. (2006b). Lenin in the Coffee-Shop: The Communist Alternative and Forms of Non-western Modernity. *Postcolonial Studies, 9*(3), 267–280.

Panayiotou, A. (2012). Border Dialectics: Cypriot Social and Historical Movements in a World Systemic Context. In N. Trimikliniotis & N. Bozkurt (Eds.), *Beyond a Divided Cyprus: A State and Society in Transformation* (pp. 67–82). New York: Palgrave Macmillan.

Papapolyviou, P. (1997). *Η Κύπρος και οι Βαλκανικοί Πόλεμοι: Συμβολή στην Ιστορία του Κυπριακού Εθελοντισμού* [Cyprus'and the Balkan Wars. Contribution to the History of Cypriot Volunteerism]. Nicosia: Cyprus Research Centre.

Peristianis, N. (1993). *Θρησκεία και Εκκλησία στην Κύπρο* [Religion and Church in Cyprus]. Lectures of the Popular University, Municipality of Nicosia Publications, No. 3, 245–262.

Persianis, P. (1978). *Church and State in Cyprus Education*. Nicosia.

Reilly, B. (2006). Political Engineering and Party Politics in Conflict-Prone Societies. *Democratization, 13*(5), 811–827.

Richter, H. (2007). *History of Cyprus (1878–1949)* (Vol. I). Athens: Estia. [in Greek].

Rokkan, S. (1970). *Citizen, Elections, Parties*. New York: McKay Co.

Smith, A. (1998). *Nationalism and Modernism: A Critical Survey of Recent Theories of Nations and Nationalism*. London and New York: Routledge.

Smith, A. (1986). *The Ethnic Origin of Nations*. Oxford: Blackwell.

Storrs, R. (1945). *Orientations*. London: Nicholson and Watson.

Tornaritis, C. (1948). *Ιστορία του Συγκεκροτημένου Κυπριακού Τεκτονισμού και Άλλαι Πραγματίαι και Ομιλίαι* [History of the Organized Cypriot Freemasonry and Other Masonic Writings and Speeches]. Limassol.

Tzermias, P. (2001). *Ιστορία της Κυπριακής Δημοκρατίας* [History of Cypriot Democracy] (Vol. I). Athens: Libro.

Yiallourides, C. (1993). Το Κυπριακό Κομματικό Σύστημα [The Cyprus Party System]. In J. Raschke & E. Katsoulis (Eds.), *Τα Πολιτικά Κόμματα της Δυτικής Ευρώπης* [The Political Parties of Western Europe] (pp. 159–205). Thessaloniki: Paratiritis.

Newspaper

Eleftheria 11.3.1931, 20.5.1931, 13.4.1927.

CHAPTER 3

National Identity, Otherness, and Bi-communal Relations Through the Cypriot Greek-Speaking Press Between 1878 and 1912

Petros Nikolaou

To Nicolas

INTRODUCTION

The prevailing perception among Greek Cypriots today views Turkey, Turks, and Turkish Cypriots as their significant "others". The prevalence of such a perception can be detected largely in the Greek national narrative which was built through the years based on the argument of eternal Turkish expansionism against Hellenism. This well-structured, "demonized" image of the "other" according to Heraclides (2006), requires the simultaneous production of a "traumatic sense of victimization" which establishes, justifies and reproduces the given image of the

P. Nikolaou (✉)
Department of Turkish and Middle Eastern Studies,
University of Cyprus, Nicosia, Cyprus

© The Author(s) 2018
T. Kyritsi and N. Christofis (eds.), *Cypriot Nationalisms in Context*,
https://doi.org/10.1007/978-3-319-97804-8_3

"other" (p. 50). Thus, the continued occupation of part of Cyprus's territory since 1974 constitutes an "unshakable" fact of affirmation, documenting this prevailing image of Turks. Although the 1974 events can be seen only as the result of a process begun decades ago, they confirm and reinforce the negative stereotypes of the "other", i.e., the national/communal enemy.

Based on this process, the dividing line between Greeks and Turks, Greek Cypriots and Turkish Cypriots is in a continuous process of reproduction and consolidation. This distinction between the "self" and the "other" implies from the outset the existence of an identity that is constructed together with otherness. As Kyriakides and Michaelidou (2006) argue, "the other exists as 'other' only through the relationship with the self and... the otherness is constituted through its relationship with the identity" (p. 134). Therefore, national identity is defined not only by its own elements, but also by its need to emphasize the distinguishing features of "others". This dialectical relationship between identity and otherness advances a better understanding of those mechanisms through which the national "other" is constructed together with national identity, since the hypothesis of a "positive national self", needs and reinforces a "coherent other" (Triandafyllidou 1998). Based on the above, the construction of Greek Cypriots' national/communal "other" goes back to the time when the Orthodox Cypriot community was exorcising its religious character and acquiring a national identity.

This chapter seeks to present relations between Greek and Turkish Cypriots as portrayed through the Greek-speaking press during the first years of the British period (1878–1912). It attempts also to discuss the dialectical relationship between identity and otherness applied in the case of Cyprus, by stressing particularly the role the Greek-speaking press played in this regard. The press, as one of the main purveyors of Greek nationalism in Cyprus, took a major part in diffusing and cultivating Greek national identity and picturing, simultaneously, an image of Turks as the "others". Nonetheless, it should be made clear here that the press is examined as a purveyor, a tool for representing and promoting the interests and aspirations of the Greek Cypriot community's elite, and following Hobsbawm's (1992) remark, in no way should the presented editorials, beliefs and attitudes be confused with public opinion (p. 11); instead, they should be seen as a means of disseminating and cultivating these perceptions to the public.

CYPRUS BEFORE NATIONALISM(S)

Several studies argue that although the process of constructing Greek Cypriots' national identity can be dated back to the mid-nineteenth century, it cannot be supported that there was a national consciousness already developed when the British arrived on the island (Kitromilides 1994). There are numerous studies supporting that throughout the Ottoman period, relations between the two religious communities in Cyprus were "friendly" and "peaceful" (Varnava 2009, p. 155; Attalides 1981, pp. 415–417). Mixed Muslim and Orthodox congregations in mosques and churches were "not a rare phenomenon", since they would celebrate each other's religious feasts together (Pollis 1998b, p. 30; Attalides 1981, p. 417), while "several inter-marriages" are reported in the literature "even though this was strictly forbidden by both religions" (Nevzat 2005, pp. 66–68; Pollis 1998b, p. 30).

It is also maintained that at least until the mid-nineteenth century, any conflicts or insurrections occurring in Cyprus did not have any national or religious character but "seem[ed] to have been along class lines" (Pollis 1979, pp. 49–50). As Pollis (1998a) notes, any conflicts taking place were "conflicts between the religious elites about privileges, power, and control" (pp. 88–89). On the contrary, though, there were indeed numerous common uprisings (1665, 1680, 1712, 1764–1765, 1783, 1804, 1830, 1833) engaged in by Orthodox and Muslim peasants and directed against local elites of Ottoman authority, bishops and Muslim and Orthodox tax collectors (Michael 2016; Hill 1952, pp. 70–119, 157–170).[1]

Even during the Greek Revolution in 1821, any conflicts occurring in Cyprus did not seem to have national or religious characteristics but were "between the Ottoman Muslim and the Orthodox elites" (Michael 2016; Pollis 1979, p. 49). Moreover, the executions of Archbishop Kyprianos, the three Bishops (Paphos, Kition and Kyrenia) and "almost the entire Orthodox elite of the island" (Katsiaounis 1996, p. 13) appeared, according to Heraclides (2006), to be part of the "pre-existing elitist conflict between the Church and the Ottoman authorities" (p. 76). The 1821 executions, however, served to produce the first national heroes, raising Archbishop Kyprianos to the status of *ethno-martyr* and passing him into what Smith (1986) calls the "mythological pantheon of national heroes" (p. 213).

The 1821 events, however, did not alter the class orientation of Cypriot society, and so Ottoman officials and the Church continued to comprise a group of elites, while the lower strata of the population continued to live and act according to local traditional values, perceiving themselves as peasants, Orthodox and Muslims, "but not yet as members of a wider national community" (Pollis 1998a, p. 87). Even after the establishment of the Greek state in 1830, the various uprisings occurring in Cyprus were based on socioeconomic reasons rather than religious, let alone national—as exemplified in the common uprisings of 1830 (Hill 1952, pp. 157–158) and 1833 (Michael 2012).

CONSTRUCTION OF THE GREEK NATIONAL IDENTITY

Historically, the emergence of Greek nationalism in Cyprus was part of the Great Idea's irredentist program, as expressed in Greece in the mid-nineteenth century. The establishment of the Greek state in 1830 made evident the need to cultivate a common identity that would "distort social contrasts", "degrade internal conflicts" and "ultimately legitimize state power" (Skopetea 1988, pp. 41–65). Accordingly, the nation-building process began in earnest, aiming on the one hand, through the cultivation of a sense of "fraternity" among in-border Greeks, to provide "national family-ties", thereby equating individuals and social classes, and on the other hand, to identify out-of-bounds populations with the Greek Kingdom (Kitromilides 2003, p. 74). Thus, Greek nationalism took the various pre-existing ethnic elements of traditional society and placed them under the service of the state, in other words "Hellenized" them (Skopetea 1988, p. 175), and produced a common national identity and a sense of "communion" (Anderson 2006, p. 6). To this end, the Greek state put in process some basic actions.

First, in 1833, through a royal declaration, the Greek Kingdom unilaterally proclaimed the Church of Greece's independence and placed it under its authority, ceasing this way the pre-revolutionary conflict between the Patriarchate and the Modern Greek enlighteners (Skopetea 1988, pp. 119–134).[2] Second, due to the presence of "foreign language idioms" that produced "linguistic heterogeneity", which presented a "real communication and comprehension problem" between both in- and out-border Greeks and within the Kingdom itself, the Greek state, through the development of a "national" education system, sought to assimilate the various idioms and dialects by establishing "a single, common and homogeneous" national language (Skopetea 1988, pp. 117–118).[3] Third, and of great importance to the nation-building process, was the transfer of the capital city from Nafplio to Athens in 1834, since Athens' ancient monuments were "the only ready national symbols" that could be used by the state to "prove" the continuation of the Greek nation in time, and to disseminate more effectively to in- and out-border Greeks the sense of a "common origin through common ancestors" (Skopetea 1988, p. 197; Smith 1986, p. 213).[4] Fourth, in an attempt to restore the Byzantine period and connect modern with ancient Greeks, thus covering "the big gap" between the two Greek worlds (Skopetea 1988, pp. 175–183), Spyridon Zambelios, in 1852, connected Byzantium with neo-Hellenism through *Greek-Christianity*, "a term introduced for a first time" (Aroni-Tsihli 2008, p. 351), while Konstantinos Paparigopoulos considered the Byzantium contribution most important, because it had "unified Hellenism politically for the first time" (Veremis 2003, p. 29).

The above actions determined and rendered the nation's distinct character, provided the Greek nation with historical continuity and offered to all Greeks a common point of origin—they originated from the ancient Greeks, with whom they were connected through language, space and traditions, and from the Byzantines, with whom they connected through religion. The Church and religion were politicized for becoming important elements of the nation's determination, and through the identification of religious and national identity, "the concepts of Christian and Greek [became] almost synonymous and defined in opposition to the identical pair of the concepts of Muslim and Turk" (Lekkas 1992, p. 159).

THE EMERGENCE OF GREEK NATIONALISM IN CYPRUS

The establishment of the first Greek Consulate in Larnaca, in 1846, can be regarded as the first official act of the Greek state to promote the newly-established ideology in Cyprus. Nevertheless, the development of any national consciousness at that time remained within the limits of a small cohort of educated elite, and even until the last years of the Ottoman period, Greek nationalism did not seem to affect the broader masses. Elias Vassiliadis, the last Greek sub-consul of the Ottoman period, reported in 1876 that "the spirit of Hellenism in some places is asleep and in others is totally non-existent" (cited in Katsiaounis 2004, p. 52). The growth of national consciousness and the gradual conversion of Orthodox into Greek-orthodox identity was a British-era phenomenon. The press had a significant role to play in this process by promoting Greek nationalism and contributing to the construction of Greek Cypriots' national identity—and therefore to the gradual differentiation of the "we" from the "others".

One of the first efforts of the Greek-speaking press in this direction was noted on the occasion of the first annual report by the Limassol Commander, Warren, in 1879. Reporting on the political situation in Cyprus, Warren alleged that a "clique of foreigners [...], led by the *Cypriote Fraternity of Egypt* and its clubs in Cyprus", had expanded into cities and "[made] every effort to create a national movement in Cyprus which [would] claim the Union with Greece" (SA03/87 1879). *Neon Kition*⁵ described these accusations as "inconsistent", criticizing the British Government for misleading *Fraternity's* "noble and high purpose" (1879a). Rejecting the claims for Greek nationalist propaganda in Cyprus, *Neon Kition* commented:

> ... as if Cypriots were not the perfect distillation of Hellenism ... [and as if Cypriots haven't] struggled – since the Phoenicians to today ... – against all of their invaders and conquerors, and for the most part Hellenized them. (1879a)

A few days later, on the same occasion, *Neon Kition*, in an attempt to "prove" Cyprus's Greekness, developed a comparative argumentation, outlining the characteristics that supposedly defined "Greeks" and separated them from "Muslims". The relationship of the "self" with the wider national community through which it is identified empowers and acquires, as Lekkas (1992) argues, its "distinct character" through "continuous stereotypical contradictions that resulted from a comparative and hetero-determination processes" (p. 131). Consequently, *Neon Kition* stressed that "apart from ethnic differences" (religion, language, customs) and "no natural dispositions and impetuosities", "Greeks" and "Mohammedans" differed also "at all material progress, as well as in moral and intellectual development" (1879b). The differences in material progress were supposed to lie in the fact that "Greeks" were engaged with agriculture, industry, and commerce, unlike "Mohammedans", who were military, porters and "truants by their nature, replenishing their livelihood needs from the Greeks" (*Neon Kition* 1879b). As for "intellectual development", the difference supposedly laid again in "inherent" characteristics. Very few Muslims knew how to read, and even fewer to write, because in their schools they were taught only the reading and writing of the Koran. On the other hand, "Greeks", "because of the Gospel's religion... and other characteristics inherent to Hellenism", had "an organized school system, even in villages", while many of them were studying at the University of Athens because according to the same source they had "progressive tendencies", they were "flowing with morality" and they were "ready for big things, looking toward the future" (*Neon Kition* 1879b).

The issue of Greek nationalist propaganda in Cyprus was raised in the House of Commons again the following year, causing further reaction from the press: "Isn't it ridiculous", *Neon Kition* (1880) wondered, "to imagine that there is a Greek propaganda in a Greek territory and among thousands of authentic Greek people?", assuring the British Government that "if there is a Greek propaganda in Cyprus, it is constituted by thousands of Greeks, whose only desire is to be governed by the new government in accordance with the principles of justice and freedom". This last comment illustrates the attitude of Greek nationalism toward the British administration at the time. Despite the reactions to the British statements, Greek Cypriot nationalism was mild in its approach to the British. Even the *enosis* demand was raised under the precondition that England would decide, for whatever reason, to leave Cyprus; if the Greek Cypriots were, however, assured that Cyprus would remain under British rule, then "their pleasure [would have] no limits and their enthusiasm [would go] beyond any description" (*Neon Kition* 1880).

The above extracts also reveal a paradox that indicates the peculiarities of Cyprus's case. Particularly, while the *enosis* demand in fact implied British withdrawal, the anti-colonialism of Greek Cypriot nationalism seemed "not [to] have an anti-British character" (Katsiaounis 2004, pp. 19–20), thus preserving, at least until the 1940s, a more oppositional stance toward the British Government's internal policy, proclaiming that Greek Cypriots complaints were "just about pounds, shillings and pennies" (*Alitheia*[6] 1893b). Conversely, being an offshoot of the Greek irredentist vision against the Ottoman Empire, Greek Cypriot nationalism began to construct the same significant other as the other of the Greeks, i.e., the Turk.

Yet the development of Greek nationalism in Cyprus was still at a limited level. The construction of national identity and otherness was a gradual process passing through different stages and levels. Thus, co-understanding between the two communities' leading members, and the collaboration between them at the Legislature in defense of common interests, remained undisturbed, while, the middle and lower strata of the population did not seem to have been affected by the nationalist ideology. Especially in Nicosia, which was "under the full influence of the Archdiocese", the development of national consciousness was slower compared to Larnaca and Limassol (Katsiaounis 1996, p. 182). For example, the 1821 anniversary of the Greek War of Independence was celebrated in Nicosia for the very first time in 1885, albeit celebrations were not repeated the following year (Anagnostopoulou 2004, p. 192), in contrast to the crowded celebrations in Larnaca and Limassol (*Foni tis Kyprou*[7] 1886; *Alitheia* 1886). The aforementioned could only confirm Hobsbawm's (1992) observation that "national consciousness develops unevenly among the social groupings and *regions* of a country" and that "whatever the nature of the social groups first captured by 'national consciousness', the popular masses [...] are the last to be affected by it" (p. 12, emphasis in the original).

Nonetheless, even in the more radical environments of Larnaca and Limassol, not only had the Ottoman past not been demonized, but it had also been compared with the British administration. Representative thereof is an incident that took place in Easter 1885. During the Orthodox religious ceremony of the *Epitaph's* procession along Limassol's streets, some British, who were at the English Club, "humiliated" the procession, causing riots throughout the city. *Alitheia* stated that the Ottoman administration not only made it easy for the Orthodox Christians to practice their religious customs, but they also "had the courtesy to provide a custodian for the procession's honorary guard" (1885). Two years later, due to the economic depression into which the island fell, *Alitheia* once again made a comparison between the old and new rulers. According to the newspaper, the Ottoman government "was ceaselessly thinking of how to heal the infertility's victims" by spending "brave sums of money" and "suspending the payment of taxes". On the contrary, the "Christian" and "civilized" British government "unconditionally continue[d] collecting taxes". The exhilaration surrounding the Sultan's tax policy remained in place during the next few years (*Alitheia* 1887). On 23 January 1891, *Alitheia* reported that the "uncivilized"

Turkish legislator had ordered the imprisonment of those debtors who were evidently able to pay but had not done so, contrary to the "civilized" British that imprisoned even those who demonstrably were incapable of paying their taxes (1891a).

INTRODUCING THE DEMONIZATION/VICTIMIZATION SCHEME

The 1890s can be regarded as a period of development for Greek nationalism in Cyprus. As already mentioned, during the construction of a national identity, a given coherent image of the "other" is needed and reinforced. Consequently, the further identification with Hellenism imposed the Ottoman past's demonization. This process began through the "rewriting" of history, and the way in which Cyprus's periods of history were narrated through the newspapers columns is characteristic in this regard.

Among others, the articles of Georgios Shiakalis and Theophanis Theodotou (both graduates of Athens University and elected MPs) can be cited as examples of the first attempts to set the basis for today's official Greek Cypriot narrative of history. Shiakalis, after demonstrating that Cypriots originated from the Ionians, made a simple reference to the "occupation" by the Egyptians and the Phoenicians and continued to focus on the "restoration" of Cyprus to the Greeks during the Trojan War—"a period when the island stood very prosperous". This "prosperous" period was interrupted in 804 AD, when the Turks "conquered" the island: "By that time, until 958 AD, when the Turks were expelled", the island met with "one of the darkest pages of its history", since "thousands of people had been killed, public auctions were ruined, and heavy taxes were imposed". The article continued by making a simple reference to the rest of the conquerors up to 1571, when Cyprus was once again "conquered" by the Turks, and "suffered again" until the British "occupation" in 1878 (*Alitheia* 1893c).[8]

Theodotou, following the same polarized scheme, placed more emphasis on the second Ottoman period, especially on the period after 1821. As he described, after the Turks "imposed" their power "with a series of cruelness", through the beginning of the Greek Revolution, "there was a true holocaust of Cypriot Bishops, who died for the freedom's sacred purpose". Furthermore:

> After slaughtering the nobles, the Turks forcibly fled against the people, and in all places the horrors of cruel warlords prevailed; they plundered all the way, they harassed virgins, crossed the bellies of pregnant women, and tortured the mothers [...], cut off the nursing babies in front of their mothers. All the Greek-speaking people had suffered from the greatest or at least the same brutality, everywhere. (*Alitheia* 1893a)[9]

Setting the historical background in that way, the Ottoman past had been demonized and the image of Turks as Hellenism's eternal enemy began to take form, together with the simultaneous production of a "traumatic sense of victimization". The press would have a key role to play in the process of cultivating and diffusing the demonization/victimization scheme through also the way by which it reported and described events and various incidents, both local and external.

For example, in regard to a number of clashes that took place in 1893 in Limassol between Greek Cypriots from Colossi and Turkish Cypriots from Episkopi, the press reported that while the former were awaiting a bridegroom from Episkopi, 300 Turks "holding the crescent" "invaded" Colossi, which they found defenseless, and "shouting beat the *gavurs*, they stabbed, broke heads, threw children into the watercourse, trampled elder people" (*Neon Ethnos*[10] 1893). Addressing, therefore, the High Commissioner *Alitheia* commented: "Where is security? Where is serenity? Where is calmness? We stand alone against the viciousness, being routed by nefarious criminals. We are destitute and poor and we are threatened in every single step" (1893d). A week later, the press reported one more incident that took place in a coffee shop in Colossi (*Alitheia* 1893e), while in March 1894 "racial rupture" was also reported in Paphos (*Alitheia* 1894a).

As indicated by the press, clashes occurred in areas where Greek and Turkish Cypriots lived in a shared community. *Alitheia* stated that "many times, quarrels are taking place [and] the Turks are often attacking [Greek Cypriots] in groups [...] [who] resist from the need to defend themselves", since "there is no power to restrain the effervescent passions" (1894b). However, the Chief-Secretary, J. Thomson, stated at the Legislature that he had been informed about these cases by newspapers, and whereas the causes of the incidents "were insignificant", these articles were intended to demonstrate that they arose from "religious rivalries", indicating that "the responsibility for undermining religious hatred" laid at the feet of the newspapers (*Alitheia* 1894c).

The Spread of Nationalism

In the immediate future, "rumors" about a possible change in Cyprus's status, as well as the wider Greek-Turkish conflict around the Cretan issue, would further influence the development of the Greek Cypriot nationalism—and therefore the further expansion of anti-Turkish sentiments.

In March 1895, in a debate in the House of Commons on Cyprus's *Grant in Aid*, several British MPs once again expressed doubts as to the island's usefulness in the British strategic policy in the region (Hansard 1895a). Moreover, Minister of Finance, W. Harcourt, claimed that Cyprus was nothing more than a "financial burden" to Britain, which could not be overcome due to the Tribute to Porte (Hansard 1895b). The aggregation of these two negative facts for Cyprus led some British MPs to support the suggestion that the 1878 Treaty should be rescinded and Cyprus returned back to Turkey (Hansard 1895c, d). As expected, the press expressed its strong reaction to these statements, describing them as "blasphemies" expressed by "2-3 pro-Turkish or Turkified British" (*Alitheia* 1895).

In the previous year, the press had also voiced its opposition to any change in Cyprus's status due to "hearsay" about the British withdrawal from the island, on the occasion of the redeployment of a large part of the British Army from Cyprus to Malta (*Evagoras*[11] 1894). Again, the case gave the press the opportunity to promulgate anti-Turkish sentiments. *Alitheia* commented on this point on 16 August 1894: "As this malicious hearsay repeats today, no-one dares to say it openly, everyone is hiding, fearing that the air of Cyprus will be polluted only by the words that has for centuries polluted everyone" (1894d). *Neon Ethnos* also stated that Cyprus's cession to its former masters "little differs from desolation and hunger, destruction and devastation" (1894). Consequently, the following year's British MPs' statement in favor of the return of Cyprus to Turkey caused demonstrations across the island, expressing the demand that "no political change in Cyprus would be accepted, other than *enosis*". The outcome of these rallies was to send a Cypriot Memorandum to Colonial Secretary Chamberlain in which, for the first time, there was a formal reference to *enosis* (*Neon Ethnos* 1895a).

The 1895 rallies also offer two important points. The first one is that although the rallies signified ostensibly a rejection of returning to the previous regime rather than *enosis* itself, the "national spirit", even in this context, had for the first time "a significant amount of public expression" (*Neon Ethnos* 1895a, b). *Alitheia* remarked on this point, noting that "never before has the national consciousness been demonstrated in such a way, and never before has such a crowd gathered in so imposing and stately rallies" (1895). The second important point regards the protesters' age composition at Nicosia's rally. The city's Commander, M. King, reported that a large proportion of the protesters "were aged 18-20, if not younger" (cited in Katsiaounis 1996, p. 209). This figure demonstrates the effectiveness of the educational system in orienting students to Greek nationalism and cultivating anti-Turkish sentiments. The following incident, cited by *Neon Ethnos* while the Cretan insurgency was underway, is descriptive of the educational system's good "national work":

> In a village, a teacher and his pupils gathered 150 dimes to buy 150 bullets. That's how it happened. The teacher recounted to his pupils about the Turkish atrocities in Crete; a pupil then raised-up to the sermon and said: "Teacher, I have one dime; with it I will buy a bullet to send it to Crete, for killing a Turk". His example excited his other classmates, and the teacher gathered 150 dimes to buy 150 bullets, in order to kill 150 Turks. (1896b)[12]

THE INFLUENCE OF 1897

Undoubtedly, the 1897 Greek-Turkish war and the Cretan insurrection had their own impact on Cyprus. For Greek nationalism, it was the first war against the "eternal enemy", and the descriptions through the newspaper columns of Turkish "brutalities" in Crete, and their recitation by teachers in schools, comprised a first-rate opportunity for acquainting Greek Cypriots (mainly the youth) with the "eternal" and "bloodthirsty tyrant" (*Neon Ethnos* 1896c).

The process of affairs in Crete was described by the press as a "long-drawn plan", which was followed by the Turks "in religious reverence", aiming at "the extinction and eradication of the heroic people". This plan was based on the "illiberal" and "despotic" traditions that were used by the Turks as "the lever of perpetual extermination and destruction of Christian populations" (*Neon Ethnos* 1896a). Thus, the Cretan question was released from its local character and commenced a struggle involving all Hellenism against the "common eternal enemy". The Cretan struggle was "a struggle of all Hellenism; the destruction of

Crete is equal to a destruction of the Panhellenic" (*Alitheia* 1896). Therefore, the practical aid to Crete was a "duty" of both unredeemed and free Hellenism (*Neon Ethnos* 1896c), so that Crete would become the "tomb of Muslim power" (*Alitheia* 1896). The crowded celebrations of March 25, 1897, by "all strata" of the population (*Foni tis Kyprou* 1897), as well as the "festive" departures of volunteers to Greece (*Neon Ethnos* 1897a), were indicative of the extent to which nationalist ideals had been spread among Greek Cypriots.

The defeat of Greece, however, constituted a "disgrace" that had to be "washed-away" (Katalanos 1914, p. 122). *Alitheia* commented on this accordingly:

> ... each one of us must become an apostle of Hellenism, armed with something that we lack of and that we need. This is the hatred for our enemies, to our tyrants. A fierce, bitter, poisoned hate... And you, oh, sweet virgins! Loving future mothers. In your heart, made for love and only love, in an aside place, fit the hatred for our enemies and tyrants. Let it be a fierce, bitter, poisoned hatred, that when you will have your baby angels in your knees or in the cradle, lolling them with kisses and saying loving words to them, to pour it into their tender hearts. And later on, when you become happy grandmothers and you narrate the tale to your cheerful grandchildren, oh, let this fairy be a story of love and hate; love for that golden country, Greece. Hate for the enemies that we all know. (1898)[13]

Despite the defeat, the progress of affairs in Crete would have a "favorable influence" on Greek Cypriot nationalism by creating suitable conditions and offering the necessary impetus for its further development in Cyprus. The autonomy status granted to Crete, under a Greek High-Commissioner and without the obligation to pay a Tribute to Porte, comprised, according to Haynes-Smith, the "most powerful influence on the Greek-speaking Cypriotes, and there [were] several of the moderate men who, watching Crete, are beginning to think that union with Greece would be for the material advantage and progress of the island" (cited in Nevzat 2005, p. 145).

Indeed, during the next period, the further identification of nationalism with *enosis* and its spread among the popular strata of the population would also be abetted by the ten-year archiepiscopal dispute (1900–1910) between *Kireniakoi* and *Kitiakoi*.[14] On the one side, the *Kitiakoi* supported the adoption of a more radical attitude in favor of *enosis* demands. On the other side, *Kireniakoi* maintained a moderate stance, in the belief that the *enosis* would be accomplished through a Greek-British agreement. Who would be at the Archbishop's throne would determine "the outcome of the national struggle" (*Evagoras* 1901a). Consequently, the 1901 Legislative elections were conducted in the most "politicized and polarized" contexts since the first elections of 1883 (*Alitheia* 1901a). The full prevalence of *Kitiakoi*, with the election of none of the candidates from the *Kireniakoi* faction—even of those who had been for years members of the Legislature and "appreciated by the farmers" (*Foni tis Kyprou* 1901a)—signaled the beginning of a new era, namely the predominance of nationalism and the popularization of *enosis* demands.

WHAT ABOUT THE TURKISH CYPRIOTS?

The 1901 elections also brought to light the question about the attitude that had to be maintained toward Turkish Cypriots. The "celebratory welcome" of the Larnaca–Famagusta constituency MP Derviş Paşa in Nicosia gave rise to a strong debate on the issue. Specifically, Greek and Turkish Cypriots, including Katalanos, a Peloponnesian teacher and newspaper editor, and Shiakalis, a newly elected MP in the Nicosia-Kyrenia constituency for the *Kitiakoi*, "warmly welcomed" Derviş to Aglantzia as an indication of their "good and sincere" willingness for "conciliation and cooperation" between the two main elements of the island (*Evagoras* 1901b). The common celebrations, due to "the large number of the concentrated people", continued at the reading club *Agapi tou Laou* (People's Love) and culminated at the Ottoman reading club at Saray Square (*Evagoras* 1901b).

The incident sparked reactions by more radicals on the issue. The joint presence of Greek and Turkish Cypriots, holding Greek and Turkish flags, along with the mutual pronouncements at Saray Square, was the subject of the symbolic reliving of traumatic historical events. *Foni tis Kyprou* criticized the common event in Saray: "where the blood of Archbishop Kyprianos and the other ethnomartyrs still steams", stressing that Greek Cypriots position "is not under the Turkish flag" (1901b). *Alitheia*, characterized what happened in Nicosia as "eyesore scenes", criticizing also the procession of the Greek flag for being "brotherly" with the Turkish one (1901b).

Moreover, the issue of cooperation between the two communities was described by *Alitheia* as a "monstrous alliance", which had "no practical purpose", because "Ottoman delegates would turn their backs to us, when the vital and greatly important issues of the island, such as the Tribute or the national restoration of Cyprus, come before us" (1901b). *Foni tis Kyprou* also noted that Turkish Cypriots "not only do not agree with its abolition or even its reduction", but they also "do not even allow the word 'Tribute' to be written in official statements". Concerning the national issue, *Foni tis Kyprou* commented that Turkish Cypriots' "heads may fall, but they will never accept such a solution", characterizing as "ridiculous" any thought of reaching an understanding with them on this matter (1901b).

In fact, *Alitheia*'s reaction was more intense on the issue, as it criticized a cooperation with the Ottomans as being "inconsistent with the big words and programs on national politics" (1901c). *Alitheia*'s criticism was directed at Shiakalis and Katalanos, accusing the former of committing "a first-rate, unforgivable slip-up" as an elected MP of the "national party" and the latter for propagating, through *Evagoras*'s columns, "his monstrous political doctrine [...] for co-operating with the eternal enemy" (1901b). The important point here is the open and direct description of Turkish Cypriots as the "enemy". Over previous years, the Greek Cypriot press had used the word "enemy" mainly for non-Cypriot Turks and mostly for non-local events, thereby maintaining a dividing line between Turkish Cypriots and non-Cypriot Turks.

For *Alitheia*, cooperation with the Turkish Cypriots, although regarded as "useful" in local matters, would "de facto turn out to be weak and chimeric" on major and important issues (1901c). Besides, during the pre-election period, *Alitheia* argued that the moderate national policy pursued by the Greek Cypriot politicians in order "not to dissatisfy" the Turkish Cypriots prevented the adoption of a more radical policy in the Legislature on more important issues (1901a). Cyprus's national restoration should be "the Alpha and the Omega of all political actions", disregarding the "small benefits that may arise" from collaboration with the Turkish Cypriots (*Alitheia* 1901c).

Katalanos perceived things quite differently during that period. As he argued, the great national issues, as well as local matters, required the maintenance of friendly relations and cooperation between the two elements. The cultivation of racial passions, "attributing to the Ottomans, by preconception or racial disgrace, all the evils", would not yield any

practical purpose, because it would neither "breach the Tribute's abolition or reduction nor make the national restoration of the island easier" (*Evagoras* 1901c). Katalanos, replying to *Alitheia*'s chief-editor,
Frangoudis, commented:

> If he had read more carefully the history of his particular country, he
> might have learned that the Greek Cypriots have excellent reasons for not
> being intransigent toward their Muslims fellow citizens and for compar-
> ing the Frankish and Venetian domination to the Turkish conquest; we will
> not hesitate to also compare it to some points to the British administra-
> tion on the island. Since the immediate domination and administration of
> Cyprus under the Turkish maladministration was absent, and both com-
> munities always bear tax burdens in the same way, there was no cause for
> division or hatred between them. In our time, there were conditions in
> Cyprus for which prosperity imposed collaboration, friendly understand-
> ing and a closer approach between the two communities in the interests
> of both, and any old hatred and passions would only achieve to abet and
> reintroduce malevolence and foolishness. (*Evagoras* 1901c)

Of course, the above statement comprised a significant modification in
Katalanos' approach to Turkish Cypriots. In 1897 (before the Greek-
Turkish war), he argued for a "need for separation", due to clashes
that took place in Nicosia between Greek and Turkish Cypriot butch-
ers. The clashes gave occasion to stress that "due to racial and religious
motives, unfortunately, any close contact between Muslims and Greeks
should not be allowed, while historical memories further widen this gap"
(*Evagoras* 1897).

A possible reason for this change in stance is that despite the "nation-
ally" favorable situation created for Crete, the recent defeat made evident
Greece's "powerlessness" in relation to the Ottoman Empire, and this
comprised a deterrent to creating a conflictual situation in Cyprus similar
to that in Crete. Besides, Cyprus was under British administration and
the Greek Cypriot nationalist movement would not want to disrupt in
any way the Greek-British friendship, through which it was hoped that
enosis would be accomplished. Thus, the argumentation in favor of the
peaceful cohabitation of the two communities resulted from the belief
that, in the event of a change in Cyprus's status, a solution based on the
majority's principle may be favored. This was probably the reason for the
frequent references to "the natural right of each community" to work
toward its national aspirations (*Evagoras* 1900, 1903a).

RADICALIZING THE *ENOSIS* POLITICS

The following year, the official connection between any possibility for *enosis* with the Turkish Cypriot opposition would bring Greek Cypriots' attention to the majority/minority scheme and increase their political actions in relation to *enosis*. Particularly in May 1902, in a debate in the House of Commons on Cyprus's *Grant in Aid*, the issue of the island's future status was raised once again (Hansard 1902a). On this contentious topic, Chamberlain stated that "even if an international agreement could be arrived" at to that effect (*enosis*), it was doubtful whether "there would be any general agreement" on the subject, since "there is a very large Mohammedan population opposed to any such transfer", making impossible any change in the island's status (Hansard 1902b).

Commenting on this point, *Neon Ethnos* stated that in such circumstances, "the historical law and the Greek Cypriots' numerical superiority are prevailing in every opposition" (1902). Chamberlain's statement, apart from causing protest and pro-*enosis* rallies across Cyprus (*Alitheia* 1902a), also pushed Greek Cypriot MPs to defend the right to the majority's principle and radicalize *enosis* politics. Specifically, on 5 June 1902, Shiakalis stated at the Legislature that Cyprus should be ceded "where the majority of the inhabitants want to be" (*Alitheia* 1902b). On 1 July, on the occasion of and in reaction to Chamberlain's statement, Greek Cypriot MPs, taking advantage on the absence of an official MP, voted on a protest resolution through which, for the first time, there was a direct reference to *enosis* demands (*Alitheia* 1902c). The following year, on 24 April 1903, Greek Cypriot MPs, taking advantage of Derviş Paşa's absence from the Legislature session, through a counter-speech to the opening speech of the High Commissioner, succeeded in including *enosis* demands for the very first time in an official British document, thus signaling a new era for Greek Cypriot nationalism and bi-communal relations (*Alitheia* 1903a). The press described this progress as the "natural aftermath" (*Evagoras* 1903d) and the "inevitable outcome of national fermentation of the previous years" (*Alitheia* 1903a).

Turkish Cypriot MPs, for their part, proposed to annex an additional paragraph in which their community's distinct national feelings would be referred to, expressing their desire to return Cyprus to its "lawful owner, when the proper time arrives" (Nevzat 2005, p. 131). Although the Turkish Cypriot proposal was rejected, on his return to Cyprus, Derviş Paşa introduced a new resolution, reiterating that "the whole

Muslim population of this island [was] strongly resistant" to any prospect of *enosis* and objecting to its inclusion in the counter-speech as "a
desire of the people of Cyprus as a whole", expressing the prospect that
if Britain left Cyprus, the island should be returned to Porte. Derviş's
resolution was eventually voted since, together with the Turkish Cypriot
MPs, the British Members of the Legislative Council also voted for it
(*Alitheia* 1903b).

This development nourished the already existing Greek Cypriot belief
about the British attempt to "split" the indigenous collaboration in the
Legislature. The Turkish Cypriots' reactions to *enosis* were perceived as
"artificial", the result of the government's "divide and rule" policy for dis-
solving the "well-established collaboration" between the two communities
(*Evagoras* 1903b, c). However, regardless of Greek Cypriots' perceptions
and the British government's policy on the issue, this was not the first
time that Turkish Cypriots had reacted to *enosis*. In 1882, for instance,
Turkish Cypriot leaders protested in London for the "Greeks' irredentist
processes", aiming at *enosis* (cited in Nevzat 2005, p. 130), while in 1893
Limassol-Paphos MP, Ahmet Raşıd, sent a petition to Porte complain-
ing about the Greek Cypriot demands for *enosis*, noting that such actions
were "infuriating the national races" (cited in Nevzat 2005, pp. 146–147).
In 1898, Haynes-Smith reported to Chamberlain that the various Greek
Cypriots demonstrations in favor of *enosis*, due to the Cretan occurrences,
had caused "resentment" within the Turkish community and "ill-will [had
been] engendered" (cited in Nevzat 2005, p. 145).

The above illustrates the weakness shown by Greek Cypriot nationalism in recognizing and realizing that its own dynamics generated the
Turkish Cypriots' reaction hence accelerating the strengthening of their
own ethnic identity. As Kızılyürek (1993, 1999) commented on this
point, the passion for *enosis* resulted in "disregard, even ignorance, of the
Turkish Cypriots' existence on the island" (1993, p. 15) who were treated
"not as political subjects but as cultural elements" (1999, p. 41). The
Turkish Cypriot elite's reaction to the Greek Cypriots' nationalism was to
strengthen their own community's national consciousness (1999, p. 35).

THE MAJORITY/MINORITY SCHEME

Of course, the Greek Cypriot side tried to quell Turkish Cypriots'
anguish and fear, stressing Greek Cypriots' will to maintain cooperation
in the Legislature. This effort, apart from always turning around

on *enosis*, was based constantly on a majority/minority scheme. *Alitheia* argued that after *enosis*, Turkish Cypriots—"although a small minority"—would be under an "honest government" following themselves "the road of progress and justice" (1902b). From the Greek Cypriot perspective, the minority "ought" to "align" with the majority's "cultural" and "national ideals" "for its own benefit", and follow it toward the fulfillment of its high destination (Kotalakides and Chalkia 2003, pp. 150–151).

This framework was expressed in 1907 via a Greek Cypriot MPs' Memorandum during the visit of Deputy Minister of Colonies, Churchill, to Cyprus. As it stated, the "historical law" of the Greek Cypriots' national desire may not be recognized by the "tiny Muslim minority", because of "religious or racial" duty:

> [B]ut, its numerical hypostasis is not strong enough to have any national fate on a Greek island, neither do its real actions in cultural and economic development have any importance... The Muslim minority, watching the national wealth of the Greek majority, not only is not harmed, but it is also benefited in many ways, because in practice, the Greek race has shown an excellent tolerance and transmissivity of all of its virtues to the foreign races from ancient times until today. (*Alitheia* 1907)

Thus, the "impartiality" and "litigiousness" which characterized the Greek race would guarantee the continuity of the two communities' peaceful coexistence when *enosis* was accomplished, thereby safeguarding, concurrently, the Turkish Cypriots' own progress. Nevertheless, in the Greek Cypriot view, the concepts of "impartiality" and "litigiousness" followed the hierarchical sequence contained in the majority/minority scheme.

The 1908 municipal elections represent a good example of the above. *Kypriakos Phylax*,[15] highlighting the elections' importance, stressed that national politics and interests "obliged" that the elected mayors in all cities "be Greeks and only Greeks" in order to demonstrate "the universal Greek character of Cyprus". This thesis, as it was exemplified, did not arise from any "racial fanaticism and passion, but from a national interest, which everyone ought to respect" (1908a). Nor should this be perceived by the Turkish Cypriots as discrimination, though it should prove to them that:

> [...] whatever authority we manage, we are conscionable, impartial and
> without any racial infatuation, we respect justice as being equal for all, and
> we behave to all with generosity which is inspired by our national courtesy
> and Greek grandeur ... Leaving behind all the tribulations that our genus
> has suffered for centuries ... Such a national action, provides the civilized
> peoples with the right to rule others, without restricting their freedom and
> consciousness, but working for their progress and prosperity. (*Kypriakos
> Phylax* 1908a)

Şevket Bey's "unexpected" election as Nicosia's mayor prompted
anti-Turkish sentiments despite what had been proclaimed during the
pre-election period. *Alitheia* described Şevket's election as a "sham and
disgrace", commenting that this "insult and stigma" resonated across
Cyprus and presented the island as "a vast theatre of the wildly intertwined, whose protagonists prefer to betray their motherland to the
enemy" (1908). *Kypriakos Phylax* also described Şevket's election as a
"sad result", clarifying, however, that reactions to Şevket's election "did
not result from racial antipathy and hatred, but from the belief that the
true prevalence of the Hellenic character must be manifested in all its
numerical and political terms", and that the non-real representation of
these proportions "constitute[d] national damage" (1908b).

TURKISH CYPRIOTS AS THE "COMMUNAL OTHER"

In the following years, external events, and in particular developments
in Greek-Turkish relations after the Young Turks movement's predominance in 1908 had a great effect on Cyprus and bi-communal relations.

Particularly, the continued engagement of the Greek Cypriot press
with the Young Turks' "atrocities" in Crete offered its own contribution to further substantiating the above case, by identifying and aligning Turkish Cypriots with the Young-Turks: "Turks remain Turks,"
Kypriakos Phylax commented in 1910, on the occasion of tensions in
Crete and the refusal of the Cretan Turks to declare "faith and obedi-
ence" to the King of Greece. It was only under the "autocracy of a *caliph*
that they [could] be governed"; otherwise, "their intolerance threatened world peace and put at risk the Christian peoples of the East".
According to this interpretation, the "continuing threat" from "Neo-
Turkish Chauvinism" to Hellenism would lead "fatally" to a new Greek-
Turkish war (1910b). *Alitheia* also commented that "the two races and

two religions, or better, the two so different worlds, Hellenism and the Muslim, perennial enemies, thousands of times conflicting" would find themselves again confronted in battle, where the "prevalence of one of the two races" would be judged (1910).

At the local level, the further alignment of Turkish Cypriot MPs with the government, thereby deflecting the Greek Cypriot majority, was perceived as a result of the Young Turks' influence on the island. *Kypriakos Phylax* commented on 14 May 1911 that Turkish Cypriots "comprise now a serious weakness and a major impediment to Cyprus's political, administrative and economic development and progress" (1911a), while on 4 June 1911 the newspaper wrote that the "Neo-Turkish bunkum, will maintain and broaden the gap between the Greeks and Mohammedans, and, intransigently, the conflict will prevail" between the two elements (1911b). The article concluded by warning the "Muslim minority" that if it continued "drifting" by neo-Turkism and maintaining its "intransigent opposition" to the Greek Cypriots "it would only hurt itself and [make] its presence on the island problematic" (1911b).

CONCLUSION

The above observations conclude the outcome of the process of shaping national identity and otherness. In the coming years, major developments in the wider region (Balkan Wars, World War I, the Greek-Turkish War of 1919–1922) strengthened the prevalence of this structure, while at the local level, the first bi-communal conflict in May 1912 in Limassol (*Alitheia* 1912; *Kypriakos Phylax* 1912; Nevzat 2005, pp. 202–212) can be considered as the first "serious" result of the identity and otherness construction process, which widened further the gap between the two communities and set the basis upon which the construction of the image of Turkish Cypriots as Greek Cypriots' "communal others" would be enhanced throughout the following years.

In conclusion, it could be said that national identity and otherness comprise social constructions that belong to a specific historical period and structure under specific socio-economic conditions. The introduction, cultivation and prevalence of the Greek national identity, which was constructed based on the irredentist program against the Ottoman Empire, inevitably produced the same "significant Other" in Cyprus as in Greece; that is the mainland Turks. As such, while Greek Cypriots saw themselves as members of the wider Greek nation, they set, at the same time, the basis for identifying the Turkish Cypriots with the mainland Turks and placed them, at the local level, in the position of their "communal Other".

Notes

1. The Church was responsible for collecting the Orthodox millet taxes. *Alitheia* (1891b) commented about this: "The Orthodox bishops systematically enjoyed the Ottoman Government's esteem, which provided them with those *zaptiehs* they needed for collecting the ecclesiastical fees, and the faithful Christians' levy was drawn through instruments not unknown to the subordinate organs of the Muslim authority".

2. It is worth mentioning that from 1833 until the recognition of the Church of Greece Autocephalous by the Patriarchate in 1850, the Church of Cyprus 'had no contact' with the Church of Greece, fully aligning its position with the Patriarchate (Katsiaounis 2004, p. 24).

3. Regarding Cyprus, Limassol Commander Falk Warren, reported in 1879, that Greek was not "the native language spoken from the five-sixths of the inhabitants", accusing a reading-club in Limassol that it 'desires to introduce the Greek language' on the island (Hansard 1880).

4. Concerning Cyprus, an article in *Evagoras* provides a characteristic example of "irredentist" populations' identification with Athens as the "national center". In a discussion regarding Turkish Cypriots' national aspirations, *Evagoras* noted: "Even if the fellow-country Mohammedans do so for fulfilling their own national aspirations, we are assuring them that we would never confront them for that, because while they will be facing Bosporus, we will be gazing at ancient and holy Acropolis" (1900).

5. The first Cypriot newspaper was *Cyprus-Kypros*, released in Larnaca a few weeks after the arrival of the British on the island. The owner and editor of the newspaper was Theodoulos Konstantinidis, who, after 'incitement and the financial help' from the *Cypriot Fraternity of Egypt*, bought and transferred to Cyprus the first typographer (Sophocleous 1995, pp. 256–257). Although the publication of the newspaper lasted only a few months, Konstantinidis would proceed in June 1879 to publish the newspaper *Neon Kition* also in Larnaca.

6. *Alitheia* released in Limassol in 1880 by Aristotle Palaeologos.

7. *Foni tis Kyprou* released in Larnaca in 1882 by Themistocles Theocharides.

8. It is important to note here the importance of the words used in image production in terms of connection or estrangement, of "good" or "bad" experiences, of identification or distinction. In the references to Greece, words are used with positive meaning (restoration, prosperity), and when referring to the Turks they are used negatively (conquered, darkness, atrocities).

9. It is worth mentioning that in 1571, the Church of Cyprus welcomed the arrival of the Ottomans on the island, having recovered the privileges lost under the Venetians, while the Archbishop was proclaimed an Ethnarch of the Christian millet. As for the 1821 events, no consul or observer in Cyprus at that time provided information on such incidents and atrocities as those described by Theodotou. For more information (see Michael 2005, 2013; Hill 1952, pp. 122–137; Heraclides 2006, p. 75).

10. *Neon Ethnos* released in Larnaca in 1893 by Cleopoulos Mesologitis.

11. *Evagoras* released in Nicosia in 1890. Pericles Michaelides was the editor of Evagoras from 1890 to 1905. From 1893 the Editor of the newspaper was N. Katalanos.

12. It is particularly important that the incident happened in a village school, because it seems that during this period, mostly due to the wider Greco-Turkish conflict over the Cretan question, national ideals had overcome the boundaries of urban centers and been extended to the most conservative and traditional rural countryside.

13. Of course, this "hatred" described in this extract was not directed against Great Britain. One month after the end of the war, Greek Cypriots participated in the celebrations for the 60th anniversary for the Diamond Jubilee of Queen Victoria as a sign of "abundant respect and deep reverence" for "the dynasty that provided Hellenism with a great support" (Katalanos 1914, p. 123; *Neon Ethnos* 1897b).

14. The great influence of the archiepiscopal dispute on the politicization of the popular strata and to the development of the Greek Cypriots national spirit was attributed by *Kypriakos Phylax* in 1910. The archiepiscopal dispute, as it noted, was the one that "aroused the crowds from side to side", and the occasion by which "in any demonstration and fair and in every gathering, either small or large, people heard and learned its duties and its rights, as a Cypriot and as a Greek, to the national mission and national destination" (1910a). For more details, see also (Michael 2004, pp. 311–380).

15. *Kypriakos Phylax* released in 1906 in Nicosia. Its owner was Ephraim Petrides and editor N. Katalanos.

REFERENCES

Anagnostopoulou, S. (2004). *The Passage from the Ottoman Empire to the Nation–States: A Long and Difficult Process: The Greek Case*. Istanbul: The Isis Press.

Anderson, B. (2006). *Imagined Communities: Reflections on the Origin and Spread of Nationalism* (Rev. ed.). London: Verso Books.

Aroni-Tsihli, K. (2008). *Ιστορικές Σχολές και Μέθοδοι: Εισαγωγή στην Ευρωπαϊκή Ιστοριογραφία: Πανεπιστημιακές Παραδόσεις* [Historical Schools and Methods: Introduction to the European Historiography]. Athens: Papazisi.

Attalides, M. A. (1981). *Οι Σχέσεις Ελληνοκυπρίων και Τουρκοκυπρίων* [The Relations Between Greek Cypriots and Turkish Cypriots]. In G. Tenekides & Y. Kranidiotis (Eds.), *Κύπρος: Ιστορία, Προβλήματα και Αγώνες του Λαού της* [Cyprus: History, ProblemsandStrugglesofitsPeople]. Athens: Estia.

Heraclides, A. (2006). *Το Κυπριακό, 1947–2004: Από την Ένωση στη Διχοτόμηση* [Cyprus Issue, 1947–2004: From Enosis to Partition?]. Athens: Sideris.

Hill, S. G. F. (1952). A History of Cyprus: The Ottoman Province; the British Colony, 1571–1948. In L. Harry (Ed.), *A History of Cyprus* (Vol. 4). London: Cambridge University Press.

Hobsbawm, E. J. (1992). *Nations and Nationalism Since 1780: Programme, Myth, Reality*. Cambridge: Cambridge University Press.

Katalanos, N. (1914). *Κυπριακόν Λεύκωμα Ο Ζήνων* [Cyprus Album Zenon]. Nicosia: Petridou & Nikolaou.

Katsiaounis, R. (1996). *Labour, Society and Politics in Cyprus During the Second Half of the Nineteenth Century*. Nicosia: Cyprus Research Centre.

Katsiaounis, R. (2004). *Η Διασκεπτική 1946–1948, με Ανασκόπηση της Περιόδου 1878–1945* [The Consultative Assembly, 1946–1948: With an Overview of the 1878–1945 Period]. Nicosia: Cyprus Research Center.

Kitromilides, P. (1994). *Enlightenment, Nationalism, Orthodoxy: Studies in the Culture and Political Though of South-Eastern Europe*. Aldershot: Variorum.

Kitromilides, P. (2003). "Νοερές Κοινότητες" και οι Απαρχές του Εθνικού Ζητήματος στα Βαλκάνια ["Imagined Communities" and the Origins of the National Question in the Balkans]. In T. Veremis (Ed.), *Εθνική Ταυτότητα και Εθνικισμός στη Νεότερη Ελλάδα* [National Identity and Nationalism in Modern Greece] (pp. 53–153). Athens: National Bank of Greece Cultural Foundation.

Kızılyürek, N. (1993). *Η Κύπρος Πέραντου Έθνους* [Cyprus beyond Nation]. Nicosia: Kasoulides & Sons.

Kızılyürek, N. (1999). *Κύπρος, το Αδιέξοδο των Εθνικισμών* [Cyprus: The Deadlock of Nationalisms]. Athens: Black List.

Kotalakides, G., & Chalkia, A. (2003). «Εμείς» και οι «Άλλοι»: Ελληνική Εθνική Ταυτότητα και η Διαμόρφωση της Ταυτότητας των Ποντίων Μεταναστών στην Ελληνική Κοινωνία [We and the Others: The Formation of Pontian Immigrants' Identity in Greece]. *Utopia, 54*, 149–167.

Kyriakides, G., & Michaelidou, M. (2006). *Η Προσέγγιση του Άλλου: Ιδεολογία, Μεθοδολογία και Ερευνητική Πρακτική* [Approaching the Other: Ideology, Methodology and Research Practice]. Athens: Metechmio.

Lekkas, P. (1992). *Η Εθνικιστική Ιδεολογία: Πέντε Υποθέσεις Εργασίας στην Ιστορική Κοινωνιολογία* [The Nationalist Ideology: Five Working Hypotheses in Historical Sociology]. Athens: Katarti.

Michael, M. N. (2004). *Η Διαδικασία Συγκρότησης ενός Θεσμού Εξουσίας. Εκκλησία της Κύπρου 1754–1910* [The Process of Establishing an Institution of Power: The Church of Cyprus, 1754–1910]. Ph.D. dissertation, University of Cyprus, Nicosia.

Michael, M. N. (2005). *Η Εκκλησία της Κύπρου κατά την Οθωμανική Περίοδο: Η Σταδιακή Συγκρότηση ενός Θεσμού Πολιτικής Εξουσίας* [The Church of Cyprus During the Ottoman Period, 1571–1878: Its Gradual Consolidation into a Political Power Institution]. Nicosia: Cyprus Research Center.

Michael, M. N. (2012). Revolts, Demands and Challenge to the Legitimacy of the Ottoman Power: The Three Revolts of 1833 in Cyprus. *Archivum Ottomanicum, 29*, 127–147.

Michael, M. N. (2013). The Loss of an Ottoman Traditional Order and the Reactions to Changing Ottoman World: A New Interpretation of the 1821 Events in Cyprus. *International Review of Turkish Studies, 3*(3), 8–36.

Michael, M. N. (2016). *Οι Εξεγέρσεις ως Πεδίο Διαπραγμάτευσης της Εξουσίας. Οθωμανική Κύπρος, 1804–1841* [Revolts as a Field of Power Negotiation: Ottoman Cyprus, 1804–1841]. Athens: Alexandreia.

Nevzat, A. (2005). *Nationalism Amongst the Turks of Cyprus: The First Wave*. Oulu: Oulu University Press.

Pollis, A. (1979). Colonialism and Neo-colonialism. Determinants of Ethnic Conflict in Cyprus. In P. Worsley & P. Kitromilides (Eds.), *Small States in the Modern World* (pp. 45–79). Nicosia: The New Cyprus Association.

Pollis, A. (1998a). The Role of Foreign Powers in Structuring Ethnicity and Ethnic Conflict in Cyprus. In V. Calotychos (Ed.), *Cyprus and Its People: Nation, Identity, and Experience in an Unimaginable Community, 1955–1997* (pp. 85–102). Boulder: Westview Press.

Pollis, A. (1998b). Η Κοινωνική Κατασκευή της Εθνοτικότητας και της Εθνικότητας: Η Περίπτωση της Κύπρου [The Social Construction of Nationality and Ethnicity: The Case of Cyprus]. *Σύγχρονα Θέματα* [*Contemporary Issues*], *21*(68–70), 25–43.

Skopetea, E. (1988). *Το «Πρότυπο Βασίλειο» και η Μεγάλη Ιδέα: Όψεις του Εθνικού Προβλήματος στην Ελλάδα (1830–1880)* [The "Model Kingdom" and the Great Idea: Aspects on the National Question in Greece, 1830–1880]. Athens: Politipo.

Smith, A. D. (1986). *The Ethnic Origins of Nations*. Oxford: Blackwell.

Sophocleous A. (1995). *Συμβολή στην Ιστορία του Κυπριακού Τύπου* [Contribution to the History of the Cypriot Press] (Vol. 1–3). Nicosia: Intercollege Press.

Triandafyllidou, A. (1998). National Identity and the 'Other'. *Ethnic and Racial Studies, 21*(4), 593–612.

Varnava, A. (2009). *British Imperialism in Cyprus, 1878–1915: The Inconsequential Possession*. Manchester: Manchester University Press.

Veremis, T. (2003). Από το Εθνικό Κράτος στο Έθνος Δίχως Κράτος: το Πείραμα της Οργάνωσης Κωνσταντινουπόλεως [From the National State to the Non-State Nation: The Experiment of the Organization of Constantinople]. In T. Veremis (Ed.), *Εθνική Ταυτότητα και Εθνικισμός στη Νεότερη Ελλάδα* [National Identity and Nationalism in Modern Greece] (pp. 27–52). Athens: National Bank of Greece Cultural Foundation.

Secretariat Archive, State Archives, Nicosia

SA03/87, Falk Warren, Commissioner of Limassol to George Richard Greaves, Chief Secretary, 29 July 1879.

Hansard Official Reports of Parliamentary Debates

Hansard (1880, June 1) *Cyprus (Orders in Council)*. 252, cols. 901–902.

Hansard (1895a) *Cyprus. Grand in Aid*. 31, cols. 683–698.

Hansard (1895b) *Cyprus. Grand in Aid*. 31, col. 689.

Hansard (1895c) *Cyprus. Grand in Aid*. 31, cols. 690–691.

Hansard (1895d) *Army Estimates 1895–6*. 31, cols. 1398–1399.

Hansard (1902a) *Civil Service Estimates 1902–3*. 108, cols. 619–644.

Hansard (1902b) *Civil Service Estimates 1902–3*. 108, col. 643.

Newspapers

Alitheia 11/04/1885, 10/04/1886, 13/10/1887, 23/01/1891a, 17/07/1891b, 9/03/1893a, 30/03/1893b, 14/04/1893c, 30/11/1893d, 8/12/1893e, 22/03/1894a, 30/03/1894b, 25/04/1894c, 16/08/1894d, 10/05/1895, 26/06/1896, 2/04/1898, 6/07/1901a, 12/10/1901b, 26/10/1901c, 8/06/1902a, 14/06/1902b, 4/07/1902c, 2/05/1903a, 9/05/1903b, 1/10/1907, 20/03/1908, 30/07/1910, 17/05/1912.

Evagoras   20/08/1894,   1/01/1897,   3/03/1900,   30/06/1901a, 4/10/1901b, 19/10/1901c, 8/05/1903a, 15/05/1903b, 19/06/1903c, 3/07/1903d.

Foni tis Kyprou 10/04/1886, 13/04/1897, 28/09/1901a, 19/10/1901b.

Kypriakos Phylax 9/02/1908a, 22/03/1908b, 30/01/1910a, 12/06/1910b, 14/05/1911a, 04/06/1911b, 19/05/1912.

Neon Ethnos 1/12/1893, 13/07/1894, 3/05/1895a, 10/05/1895b, 13/06/1896a, 20/06/1896b, 4/07/1896c, 1/04/1897a, 4/06/1897b, 21/06/1902.

Neon Kition 3/10/1879a, 15/10/1879b, 14/02/1880.

CHAPTER 4

The Legislative Council and Its Historical/Political Implications in Cyprus (1882–1931)

Meltem Onurkan-Samani

INTRODUCTION

The process of transformation—from traditional to modern socioeconomic and political structure, and from a religious identity to national identity in Cyprus—took place during the British colonial rule lasting from 1878 to 1960. Colonial policies pursued during this eighty-two years period and the Legislative Council, which constitutes the main focus of this study, inevitably influenced the modernization dynamics and the configuration of the political culture and institutions of the island's societies. The Legislative Council was established in accordance with the 1882 Constitution during the British Period in Cyprus. The local elected members in the Council consisting of Greek and Turkish Cypriots were twice as numerous as its appointed British official members. Through this council participation of the colonized community in the governance of the country—at least in the legislative sense—was ensured, albeit partially.[1] The longevity of the Council totaled only about 50 years out of

M. Onurkan-Samani (✉)
European University of Lefke, Lefke, northern Cyprus
URL: https://www.eul.edu.tr

© The Author(s) 2018   75
T. Kyritsi and N. Christofis (eds.), *Cypriot Nationalisms in Context*,
https://doi.org/10.1007/978-3-319-97804-8_4

the 82 years of British colonial rule, the time period in which eleven gen-eral elections and a number of by-elections were held on the island.

The British administration maintained the traditional religious-based social differences existed during the Ottoman Cyprus (1571–1878) defining the population on the island as Muslims and non-Muslims; allo-cating twenty-five percent of the seats in the Council to Muslims and the remaining seventy-five percent to the non-Muslim community, based on their respective proportions in the population. This allocation caused the Council membership to be constituted by a great majority of Orthodox Christian Greek Cypriots and Muslim Turkish Cypriots, leaving rela-tively small communities living on the island—such as the Maronite, Armenian, and Jewish—unrepresented. To illustrate, representatives of the Maronite community were able to gain access to the Council only during the period when Orthodox Christian Greek Cypriots were boy-cotting the Council (*The Cyprus Gazette* 1922; Georghallides 2004, pp. 209–210, 292).

The Council can be considered as constituted by three wings, namely, Muslim, non-Muslim, and Governmental. However, particularly, dur-ing the first twenty years when the demand for *enosis* was not on the Council's agenda, it would be more accurate to speak of two wings: the Muslim and non-Muslim elected locals and the Governmental Wing rep-resenting the British colonial administration.

Although the appointed British official members had only thirty-three percent of the total seats, they constituted the Governmental Wing, which possessed excessive power over the Council. In spite of the fact that the Colonial Administration pursued a policy that did not employ the overt and covert powers unless absolutely necessary passing the deci-sions they deemed necessary through the Council—by persuasion—as they were unable to persuade the appointed local members who occu-pied more than sixty-six percent of the seats on most issues they started to implement these powers quite soon. This brought the opposition of non-Muslim and Muslim members, who constituted the majority of the Council, against the Governmental Wing (Onurkan-Samani 2007, pp. 43–62, 128–142, 165–310).

The numerical composition of the Council necessitated various groups—formed depending on the nature of the agenda—to reach a consensus for any decision to be passed by the Council. In fact, none of the existing three groups was able to gain sole control of the Council.

Turkish Cypriot members—as the smallest group in the Council—occupied a strategic key role due to frequent oppositions between British and Greek Cypriot members.

Against the possibility of Greek Cypriot members who would aim at *enosis*, the British assumed—to become the majority with the votes of the "loyal" Muslims.[2] Of the eighteen members of the Council, nine were Greek Cypriots, three Turkish Cypriots and six appointed (British) officials indicating that the sum of British and Muslim votes would equalize the Greek Cypriot votes. However, although not counted as a member of the Council, the President of the Council (High Commissioner) would have the casting vote, with which the British and Muslims together would have the majority.[3] In case of collective boycott, resignation, or any other form of absenteeism of local members, the operation of the Council would not be hampered as the quorum was kept equal to the number of British members.

BRITISH COLONIAL POLICIES, INSTITUTIONS, AND THEIR EFFECTS

With their pragmatic Indirect Rule policy, the British constructed administrative structures in the colonies under their rule subject to change, depending on the individual conditions of each colony (Chamberlain 1998). The British Indirect Rule policy required that the colonies be governed by traditional institutions together with an administrative elite which means that the traditional institutions were somehow preserved, conflicting with the "civilization" and "modernization mission" of colonialism, sometimes leading to undesired consequences (also, Stout 1953; Lugard 1926; King-Hall 1937; Bates 2000; Said 1998; Young 1994; Chatterjee 1996; Taylor 1975; Wade and Phillips 1934; Porter 1996). Traditional institutions harmonized with the colonizer's interests and the traditional administrative elite—preserved as long as they cooperated—were supported against the advocates of Western-style reforms within the colonized communities (Kitromilides 1977).

Emerging progressive versus conservative, and/or traditionalist versus modernist conflicts and divisions within societies made it easier for the colonizer to find supporters. Meanwhile, traditional structures and personnel were redefined on the basis of the colonizer's interests gaining more power than before, with certain titles of nobility. For example, the traditional role of Evkaf (the administration of Muslim pious foundations) was to be the main body responsible for the administration of almost all Muslim institutions meaning that the Evkaf heads appointed by the Colonial rule would also be community leaders (Onurkan-Samani 2007, pp. 161–164, 203–254). Along with many other titles, one of the Evkaf heads, Mehmet Münir Bey was to be given the "Sir" title (An 2002, pp. 381–383).

Representative type of legislative councils generally providing the separate and mostly proportional representation of various ethno-religious groups with traditional social structures accommodated in the pre-nation period (Wade and Phillips 1934, pp. 348–350; Stout 1953, pp. 407–408; Chamberlain 1998, pp. 3–7). The British administration refused certain demands mostly nationalistic ones—as in the Cyprus example—of these groups using the opposition of another group against these demands as an excuse. The administration tended to employ members of communities with a smaller proportional population, particularly those who were both loyal and more inclined to cooperate, such as Muslim Turkish Cypriots as in the Cyprus case. In some institutions outside the council, such as in the police force, the British contributed to the development of competing nationalisms through placing the "loyal" group against the "problem-causing" group (Rızvi 1993; Young 1994).

On one hand, the British administration was playing the role of strengthening competitive nationalisms for its own interest in order to continue its existence in the colony and on the other trying to weaken the now powerful nationalists who were against it. British colonialism neither pursued assimilation or Anglicization policies nor encouraged development of a common local identity of different ethno-religious groups—thinking they might start a common struggle against them.[4]

THE CASE/STATUS OF CYPRUS

The island of Cyprus, a protectorate[5] between the years 1878–1914/25 and a royal colony[6] afterward, was not given any form of a self-government or a responsible government status by the British rulers. Despite that, the majority of the members of the Legislative Council were local representatives and the British official members were in minority. This was not a common condition within the British royal colonial system (King-Hall 1937, p. 73; Chamberlain 1998, pp. 3–7; Onurkan-Samani 2007, pp. 59–62). The reason for this might be that the demographic configuration of the island made up of Muslim Turkish Cypriots and

Christian Greek Cypriots involved in political oppositions that would not render it possible to engage a common resistance/struggle against the British (as colonizers) in the Council. The already existing oppositional elements had the potential to be sharpened or exploited by employing British tactics like divide and rule.

In the case of local members' unification and acting together, other safety valves were thought of in order not to lose the Colonial Rule's legislative control over the Island. The Island Constitution enabled the Government to veto the Council decisions rendering them ineffective imposing laws on the Island by royal decrees. The Council could not make any changes in the Constitution. While giving some legislative power to the local representatives, the Constitution prevented their participation in executive power.[7] The government was not formed with the majority vote of the Council and the Executive Council, which served as a kind of cabinet, solely consisted of appointed members.[8] When some proposals like the Annual Budget which were vital for the administration of the Island were rejected, the Government did not fall. The local members had no significant say in important financial issues such as taxation, poll taxes, and high-ranking official salaries.

Local representatives, as a reaction, began from the very beginning of the Council to voice their discomfort in many subjects such as the denial of execution of certain decisions they had taken in order to solve common problems of the Island, the representation of proposals/bills of law they had already rejected without any changes or their imposition by order in councils, the preparation of the annual budget without their consent and its presentation to the Council with London's approval, unrecognition of the cuts, changes and suggestions they made in the budget, and their lack of say in decisions regarding execution. This gave the image of an opposition party to the group made up of local representatives against the Governmental Wing. They almost always criticized any proposal brought by the government and its decisions justifying their opposition as an effort to protect the people of the Island. Local members also criticized the insufficiency of the Government's actions with regard to infrastructure and public service (Onurkan-Samani 2007, pp. 258–287).

Some issues which often caused an opposing stance against the Government by the local members of the Council were the colonial administration's financial and economic policy sending a significant amount of the Island's income under the name of tribute payment to London, collecting harsh taxes,[9] and spending the remaining income on what the locals considered to be very expensive. Moreover, public expenditure such as British officials' salaries, sparing no sources for education and agriculture, which the local members of the Council considered to be priorities caused problems (Onurkan-Samani 2007, pp. 258–288). In fact, according to the Constitution, the powers of the Council regarding financial issues, particularly tribute payment, taxation, and budget were highly limited and the Council did not even have the right to present a proposal in the related fields. Therefore, the local members of the Council either made changes or totally rejected the relevant proposals and budget items suggested by the Government. In such cases, the Colonial Administration, usually executed the budget and other proposals they deemed necessary through mandates, thereby ignore the Council's decisions.

During the whole period of the Legislative Council, the British administrators, clearly expressing how seriously disturbed they were by the situation, said that the rights and powers "granted" to the Cypriot communities were abused warning that the "privileges" they had might be taken back if they continued like this (Orr 1972, p. 108; Onurkan-Samani 2007, pp. 160, 288–290, 316). On the other hand, particularly the Greek Cypriot members, from the very beginning of the Legislative Council, demanded that constitutional rights and powers were expanded (*LCM* 1883, pp. 2–3; Gürkan 1989, pp. 164–168; Kyrris 1996, p. 307; *The Annual Reports* 1889–1890; 1890–1891, pp. 1–5), that the Government's veto power was lifted (Onurkan-Samani 2007, pp. 142, 168), and that high-ranking offices were occupied by locals; as a result they demanded wider participation of the communities in the administration (*LCM* 1900, pp. 15–16; Onurkan-Samani 2007, pp. 288–290). The Greek Cypriot members also believed that tribute payment had to be removed. Yet, Turkish Cypriot members were cautious about the Greek Cypriot demands of removing tribute and appointing locals for high-ranking government offices (Onurkan-Samani 2007, pp. 166–167, 175, 204, 209, 255–258). It was observed that the Turkish Cypriot members objected to opening high-ranking positions to the locals worrying that these positions would be occupied more by the Greek Cypriots and were cautious about the removal of tribute demands thinking that it represented maybe the last connection between the Ottoman State and Cyprus so as to not harm any Ottoman interest on the Island. Still, the Turkish Cypriot members, although not on the removal of tribute, agreed with the Greek Cypriot members that the sum be paid by British central treasury.[10]

Within the first twenty years of the Council's life, when the *enosis* demands were not brought to the Council agenda, Turkish Cypriot members acted in unison with the Greek Cypriot representatives almost on every issue disappointing the British administration hoping to control execution relying on the Muslim vote in the Council. Going into the twentieth century under these circumstances, the Colonial administrators more regularly attempted to indirectly interfere with the internal affairs of the communities in order to have control over the Muslim vote and help the election of "moderate" candidates who would cooperate with them in the Council. Along the history of the Council, the Colonial Administration directly or indirectly attempted to interfere with the elections by bringing people who would work in harmony with them to high-ranking offices in order to increase their prestige in the eyes of the community, thereby increasing their chance to win the elections, or by appointing certain sharp opponents to official positions which were difficult to reject so as to pacify them (Onurkan-Samani 2007, pp. 125, 161–163ff.; An 2002, pp. 126–127; Atesin 1996, p. 293).

The intercommunal equilibrium and inner dynamics of each community—Muslim Turkish Cypriots in particular—were under close scrutiny by the British administration at the beginning of the twentieth century. Notable Turkish Cypriot and Greek Cypriot members protested the government for interfering with the 1901 elections (*LCM* 1902, pp. 35, 49–53, 57–66; Georghallides 2004, p. 72; Onurkan-Samani 2007). Some new Greek Cypriot members put their *enosis* demands on the Council agenda in the years 1902–1903 in the absence of a Muslim member Dervish Pasha (*LCM* 1903, pp. 1–6; 1904, pp. 33–35, 39). This event was used both by the Government and the opponents within their own community to wear out some Turkish Cypriot members like Dervish Pasha and Haci Hafiz Ziyai. The Turkish Cypriot members were blamed for "Supporting the Greek ambitions" and put them in an awkward position in the eyes of their community (Onurkan-Samani 2007, pp. 180–184, 209–210).

It should be noted that Dervish Pasha and Ziyai Effendi (the Legislative Council members from 1896 until 1904–1906) were among the supporters of the group who demanded that the institutions and sources of the Muslim community should be governed by the community itself before the Chief Judge (*Kadı*) of the traditional Muslim Sharia Court, considered as relatively autonomous from the British government in Cyprus (*LCM* 1898, p. 134). What they actually meant was the governing of the Evkaf (the administration of Muslim pious foundations) controlling the material wealth of the Muslim community on the island and holding material and moral significance before the society. Targeting to manipulate the Muslim community through Evkaf, the British administration, however, appointed Mehmet Sadık in 1894 and later Irfan Bey in 1904 as the head of Evkaf. Irfan Bey was elected to the Council in 1913 serving as a member of the Council for about three incessant periods until his death in 1925, voting generally in favor of the Governmental Wing. With Ziyai Effendi's accession as the Mufti, the highest official of Islamic religious law, in 1909, the Turkish Cypriot notables were divided as Mufti supporters and Evkaf supporters (An 2002, pp. 107–109; Onurkan-Samani 2007, pp. 211–212, 221, 318–319, 327).

While Mufti supporters were against the governing of Evkaf by "Irfanites collaborating with the British," Evkaf supporters accused the opposing group as "serving to Greek ambitions" (Onurkan-Samani 2007, pp. 209, 212–213, 227, 317–319). This conflict, with also an intense level of personal antagonism involved, was more a competition regarding who would be leading the society and governing the community sources and institutions. Although they criticized each other for it, one of the common points in this competition was to look for an external support from British and/or Turkish governments. In time, the successors of Mufti supporters who saw themselves as "Kemalists," were to be defined as progressive or modernist because they were demanding social reforms in line with Mustafa Kemal Ataturk's Turkey (Atesin 1996; Onurkan-Samani 1999, 2007, pp. 125–126, 195, 206, 223, 319; An 2002). Evkaf supporters were to be remembered as traditionalists or conservatives since they were against the reforms that might change the status quo in their control.

In the time period this study covers, there seems to be no firmly and clearly defined ideological division. For example, people sometimes were accused of being conservative and pious because they were against the abolition of Islamic Law Courts. Yet, they were not necessarily more religious than the others and often represented the fervent supporters of the continuation of the "secular" British administration. Moreover, assuming that Evkaf supporters of the period, like Dr. Eyyub, who did not mind having a British headmaster for the Turkish Lycée and approved of establishing a college department, whose medium of education would be English, were less nationalistic would be misleading.[11] Similarly, Mufti supporting group's collaboration with Greek Cypriot members on issues regarding common problems did not mean they were "Supporting the Greek"; on the contrary, the members of this group would in time define themselves as "nationalists/Kemalists." Also, Evkaf supporting members, other than Irfan Bey, voted in agreement with the Greek Cypriot members on socioeconomic issues. It is also observed that Mufti supporting members of the Council who blamed the Evkaf supporting members for collaborating with the British, neither took a firm anti-colonialist stance nor demanded Britain's evacuation of the island.

With regard to their opposition to *enosis*, both groups had similar views and all Turkish Cypriot members of the Council openly stating at every opportunity that they were against *enosis*. It must be pointed out that apart from their opposition to *enosis*, they did not resort to nationalist discourse much and compared to Greek Cypriot members they did not assume a nationalist attitude during the negotiations in the Council. Yet, it must also be acknowledged that they were sensitive to protect and improve the Turkish Cypriot community's status under the British rule and against the Greek Cypriot dominancy. Despite declaring an affinity and open loyalty to "Motherland" Turkey, they did not demand to unite with Turkey, as a move against *enosis* in the Council.

Politically, the Greek Cypriot members, after the 1901 elections onwards, idealistically and excitedly based their arguments on the contemporary ideals of nationalism, insisting on the principle of nationalities, the right to self-determination, the rule of the majority, and similar concepts and principles, and thus, demanding that Britain hand the Island over to Greece (Onurkan-Samani 2007, pp. 180–202, 228–254). On the other hand, Turkish Cypriot members, who were strongly against *enosis*, expressed their trust in the British in this matter and did not make any demands for a change in administration. They preferred a more pessimistic tone in their arguments, using statements that evoked a realistic political approach and universalism instead of nationalism. They put forward principles such as pursuing human and individual rights instead of nationality rights, and a balance between peoples, groups and even individuals rather than the dominance of the majority (*LCM* 1903, pp. 30–44, 343–351, 470–473; 1915, p. 7; 1917, pp. 14–15, 25; 1931, pp. 13–18, 300–310).

The Council's Greek Cypriot and Turkish Cypriot members had differing opinions toward the claims made by the British administration that British Colonialism would "civilize" its colonies and bring them to an adequate level of development for greater constitutional powers that would eventually lead to independence. Fearing that this would result in the rule of the majority on the Island, the Turkish Cypriot members were against most of the proposals for constitutional changes, claiming that the people of the Island were not ready yet, and had not reached a sufficient social-cultural level (*LCM* 1930, p. 40). On the other hand, the Greek Cypriot members claimed that the people of the Island were mature enough declaring that there were no objective criteria to show which one, the "Invader (colonial)" or the "Invaded (local)" was more "civilized." Moreover, the Greek Cypriot members would also suggest that not much development could be expected under limited and isolated conditions created by the invader power in a colony country (*LCM* 1931, pp. 14–15).

Since they were advocating the continuation of the British rule and in fact, were against autonomy due to their fear of *enosis* or of a possible Greek Cypriot dominance, Turkish Cypriot members were being accused of collaborating with the colonial rulers and of not being nationalistic by the Greek Cypriot members, who preferred Turkish nationalists to enter the Council as in the elections held in 1930 hoping to resist the colonial rule together (*LCM* 1917, p. 23; 1918, pp. 4–6; 1920, pp. 7–9). However, as long as the Greek Cypriot members' main objective was *enosis*, the desired cooperation—as was the case throughout the history of the Council—could only be possible on common socio-economic problems with each community ruling its institutions independently of the Colonial Administration.

After the 1925 elections, "moderate" Greek Cypriot and Turkish Cypriot members of the Council rejected the 1927 Budget.[12] This was seen as an uprising by the British administration. The local members were forced to act in accordance with the Island's communities' expectations hoping that their socioeconomic problems would be solved. The members at the time had been elected to the Council with the promise that the problems in question could be solved more easily through "moderate" policies and politicians. However, even their rejection of the budget came to nothing and the British Administration put the rejected Budget into effect with an ordinance. As a result, both Turkish Cypriot and Greek Cypriot "extremists/nationalists" won the seats in the 1930 elections. The British were afraid that the new Council would adopt an anti-colonialist attitude. However, this never happened as the Council was dissolved within a year.

According to the 1930–1931 Legislative Council Minutes, there was nothing new or different about the atmosphere in the Council. Neither was there an atmosphere of rebellion, which would make the British administration complain. On the contrary, Greek Cypriot and Turkish Cypriot members were engaged in lengthy discussions over socioeconomic issues. Apparently, the Greek Cypriot members, who could not find the support they received during previous representatives, were in particular disappointed with new member and leader of the Kemalist group, Necati Bey during the talks on the budget and several other socioeconomic issues. There were still instances, where, as in the past, local members voted together—like voting against the additional customs official draft law—and "angered" the British administration.

From 1901 elections onwards, *enosis* supporter Greek Cypriot members of the Legislative Council were roughly divided between moderates and extremists accusing each other of cooperating with the British and/or the Turks and not protecting the community's interests (Onurkan-Samani 2007, pp. 171–202). While the moderates advocated putting more emphasis on socioeconomic and other internal administrative issues in the Council and making as many acquisitions as possible, provided that the ultimate goal of *enosis* remained on course, the extremists advocated giving priority to the struggle for *enosis*.

During the first twenty years of its existence, the Council was composed of traditional elite members including influential and rich taxmen, tradesmen, money lenders, and landowners. At the time, moderate attitude and policies were brought to the forefront leaving *enosis* off on the agenda of the Council. At the beginning of the twentieth century, there was a demand to put it at the top of the agenda due to the change in the members' profiles. The new generation council members—lawyers, doctors, teachers who had generally studied abroad—became agents of nationalist ideas. This group known as the extremists-gradually gained power, advocating implementing certain methods that includes boycotting the Council, resigning, not attending sessions with the aim of forcing constitutional changes as well as protesting against the current regime (Hill 1952, pp. 534–536, 540; Georghallides 2004, pp. 171–206ff.; Onurkan-Samani 2007, pp. 181–192, 232–234; *The Cyprus Gazette* 1924 and 1.9.1925; *LCM* 1919, pp. 28–32, 39; 1920, pp. 6–7, 9).

The moderates argued that such methods would not work as there would always be people who would enter the elections winning the non-Muslim seats, and without their presence in the Council, British and Turkish Cypriot votes could take decisions that were against the interests of the people. Consequently, the moderates' forecasts pretty much came true, but the extremists' view that no further rights could be obtained through the existing constitutional powers, or lack of, was also true (*The Cyprus Gazette* 1922; *LCM* 1923, pp. 5–6, 19–20; Georghallides 2004, pp. 209–210, 292; Onurkan-Samani 2007).

It can be said that the improved constitutional rights and powers given to the Cypriot people by the Legislative Council did not satisfy any group, including the British themselves. In time, even if it was for different reasons, the Council turned out to be a disappointment for all groups.

Greek Cypriot members could hardly pass any political decision such as improving constitutional rights and powers, opening high official posts to the locals, which the Turkish Cypriot members did not support, let alone passing decisions aimed at *enosis* (see *LCM* 1884, 1897, 1902, 1903, 1904, 1911, 1914, 1924, 1931). And this was considered as a big injustice for them. As stated by the Greek Cypriot members of the Council, the British claimed to give importance to the colonial people's feelings and opinions, integrating them into their country's government, at least giving them the right to speak, by siding with the minority against the majority or using the minority, did not allow the majority to express their views even as a Council decision (see *LCM* 1914, pp. 6–7; 1915, pp. 10–15; 1917, pp. 11–28; 1918, pp. 4, 8; 1930, p. 40; 1931, pp. 14–15). The British officials were often citing the Muslim Turkish Cypriots' opposition as an excuse to reject Greek Cypriot demands, arguing that the feelings and wishes of Muslim Turkish Cypriots had to be taken into consideration as well, otherwise unrest would break out on the Island. However, not only the Muslim Turkish Cypriots but the British were also against the Greek Cypriot demands. In the case of a British–Greek Cypriot alliance in the Council eighty-five percent majority would be established and the Turkish Cypriots' votes would have no bearing on the outcome. In other words, the main obstacle in front of the Greek Cypriot members' failure to pass the decisions they wanted, including *enosis*, was not the Muslim Turkish Cypriots, but the British.

Even though Turkish Cypriot members could play a strategic key role in Council votes, they were also not content with their role in the

Legislative Council. As the smallest group of the Council, the Turkish Cypriots did not have the power to be influential on any decisions taken by the Council preventing them from developing an independent will from the other groups and establishing policies. Turkish Cypriot members had to act together with the British advocating the continuation of the British rule in order to prevent Cyprus uniting with Greece that would lead the establishment of a Greek Cypriot dominance on the Island. Moreover, they were trying to get or maintain Turkey's interest and support in case the British left the Island making it difficult for them to develop a political self-confidence with respect to the establishment of policies independent from Britain and/or Turkey.

In terms of its desired function, the Legislative Council did not satisfy the decision-making mechanisms in London or its officials on the Island. Contrary to the generally accepted knowledge, even though the Greek Cypriot–Turkish Cypriot cooperation in the Council had seriously deteriorated since the Greek Cypriot members began to raise the demand for *enosis* on the Council's agenda in 1902–1903, the cooperation continued on socioeconomic issues. Disparities were emerging only on issues regarding differences in political objectives. Local members voted against many laws that the Colonial administration wanted to pass particularly the ones that were related with the budget, salaries of the top British civil servants and certain other public expenditures.

The British officials argued that the local members were opposing for the sake of opposition, were not honestly interested in the Island's main problems, and did not take the budget's constraints into account when making demands. In other words, as stated by the British officials, local members were acting irresponsibly. In this respect, the British suggested that the local members were abusing the rights and powers they were entrusted with (Onurkan-Samani 2007, passim; Orr 1972, p. 108; *LCM* 1883, pp. 1–3; 1888, pp. 70–87; 1894, pp. 48–56). Actually, in a council with such a structure, it could be true that the local members did not feel responsible because, as the British officials often stated themselves, it was the Colonial Government which was responsible, not the Council (Onurkan-Samani 2007, pp. 169–170, 186). Therefore, they had no desire to share the responsibility with the Colonial administration by approving proposals such as the budget, which had been drafted without their consultation and which they usually did not find acceptable. In this respect, from time to time they would vote against the proposals of the administration that could be beneficial to the Island knowing that rejecting the budget would not cause chaos. Such a situation was an obstacle to undertaking responsibility and gaining experience in ruling their country in real sense.

One positive contribution of the Legislative Council to the development of the Island's political culture was freedom of speech. Freedom of opinion and speech was secured in the Legislative Council on almost every issue including political demands and thoughts stipulating that the British should leave the Island. This prevented the opposition to the colonialist from turning into violence or going underground; kept their hopes that British would help them realize their political objectives or keep them alive; and allowed the sides to know about each other's intentions and thoughts.

On the other hand, allowing especially the demand for *enosis* to be voiced openly in the Council, resulted in devoting a significant amount of its time to this issue and in time, looking at every issue from the perspective of long-term political objective. This situation also led to a polarization between the Greek Cypriot and the Turkish Cypriot members. Moreover, the internal political process in each community was developed on the grounds of *enosis* among Greek Cypriots, and opposition to *enosis* among Turkish Cypriots. It was a factor in which internal group in each community was more pro or anti-*enosis* during the election campaigns. In other words, this competition moved to the level of patriotic-traitor. As a result, rather than establishing their policies according to their economic policies or knowledge, observations and experiences in other fields, the tradition of making easy politics over the Cyprus problem would take root. Making politics over communities' general vulnerabilities, like a vicious cycle, was resulting in the people, politicians and individuals' putting one another under political pressure.

In conclusion, despite all the detailed negative aspects presented in this study, the Legislative Council—with its one round/direct election system and other features—had the potential to provide the people of the Island with a serious experience toward the development of a parliamentarian representative democracy. It was observed that the Turkish Cypriot and Greek Cypriot members, in the established law system, generally respected the Constitution and the laws, making efforts to carry out their struggle through legal avenues, abiding by the rules and statutes pertaining to the Council internal regulations. Since the provision of freedom of speech (the Council's composition required the members' groups to compromise), there was a potential for a culture of compromise in the modern sense. However, the failure to be granted the powers requested through the local members in the Council disregarding views on how and where the Island resources should be spent and on other issues too, not only prevented local members from gaining experience in ruling by taking part in the Island administration, but also resulted in their questioning the Council's functionality and benefit. It is obvious that this situation strengthened the hand of the Greek Cypriot nationalists/extremists who wanted *enosis* to be prioritized play a role in deepening the feeling that they would not be able to carry out their struggle on legal grounds with colony rules. As a result, in 1931, the *enosis* Rebellion broke out, and the British administration—it was looking for an opportunity anyway—suspended all democratic procedures and institutions abolishing the Legislative Council.

NOTES

1. For the 1878 and 1882 Constitutions and for the constitutional additional orders see *The Cyprus Gazette* (1882), *Cyprus Civil List* (1905, Appendix B: v–xi; 1908, p. 3; 1905, Appendix C, D, E: xii–xxiii; 1908, p. 3).
2. In his memoirs published in 1953, L.S. Amery, who held significant positions such as the Ministry of Colonies, states that Muslim Cypriot community was given "disproportionate representation" so that they could form a counterpoise against *enosis*. Amery also claims that they anticipated the emergence of *enosis* as a serious problem sooner or later. Cited in Georghallides (1985, p. 5).
3. Although the number of Greek Cypriot members was raised from nine to twelve with the 1925 Constitution, the equilibrium in the Council was preserved as the number of British members was raised proportionally (six to nine). For the 1925 Constitution see *The Cyprus Gazette* (1925a).
4. For example, Georghallides (1985) recounts the feasibility studies of decision-making bodies in London in early 1928 on developing "Cypriot patriotism" in schools and even suggesting a Cyprus flag (p. 6).
5. Between the years 1878 and 1914/25, the local communities of Cyprus, who were under the rule of "High Commissionaire and Commander in Chief," were not given British nationality and were still considered Ottoman subjects. For the nationality issue see also Dendias (1937, p. 187), Hill (1952, p. 408), *The Annual Reports* (1914–1915, p. 41), *LCM* (1915, p. 30). Only the island's administration was taken over after a diplomatic treaty; the island itself was not the direct property of the Queen. It could be said that all these and all other features examined in this study fit the definition of Protectorate.

6. In the years 1914/25, Cyprus was unilaterally annexed and became a part of the Empire. With this, the highest level administrator was called the "Governor and Commander in Chief" and the Island communities became British subjects. See Onurkan-Samani (2007, pp. 64–66), *The Cyprus Gazette* (1925a, b).

7. This was in accordance with the general British colonial policy which aims to keep the execution rather than the legislation under control. For example, see Chamberlain (1998, p. 44), Onurkan-Samani (2007, pp. 57–70, 137–143).

8. Although civilian representatives, among whom were some local members of the Legislative Council, were appointed to the Executive Council as "Additional or Extraordinary member," they were summoned for the meetings only when deemed necessary. For examples, see Hill (1952, p. 423), Orr (1972, pp. 103–104), Onurkan-Samani (2007, pp. 137–141), *Cyprus Civil List* (1905, p. 30; 1908, pp. 41–50).

9. The British preserved the Ottoman period's taxation system to a large extent—although they started a serious revision process—and although they did not propose a raise in total tax amount, there was an increase in tax income as the system was made more efficient and tax evasion was minimized (Samani 2006, pp. 214–251).

10. Starting in 1886, Greek and Turkish Cypriot members of the Council collaborated to have the tribute paid by England's central treasury. For example, see *LCM* (1888, pp. 70–87; 1897, pp. 33–34; 1904, p. 39). Two of the Muslim members voted yes for the Greek member N. Rossos' 16 March 1887 dated resolution presented to the Council regarding the payment of tribute by British central treasury, and thus the resolution was passed by the Council. Resolution was passed with the affirmative votes of Hüseyin and Rashid Efendis, while Naim Efendi voted in the negative along with the British members (*LCM* 1887). Turkish Cypriot members also agreed with the Greek Cypriot members on the abolishing of tribute after the Island's annexation by Britain (*LCM* 1923, p. 177; 1925, pp. 1–2; 1926, pp. 141–157).

11. Dr. Eyyub accused the "Kemalist Populists", who he characterized as "Forced Nationalists," of making "ugly and shameful" propaganda in the 1930 elections and wrote: "they raised hell and put on airs as if they were the great saviors... They put the British headmaster issue on top of their opposition program and became nationalists while others became British collaborators. However, they know as well that Commission members who are Turkish and most of whom graduated from universities in Turkey were obliged to appoint a British headmaster. I wonder which one of great patriots respected the Turkish headmaster notion and defended the idea of a Turkish headmaster as much as we did? On the

contrary, each one of them was against a Turkish headmaster…" The newspaper *Hakikat*, 1931 (470–480), published eight articles between the dates 24 January–9 May; Fedai, 1985–1986; cited in An (2002, pp. 264–266).

12. For the rejection of the 1927 Budget and the developments that followed, see Onurkan-Samani (2007, pp. 285–286); *LCM* (1926, pp. 141–157), *The Cyprus Gazette* (1926, 1927a, b).

References

An, A. (1996). *Kıbrıs'ta İsyanlar ve Anayasal Temsiliyet Mücadelesi (1571–1948)*. Lefkoşa: Mez-Koop.

An, A. (2002). *Kıbrıs'ın Yetiştirdiği Değerler*. Ankara: Akçağ.

Ateşin, H. M. (1996). *Kıbrıs'ta İslâmi Kimlik Dâvâsı*. İstanbul: Marifet.

Bates, C. (2000). *Communalism and Identity Among South Asians in Diaspora* (Heidelberg Papers in South Asian and Comparative Politics, Working Paper No. 2). [Online] Available at: http://archive.ub.uni-heidelberg.de/volltext-server/4007/1/hpsacp2.pdf. Accessed 28 Nov 2017.

Chamberlain, M. E. (1998). *European Decolonisation in the Twentieth Century*. London: Longman.

Chatterjee, P. (1996). *Milliyetçi Düşünce ve Sömürge Dünyası* [Nationalist Thought and the Colonial World] (S. Oğuz, Trans.). Istanbul: İletişim (in Turkish).

Dendias, M. (1937). *The Cypriote Question*. Athens: Pyrsos.

Georghallides, G. S. (1985). *Cyprus and the Governorship of Sir Ronald Storrs: The Causes of the 1931 Crisis*. Nicosia: Cyprus Research Center.

Georghallides, G. S. (2004). *A Political and Administrative History of Cyprus 1918–1926 with a Survey of the Foundations of British Rule*. Nicosia: Cyprus Research Center.

Gürkan, H. M. (1989). *Dünkü ve Bugünkü Lefkoşa*. Lefkoşa: Galeri Kültür.

Hill, G. (1952). *History of Cyprus* (Vol. IV). Cambridge: Cambridge University Press.

King-Hall, S. (1937). *The Empire Yesterday and To-Day*. London: Oxford University Press.

Kitromilides, P. (1977). From Coexistence to Confrontation: The Dynamics of Ethnic Conflict Cyprus. In M. Attalides (Ed.), *Cyprus Reviewed* (pp. 35–70). Nicosia: Jus Cypri Association.

Kyrris, K. (1996). *Peaceful Co-existence in Cyprus Under British Rule (1878–1959) and After Independence: An Outline*. Nicosia: Cosmos.

Lugard, F. (1965). *The Dual Mandate in British Tropical Africa*. London: Frank Cass.

Onurkan-Samani, M. (1999). *Kıbrıs Türk Milliyetçiliği*. İstanbul: Bayrak Matbaacılık.

Onurkan-Samani, M. (2007). *Kıbrıs'ta Bir Sömürge Kurumu: Kavanin Meclisi (1882–1931)*. Ph.D. dissertation, Hacettepe University, Ankara.

Orr, C. W. J. (1972). *Cyprus Under British Rule*. London: Zeno Publishers.

Porter, B. (1996). *The Lion's Share: A Short History of British Imperialism 1850–1995*. London: Longman.

Rızvi, G. (1993). Ethnic Conflict and Political Accommodation in Plural Societies: Cyprus and Other Cases. *Journal of Commonwealth and Comparative Politics, 31*(1), 57–83.

Said, E. (1998). *Kültür ve Emperyalizm* [Culture and Imperialism] (N. Alpay, Trans.). İstanbul: Hil (in Turkish).

Samani, H. (2006). *Tanzimat Devrinde Kıbrıs (1839–1878)*. Ph.D. dissertation, Hacettepe University, Ankara.

Stout, H. M. (1953). *British Government*. New York: Oxford University Press.

Taylor, A. J. P. (1975). *The Second World War: An Illustrated History*. Middlesex: Penguin Special.

Wade, E. C. S., & Phillips, G. G. (1934). *Constitutional Law*. London: Longmans.

Young, C. (1994). The Colonial Construction of African Nations. In J. Hutchinson & A. Smith (Eds.), *Nationalism* (pp. 225–231). Oxford: Oxford University Press.

Newspaper and Periodicals

LCM (Legislative Council Minutes), Cyprus House of Parliament
1883, Issues 1–2, pp. 1–3; 1884, Issue 2; 1887, Issue 3; 1888, Issue 4, pp. 70–87; 1894, Issue 7, pp. 48–56; 1897, Issue 9, pp. 33–34; 1898, Issue 10, p. 134; 1900, Issue 12, pp. 15–16; 1902, Issue 14, pp. 35, 49–53, 57–66; 1903, Issue 15, pp. 1–6, 30–44, 343–351, 470–473; 1904, Issue 16, pp. 33–35, 39; 1911, Issue 23; 1914, Issue 26, pp. 6–7; 1915, Issue 27, pp. 7–15, 30; 1917, Issue 29, pp. 11–28; 1918, Issue 30, pp. 4–8; 1919, Issue 31, pp. 28–32, 39; 1920, Issue 32, pp. 6–7, 9; 1923, Issue 35, pp. 5–6, 19–20, 177; 1924, Issue 36; 1925, Issue 37, Volume 2, pp. 1–2; 1926, Issue 38, pp. 141–157; 1930, Issue 42, Volume I, p. 40; 1931, Issue 43, Volume I, pp. 13–18, 300–310.

Cyprus Gazette:
Number: 83 (23/3/1882), 1553 (11/12/1922), 1561 (19/1/1923), 1656 (24/10/1924), 1691 (1/5/1925a), 1717 (1/9/1925b), 1820 (31/12/1926), 1834 (7/3/1927a), 1870 (13/9/1927b).

Cyprus Civil List
1905; 1908.

Cyprus Annual Reports
1889–1890; 1890–1891; 1914–1915.

CHAPTER 5

Engendering Nationalism in Modern Cyprus: The First Women's Organizations

Thekla Kyritsi

INTRODUCTION

In 1861, a Greek school for girls opened its gates in the coastal city of Limassol. It was the first public[1] school for girls in the city and the second one in Cyprus—the first public school for girls in Cyprus had been established two years earlier, in 1859, in the capital city of Nicosia (Filippou 2000, pp. 173, 191). Like their equivalent schools in the newly independent state of Greece,[2] these girls' schools were called *Parthenagogeia*—which in the Greek language means the places for virgins' education. At a time when illiteracy was the devastating norm,[3] a few girls had the privilege to stand in the grounds of the new school of Limassol and listen to the speech of their first director, the Athenian Marigo Lazaridou (Loizias 2011a, p. 573) who—like many women teachers of her time—had graduated from the famous *Arsakeion* school of Athens, a prestigious educational institution for the training of women teachers (Dalakoura and Ziogou-Karastergiou 2015, pp. 61–71).

Reflecting the importance attributed by Cypriots to the first organized education, the day of Lazaridou's arrival, students as well as women and men of the "respectable" society of Limassol were gathered at the

T. Kyritsi (✉)
Political Science and History,
Panteion University of Social and Political Sciences, Athens, Greece

© The Author(s) 2018
T. Kyritsi and N. Christofis (eds.), *Cypriot Nationalisms in Context*,
https://doi.org/10.1007/978-3-319-97804-8_5

93

Parthenagogeion to welcome her and listen to her speech (Loizias 2011a, p. 573). The latter was given in an archaic form of the modern Greek language used by Greek literates named *katharevousa*,[4] which was probably not comprehensible to most of her younger audience but, being the official language of the Greek state it commanded respect and admiration for anyone who could use it, even if that person was a woman. Among the audience was the student Polixeni Loizias who would later be recognized as one of the first feminists in Cyprus and a tireless advocate of Greek nationalism (Pylarinos and Paraskeva-Hadjicosta 2011).

Some decades later, Loizias would describe Marigo Lazaridou, as "an angel bearing the national message of mother Greece" who had arrived in Cyprus to take the Greek women of Limassol out of their national "lethargy" (Loizias 2011a, p. 571). Loizias would especially commemorate how Lazaridou opened that first speech by addressing the students as *ellinides*, the female gender of Greeks, which can be translated as Greek women. "How much *joy*", Loizias narrated, "how much *pride* and *glory* those words meant to us. And we dreamed that *freedom*, crowns of *honor* and glory [would come] if we were educated as Greeks and if we sacrificed ourselves for Faith and Nation [italics mine]" (Loizias 2011a, p. 573).

Although women, such as Marigo Lazaridou and Polixeni Loizias, are sometimes—though not often—commemorated in national narratives, their story is rarely considered—if ever—from the perspective of nationalist studies. This chapter argues that this missing piece, namely the role of women as early agents of nationalism, is important for understanding the whole story. More particularly, this chapter refers to the role of the first women's organizations in Cyprus and their relationship with the early steps of the Greek nationalist ideology. These organizations were formed by literate middle-class women—mainly women teachers—in the years around 1900. The focus of the analysis is on two particular organizations of women which were both established in the city of Limassol. The first one, established in 1898, was an initiative of Polixeni Loizias and was named Greek Women's Union (*Enosis ton Ellinidon*).[5] The second one was Alexandra Charitable Association (*Philoptochos Alexandra*) and it was established a year later by Kassandra Zinonos, a woman writer of Athenian and Istanbulian origins staying in Limassol (Siakalli 2011, p. 49; Pylarinos and Paraskeva-Hadjicosta 2011, p. 90).

In 1906, the two organizations published together their own periodical, *Parthenon*, a biweekly magazine that circulated from 15 October 1906 to 1 July 1907, and was the first women's magazine in Cyprus (Sofokleous 2003). Although the editor of the magazine was a man journalist and intellectual, Euripides S. Chourmouzios (for a short biography see Koudounaris 1989, p. 189), the soul of the periodical was Polixeni Loizias and the slogan of the magazine declared that this was a women's publication, "under the protection of the women's organizations of the city, namely Greek Women's Union and Alexandra Charitable Association". *Parthenon* is one of the rare historical sources where the historian can trace the views of the women themselves, rather than a male perception of them.

The chapter is therefore based on the study of *Parthenon*, as well as a close analysis of the works of the leading Cypriot feminist Polixeni Loizias. As will be shown, the story of the first attempts of women to self-organization unfolds a relationship between early feminist consciousness and early nationalist ideology which resulted in a form of "feminist nationalism" or "nationalist feminism". Even though this may seem contradictory to the contemporary eye—due to the universality of women as a category and the particularity of nationalism—this relationship made sense in its historical context. It is also an exciting source of information for understanding the *appeal* of nationalism as an identity, an ideology, and a political movement.

CYPRIOT MODERNITY, GREEK NATIONALISM, AND WOMEN'S PLACE

The late nineteenth century was a period of transformation for the Cypriot society. The fact that Cyprus went under the administration of Britain in 1878 brought to an end the Ottoman era in the island along with the *millet* system according to which the subjects of the Ottoman Empire were categorized in ethnoreligious communities, and the leadership of the community was a priori in the hands of the (male) religious authorities—given to them by the supreme authority, the Sultan.[6] This resulted in a series of institutional and legal changes (Georghallides 1979, pp. 37–87). On the administrative level, immediately after the arrival of the British in 1878, a form of legislative body was established—the Legislative Council (Onurkan-Samani, this volume; see also Georghallides 1979, pp. 39–40). After a reform of 1882, the Legislative Council became closer to western forms of political representation

(Onurkan-Samani, this chapter; Georghallides 1979, pp. 41–42); though until then it included four nominated official members and three unofficial representatives of the local religious communities (Georghallides 1979, p. 40), now the twelve out of the total eighteen members of the Council would be directly elected by the local communities (nine from the "non-Muslim" and three from the Muslim community, see Onurkan-Samani, this volume).

At the same time, 1878—the year that Britain obtained Cyprus—was also the year of the appearance of the first Greek newspaper in Cyprus, *Kypros-Cyprus*, which was soon followed by a rapid development of the Greek language press (Sofokleous 1995). In the meantime, during the second half of the nineteenth century, Greek educational institutions met an important growth (Filippou 2000). The new modern institutions of representative politics, mass education and press circulation, along with the development of new professions—merchants and traders, owners of workshops and manufactures, lawyers, doctors, teachers, journalists et cetera—in other words, the expansion of the middle classes of the cities, that were attracted to the modern ideas of enlightenment and "progress", consisted the pre-conditions for the emergence and the development of the ideology of Greek nationalism.

Therefore, after the arrival of Britain and the institutional changes which accompanied it, these elites would expand and would become more and more loyal to the nationalist aspirations. By the end of the nineteenth century, considering that an independent state of Greece existed since 1832, a body of the secular, literate elites, along with a few educated clerics had already become loyal to the ideology of Greek nationalism and the Greek irredentism, that is, the belief that their community would only be "free" if they became citizens of the Greek state.

Meanwhile, all these developments—organized education, representative politics, press circulation, and the simultaneous creation of a "public opinion" (Bryant 2004, p. 32)—constituted for many Cypriots their first encounters with notions of modernity, such as "representation", the condition of being a "citizen", rather than a "subject" of an Empire, the ideas of "equality" and "rights". However, as noted by Rebecca Bryant (2004, p. 5), within modernity "supposedly universal ethical principles of democratic representation and rights were realized in culturally specific, and often contradictory, terms".

In the case of women, the universal principle of representation was not applied; only males—over the age of 21 and with particular property or financial situation—were allowed to vote or get voted in the Legislative Council (Katsiaounis 1996, pp. 84–92; see also Protopapas 2012). Women were banned from the electoral body of the Council or any kind of political rights, regardless of their financial situation (Protopapas 2012). For women—as for the men of the popular strata for this matter—the contradiction between their real, everyday life and the concepts of representation and equality was quite devastating. All institutions, from religious ones to the press and the educational system reproduced gender norms and inequalities while patriarchy and sexism, as systems of values and social attitudes, continued to be the basis of family, social structures, and communal life.

Beyond some urban development and the expansion of the Cypriot middle class, at the end of the nineteenth century Cyprus remained a rural economy and a traditional society. Most women as well as most men lived in poor rural households, earning their living from family-based, agricultural production, farming and animal-related activities, and/or agricultural labor. The vast majority of the population were illiterate; in 1879 the British High Commissioner, Robert Biddulph, reported that in many villages there was no individual able to read or write, while he noted a total negligence of women's education (Filippou 2000, p. 39). Even in 1911, approximately 93% of the female population were illiterate (Persianis 1998, p. 36).

Overall, Cyprus was a patriarchal and hierarchical society based on class, age, and gender hierarchies, with religious leadership having a significant proportion of power. Considering that the social history of women in Cyprus is extremely under-researched and it is not in the aims of this chapter to bridge the gap, it is enough to say here that gender segregation was a structural characteristic of all aspects of private and communal life both in villages and in the cities. Nevertheless, although women's subjection as such was a universal characteristic in the Cypriot space at the time, the experience of women's roles and lifestyle varied according to region—e.g., urban or rural areas—and socioeconomic class (Ragkou 1984). The literate women of the middle and upper middle classes of the cities, although very few in numbers, are the focus of this study since they would be the first women in Cyprus to attempt to organize their gender in all-female associations.

As apparent in the early Greek press which began to circulate in the cities of Cyprus at the end of the nineteenth century, this category of women was expected to remain in the private sphere, taking care of their husbands and their children. Their socialization in the public sphere was limited to going to the Church, or getting dressed according to the growing influence of the European fashion, and accompany their husbands to the few social gatherings and events organized by the "respectable" society (Kyritsi 2018, p. 251). The press and the educational system put particular emphasis on separate gender spheres and a distinctive "woman's nature" while a deeply rooted misogyny and prejudice against women was evident in the first Greek newspapers (Alekou 2018; Kyritsi 2018). Women's work was seen as shameful and inappropriate by the rising bourgeoisie as well as by the British administration. Women were excluded from most professional occupations which developed during the nineteenth century—such as merchants, doctors, lawyers et cetera. The only professional opportunity for an educated woman was to become a teacher.

Nevertheless, women educators were also excluded from decision-making bodies, even regarding women's education. With the arrival of the British and the new politics, although the traditional power of the Church in the Orthodox community seemed for a moment to be threatened (Papageorgiou 1996), the Church continued to have a significant role in the Cypriot society, only now, it had to operate in a modern context.[7] Thus, the School Committees which were the administrative authorities of the Greek educational institutions (Filippou 2000, pp. 164–173) remained under the control of the Church. These Committees had the authority to employ or fire the directors and teachers of the *Parthenagogeia*, which meant that the career and the living of women educators were entirely dependent on the Church and the men of the Committees (Persianis 1998, p. 30).

In many cases, women educators were fired according to the will of the school authorities without any kind of protective regulations against arbitrary termination (Persianis 1998, p. 30). Furthermore, particular regulations—during both the Ottoman era and the British rule—forbade the employment of married women to the teaching profession, or made them resign their position once they got married (Persianis 1998, p. 29); the dominant belief was that women could not work and be simultaneously "good" wives and mothers. Moreover, women educators were paid approximately half the wage of male educators in similar positions (Persianis 1998, pp. 261–264).

THE FIRST WOMEN'S ORGANIZATIONS IN CYPRUS: A NATIONALIST FEMINISM

Having said this, modern institutions still marked the end of the *Ancien Régime* which in the Cypriot context meant—as already explained—a patriarchal communal order based on the principles of the Ottoman *millet*. Therefore, despite the new role of religion in the modern context, and despite the reproduction of gender inequalities and the exclusion of women from power, a society where traditional hierarchies rupture, political power, and forms of representation change, still offers some space for the negotiation of new roles. Thus, although the new institutions excluded women from power, the modern context simultaneously brought contradictory messages regarding women's place, and offered them new opportunities however limited.

On the one hand, the misogynist discourse of the press was found next to news about international women's movements that demanded political rights: the Greek feminists demanded education and work for women (Varika 2004), the British suffragists demanded women's vote (Purvis 1995), and some states, such as New Zealand and South Australia had already allowed women's vote in 1893 and 1894, respectively. However, the lack of an organized women's movement before the end of the nineteenth century meant that these messages remained to most some "peculiar" facts occurring in the world outside Cyprus.

Eventually, the institution which would constitute an actual threat to the *status quo* of gender relations and the culture of misogyny at the turn of the century would be women's education. The latter would become the center of women's politicization and early feminist consciousness, resulting in the formation of the first women's organizations. Indeed, in 1898, the formation of a women's organization named Greek Women's Union (*Enosis ton Ellinidon*) was announced in the local press of Limassol (Siakalli 2011, p. 47; Pylarinos and Paraskeva-Hadjicosta 2011, p. 90). This organization was the first all-female initiative in Cyprus—or the first that we know of—toward women's self-organization with feminist aspirations and early political demands.[8] It was established by Polixeni Loizias who was now the director of the city's *Parthenagogeion*. Loizias was encouraged to establish the organization by the Greek feminist Kalliroi Siganou-Parren who two years earlier had formed an analogous organization in Greece (Varika 2004, p. 366). The name chosen for the Cypriot organization was exactly the same because it was intended as a "branch" of the Greek organization.

The first president of the Greek Women's Union—suggested by Polixeni Loizias—was Melpomeni Rossidou who had an upper middle class background as her husband was an important merchant in Limassol (Koudounaris 1989, pp. 151–152). During the first year of its existence, the members of the Greek Women's Union were about thirty-eight (Siakalli 2011). Aiming to expand women's education, among the first decisions of the organization was the establishment of a Sunday school where members of the organization would give free courses of Greek reading, writing and Orthodox religion (Siakalli 2011, p. 48; Pylarinos and Paraskeva-Hadjicosta 2011, p. 157) to "the women of the people"—a term used by the upper classes at the time to describe the women of the popular strata. Other early activities included the organization of exhibitions to promote local women's work—such as embroidery and knitting—and the formation of a textile mill to teach weaving to orphan women (Pylarinos and Paraskeva-Hadjicosta 2011, p. 158). Their activities targeted to help women of all classes to receive a basic education and to help poorer women to gain useful skills that would allow them to earn their living or contribute to their family income.

After the formation of the Greek Women's Union Branch in Limassol—particularly, one year later—another women's organization was established in the same city named Alexandra Charitable Association (*Philoptochos Alexandra*) by Kassandra Zinonos (Siakalli 2011, p. 49; Pylarinos and Paraskeva-Hadjicosta 2011, p. 161). Like Loizias', Zinonos' initiative also occurred after her encouragement by a Greek woman, Sotiria Aliberti. The latter was the leader of a charitable organization of Greece named "Ergani Athena" (Pylarinos and Paraskeva-Hadjicosta 2011, p. 161). Similarly to the Greek Women's Union, Alexandra Charitable Association was also seen as a Cypriot "branch" of its Greek equivalent organization, "Ergani Athena" (Pylarinos and Paraskeva-Hadjicosta 2011, p. 161). Around this period, similar organizations would emerge in the cities of the island and would operate both as agents of an early feminist consciousness and as militants of the national cause. Some of the organizations mentioned in the literature include the "Alexandra Charitable Organization" of Larnaca and the "Greek Women's Charitable Association of Famagusta" (Siakalli 2011). In Nicosia, an effort by the director of the city's *Parthenagogeion*, Theano Parouti, was initially made for the formation of a Nicosian branch of a "Greek Women's Union" (*Foni tis Kyprou 1898*); however, it seems that the initiative did not flourish before the 1914 when the "Greek Ladies' Association, the Union" was established in Nicosia (Siakalli 2011).

These first attempts to women's self-organization were initiatives of literate women belonging mainly to the middle class of the major cities. They were obviously and directly influenced by the Greek women's movement. The soul of the movement was women educators—especially the directors of *Parthenagogeia*. As already explained, they focused their activities on charity work, the expansion of women's education and women's opportunities to work. They were also extremely attached to the ideology of Greek nationalism and zestfully devoted themselves to the national cause.

EDUCATION AND THE POLITICAL SOCIALIZATION OF WOMEN

The fact that the first category of women to express a collective voice and aim to negotiate women's role in the new context were the literate women—mainly women teachers, and especially the directors of *Parthenagogeia*—is not peculiar. The latter shared some characteristics which distinguished them from other groups of women. A key factor was that literacy as such promoted "self-awareness of one's own condition, more exigent needs and higher aspirations" (Katsiaounis 1996, p. 93) therefore it allowed women to imagine new roles and better conditions for themselves. At the same time, literacy commanded the respect of the community and operated as a Bourdieuian[9] "symbolic capital". In other words, literacy alone upgraded the social position or the status of an individual; especially in a period when the limits between social classes were not quite fixed or clear.

This is particularly evident in the case of women teachers. Due to the culture which assumed that working outside the house was degrading for women, the women of the upper middle classes would not be interested in becoming teachers (Persianis 1998, pp. 84–85). This way, women of the popular strata were encouraged to cover this need. They would receive financial help by the School Committees (Persianis 1998, p. 85), or by wealthier relatives and charity establishments in order to continue their studies and be trained as teachers. Although women teachers received very low wages—approximately half of their male colleagues as already explained—they still passed from the poor and illiterate popular strata to the respectable and prestigious minority of Greek educators.

Therefore, although their career and their living were entirely dependent on the Church and the men of the School Committees (Persianis 1998, p. 30), women educators—as educated and financially independent—enjoyed an extent of respect, freedom, and self-reliance that no other category of women enjoyed. Moreover, due to the regulations against the employment of married women to the position of the teacher (Persianis 1998, p. 29), women educators were single and in this sense not bounded by the will of their husband.

Beyond their socioeconomic characteristics, women educators became politicized due to the framework of their occupation. As the first educational institutions for girls became centers for women's intellectual activity and aspirations, the first attempts of women to organize themselves emerged by women scholars. Indeed, in the context of the nineteenth century, education in general became "a major agency of political socialization" (Katsiaounis 1996, p. 92) for both men and women. For women, however, schools became the only space of politicization. As already explained, the women of the middle classes were expected to stay at home and be concerned with their everyday duties as housewives, daughters or mothers while men could sit in traditional coffee shops, reading the press and "battling among themselves over modernization and 'national' causes" (Bryant 2004, p. 7). However, in the first *Parthenagogeia* women could talk about the "important" staff, the "high" politics and the "sacred" national cause. As the men in their coffeehouses "claimed to speak for the people, at the same seeking to describe a consensus that would support their claims to authority" (Bryant 2004, p. 7), a distinct female culture flourished in girls' schools where women scholars would begin to speak for their gender and thinking of ways to gain a place and a say in the new world.

However, *Parthenagogeia* were also centers of promoting the nationalist project of the *Megali Idea* (Great Idea) and the Greek irredentism. Women's education itself in regard to the Orthodox community of Cyprus owed its existence to the Greek state and the ideology of Greek irredentism. Women teachers were educated in Greek educational institutions, where they were taught that their highest duty as teachers was to promote the national cause among the young generations of women. For some researchers, this could be a sufficient explanation for the coexistence of feminist consciousness and nationalist ideology in modern Cyprus: education as such promoted both the Greek nationalism and an awareness of one's position, which in the case of women would result in both nationalist and feminist ideas.

However, the study of women's nationalism and the first women's organizations indicates that this relationship was more than the result of a nationalist "brainwash" to women from above. A close analysis of the first women's organizations, the works of Polixeni Loizias and the discourse of *Parthenon* shows that this process was not a *passive* acceptance of a nationalist narrative invented by the men and the Greek state. These developments were obviously part of the material and historical pre-conditions which allowed the construction and the social relevance of the nationalist narrative. Beyond that, however, middle class women emotionally and sincerely identified with the nationalist project because, among other reasons, it made sense to their search of a positive identity and offered them a safe symbolic space in the framework of Cypriot modernity.

NATIONALISM, FEMINISM AND THE SEARCH FOR A POSITIVE IDENTITY

In her pioneer work on the history of Greek feminists, Varika (2004, p. 22) observed the contradiction between a "delirious" nationalism and an internationalist feminist engagement. However, this delirious nationalism, as experienced also by the Greek Cypriot feminists, was not seen by them as contradictory to feminism. Instead, they saw nationalism as a synonym of humanism, freedom, and equality, while they found in nationalism a positive and meaningful female identity, and an ideology which could justify their demands for women's work and women's education. This scheme was expressed by Loizias (2011a, pp. 573–574) when she explained that her first teachers—such as Marigo Lazaridou and others—taught her and her female co-students, "during the Turkish rule in this far-away corner of Hellenism [Cyprus]", that "they too were human beings". In the same sentence, Loizias also explained that their teachers taught them that "humanism" meant "to belong to a nation, to know the history of one's country and one's Church".

These women—as well as their male compatriots—saw the world as already divided in nations; some nations were "free", some still "enslaved". In a text written by Loizias and used as a textbook in girls' education in Cyprus, the teacher assured the students that the day was close when their nation—"and all of the enslaved nations"—would be "liberated"

(Loizias 2011b, p. 352). And then, Cypriot women would be called "free" because, as the text explained, "when Cyprus is a slave, that is, when it has a foreign ruler", "all its inhabitants are named slaves, men and women and children" (p. 352). National freedom and individual freedom were therefore experienced as synonyms. Moreover, nationalism suggested a scheme which could explain their situation in a seemingly meaningful way—their current misery was due to the foreign ruler—while it also gave them hope and a clear solution to all their problems, the union with Greece.

Meanwhile, nationalism presumed a kind of equality, at least on an abstract or spiritual level which, as argued by Benedict Anderson (1991, p. 7), was a characteristic of all nationalisms: "Nation", Anderson observed, "is imagined as a community, because, regardless of the actual inequality and exploitation that may prevail in each, the nation is always conceived as a deep, horizontal comradeship". This was reflected in a speech dedicated to the Greek women conducted by Nikolaos Katalanos (1894), a leading figure and a militant intellectual of the Greek nationalism in nineteenth-century Cyprus (see Katsiaounis 1996, pp. 215–223). Although Katalanos accepted that women were "servitorial" by nature and less capable of analytical thinking than men, he also declared that women were equal to men in front of God and no different than men regarding "the universal idea of humanity". In other words, he declared that women too were human beings rather than some kind of a different genre; an idea often suggested at the time in the misogynist discourse (Alekou 2018; Kyritsi 2018).

This was a powerful and appealing message to women, namely that whatever inequalities existed between men and women, women too were members of the great Greek nation and they too had an important role to play to the national cause. As Dekker (1998, p. 13) observed in his search for explaining nationalism, "people strive not to an identity, as such, but rather to have a positive identity and high self-esteem". This, he explains, is one of the psychological needs which are linked to national attitudes. In other words, nationalism wasn't just a way to belong but it was a way to belong in something great. Indeed, the first women educators and their organizations experienced their "Greekness" as an "uplifting" and "glorious" identity. Not only women were "human beings" but they also were the descendants of a great nation. The search for a positive female identity is evident in the way women educators looked repeatedly for admirable women in the history of the nation to find examples of Greek women's bravery and morality. Loizias' work—both her pedagogic textbooks aimed to be taught in the class and her personal work such as her poems—is characterized by a turn to women's history and a search for positive female figures in the history of Greece and Cyprus.[10]

It is not then a coincidence that the study of the first newspapers of Nicosia for the period 1887–1900 (Kyritsi 2018), namely *Foni tis Kyprou* and *Evagoras*, makes it evident that the passages where women were positively presented and idealized were the ones that were connected to the national cause. In those cases, women were presented as Greek heroines or Greek mothers (Kyritsi 2018, p. 260). In contrast, when women were depicted outside the nationalist narrative, they were presented as vain, dangerous, evil, and manipulative (Kyritsi 2018). In other words, the alternative identity for the women of the middle and upper classes was to accept that they were vain and useless creatures, destined to be the jewelries of their husbands or eternally doing a dull never-ending and invisible work of house chores and child care. Instead, nationalism suggested a positive way to belong and it also offered a meaningful narrative of one's situation, along with a sense of purpose and hope; in this view, housework and motherhood were sacred duties to the national cause, and women not only weren't useless but they should also be educated in order to fulfill those duties.

Besides the role of the Greek *oikodespoina*, a term which can be translated as the lady of the house who was expected to support her husband and provide her home with warmness and comfort, a key element linked to the construction of the Greek female identity was the role of the Greek mother. While the emphasis on the future of the community became more and more connected to the aspirations of Greek nationalism, motherhood became more and more attached to the needs of the nation. The arguments in favor of women's education were almost always linked to "motherhood" which was presented as a "sacred" duty to the nation. During the two years of the circulation of the women's newspaper *Parthenon*, the appeal to "motherhood" and its importance to the nation was rarely absent from an issue.

Thus, in the first issue (15.10.1906, p. 1), the editor's note explained that the purpose of the newspaper was to provide the "female sex" with an organized space for the "Greek education and intellectual development of the Cypriot woman" and to "contribute to the making of mothers who will be worthy of their high destination". The front page of the second issue of the newspaper was titled "The woman as a mother" and the front pages of the next three issues (3–5) were titled "On the education of the Greek mother". In these texts, motherhood is mainly valued and idealized due to its importance to the national cause. The relationship between motherhood and the national cause was repeatedly used to justify women's rights to education and legitimize this demand. In this context, even if society found that women were not supposedly destined to form the politics of the nation or to follow professional occupations, they should still agree that women's education was necessary in order for them to fulfill their duty to the future generations, namely to be good mothers who would raise good Greeks.

CLOSING REMARKS: NATIONALISM AS AN ALTERNATIVE PATH TO CITIZENSHIP

The relationship between women's education and nationalism was therefore interdependent: it wasn't only that education promoted nationalism but also vice versa, it was nationalism that actually legitimized women's education. At the same time, nationalism legitimized the only prestigious occupation for women, that is, women educators. When literate women made their first attempts to speak or write publically, they chose the subject of the national cause, and their attempts were accepted to a great extent by the community because of the important role of women educators as the "cultivators" of the new generations of Greek mothers. Women educators were the first women to speak in front of a public audience and write in the press on public issues, and they commanded their say precisely as the educators of the future generation of Greek mothers.

It was in this context that the first women's organizations of Limassol were to a great extent accepted by the community. Women's organizations, same as the articles of their magazine, *Parthenon*, did not question directly the ideology of separate spheres. They accepted the assumption of a distinctive "woman's nature" destined to be the guardian of the house and the caretaker of her children. However, these roles were reframed to justify the demands for both women's education and women's participation in the national affairs. Although women's organizations accepted particular stereotypes—for example that charity is supposedly more appropriate for women as a continuation of the role of the mother and the caretaker—through this they justified their presence in the public sphere.

While nationalism legitimized women's right to education through assuming a higher purpose to "motherhood", it also offered a different path to women's *citizenship*. In other words, although modern institutions and the new representative politics as well as the traditional institutions of the community, such as the Church and the School Committees, refused political rights to women and therefore did not recognize them as *citizens*, nationalism offered a different path to citizenship and a justification for women to demand a say in public affairs. Even if women were denied political rights, they became nevertheless citizens once they became Greeks. In this context, for Loizias (2011a, p. 671) and the first feminist organizations, women's role as *oikodespoina* or *estiada* (lady of the house) went hand in hand with their role as *politida*, that is, the female citizen, the equivalent of the French *citoyenne*. If they were Greek mothers, they should receive decent education; if they were the mothers of Greeks, they were Greek citizens; and as long as public affairs were national issues, women should have a say in public affairs. In a Hegelian process, the acceptance of a private woman's nature (motherhood, caretaker) in the framework of the nationalist worldview was used by the Cypriot feminists of the nineteenth and early twentieth century to justify the first demands for women's involvement in public sphere and political affairs.

NOTES

1. These schools were public in the sense that they were not private but community-based institutions—where community here means the Greek Orthodox community of Cyprus. Namely, the particular schools for girls were part of a wider educational system which was developed within the Orthodox community of Cyprus during the nineteenth, and especially the second half of the nineteenth century (Filippou 2000, p. 172). These schools were governed by provincial bodies named "School Committees". The head of the Committees was the Archbishop of the Church or the Bishop of the relevant province and the members of each Committee consisted of high ranking clerics as well as individuals from the lay squirearchy and the rising bourgeoisie.

2. For a history of modern Greek education see Dalakoura and Ziogou-Karastergiou (2015).

3. Even in 1881, twenty years after the establishment of the *Parthenagogeion* of Limassol, this remained the only elementary school for girls in the city with approximately 140 students (cited in a table regarding the number of students in Cyprus in 1881, 1891, and 1901 by Persianis 1998, p. 124). Even four decades later, in 1911, 93.22% of the female population were illiterate (Persianis 1998, p. 36).

4. *Katharevousa* was an archaic form of the modern Greek language used by literates during the nineteenth and the twentieth century. In contrast, the popular form which was spoken in Greece at the time was called *demotiki*. *Katharevousa* was the official language of the Greek education and the Greek state until 1976 when it was replaced by *demotiki*.

5. The Greek Women's Union, established in 1898, is the second in time women's organization mentioned by the literature. One earlier organization was established before the end of the Ottoman era, in 1870 (Siakalli 2011, p. 34). It seems that this was an initiative of the Bishop of Kition, Kyprianos Oikonomidis, who suggested to some upper and middle-class women of Larnaca to get organized in order to help the church do charity work—such as giving bread to the population. This charitable women's organization was named Larnaca's Charitable Association of Ladies (*Philoptochos Adelfotita Kirion Larnacas*).

6. For an analysis of the *millet* system and the Greek Orthodox Communities, see Anagnostopoulou 1998.

7. Many clerics, for example, gained positions in the Legislative Council although the legitimization of their political power in the modern context did not derive from them being clerics, but from the approval of the electoral body which offered them this position. As Bryant (2004, p. 29) explains, "a younger, dynamic clergy and other elites tied to them were prepared to manipulate the new forms of representation" and to "stake their own claims in the political arena".

8. As mentioned in a previous endnote, the literature refers to one earlier organization of women which was established in 1870 named Larnaca's Charitable Association of Ladies. However, that was a purely charitable association and an initiative of a male priest, the Bishop of Kition.

9. Pertaining to the French intellectual Pierre Bourdieu.

10. Most of Loizias' work is found in Pylarinos and Paraskeva-Hadjicosta (2011).

References

Alekou, S. (2018). Γυναικοφοβία ή Θηλυκοποίηση του Φόβου: Από την Αρχαία Μυθολογία στην Ευρωπαϊκή Απομυθοποίηση του Κυπριακού Μισογυνισμού [Gynaephobia or Feminisation of Fear: From the Ancient

Mythology to the European Demystification of the Cypriot Misogyny]. In A. Alecou (Ed.), *Ο Χρήσιμος Εχθρός: Δοκίμια για την Κατασκευή του «Άλλου»* [The Useful Enemy: Papers on the Construction of the "Other"] (pp. 209–242). Nicosia: Cyprus University Press.

Anagnostopoulou, S. (1998). *Μικρά Ασία, 19ος αι.– 1919. Οι Ελληνορθόδοξες κοινότητες. Από το Μιλλέτ των Ρωμιών στο Ελληνικό Έθνος* [Asia Minor, 19th Century—1919: The Greek Orthodox Communities: From Rum-Millet to the Greek Nation]. Athens: Ellinika grammata.

Anderson, B. (1991). *Imagined Communities: Reflections on the Origin and Spread of Nationalism*. London and New York: Verso.

Bryant, R. (2004). *Imagining the Modern: The Cultures of Nationalism in Cyprus*. London and New York: I.B. Tauris.

Dalakoura, K., & Ziogou-Karastergiou, S. (2015). *Η εκπαίδευση των γυναικών - Οι γυναίκες στην εκπαίδευση, 18ος-20ός αι* [The Education of Women—Women in Education, 18th–20th Century]. Athens: Syndesmos Ellinikon Akadimaikon Vivlion (SEAB).

Dekker, H. (1998). *Nationalism, Its Explanations, and National Socialization*. Paper prepared for presentation at the second Dutch–Hungarian Conference on Interethnic Relations, p. 13.

Filippou, L. (2000). *Τα ελληνικά γράμματα εν Κύπρω κατά την περίοδο της Τουρκοκρατίας, 1571-1878* [Greek Literacy in Cyprus During the Turkish Rule, 1571-1878]. Nicosia: Epifaniou.

Georghallides, G. S. (1979). *A Political and Administrative History of Cyprus, 1918-1926: With a Survey of the Foundations of British Rule*. Nicosia: Cyprus Research Centre.

Katalanos, N. (1894). Ο λόγος του Καταλάνου [The Speech of Katalanos]. *Ευαγόρας* [Evagoras], Issue 223.

Katsiaounis, R. (1996). *Labour, Society and Politics in Cyprus: During the Second Half of the Nineteenth Century*. Nicosia: Cyprus Research Centre.

Koudounaris, A. L. (1989). Βιογραφικόν ΛεξικΔν Κυπρίων [Biographical Dictionary of Cypriots]. Nicosia: Pierides Foundation.

Kyritsi, T. (2018). Μισογυνισμός στα τέλη του 19ου αιώνα στην Κύπρο: οι πρώτες εφημερίδες της Λευκωσίας [Misogyny in Cyprus at the End of the 19th Century: The First Newspapers of Nicosia]. In A. Alecou (Ed.), *Ο Χρήσιμος Εχθρός, Δοκίμια για την Κατασκευή του «Άλλου»* [The Useful Enemy: Papers on the Construction of the "Other"]. Nicosia: Cyprus University Press.

Loizias, P. (2011a). Κυπριακή Κυψέλη [Cypriot Hive]. In Th. Pylarinos & Y. Paraskeva-Hadjicosta (Eds.), *Πολυξένης Λοϊζιάδος, Τα Έργα* [Polyxeni Loizias, the Works] (pp. 533–680). Nicosia: Kentro Epistimonikon Erevnon.

Loizias, P. (2011b). Πατριδογραφία Κύπρου [Patriography (Meaning the Mapping of One's Home Country) of Cyprus]. In Th. Pylarinos & Y. Paraskeva-Hadjicosta (Eds.), Πολυξένης Λοϊζιάδος, Τα Έργα [Polyxeni Loizias, the Works] (pp. 347–382). Nicosia: Kentro Epistimonikon Erevnon.

Papageorgiou, S. (1996). Η πρώτη περίοδος της «αγγλοκρατίας» στην Κύπρο, 1878–1914: πολιτικός εκσυγχρονισμός και κοινωνικές αδράνειες [The First Period of the British Rule in Cyprus, 1878–1914]. Athens: Papazisis.

Persianis, K. P. (1998). Ιστορία της εκπαίδευσης των κοριτσιών στην Κύπρο [History of Girls' Education in Cyprus]. Nicosia: Persianis.

Protopapas, V. (2012). Εκλογική ιστορία της Κύπρου: πολιτευτές, κόμματα και εκλογές στην Αγγλοκρατία, 1878–1960 [Electoral History of Cyprus: Politicians, Parties and Elections in British Rule, 1878–1960]. Athens: Themelio.

Purvis, J. (Ed.). (1995). Women's History: Britain, 1850–1945: An Introduction. London and New York: Routledge.

Pylarinos, T., & Paraskeva-Hadjicosta, Y. (2011). Εισαγωγή [Introduction]. In T. Pylarinos & Y. Paraskeva-Hadjicosta (Eds.), Πολυξένης Λοϊζιάδος, Τα Έργα [Polyxeni Loizias, the Works] (pp. 37–304). Nicosia: Kentro Epistimonikon Erevnon.

Ragkou, E. (1984). Η γυναίκα της Κύπρου το 18ο και 19ο αιώνα [The Cypriot Woman in 18th and 19th Century]. In Η Ζωή στην Κύπρο τον ΙΗ' και ΙΘ' αιώνα [Life in Cyprus in 18th and 19th Century] (pp. 107–120). Nicosia: Nicosia Municipality.

Siakalli, A. (2011). Γυναικεία Σωματεία [Women's Clubs]. Series: Enthymion (Vol. 6), Fileleftheros.

Sofokleous, A. (1995). Συμβολή στην ιστορία του κυπριακού τύπου [Contribution to the History of the Cypriot Press] (Vol. A) (Series). Nicosia: Intercollege Press.

Sofokleous, A. (2003). Συμβολή στην ιστορία του κυπριακού τύπου [Contribution to the History of the Cypriot Press] (Vol. C) (Series). Nicosia: Intercollege Press.

Varika, E. (2004). Η εξέγερση των κυριών [The Uprising of the Ladies]. Athens: Katarti.

Newspapers

Ethnos (5.7.1985) [Cypriot Newspaper].

Foni tis Kyprou (21.12.1894) [Cypriot newspaper].

Foni tis Kyprou (12.07.1898) [Cypriot Newspaper].

Parthenon 15/10/1906 (1), 31/10/1906 (2), 15/11/1906 (3), 30/11/1906 (4), Undocumented date (5).

PART II

Moments of a Mass Movement

CHAPTER 6

Cyprus in the 1940s: The Nationalization of Greek Cypriot Politics

Dimitris Kalantzopoulos

INTRODUCTION

This chapter explores the shaping of Greek Cypriot politics during the 1940s, focusing on the consolidation of nationalism within the community and examining mainly the politics of two principal actors, the Orthodox Church and the *Progressive Party of the Working People* (*Ανορθωτικό Κόμμα Εργαζόμενου Λαού*, AKEL). Throughout the 1930s and 1940s the Church, the main actor to promote nationalist politics, strove, not least by putting forward the claim of *enosis*, to emerge as the ethnarchic leadership, or the national authority of the community. By 1950, this primacy would be achieved, despite two major challenges to the Church's politics. From the aftermath of the 1931 revolt and during the largest part of the period under examination, the colonial government sought to restrict the political activities of the Church and control the advance of Greek Cypriot nationalism.[1] The main exceptions to this policy were the cases of cooperation between the two institutions against the new forces representing the ideologies of communism and socialism.

D. Kalantzopoulos (✉)
Athens, Greece

© The Author(s) 2018
T. Kyritsi and N. Christofis (eds.), *Cypriot Nationalisms in Context*,
https://doi.org/10.1007/978-3-319-97804-8_6

113

Indeed, the most significant challenge to the confessional politics came from the broad secular political space of the Left, which had a key influence on Greek Cypriot political life during a great part of the 1940s. Nevertheless, the political discourse of the Left came to be increasingly nationalist after the foundation of AKEL in 1941, leading to the complete adoption of *enosist* politics by the party and gradually to the recognition of the Church as the national leadership of the community.

THE *NATIONAL QUESTION*: TOWARD A CONSENSUS

In the wake of the 1931 revolt the colonial government imposed an authoritarian regime in Cyprus, suspending the elections; repealing the semi-liberal institutional framework of the previous period; and imposing a series of measures, mainly against the Church and the Communist Party of Cyprus (*Κομμουνιστικό Κόμμα Κύπρου*, KKK), which was outlawed in 1933, with a view to eliminate communal autonomy and suppress all political activities. Many of the measures were eventually lifted during the Second World War years, yet the suspension of constitutional government in Cyprus was, uniquely in British colonial policy, never restored until the end of colonial rule in the island.

Part of the measures taken by the government against the Church was the deportation of two of the island's three bishops—the Bishops of Kyrenia and Kition. After Archbishop Cyril's death in 1933 the Bishop of Paphos, Leontios, the only bishop remaining in the island, assumed the position of Locum Tenens of the vacant archiepiscopal see. The absence of the two bishops outside Cyprus constituted an obstacle for a canonical election of a permanent successor to Cyril as the holding of the Holy Synod—composed of the three bishops, according to the Charter of the Orthodox Church of Cyprus—was impossible (*Charter of the Most Holy Church of Cyprus*, article 2). The government's refusal to authorize the exiles' return and the decision of the exiles and the Locum Tenens to postpone the elections until they would be held canonically, created a deadlock. In 1937, the government passed legislation providing that the three bishops could not be candidates for the archiepiscopal see and that the elected archbishop would have to be approved by the governor, giving a new turn to the *Archiepiscopal Question*, which emerged as a strong political confrontation between the Church and the government and would not be solved until 1947.[2]

Throughout this period, the Locum Tenens stressed, both publicly and in his correspondence with colonial officials, his ethnarchic role and the desires of Greek Cypriots for *enosis* (CO 67/313/11). While the confrontation between the Church and the government was growing, the appearance of a new party would gradually bring major transformations in the Greek Cypriot political landscape. In the early 1940s the KKK—which had been established in 1926 and was illegal during the 1930s—moved to form a new, legal left-wing party which would claim dynamically labor and civil rights and the end of colonial rule in the island. The foundation of AKEL in April 1941 signaled the formation of a broad secular political space, which posed a serious threat to the traditional political establishment. Being particularly active in trade union organization, the new party played a key role in supporting mass labor mobilizations throughout the 1940s. The politics of AKEL met with large popular support, as indicated by the results of the municipal elections, reinstituted in the island during the war years, and by the end of the war, the party had emerged as the most significant opponent to both the nationalist Greek Cypriot elite and the government, causing their reaction.

A few days after the party's appearance, the Locum Tenens founded a six-member *Popular Council*, composed of nationalist figures from all districts of the island (*Eleftheria* 1941). As early as April 1942, the governor suggested the deportation of the General Secretary, Ploutis Servas, while a year later, following AKEL's success in the 1943 municipal elections, right-wing politicians moved to the foundation of the *Cypriot National Party* (Κυπριακό Εθνικό Κόμμα, KEK).[3] The party sought to impede the expansion of AKEL's influence and form an anti-communist nationalist pole within Greek Cypriot politics which would put forward the claim of *enosis* within the framework of Anglo-Hellenic friendship and by legal means (FCO 141/2819; *Eleftheria* 1943b). As most leading figures of KEK, the General Secretary of the party and mayor of Nicosia, Themistocles Dervis, had been closely cooperating with the government for over a decade, while in 1935 he had been awarded the title of Officer of the British Empire and three years later he had suggested that the elections should not be restored in the island (Katsiaounis 2000, pp. 43, 47). In this context, and as right-wing nationalist politics was dominated by the Church, the appeal of the new party remained limited, yet its very appearance signified the great concern of the Greek Cypriot elite about the growing influence of AKEL, considered as an "internal enemy" (*Eleftheria* 1943a).

However, the politics of AKEL and the Greek Cypriot elite intersected on a major question: the *national question*. In fact, as much as the foundation of AKEL marked the emergence of a political dynamics which challenged the confessional right-wing Greek Cypriot politics, it also signaled the nationalization of the discourse and politics of the Left. Since its very early steps, the new party adopted the dominant nationalist discourse of *enosis*, hitherto monopolized by the Church and the nationalist politicians, while it would gradually also recognize the head of the Church as the ethnarch, or the natural leader of the Greek Cypriot community and the national liberation struggle.

In February 1942, Servas submitted an extensive memorandum to the governor—resembling the program of the First Congress of AKEL—which suggested cooperation of the party with the government for the better administration of the island and the protection of the working class (CO 67/314/14). Servas criticized the colonial authorities since the beginning of the occupation and suggested a series of reforms, concerning mainly the democratization of the administration, the establishment of representative institutions, the economic relief of the inhabitants and the protection of the working class. Strikingly, the introductory paragraph of the memorandum stated that the party wished to cooperate with the government "in the interests of the community", among others; the statement, referring to the Greek Cypriots, made no reference to the Turkish Cypriot community, constituting a radical shift from all the KKK's documents, but also the documents hitherto produced by AKEL. Even more significantly, the memorandum conceptualized the right of the Greek Cypriots to "national restoration" on a line of arguments identical to that of the Church. The text referred to Greek Cypriots' hopes for *enosis*, stating that the island had been inhabited by *Greeks* for 3000 years, and stressed that national restoration should be expected after the war. Furthermore, the memorandum criticized the government's policy on the national character of education and backed the Church, asking for the lifting of the legislation on the archiepiscopal election.

In May 1942, AKEL addressed a memorandum to the governor, asking that the Atlantic Charter's provisions for self-determination be implemented in Cyprus. The memorandum stressed that this should be applied in the context of the statement of Greece's prime minister, who spoke of *enosis* (*Anexartitos* 1942b). The memorandum was published in the party newspaper *Anexartitos* (Independent), under the title "enlistment under the condition of securing the union of Cyprus with mother Greece", together with a similar memorandum by the Locum Tenens, which openly asked for *enosis*. A month later AKEL called the government to recognize the "national status" of the Greek Cypriot schools, which should promote the "national consciousness" of the people (*Anexartitos* 1942c). In the end of the year, the General Secretary of the party addressed a memorandum to the Secretary of State, protesting among others for the teaching of Greek history in schools and government's refusal to allow the reposting of pictures of heroes of the Greek revolution on school walls (CO 67/314/15). All memoranda as well as all documents submitted by the party received no attention by the Cyprus government. However, AKEL gave great publicity to them and supplied copies to organizations and politicians in Britain (e.g., *Anexartitos* 1942d).

Due to lack of evidence, it remains unclear how and when the shift on the *national question* started, but it seems that it can be traced to the second half of the 1930s, after the official election of Ploutis Servas as General Secretary of the KKK in 1936 by the Third Congress of the party.[4] The new Secretary introduced two main transformations in the policy of the KKK: he emphasized on the organization of trade unions, insisting that communists in the unions should be sensitive to gain public opinion; and insisted that the party should avoid appearing too hostile to the Church and the nationalist discourse on *enosis*. Although it is not known how influential Servas' position on the KKK's national politics was, the stance of AKEL—of which Servas was also the General Secretary since its foundation until 1945—on the *national question* indicates that a turn in the KKK's policy must have started some years before the foundation of AKEL.

In January 1943, the Second Congress of the party declared that "our only claim, [is] the national claim" and demanded "national restoration" (*Political Decisions* 2014, pp. 61–71). AKEL's new position on the *national question* was extensively reported in the party's newspaper, while many articles revealed its attempt to come to an understanding with the Church (*Anexartitos* 1942a, e). The effort seemed to have had an initial success, as the Locum Tenens responded positively to the party's request of his help to re-establish political life in the island and held a neutral position at the March 1943 municipal elections, in which AKEL's politics would be tested (Private Papers of Archbishop Leontios 1942a, b).

During the preelection period, the candidates supported by the Left emphasized labor issues as well as the *national question*, while they also denounced the candidates of the Right who had been appointed to official positions by the colonial authorities during the previous decade and had cooperated with the government.[5] A few days before the elections the candidate of the Left in Limassol and General Secretary of the KKK and AKEL stressed repeatedly that the national goal of communists was *enosis* (see *Anexartitos* 1943a).

The elections proved a great success for AKEL: the party's candidates in Limassol and Famagusta were elected mayors, while the overall share of the vote for the candidates supported by AKEL was 50% in the island's towns, compared to a 54% for the right-wing candidates.[6] On the eve of its success, the party embarked on a new nationalist campaign, calling for the cooperation among all political forces in the Greek Cypriot community on claiming *enosis*.

ATTEMPTS AT THE FORMATION OF A COMMON NATIONAL FRONT

Following the municipal elections, which demonstrated that the nationalist political discourse developed by AKEL had popular appeal, the party intensified its direct calls for *enosis* and called for the formation of a *National Council* (e.g., *Anexartitos* 1943e). Such a body, in which all Greek Cypriot organizations would participate, and which would be presided over by the Locum Tenens, would have the sole goal of promoting *enosis*. The initiative was rejected by the right-wing politicians and organizations, while it was received positively by the Locum Tenens. Leontios often supported AKEL's policy, causing a strong reaction by conservative politicians, such as Dervis, and by the circle of the Bishopric of Kyrenia. A few weeks after the elections, right-wing politicians criticized Leontios for meeting with and praising the national activities of the members of the newly elected municipal council of Famagusta (*Anexartitos* 1943c). Similarly, a visit to the Archbishopric by a delegation of Morfou cultural clubs affiliated to AKEL was met with disapproval (*Anexartitos* 1943d). A series of articles in *Neos Kipriakos Filax* (The New Cypriot Guardian) criticized the Locum Tenens' overall attitude toward the party and called him to abandon any effort on the foundation of a National Council which would include the Left (*Neos Kipriakos Filax* 1943a, b, c, 1954). The Locum Tenens, however, attempted to arrange a meeting with delegates from AKEL, KEK, the Pan-Cypriot Farmers' Union (PEK) and from the press, as well as all elected mayors of the island and some prominent political figures of the Greek Cypriot community, to discuss the formation of such a body (Yiangou 2012, pp. 104–105). The appeal failed, as only the Left responded positively, with KEK and right-wing organizations demanding the exclusion of AKEL as a condition for their participation (*Eleftheria* 1943b).

In April 1944, AKEL held its Third Congress, which focused on the war effort, peasant and labor issues, civil rights and the *national question* (*Political Decisions* 2014, pp. 73–82). The congress documents suggested a series of reforms for the protection of the peasant and working classes and called for "national restoration", in the spirit of the Atlantic Charter. The congress also addressed a resolution to the governor, which systematized the party's political priorities. The text reflected the anti-colonial discourse which the party had been articulating since its foundation and codified the national and sociopolitical claims of the Left. On the one hand, the now nationalist-tinged politics of the party considered *enosis* as the ultimate goal of the Greek Cypriot community; nevertheless, AKEL also put forward a social program based on civil rights and a democratic administration. This duality of the party's anti-colonial discourse would be, with some variations, constantly stressed until the end of colonial rule.

Overall, AKEL aspired to play a significant role in Greek Cypriot politics, a goal for which it strove to prove its national credentials and to come to an understanding with the Church, now seen by the party as the natural leadership of the community. The very fact that the archiepiscopal see was occupied by the Locum Tenens, Leontios, a moderate religious leader, favored this policy. In late 1943, the party and its affiliated organizations sent a dispatch to the governor, asking specifically for the abolition of the laws which impeded the archiepiscopal elections (*Anexartitos* 1943f). The move was warmly received by the Locum Tenens, who sent a dispatch to AKEL, praising its repeated efforts toward the solution of the question (*Anexartitos* 1943g). The rapprochement between the Church and AKEL continued in the following years, until late 1947, when Leontios died and Makarios II was elected archbishop.

In mid-1944, the Locum Tenens attempted once more to form a National Council, which would embrace all political parties. This short-lived initiative was also bound to fail: KEK not only considered AKEL as a treacherous political force, but was critical of the attitude of Leontios, who refused to denounce AKEL's appeals in support of "Greek communist insurgents" (Private Papers of Archbishop Leontios 1942, pp. 249–259). In August of the same year, the visit of the Undersecretary of State, Sir Cosmo Parkinson, to the island made a coordination of Cyprus' political forces more imperative than before, with Leontios inviting all parties to submit a common memorandum demanding *enosis* immediately after the war (*Anexartitos* 1944a). AKEL responded positively, though its participation was again an obstacle for the Right, with the Bishopric of Kyrenia announcing its dedication to the fight against communism (*Eleftheria* 1944a). Doubting the sincerity of the Left's unionist discourse, KEK eventually refused to participate in any collaborative moves and sent its own dispatch to the Undersecretary (*Pirsos* 1944a). On his arrival in Cyprus, Parkinson received a series of telegrams from various Greek Cypriot organizations, mainly requesting union with Greece (*Anexartitos* 1944b). AKEL and KEK issued separate proclamations demanding *enosis*, while both parties requested interviews with the Undersecretary.

Despite the tension between the Left and the Right, cooperation would pay off soon after the visit of the Undersecretary, in the context of the imminent liberation of Greece and the discussions on the formation of a national unity government which would include the Greek Left. In September 1944, AKEL called for the formation of a common Greek Cypriot political organization which would collect funds for Greece (*Anexartitos* 1944c). The suggestion was positively received by part of the right-wing press, who urged the Locum Tenens to launch the initiative (*Neos Kipriakos Filax* 1944). With KEK's declared intention to support such a move Leontios organized a meeting of representatives of all political parties, organizations and newspapers at the Archbishopric, which led to the formation of a pan-Cypriot Committee to work on that purpose (*Eleftheria* 1944b; *Pirsos* 1944b; CO 67/323/3).

Strikingly, KEK called, a few days later, for the formation of a National Council, encouraging the Locum Tenens to request the overcoming of political differences among the parties of the island, in order to form a political organization to demand *enosis* (*Eleftheria* 1944c; *Anexartitos* 1944d). AKEL and KEK, indeed, agreed to cooperate, under the leadership of the Locum Tenens, and after a period of negotiations among all parties and organizations an agreement was finally reached in November 1944 (*Anexartitos* 1944e, f, g, h; *Eleftheria* 1944d, e, f). The right-wing organizations' doubts regarding AKEL's unionist politics was the main obstacle, which was eventually surpassed, thanks to reassurances by Leontios. The conciliation, however, would prove short-lived, as the national unity spirit in Greece, which had initially triggered the understanding among Greek Cypriot political forces, totally collapsed in the early December with the outbreak of the "December events" (*Δεκεμβριανά*). In January 1945, a seven-member Ethnarchy Office was founded, composed of nationalist figures from all over the island, appointed by the Locum Tenens (*Eleftheria* 1945). In the same period, right-wing politicians started a campaign of expelling left-wing teachers from schools, including the mayor of Famagusta, Adam Adamantos, who was prohibited from teaching in the high school (Panayiotou 1999, p. 354).

After a period of open calls to all Greek Cypriot parties and the Locum Tenens to cooperate on the campaign for *enosis*, AKEL eventually managed in June to hold a *National Conference* in Limassol, in which centrist and moderate right-wing politicians attended (*Anexartitos* 1945a, b). Willing to prove its dedication to the national cause the party submitted an extensive declaration to the conference, stressing AKEL's constant devotion to *enosis* and denouncing the politics of the KKK on the *national question*. The conference led to the formation of the *Limassol Association of National Collaboration* (ELES), which called on the Locum Tenens to form a new, democratically based and representative National Council (*Anexartitos* 1945c, d). Despite Leontios' attempts the suggestion was rejected by the majority of the council, which wanted to prevent the Left from participating.

AKEL's position for the formation of a *National—Liberation Front* was repeated a few months later, at the party's Fourth Congress, held in August 1945, which elected Fifis Ioannou as the new General Secretary (*Anexartitos* 1945f). The dual anti-colonial discourse employed at the previous Congress was maintained, with the party calling for *enosis*—characterized as "national destiny" and seen as a condition for the definite solution of any political and economic problem—and for a democratic administration based on civil rights (*Anexartitos* 1945e). The new leadership amplified the calls for *enosis* and for the formation of a national liberation front. At the same time, the party made clear that the front should be formed under the leadership of the Locum Tenens. This concession of the leadership of the anti-colonial struggle to the Church came as a result of the realization that the moderate Leontios was the only personality that could unite the action of the Cypriot Left and Right, given the latter's intransigence in cooperating with the Left, let alone allowing it to lead *enosis* politics.

Although the attempts to form a front failed, AKEL's tactics was soon to be proved successful: in the May 1946 municipal elections the party and its allies, campaigning on a platform of national unity, prevailed in four out of six municipalities of the island (Limassol, Famagusta, Larnaca and Nicosia), as well as in many rural municipalities, with approximately 56% of the vote in total (See indicatively *Anexartitos* 1946a, b; Protopapas 2012, p. 373). The Right maintained power only in the small municipalities of Kyrenia and Paphos. Most significantly, the hitherto mayor of Nicosia and General Secretary of KEK, Dervis, lost to the centrist candidate of the Left, Ioannis Clerides. In the wake of its great victory, however, AKEL did not seek to function exclusively outside the space of the Church, but rather to expand further its organizational structures and transform the electoral alliances into a broad pan-Cypriot national liberation organization under the leadership of the Church (See indicatively *Anexartitos* 1946c). Nevertheless, despite the attempts of the Locum Tenens any such moves were bound to fail, given the refusal of the right-wing politicians and the conservative leadership of the Church to cooperate with the Left. By contrast, the success of AKEL motivated figures of the Right and the Church that previously did not support the Locum Tenens to rally around the emerging ethnarch.

The Consolidation of the Ethnarchic Politics of *Enosis*

The success of the Left in the municipal elections alarmed both the Greek Cypriot elite and the government, while further developments within and outside Cyprus in the same period led to the reshaping of Greek Cypriot politics.

Firstly, the decision of the government to repeal the laws on the archiepiscopal election would lead to the long-awaited solution of the Archiepiscopal Question, creating new conditions for the relations between the Church and the Left, as well as between the two and the government. The 1937 legislation was repealed in October 1946, to a great extent due to the colonial authorities' determination to strengthen the position of the Church so as to restrict the continuously growing appeal of the Left, evinced at May's municipal elections.[7] The growing appeal of AKEL was attributed to a great extent to the diminishing of the influence of the Church, while Leontios was considered "little more than a puppet in the hands of politicians" (CO 67/324/4). The party itself was since the end of the war considered as the island's primary political driver and as the government's greatest threat.

The candidates for the archiepiscopal see were the Archbishop of Sinai, Porfyrios, and the Locum Tenens. Porfyrios was supported by the Bishopric of Kyrenia, the Ecumenical Patriarchate, the Archbishopric of Athens and KEK (*Ethnos* 1947a). The Locum Tenens was supported by the abbots of the monasteries of Chrisoroyiatissa, Machaira and Stavrovouni, AKEL and several leftist and centrist politicians. At the elections of 4 May 1947, 900 out of 1000 elected special representatives supported the Locum Tenens, who was elected at the archiepiscopal see in June 1947.[8] Having waited so long for his enthronement, he died a month later and the Bishop of Kyrenia, Makarios, now allowed back from exile, succeeded him in December 1947.

The final solution of the Archiepiscopal Question and the election of Makarios II had a twofold significance for Cypriot politics. On the one hand, the government's accession to the Church's demands and the ascendancy of Leontios to the archiepiscopal see, whose election the British had tried to prevent for over a decade were a sign that the Church had prevailed in its confrontation with the colonial authorities. On the other hand, the very election of Makarios marked a definite rupture of the relations between the Church and the Left. Less than a year after his election the Holy Synod issued a circular against communism, while numerous anti-communist articles were constantly published in the Church's journal (*Apostolos Varnavas* 1948, 1949a). The fragile rapprochement between the Church and the Left, observable mostly after the foundation of AKEL, relied almost exclusively on the policy of the moderate Leontios. The new Archbishop attacked constantly AKEL, while in late 1940 the newspaper *Efimeris* (*Newspaper*), edited by the Secretary of the Bishopric of Kyrenia, Polykarpos Ioannides, called openly for the proscription of the party (Katsiaounis 2007, p. 457). In fact, government's decision for the return of Makarios was also taken under the expectation that in his person a strong ally against AKEL could be found. The fact that the Bishop was an ardent anti-communist and had made serious attempts to prevent AKEL's effort to form a united front promoting *enosis* had led the governor to consider his presence in the island as politically advantageous (CO 67/321/8).

The policy of Leontios, during the term of whom as Head of the Church (1933–1947) some preconditions for an understanding with the Left were formed, was in fact as much undesirable for the Greek Cypriot elite as it was for the colonial authorities. Before and after his term, anticommunism was a constant feature of the prelacy's discourse and policy, drawing Church and government together and providing on many occasions ground for common action. As an official of the Colonial Office put it in 1939, "it is prejudicial ... to the British Empire to that the Christian religion, even in the form in which it is nominally imparted by the Cypriot branch of the Orthodox Church, should be allowed to die out", as "the alternative ... to the Christian philosophy can only be pagan materialism, which, in non-Fascist countries with inhabited by a poor population, invariably tends towards proletarian Communism" (CO 67/297/4). In the same spirit, a 1941 memorandum of the government on the Cyprus Archbishopric stated that "the Government should have in the Church after the war a strong ally against the spread of communistic doctrines which are tending to make a good deal of headway in the colony" (CO 67/313/8).

Indeed, the confrontation between the Church and the Left would soon culminate, justifying the government's tactics. At the end of 1945, as the anti-colonial climate was growing internationally after the end of the war, and in the face of the growing political pressure of the anti-colonial movement in the island the new Labor government in Britain, in power since July 1945, hinted the possibility of granting a constitution in Cyprus after consultation with representatives of the local population. In July 1947, the governor announced the government's plans for the introduction of a constitution and declared his intention to form a Consultative Assembly composed by representatives from both communities to consult the government (Katsiaounis 2000, pp. 201ff.). The convocation of the Assembly would stand as a critical point for the contest between the politics of AKEL and that of the Church.

AKEL and the Pancyprian Federation of Labor (PEO), controlled by the party, were the only groups from the Greek Cypriot community to participate in the Assembly, while the Church and KEK denounced any negotiation with the government. Most importantly, AKEL participated in the Assembly with a new position on the *national question*, adopting the slogan "self-government—*enosis*", which caused the strong reaction of its rivals, who accused the party of betraying the national cause. In December 1947, the Bishopric of Kyrenia, under Bishop Makarios—now

Locum Tenens—issued an announcement, making clear its position against the politics of AKEL:

> His Reverence the Locum Tenens stressed that Cyprus constantly ... insists on its national demand and will never lower the flag of Enosis ... In view of the extent to the party's continuous attempts to take over the political initiative on the *national question* against the Greek Cypriot elite and lead the national-liberation struggle itself. A moderate realistic success of the Assembly and an advantageous temporary solution could render the Left the winner of the confrontation. In December 1947, two months after the Fifth Congress of AKEL, the party moved to the foundation of the *National Liberation Alliance* pathetic attitude of the few communists who separated from the national body and ask for autonomy, His Reverence the Locum Tenens said that the national struggle of the Island is inevitably on two fronts from now on. Namely, the people have to withstand both England and its allies, the autonomists. (*Eleftheria* 1947b)

The change of AKEL's line and the participation to the Assembly should be attributed to a great extent to the party's continuous attempts to take over the political initiative on the *national question* against the Greek Cypriot elite and lead the national liberation struggle itself. A moderate realistic success of the Assembly and an advantageous temporary solution could render the Left the winner of the confrontation. In December 1947, two months after the Fifth Congress of AKEL, the party moved to the foundation of the *National Liberation Alliance* (EAS), aiming at escalating the mobilizations for self-government—*enosis*. The organization included leftist politicians as well as middle-class centrist allies, such as Clerides, who was the head of the alliance.

However, a few months later, in May 1948, faced with the government's refusal to grant self-government, and under intense criticism by its opponents, the Left withdrew from the Assembly. In July of the same year, the Holy Synod decided on the enlargement of the Ethnarchic Council, excluding AKEL, and the foundation of the Ethnarchy Office. This would be elected by the Ethnarchic Council and function as its executive body. Its first president was the Bishop of Kition, Makarios, later Archbishop Makarios III (Anagnostopoulou 1998, p. 212). AKEL's participation in the Consultative Assembly had given the Church the opportunity to establish more steadily its position as the ethnarchic leadership of the Greek Cypriot community and achieve its principal goal: the monopolization of the slogan of *enosis*. The strengthening of the Church's stance became immediately apparent. In September, the Archbishopric issued a circular against communism, and in October, the Holy Synod amended the Charter of the Church, so as to exclude communists and left-sympathizers from the process of ecclesiastical elections.

Six months later, in view of the upcoming municipal elections, the Ethnarchy Office denounced any cooperation with communists, characterizing it as equal to national treason (*Apostolos Varnavas* 1949a). The danger that AKEL constituted for the confessional politics of the Church necessitated an alliance among all anti-communist political actors. As the position of the Church had been seriously reinforced after the election of Archbishop Makarios and the subsequent organizational moves, the undertaking of such an initiative from the Church led many right-wing politicians and other bourgeois figures to rally around it. The new Archbishop urged continuously the lay elite to terminate their close relations with the government, evinced as late as mid-1949, when prominent Greek Cypriots attended the ceremonial parade and social reception, organized at the Government House on the occasion of King George VI's birthday (Heraclidou 2011, p. 161).

Meanwhile, political developments in Greece following the end of the war influenced directly Greek Cypriot politics: the repercussions of the Greek Civil War (1946–1949) in Cyprus enhanced the conflict between AKEL and the Greek Cypriot nationalist elite. Throughout the war, AKEL was in direct communication with the Communist Party of Greece, while it also organized fundraising campaigns to support the *Democratic Army of Greece (DSE)*. Furthermore, in 1946 members of the Greek extreme right-wing organization "X" (*Chi*) had arrived in Cyprus, to form a linked organization in the island (see Alecou in this volume). The first group of Chi was particularly active during the 1947 archiepiscopal elections, while two years later the *National Peasant Party of Chi-ites* [members of X] *of Cyprus* was founded (Alecou 2011, pp. 110–111).

The inauguration of the Truman doctrine in 1947, which provided for the replacement of Britain by the USA in supplying military and economic aid to the Greek government, enabled the latter to adopt a much more active policy on the question of *enosis*, as constantly requested by the Greek Cypriot nationalist elite. In late 1947, a statement of the Greek prime minister supporting *enosis* reinforced the position of the ethnarchy, accusing again the Left of treason for participating in the Consultative Assembly (Alecou 2011, p. 119).

The confrontation between the Left and the Right-wing, now ethnar-chic, political space was vividly expressed in the 1949 election campaign period, with the latter receiving the support of the government. In his address to the commissioners of the island in February 1949, the acting governor stated:

> [A] glancing blow was delivered at the Right. For a long time now we have turned a blind eye to the seditious aspect of the advocacy of eno-sis. We shall continue to do so... We must concentrate upon the commu-nists... The religious influence of the Church is ... especially important at this time because of its anti-communist nature. What I should like to secure would be an implicit truce between Government and the Church on the question of enosis... [I]n promoting them there must be no sug-gestion of ... a license to override the law.... (CO 537/4309)

A few weeks before the May municipal elections, the Cyprus government was urged by the US government to "assist ... the nationalist parties in Cyprus to develop a strong line ... and to win as many votes as possible". It was also suggested that "the Orthodox Church should be urged to make a public display of its interest in the elections and that the bishops should openly support nationalist candidates" and that "American influ-ence might be exerted to this and through Archbishop Damaskinos and his friendship with Archbishop Makarios", as well as by taking respective action in Greece and Turkey (CO 537/4974).

Indeed, the Left faced a serious blow at the elections of May 1949, marking the elimination of the possibilities for the formation of a com-mon front with the Right, which continued accusing AKEL for having betrayed the national struggle. AKEL and its allies maintained only the municipalities of Limassol, Larnaca and Famagusta, receiving a total 48% of the vote, compared to the 56% three years earlier (Protopapas 2012, p. 468). The participation in the Consultative Assembly and the support of self-government had proved detrimental for its appeal, as admitted by AKEL itself, while it also triggered a severe crisis within the party (ASKI, F-20/21/20). Following a series of meetings of the General Secretary and the cadre Andreas Ziartidis with the leadership of the Communist Party of Greece, the Central Committee of AKEL denounced, in January 1949, the shift of the party politics in favor of constitutional reforms and the participation to the Assembly. It further denounced self-government and stressed that the only goal of the party should be *enosis* (ASKI, F-20/21/19; F-20/21/21; F-20/21/47). Two months later the Central Committee resigned and appointed a Temporary Central Leadership (*Καθοδήγηση*) to guide the party until the Sixth Congress (*Anexartitos* 1949a). The new line was extensively covered by the left-wing press, while the Congress, held in August 1949, denounced again the support of self-government and the participation to the Consultative Assembly, and called for the intensification of the struggle for *enosis*.[9]

As ethnarchic politics had prevailed within the Greek Cypriot community, AKEL was now forced to readopt the intransigent line of *enosis*. Most importantly, this signified the failure of the party to emerge as a political actor able to lead a national liberation anti-colonial struggle, a main goal of its policy since its foundation in 1941. AKEL's national politics would until the end of the colonial rule remain under the shadow of the Church. In August 1949, on the occasion of the arrival of Governor A.B. Wright, the party organized mass demonstrations across the island, signings of resolutions demanding *enosis* and announced the holding of a plebiscite on the question of union with Greece. However, the ethnarchy managed to take back the political initiative, announcing in November the holding of its own plebiscite, to be organized by the Ethnarchic Council. AKEL canceled its own plebiscite and supported the plebiscite organized by the Church, campaigning for voting in favor of *enosis* (*Apostolos Varnavas* 1949b; *Anexartitos* 1949c, 1950; ASKI, F-20/21/24). According to the decision of the Council the plebiscite would be held on 15 January 1950 and a circular would be sent to the government, inviting it to conduct the plebiscite. In case of refusal, the plebiscite would be organized by the ethnarchy. All Cyprus' inhabitants above 18 years old, both men and women, would have the right to vote.

The government naturally refused to conduct the plebiscite and stressed that the question of Cyprus' union with Greece was closed, with the agreement of the Greek government. However, it did not prohibit the holding of the plebiscite, whose results would of course not have any official validity (*Apostolos Varnavas* 1949c). The plebiscite, organized by the Church and supported fully by the Left, would raise even greater concern to the colonial authorities, mostly the potentiality of an alliance between the Right and the Left. However, as the Left was becoming all the more subordinated to the politics of the Church, it would be the latter that would soon lead a militant anti-colonial movement in the island. According to the results of the elections, approximately 96% of the Greek Cypriot population was in favor of *enosis* (Protopapas 2012, p. 490).

The plebiscite was quickly internationalized, as it was extensively covered by the Greek and international press, while copies of the signed ballot papers were handed to the president of the Greek parliament and the Secretariat of the United Nations.

CONCLUSION

By the end of the 1940s the politics of *enosis* had conclusively prevailed, being supported indistinguishably by all political forces in the Greek Cypriot community; and the main advocator of *enosis*, the Church, had emerged as the most powerful political actor in the island. Most significantly, the consolidation of Greek Cypriot nationalism brought about a homogenization of Greek Cypriot politics. By managing to make its political discourse dominant within the Greek Cypriot community the Church succeeded in heading off the secular political actor that had most successfully threatened its political space. By the early 1940s, a broad, Left political space had formed, whose politics and discourse were formulated along class lines, claiming to represent the interests of the Cypriot working class. However, despite the significant successes and the growing appeal of the Left, dominating Greek Cypriot politics until 1947, the nationalist discourse put forward by the Church remained unchallenged by the main party of the Left, AKEL. By the end of the decade, despite certain variations in its position on the *national question*—most vividly manifested at the Consultative Assembly—the Left eventually adopted completely the *enosist* politics promoted by the Church. Following the collapse of the Assembly, and despite the renewed cooperation between the government and the Church against the party, AKEL would largely define its politics according to the political context set by the latter. In 1950, AKEL's support for the Church in organizing the plebiscite on *enosis* would illustrate the latter's emergence as the political actor to define the politics of the community against the British authorities, a role it would maintain until the end of colonial rule in the island.

Furthermore, the Church dominated right-wing politics, helping to prevent the emergence of an organized, and most notably, secular, right-wing party. In the late 1940s, the political initiatives and tactical moves of Archbishop Makarios II forced the largest part of the lay elite, including those with a long history of close relations with the government, to rally around him. Finally, the Church prevailed in its confrontation with

the colonial authorities and managed to impose a large part of its politics on the government. The 1933–1947 Archiepiscopal Question, a
major point of conflict between the Church and the government, was
ultimately solved according to the terms set by the former from the very
first moment. The very election of the Locum Tenens, who had emerged
as one of the most prominent anti-government figures during the colonial rule, demonstrated the failure of British policies to accomplish one
of the government's main objectives, namely to control the power of the
Church and the appeal of nationalist politics to Greek Cypriots, seeking
to turn them into loyal British subjects. The Church's radical politics
of *enosis* would set the tone of the anti-colonial movement in the island
until the end of British rule. During the 1950s Cyprus would witness a
militant national liberation struggle headed uniquely in the experience of
decolonization by a deeply conservative religious institution, the Church
of Cyprus.

NOTES

1. Political developments during the 1920s and the rising social discontent
   at the end of the decade and the early 1930s, owing mainly to the economic hardship of the population, led to one of the most significant political crises in the island's history: the 1931 October revolt. On 21 October,
   opposing to government's economic policy, all Greek Cypriot members of
   the Legislative Council resigned and proceeded to the Nicosia Commercial
   Club to address the gathered crowd. After the councillors finished their
   speeches, some 5000 Greek Cypriots marched towards the Government
   House, carrying sticks, torches, banners and Greek flags. Shouting slogans in favor of *enosis* and the end of British rule, they eventually set the
   building on fire. Soon afterward, riots broke out across the island, in both
   urban and rural areas. Instances of violence were reported in every major
   town in Cyprus as well as 209 of the island's 598 Greek Cypriot or mixed
   villages. The revolt was quite easily suppressed by the British within a week
   (NA, CO 67/240/11; CO 67/240/13; CO67/243/1; CO 67/243/2;
   The Cyprus Gazette 1931, pp. 781–788). See also Georghallides (1985,
   pp. 570–574, 679, 686–695), Styllianou (1984, pp. 59–151), Rappas
   (2008, pp. 18–20), Holland (1998, pp. 1–5), Grekos (1994, pp. 11–15).
2. Immediately after Leontios assumed duties as Locum Tenens, the exiled
   Bishops made clear that they rejected the possibility of a settlement before
   their return to Cyprus. The Bishops of Kition and Kyrenia attempted to
   pre-empt an intervention by the Ecumenical and the other Patriarchates
   during their absence from the island, which could cost them their future

election. For Leontios, the exile of the two leading bishops presented him with a great opportunity. A lengthy postponement of the elections would only provide him time to gradually consolidate his position within the Church and among the congregation, and convert his temporary status into a permanent arrangement.

3. A few months later Servas was searched and arrested for being suspected as carrying a revolver and revolutionary documents. He was eventually released, while all documents found on him were seized (CO 67/314/14; *Anexartitos* 1942f; CO 67/314/15).

4. Since its foundation in 1926 and for the next decade the CPC did not endorse the cause of *enosis*, calling instead for the establishment of an independent, socialist republic. Its policies questioned the confessional politics of the Greek- and Turkish Cypriot elites, attempting to fashion an all-Cypriot political space, and developing a political discourse that called both Greek and Turkish Cypriots to the struggle for liberation from colonial rule.

5. Such was the case in Nicosia, Paphos and Famagusta. Criticism was mostly against Themistocles Dervis, the hitherto appointed mayor of Nicosia, who ran for mayor as the leader of Nicosia's *National Combination* (See indicatively *Anexartitos* 1943b).

6. The voters could vote for candidates from both ballot papers (Protopapas 2012, p. 373).

7. Such a policy was followed by colonial Governments in many regions of the Empire. After the Second World War the colonial authorities in Malta and the local Catholic Church were united against the Malta Labor Party. In Cyprus' case, however, the Church's early dynamic position for *enosis* and the fact that the Left had lagged behind the former by the end of the 1940s precluded a permanent rapprochement between the Government and the Church (Holland 2009, pp. 5–6; for a comparison with Malta, see also Marovich-Old in this volume).

8. According to the Charter of the Church of Cyprus, the male Greek Cypriot Orthodox Christians elected a number of special representatives, who then elected a number of general representatives, laymen and clerics. The general representatives together with officials of the Church elected the Archbishop (*Eleftheria* 1947a; *Ethnos* 1947b).

9. The Congress also elected Ezekias Papaioannou as General Secretary (*Political Decisions* 2014, pp. 131–145; *Anexartitos* 1949b).

References

Alecou, A. (2011). *Οι Πολιτικές Εξελίξεις στην Κύπρο, 1945–1955* [The Political Developments in Cyprus, 1945–1955]. Ph.D. dissertation, Panteio University of Social and Political Sciences.

Anagnostopoulou, S. (1998–1999). Η Εκκλησία της Κύπρου και ο εθναρχικός της ρόλος: 1878–1960 [The Church of Cyprus and Its Ethnarchic Role: 1878–1960]. *Σύγχρονα Θέματα* [Contemporary Issues], 68–69–70, 198–227.

Georghallides, G. (1985). *Cyprus and the Governorship of Sir Ronald Storrs: The Causes of the 1931 Crisis.* Nicosia: Cyprus Research Center.

Grekos, K. (1994). *Τα Οκτωβριανά και το Κ.Κ.Κ.* [The October Events and K.K.K.]. Nicosia.

Heraclidou, A. (2011). *Politics of Education in Colonial Cyprus, 1931–1956, with Special Reference to the Greek-Cypriot Community.* Ph.D. dissertation, University of London.

Holland, R. (1998). *Britain and the Revolt in Cyprus 1954–1959.* Oxford: Oxford University Press.

Holland, R. (2009). *The British, the Mediterranean and the Anglo-Cypriot Relationship: What Went Wrong and Can It Be Put Right?* ERPIC (European Rim Policy and Investment Council) Report, 5–6.

Katsiaounis, R. (2000). *Η Διασκεπτική 1946–1948· Με ανασκόπηση της περιόδου 1878–1945* [The Consultative Assembly of 1946–48; with a Review of the Period 1878–1945]. Nicosia: Cyprus Research Center.

Katsiaounis, R. (2007). Cyprus 1931–1959: The Politics of the Anti-colonial Movement. *Yearbook of Research Center* (Nicosia), XXXIII, 441–469.

Panayiotou, A. (1999). *Island Radicals: The Emergence and Consolidation of the Cypriot Left, 1920–1960.* Ph.D. dissertation, University of California.

Protopapas, V. (2012). *Εκλογική Ιστορία της Κύπρου· Πολιτευτές, κόμματα και εκλογές στην Αγγλοκρατία· 1878–1960* [Electoral History of Cyprus; Politicians, Parties and Elections During British Rule; 1878–1960]. Athens: Themelio.

Rappas, A. (2008). *The Elusive Polity: Social Engineering and the Reinvention of Politics in Colonial Cyprus, 1931–1941.* Ph.D. dissertation, European University Institute.

Styllianou, P. (1984). *Το Κίνημα του Οκτώβρη του 1931 στην Κύπρο* [The October 1931 Movement in Cyprus]. Ph.D. dissertation, University of Ioannina.

Yiangou, A. (2012). *Cyprus in World War II: Politics and Conflict in the Eastern Mediterranean.* London: I.B. Tauris.

Archival Material

Official Records
The National Archives of the United Kingdom, London.
Αρχεία Σύγχρονης Κοινωνικής Ιστορίας, ASKI [Archives of Contemporary Social History], Athens.

Unofficial Records
Αρχιεπισκοπή Κύπρου [Cyprus Archbishopric], Nicosia.
Private Papers of Archbishop Leontios, Book 15, 16.6.1942a; 18.6.1942b.

Primary Printed Sources
Καταστατικόν της Αγιωτάτης Εκκλησίας της Κύπρου [Charter of the Most Holy Church of Cyprus]. (1914). Nicosia.
Πολιτικές Αποφάσεις και Ψηφίσματα Συνεδρίων του Κομμουνιστικού Κόμματος Κύπρου (ΚΚΚ) και του Ανορθωτικού Κόμματος Εργαζόμενου Λαού (ΑΚΕΛ) [Political Decisions and Congress Resolutions of the KKK and AKEL]. (2014). Nicosia.

Newspapers and Periodicals
Anexartitos (The Independent), 29/05/1942a, 31/05/1942b, 14/06/1942c, 16/06/1942d, 4/11/1942e, 12/11/1942f, 18/03/1943a, 20/03/1943b, 18/04/1943c, 21/04/1943d, 14/05/1943e, 27/11/1943f, 5/12/1943g, 1/08/1944a, 12/08/1944b, 13/09/1944c, 1/10/1944d, 10/10/1944e, 1/11/1944f, 11/11/1944g, 25/11/1944h, 26/04/1945a, 01/06/1945b, 20/06/1945c, 21/06/1945d, 24/08/1945e, 26/08/1945f, 25/01/1946a, 24/04/1946b, 1/08/1946c, 10/03/1949a, 17.03.1949b, 21/12/1949c, 16/01/1950.
Apostolos Varnavas 6/09/1948, 6/04/1949a, 8/12/1949b, 17/12/1949c.
Cyprus Gazette (The), 9.9.1931.
Eleftheria (Freedom), 4/06/1941, 5/06/1943a, 7/06/1943b, 10/08/1944a, 21/09/1944b, 26/09/1944c, 09/10/1944d, 10/10/1944e, 20/10/1944f, 4/01/1945, 5/05/1947a, 21/12/1947b.
Ethnos (Nation), 25/04/1947a, 21/06/1947b.
Neos Kipriakos Filax (The New Cypriot Guardian), 17/05/1943a, 18/05/1943b, 5/06/1943c, 16/09/1944, 22/05/1954.
Pirsos (Torch), 9/08/1944a, 26/09/1944b.

CHAPTER 7

Imported Nationalism: The Appearance and Evolution of "X" Organization in Cyprus

Alexios Alecou

INTRODUCTION

The history of especially the Cypriot, as well as the Greek far-right, is one of the many that have not been analyzed adequately. The particular omission, however, is worthy of attention as the far-right—below is explained what is meant by using this terminology—has played a role anything but marginal in the twentieth century. For nearly three quarters of the century, and especially from 1920 to 1974, the far-right had either starred in the political life of Greece and Cyprus or acted in the foreground. On the other hand, what is considered one of its greatest failures during this period is the fact that it failed to achieve a political or

An earlier version of this paper was presented at the Conference on *Extreme right in Cyprus, Turkey and Greece* on 1 November 2014 (University of Cyprus) under the title "Far-right in Greece and Cyprus: Evolution and radicalization in the 1940s".

A. Alecou (✉)
Department of History, University of Cyprus, Nicosia, Cyprus

© The Author(s) 2018
T. Kyritsi and N. Christofis (eds.), *Cypriot Nationalisms in Context*,
https://doi.org/10.1007/978-3-319-97804-8_7

ideological unity, or to secure a wider legitimacy even though it used the dominant vocabulary of nationalism and drew on the already widespread political feelings.

There are great works that approach the evolution of extreme right in both Greece and Cyprus but also in the Western Europe under an analytical and in-depth examination. The work of Antonis Ellinas (2013) about the rise of Golden Dawn (Χρυσή Αυγή, GD); Cas Mudde (1996) about the extreme right party family; the work of Swank and Betz (2003) on the right-wing populism in Western Europe; Yiannos Katsourides (2013a, b) work on the crystallization of Greek Cypriot nationalist party politics and also his work on ELAM (2013a), are just few of the works that are necessary in understanding right-wing extremism. What new this analysis brings into discussion is that it focuses on the evolution and radicalization of extreme right groups in both Greece and Cyprus, marking the main similarities at least in their rhetoric in such a way that we could assert that Greek Cypriot right-wing extremism duplicated the rhetoric of their Greek counterparts.

THE GREEK FAR-RIGHT: APPEARANCE, CHARACTERISTICS, IDEOLOGY

The Greek far-right, during the period of its substantial presence, played a role anything but marginal, having provided support to dictatorships, organizing coups, had cooperated with the invaders at times, and in order to reduce the social dispute created mainly by the German occupation during the 1940s, acquired a massive base and organization (Marketos 2009, p. 3). It was consolidated in the state apparatus, a fact that offered its political members as well as its plain supporters a social rise, and finally it managed to consolidate nationalism as the official public discourse which was the reason that was legitimized for years. Nevertheless, it failed to be represented as a unified political or ideological whole, and more importantly it failed to ensure a greater social legitimacy (Marketos 2009).

During the Interwar, the Greek right had specific conservative ideological references adapted to the European conservatism of the period (Weiss 1977, p. 7), giving a particular emphasis on the dominant version of Orthodoxy and the defense of the established power (mainly of monarchy). A great part of the Right during this period remained oriented in the parliamentary system, and usually supported the traditional politicians. Occasionally though, a greater part of the Right that was initially linked directly to the throne and was gradually radicalized, it was characterized by authoritarian tendencies and often biased toward the far-right (Marketos 2006). In the 1940s the far-right began to strengthen significantly, mainly because of the deadlock options made by the traditional conformists during the German occupation, and then because of the persecutions preached by the bourgeois against the Left (Marketos 2009, p. 4).

Referring to the far-right, we mean the groups, movements, and governments that exhibit extreme hostility mainly against the Left and the Liberals and thus oppose to the democratic institutions which legitimize the existence of these political fields, meaning the Left and Liberals (Passmore 2002, p. 24). Therefore, this is about a range consisting of different forces, ranging from fascism to urban groups that support conservative authoritarian dictatorships. In Greece, these forces are expressed mainly through the (urban) opposition to political or social reforms, such as the integration of refugees or any other minorities in the political and social covey and the agrarian reform (Marketos 2009, p. 5). During the Interwar, even though they failed to acquire a common language or to at least form even a loose bond between them, they nevertheless remained powerful. Different sides of them dominated from time to time in the political life and public discourse, while their ideas were disseminated by the major newspapers (Marketos 2009, p. 5).

Fascism, a powerful group within the whole that we call far-right, it practically differs from the conservative tendencies of the far-right, especially in trying to create a mass movement (Paxton 2007). Despite all the post-war attempts to conceal this bitter truth, available data shows that among the bourgeois, fascism had generally a positive and not a negative meaning (Marketos 2009, p. 6).

The far-right and especially fascism, reflexively regroup in a massive way when and where they are evoked by the Left, and this challenge arose rapidly: the possibility that the leftist EAM (Εθνικό Απελευθερωτικό Μέτωπο/National Liberation Front) would attempt to seize power during the period of Occupation and the democratic reforms after the liberation, constituted a violent challenge for the Right which being weak to face the danger they could see coming, strengthened the massive increase of fascist groups, ranging from the Security Battalions to the National Party of Chites, aiming to limit EAM and dissolute the Left.

Both, Metaxas' dictatorship and the authoritarian measures of the previous governments succeeded in greatly reducing the action of the Left, mainly through the persecution of the mass organizations and trade unions. This repressive policy though did not solve any social problems, but on the contrary in conjunction with these, it enhanced the social questioning.

From the early months of the occupation, EAM managed to rally the majority of the progressive forces and immediately became the main body of resistance, partly due to the experience of the veteran leftists who were the first to regroup around it, and partly due to the strategy that it followed. The great success of EAM in the mass mobilization of the people awakened the reflexes of the bourgeois who realized that it would be impossible to deal with it by peaceful means and therefore turned to the strengthening of the far-right (Marketos 2009, p. 12).

EAM, by putting aside the class discourse for the sake of the national, with a program which could be characterized progressive and liberal left in general lines and by no means communist or even socialist, managed to convince that the social and political content of its national discourse was quite opposite from that of the Right. The combative national democratic discourse of EAM (Social/Justice/Sovereignty/Democracy) identified the nation with the people (Fleischer 1995, p. 56) and virtually excluded from the nation those layers of the population that benefited from the Occupation. The dipole of the concepts embodied in this period (and which later on were carried intact in Cyprus) had been on the one hand the positively marked concepts of the nation for the one side and democracy for the other side, while the main accusations addressed to their opponents had been communism for the one side and monarchy-fascism for the other side (Alecou 2016, p. 78).

To remedy therefore the "galloping" Left, far-right mass organizations and paramilitary groups were formed, with the Security Battalions and the "X" organization being the major ones. Resistance to the occupier, even when declared, was merely a pretext. As reported by a British officer, "the right elements drown mostly by the Axis and their organizations played a double game. Their main purpose was clearly the opposition to the Left. As long as the Axis would guarantee the repression of communism, they did not attempt to seriously fight it" (Stevens 1982, p. 5).

SECURITY BATTALIONS

During the occupation, the state apparatus remained substantially the same authoritarian and oppressive mechanism of Metaxas' dictatorship, but under the new conditions, it was impossible to carry out its task of repressing the Left. So it had been enhanced in 1943 by the creation of the Security Battalions. These squads, which were numerous and well equipped (came to numbering around thirty thousand armed men) (Margaritis 2001, p. 59), were actually support groups of the occupational forces. They were controlled and equipped by the Germans, and they worked together on a daily basis to crack down the Left and to terrorize the rest of the population (Alecou 2016, p. 78).

According to Rallis himself, the main cause of the creation of the Security Battalions was that without them the country was "at risk of falling under the communist regime" (Rallis 1993, p. 301). Due to the threat by the Left therefore, for the very first time the Venizelists and anti-Venizelists were united: the Security Battalions were their common creation, and prominent politicians from across the middle-class spectrum applauded their action. This very important change is the one that brought in Greece for the very first time the massive increase of fascism (Marketos 2009, p. 22).

"X" AND CHITES

The initial basic core of "X" was founded in 1941, but by 1943 the organization remained unknown and insignificant. Head of the organization was the Cypriot origin, and Lieutenant Colonel of the Greek army, George Grivas. During the occupation, Grivas' organization attempted unsuccessfully to come in contact with the German forces. According to Hagen Fleischer:

> The "X" organization escaped the stigma of being an infidel not because of its consistency, but because of lack of interest on behalf of the Germans. In 1943, its leader, Colonel George Grivas, had offered to cooperate with the Occupation authorities, stressing out his Anglophobia and his anti-communist beliefs. The German General Staff, however, had replied that they will not converse with a "bandit", and much more with someone that was considered as insignificant as the Colonel was. (1982, p. 82)

Thanasis Hatzis' opinion for the appearance and the role of "X" is quite informative:

> At this time (Spring of 1943) make their appearance the Bourandas police-men too, the Mantouvalaioi in Piraeus, the social scums of the Special Security, Grivas' Chites, Papageorgiou's Edesites and a series of other traitors of the nation who were guided by the nation's savours of the Military hierarchy like Ventiris, Spiliotopoulos, Zervas, Antonopoulos and Stathopoulos, all of which were under the commands of Rallis and through him both of the Germans and the British. (1982, p. 433)

It is a fact that the "X", during the period of the occupation failed to become a massive movement, and remained a paramilitary movement with a strict military-like structure and discipline. In its first steps, it relied on Cypriot officers and maintained close (mainly economic) rela-tions with two religious factors of Cyprus, the late Archbishop and for-mer Archbishop of Athens, Chrysanthos, as well as the Bishop of Kyrenia and later Archbishop of Cyprus, Makarios II. According to Woodhouse (1948), "the name of "X" was unknown until just before the departure of the Germans, but even then it had no connection to the Resistance. Only in the years following the post-war it had acquired significance: the very same horrible meaning that the Ku Klux Klan had" (p. 31).

The organization "X" gained existence in the fall of 1943, when the British had decided to use it in the war they had been preparing in order to exterminate EAM. That period arrived in Athens the New Zealand Army Captain of the British, Donald Stott, who used the nickname Don. Don's mandate was to bring together all the far-right organizations active in Greece. The ultimate goal was to create a common frontier of the conservative forces in order to be used the right time against EAM, in an effort to bring Greece under the Western influence when the war would end (Athanasiades 1994, pp. 222–223).

In October 1943, Don began consultations with various organiza-tions in Athens. In the same month, a meeting took place with Don, Grivas and the leaders of other right-wing organizations, which resulted in the signing of a new protocol of cooperation. Thereafter, Grivas called a meeting of the members of "X", at which he announced them that a protocol had been agreed and signed which provided coopera-tion between all the extreme right-wing organizations for "the National struggle" and which mentioned that everyone was willing to "put under the commands of the Middle East Command all their will and strength to fight" (Drousiotis 2000, p. 27).

According to the signed protocol, their final target was to take such measures so that after the liberation, any possibility of an "EAM coup" would be excluded, so that the country would pass from the hands of the Germans to the hands of the British (Papageorgiou 2004, p. 124).

Grivas used the services of the British to unite various far-right groups against EAM while a bit later accepted in "X" a great number of members of the Security Battalions, as well as other well-known collaborators of the Nazis. It also seems that just before the departure of the Germans he was helped by the British to receive guns from the Germans, which were delivered to him with the help of Rallis' government (Woodhouse 2002, p. 98). The dramatic enhancement of EAM during the last months of the Occupation made it necessary for the opponent party to consolidate, putting aside the issue of the Axis friendly and British friendly preferences of its members.

Immediately after the withdrawal of the Germans, "X" realized the need to rally and become massive, and simultaneously acquired the ability to do so by drawing manpower from the "tagmatasfalites" (members of the Security Battalions) which included besides officers many middle-class citizens, outcasts of the cities, and even more so, farmers (Marketos 2009, p. 33). "X" now acquires the typical profile of a fascist movement (Paxton 2007, p. 30). As Grivas (1947) bluntly described it: "TOTAL WAR. Don't just attempt to take temporary measures. Gaze far away and beat firmly to prevent them from lifting their heads up not only for tomorrow, or after one, five, ten years, but never again on our generation or the generations to come".

A turning point in the evolution of "X" was the Battle of Athens, in December 1944, during which the leadership of the organization was fortified around Thisseio and was threatened to be badly defeated by the leftists (Marketos 2009, p. 33), but at the end it was rescued by the intervention of the British forces.

On December 3, 1944, date on which conflicts broke out in Athens, *Chites* were the vanguard of the government forces supported by the British forces that invaded Greece. The next day, as the protesters were returning from the Syntagma Square, where they had gathered under the framework of a general strike against the bloody events, they had been attacked by armed *Chites*, resulting in 40 dead and seventy wounded who painted with their blood the streets of Athens.

In February 1945, and after the British had won the battle of Athens, the Varkiza Treaty was signed between the government forces and EAM, which provided the disarmament of all organizations. This agreement was broken by the militia forces and by the right-wing extremist groups who were recruited in order to defeat EAM/ELAS. On the day of the Treaty, the newspaper *Eleftheria* (Freedom), in its first comments mentioned in sarcasm:

> Keeping all the rules of the German tactics, a "block" took place yesterday morning. National Guard and many constables arrived in the suburb, awakened by gunfire all the residents and gathered all males from the age of 14 to 60 years old. Then, after arraying them by occupations, ordered them to declare by themselves who belonged to EAM. Then some people, who did not wear a visor, suggested to the policemen at their discretion which of EAM's members were dangerous. Those, then, were violently forced to climb on tracks and were driven to different lockups. This brilliant ceremony lasted for five hours, to the great satisfaction of the citizens who thought that Germany has been defeated but its processes remain immortal. (*Eleftheria* 1945)

The conditions prevailing after the Varkiza Treaty, offered "X" the chance to have an enormous growth and in early 1945 became the basic pole of the far-right, a development that is organizationally reflected in the establishment of branches all over the country. The gigantic empowerment of "X" after the Varkiza Treaty, a time when it became "the most famous secret armed organization of the far-right in Greece" was not because of Grivas' organizational majesty but because of the need of the infidels to find a political shelter, and of the other political conservationists to crush the Left (Marketos 2009, p. 34).

The historian Mark Mazower makes a similar assessment: "In the streets below the temple of Thiseio, the gunmen of "X" exchanged gunfire with the patrols of ELAS and fought beside the Security Battalions. "Today they are with the Germans, tomorrow with the ones that will bring back the blessed King" (Mazower 1994, p. 378).

The clashes during the period of the Varkiza Treaty and the elections of 1946, resulted in 1289 murders, and 6671 injured people, while over 30,000 persons had been tortured and 20,000 of offices or homes were looted and destroyed (Nikolakopoulos 2005, p. 13).

The cooperation between Grivas and the British kept on until the early 50s, when Grivas had already begun preparing his plans on Cyprus. This fact raises legitimate questions as to the purpose of Grivas' action on the island, since while he was in Greece he collaborated and was equipped by the British and he was trusted as their loyal ally, and at the same time he made plans—at least according to the prevailing historical records—so as to evict them from the island (Alecou 2016, p. 82).

THE NATIONAL PARTY OF *CHITES*

In May 1946, Grivas presented to the members of his organization his decision to proceed with the establishment of the National Party of *Chites* and set some key direct objectives of the party: restore the King and crash the Greek Communist Party (KKE). Trying to minimize the importance of this mutation, he stressed the need for the organization to be given a facade in order to reduce the international reactions against it (Marketos 2009, p. 56). The National Party of *Chites* according to Marketos was qualified as a fascist party,

> [...] not only in terms of its policy and objectives and the driving forces of its members' passions, but also because of its organizational structure and practice. In fact it was the only right-wing party before 1974 that had attempted to become seriously massive. Actually, *Chites* tried to express besides the great feelings of anti-communism of those who had to gain a lot from the Occupation or who were frightened of the democratization of the country, the much broader dissatisfaction of the "politics of notables" (Honoratiorenpolitic) which looks like it had spread among the middle class even before the Occupation. (2009, p. 57)

Grivas' organization managed to gather members from all the social layers, with a proportionately greater involvement of the police and the military. *Chites* held a partisan identity, signed by Grivas himself, which had to be renewed at regular intervals. The official salutation of *Chites* was indistinguishable from Hitler's (taut palm and clasped fingers) (*Efimeris ton Chiton* 1946). In almost two years of the party's existence, The National Party of *Chites* was renamed to National Agrarian Party of Chites (EAKX) (*Efimeris ton Chiton* 1948a).

Chites party had its own Working Youth as well as a National Trade Union Movement of Chites' Labourers, which was organized according to professions and which led in breaking strikes. At its regular weekly meetings, their commitment against the struggle of classes and slavish-communism was explained, and it promoted the peaceful cooperation of the classes in a national context of Country, Religion, and Family (*Efimeris ton Chiton* 1948c).

Grivas' party emphasized promoting a distinct ideological stigma so as to be distinguished from the rest far-right parties. The fundamental principle of *Chites*, as this came out from the official organs of the party, was expansionist nationalism, adherence to the middle-class regime and monarchy, assertion of individual freedom and the harmonious cooperation between the capital and the workers. Basic tool of its propaganda was the weekly newspaper of Chites, which was published from May 1945 until the party's electoral crush in 1950. The newspaper was edited so as to continually promote their nationalist, irredentist, and anti-communist slogans. Characteristic examples are the following (*Efimeris ton Chiton* 1945):

> We will fight for a Great Greece which will include: NORTH EPIROS, THE SERBIAN AND BULGARIAN MACEDONIA, and EAST ROMILIAN AND CYPRUS.UNDER THE COMMANDS OF THE KINGS AND EMPERORS GREECE SUCCEDED GREAT THINGS. NATIONALISTS! Let's give an oath to our homeland and our king that we will rout out communism from Greece. Nationalists, protect yourselves from fake proclamations for reconciliation with which the communists try to deceive you. Nationalists! The slogan for reconciliation is a pure fraud. Those who proclaim are preparing something suspicious. Answer to this with: "Unconditional submission of the ones who slaughtered the Greek people and the Greek state." Safety is not restored with soft answers. The entire nationalist world should ask from the government to organize a local security system in every village and town by recruiting locals to fight against them.

The marginalization and eventually the dissolution of the Chites party was something natural after the elections of 1950. On the one hand, Grivas' personality—his authoritarianism drove away the capable members, and his fanaticism stood in the way of having any sort of consultation with potential allies—and the political situation, on the other hand, led the party to dissolution. Each step toward the stabilization of the political situation made it less necessary for the government to support Grivas. So at the end of the civil war in 1949 although it signaled the defeat of the Left, it also constituted the defeat of the fascist far-right (Marketos 2009, p. 60). In addition to that, the economic survival of the party was an insurmountable obstacle. The financing of the party from the Greek capital was interrupted in the spring of 1946, when Chites decided to detach themselves from the right wing.

By the end of the Civil War, they even ceased to have an acceptable reason for their existence by anyone else, and even worst their action threatened to expose the regime internationally. Their party managed to survive until the next elections of 1950 when it experienced a crushing defeat for once more and a bit later it dissolved. The next plan of their leader was against the British rule in Cyprus. The leaders of the conservative Right assisted him in order to do so; something like what Franko did during the Second World War, who sent the Spanish fascists to the Eastern front in order to get rid of them (Jurado and Bujeiro 2009, p. 34).

The "X" Organization in Cyprus

1948 was the year with the most rapid developments in Cyprus, both for the labor movement as well as for the Greek Cypriot demand for *enosis*, namely the union of Cyprus with Greece. The British proposals for constitutional regulations in Cyprus that started as just an idea in 1946 were placed as official proposals in 1947. A year later, in 1948, they would reach a conclusion with multiple effects in the later course of the *enosis* as well as for the different parties accordingly, based on the attitude they had kept on these proposals. At the same time, the large strikes that broke out the same year set fire in the climate between the Colonial Government and the Right-wing on the one hand, and the Left on the other, and they formed the reference point for the future development of the Trade Union movement in Cyprus. The Left had achieved through strikes in which pioneered, to become even more massive, scoring victories therefore in a field that it was anyway expected to prevail. The Right managed to gain access to the working class, break the monopoly of the Left and establish a new trade union (SEK), as a different option for the workers who wanted to organize around a trade union (Alecou 2012, p. 198).

All the above developments were parallel and they were linked to a great degree to what was taking place in Greece at the same time. The influence of the civil war on the stance of the political parties in regard to the strikes was quite evident. The transfer of the civil war atmosphere was even clearer in the radicalization of the Cypriot nationalism, with the appearance of *Chites* in Cyprus and the establishment of a corresponding party according to its Greek standards.

In the late 1946, members of the Greek organization "X", mainly royalist youth had made their appearance in Cyprus. Two officers of the Greek army, Kostantinos Ntabios, and Charidimos Frankgeskou, had arrived in Cyprus in order to establish the movement of *Chites* on the island (Katsiaounis 2000, p. 287). The first activities of the organization began at the end of 1947 during the elections for the Archbishop of Cyprus. "X" sought to intimidate its rivals by sending them anonymous threatening letters, and in many cases, while wearing a visor, members of "X" would go to the houses of the Leftists to threaten them (CO 67/341/7, 1947). *Chites'* presence contributed decisively to the Archbishop elections of 1947 under conditions of unprecedented political tension and violence (*Demokratis*, 27.9.1947).

The far-right elements, some of whom were directly imported from the Greek Civil War, defined the policy of the Church. Through their newspaper, they demanded that a body of *Chites* should be officially established in Cyprus. Typically the newspaper wrote:

> To establish a body of *Chites* in order to deal not with the communists– they are treated accordingly by the religious and patriotic people of the island – but to carry out the urgent and honourable duty of rehabilitation of those "nationalists" who have been the most generous and regular sponsors of the communist mafia. By this we mean the ones that project themselves as "nationalists" but at the same time they do not hesitate to continuously supply the communist media with commercials and other ads. [...] those will be stigmatized, they will be spited upon by the patriotic youth, privately and publicly; they will be torn apart and through in their face the yellow papers with their commercials and other ads that they will find in their offices or their pockets or houses. Then these people will be delivered to the public for pillory and mocking through the publication of their names as cheap associates of the fundamentals of slavish-communism. (*Efimeris* 1948)

The scepters in the anti-communist struggle, until the official appearance of *Chites* on the island, were held by the Cyprus Workers Confederation (SEK), which organized campaigns and rallies against AKEL and EAM. According to Spyros Papageorgiou, a committed defender of "X", the organization of the anti-communist and "anti-slavish" rallies was an action of courage and patriotism of SEK, which "led the way of confronting communism and organized in the September of 1946, massive anti-slavish rallies". In an encyclical of hem toward the nationalist organizations (9.9.1946), SEK reported:

At these demonstrations, representatives of all the nationalist organizations will greet, and pamphlets will be handed out as well as banners with phrases like: "Down Communism", "AKEL and EAM are the traitors of our Nation", "Death to the Slavish and their allies", "Glory and honour to the friends of Greece", "Long live the Union of Cyprus with Greece" etc. (Papageorgiou 2004, p. 640)

On the relationship between SEK and "X", Papageorgiou said:

The tricks and the behaviour of the Cypriot communists are similar with those of their Greek brothers. Like a 'Little Greece', Cyprus, lived on the far corner of the Mediterranean, marching in a pace comparable to that of its mother country. It has followed this collateral course in both minor and major issues. But the common facts were not only about the Communists, but about the reaction of the nationalists as well. SEK, from where Chites fighters of EOKA also originated, was at the time the vanguard of the anti-communist fight. When in 1 April 1947 King George died, Cyprus participated in the national mourning of Greece, except of course from AKEL and its offshoots. [...] the phraseology of SEK for the King impressively evokes the Greek origin texts of the royalists and Chites. (2004, pp. 646–648)

A few days after the requests of the nationalists for the establishment of an official body of Chites in Cyprus, the Ministry of Law and Order of Greece through a note sent to the Ministry of Foreign Affairs of Cyprus confirms the establishment of *Chites* on the island:

We have been informed that a special group of Cypriot nationalists is going to be established in Cyprus, and it will be named Group of Chites. It will take up the monitoring of the traders and businessmen who supply with commercials and other ads the communist press, as well as those who buy these newspapers. This procedure will address the Cypriot Leftists and will aim to the interruption of the cooperation and aid of them and of AKEL supporters. (Y.D.I.A. 1948)

In a subsequent note of the Ministry, the information about the action of the Body of Chites on the island is confirmed and it is stated that:

> Fortunately in this darkness, a movement has started to be formed which becomes continually more intensive on behalf of the youth, having highly nationalist ideals and all the passion and yearning needed to work for the National redemption, against all obstacles, marching upon the flaw-less path set by Greece. They boast for being called Chites of Cyprus and wherever they participated they defeated the communists even with the use of a bat. They have the tolerance of the Police. These youth are members of the sports club "OLYMPIAKOS" Nicosia. The club's aim is to evolve as a club of fighters against communism. All of them are enthusiastic young people who lack an organization and a man who would lead them. (Y.D.I.A. 1948)

Despite the fact that the organization was characterized as nationalist and was motivated from Athens, it had not in its assets any kind of action against the colonial regime. As it happened in Greece during the occupation, in Cyprus as well the action of "X" turned not against the foreign sovereign but against the inner enemy, which was in other words, the movement of the Left. Even from Greece Grivas' "X" had expected from the British to marginalize the Leftists in Cyprus. The newspaper of the Greek "X" characteristically indicates: "In the mean-while, all nationalists expect from the Government of Mother Greece to request in a diplomatic way from the Ally British Government, a change of tactics against the audacity of the communist dogs. Because they must return Cyprus back to Greece with as few communists as possible" (*Efimeris ton Chiton* 1948b).

Leader of *Chites* in Cyprus was Dr. Euripides Zemenides, who was also the president of the Football Club "Olympiakos". The newspaper of the Greek "X" writes: "The leader of Cypriot *Chites* and President of the "National Club Olympiakos", Dr. Euripides Zemenides, plays a primary role in the dramatic action of the anti-communist fight in Cyprus" (*Efimeris ton Chiton* 1948d).

The action of Grivas' men in Athens during 1943–1944, who were enforcing law and order in collaboration with the Germans against EAM, was similar to what was happening in Nicosia in 1948, where the Greek Cypriot like-minded were helping the colonial police to maintain the order against the Left trade-unionists. The newspaper *Ethnos* in Nicosia, mentioned on 24 October 1948:

> The communists see Chites everywhere, even when they are asleep, punishing their crimes. Does the fear of Chites seize them? Or are the loud daily protests of them a proof of the effective labour a few good men of the national- guard offer to the police in order to assist them to protect the city from the Red Terrorists? The peaceful and lawful people of the capital show great gratitude to the good lads who guard the city and thwart the satanic, criminal designs of the communists. "Chites" are the guard, the vigilantes of the city, and panic seizes the communists with the view and only of them. This measure was what the communists need, and they got what they were asking for.

The collaboration with the colonial police included activities like arrests by the members of "X" of anyone considered to be suspicious or a troublemaker and the handing over of these suspects to the police. Typical was the complaint of a Trade Unionist, who on 19 September 1948 was arrested by members of "X" and transported to the sports club "Olympiakos". There he was guarded by two men carrying bats until they surrendered him to the police. In another occasion, during the trial of a case on 1 November 1948, some of the leaders of "X" testified that they had been given an oral permission from policemen to arrest citizens at their discretion (Alecou 2012, p. 149).

In July 1949, the National Agrarian Party of Cyprus Chites was founded, synonymous and parallel to that of Greece. The new party, which was established in order to fight communism, "will show interest in helping to raise the living standard of the working people, ... it will require the generous contribution of the rich to enhance the fight of the Cypriots for the Union with Greece and the disbandment of the communists" (*Efimeris ton Chiton* 1949). Considerable help in the party's campaign to enlighten the Cypriots offered the General Secretary of SEK, Michalakis Pissas, who undertook the onrush in the country side (Papageorgiou 2004, p. 662).

Our research was limited in finding any additional information on this party's course in Cyprus after 1950. References to the "X" organization in the press of the period are significantly restricted, while no official announcement is recorded that indicates the termination of the activities of the organization. A conjecture could be made that the end of the civil war in Greece and the defeat of the Greek Left, in parallel with the (electoral) rollback of the Left in Cyprus at the same period, reassured and gradually led to the inactivation of the majority of the members of the organization, some of which possibly reactivated five years later, through the ranks of EOKA.

CONCLUSION

The present article has not addressed all issues related to extreme right mobilization in these countries, and future research could focus more on other aspects such as the organizational infrastructure and leadership to explain their influence on the political speech or the electoral campaigns. This article has examined the factors pertaining to the appearance and evolution of the extreme right in Greece and Cyprus, analyzing the ways in which it formed its identity.

The far-right in Greece grew up in a massive way as a response to the possibility that EAM would attempt to seize power during the period of occupation. This could constitute a violent turnover for the upper class which aimed to limit and dissolute the influence and power of the Left. Toward this, the tolerance at first, and then the strengthening of far-right groups was the only way for the right-wing elite to keep the reins of the political life of Greece. At the same time in Cyprus, AKEL managed to establish its power during the municipal elections of 1946 and also achieved through strikes in which pioneered, to become even more massive, scoring victories therefore in a field that it was anyway expected to prevail. The appearance of *Chites* in Cyprus could be seen as a response to the right-wing's weakness to face the upward power of AKEL.

In both countries, the marginalization of the far-right was something natural after the developments of 1950. The political situation after the elections of 1950 in Greece led the "X" party to dissolution. The stabilization of the political situation made it less necessary for the right-wing politicians to forbear and support Grivas. Since the end of the civil war signaled the defeat of the Left, it was natural for the far-right to come to its completion. At the same time in Cyprus, the Left defeated in the municipal elections of 1949 and a year later archbishop Makarios was elected, marking a new era in the process of the struggle for *enosis*.

A common element for the far-right in both countries was the anti-communist struggle. The propaganda against the communists which rose up in Greece during the civil war, offered the budding far-right of

Cyprus valuable ideological ammunition. We must stress out that these important tools for spreading the anti-communist propaganda had been the history lessons at schools, in the army and the church. The Greek Cypriot far-right would be essentially deprived of important ideological background without having the historical consciousness of the Greek past to exhibit to Cyprus present. The radicalization of the far-right became even more intensified in the 1950s, when it was organized and equipped toward the goal of consolidation in Cyprus of the attempt that failed to consolidate in Greece. Grivas, considering that the fundamental principle of the ideology of *Chites* could find greater response in Cyprus than in Greece, carried the ideological framework of anti-communism in his homeland. This time, however, the movement's privileged relationship with the Church of Cyprus and with Greece as a National Center, allowed him to disguise his anti-communist struggle with the mantle of a struggle against a common enemy: the British colonialism.

REFERENCES

Alecou, A. (2012). *1948: Ο ελληνικός εμφύλιος και η Κύπρος* [The Greek Civil War and Cyprus]. Nicosia: Power Publisher.

Alecou, A. (2016). *Communism and Nationalism in Postwar Cyprus, 1945–1955*. New York: Palgrave.

Athanasiades, G. (1994). *The First Act of the Greek Tragedy* [Η πρώτη πράξη της ελληνικής τραγωδίας]. Athens: Syghroni Epohi.

Betz, D. S.-G. (2003). Globalization, the Welfare State and Right-Wing Populism in Western Europe. *Socio-economic Review, 1*, 215–245.

Bujeiro, C. C. (2009). *Blue Division Soldier 1941–45: Spanish Volunteer on the Eastern Front*. Oxford: Osprey.

Drousiotis, M. (2000). *Πως φτάσαμε στην ΕΟΚΑ* [How We Ended up to EOKA]. Nicosia: Alfadi.

Ellinas, A. A. (2013). The Rise of Golden Dawn: The New Face of the Far Right in Greece. *South European Society and Politics, 18*(4), 543–565.

Fleischer, H. (1982). Επαφές μεταξύ των Γερμανικών Αρχών Κατοχής και των Κυριότερων Οργανώσεων της Ελληνικής Αντίστασης [Contacts Between German Occupation Authorities and the Major Greek Resistance Organizations: Sound Tactics or Collaboration?]. In J. Iatrides (Ed.), *Η Ελλάδα στη Δεκαετία του 1940–1950: Ένα Έθνος σε Κρίση* [Greece in the '40s: A Nation in Crisis] (pp. 91–115). Athens: Themelio.

Fleischer, H. (1995). The National Liberation Front (EAM), 1941–1947. A Reassessment. In J. Iatrides & L. Wrigley (Eds.), *Greece at the Crossroads. The Civil War and Its Legacy* (pp. 56, 48–89). New York: Pennsylvania State University Press.

Grivas, G. (1947, August 25). Το αμείλικτον κατηγορώ. *Newspaper of Hites.*

Hatzis, T. (1982). *The Lost Winning Revolution* [Η νικηφόρα επανάσταση που χάθηκε]. Athens: Dorikos.

Jurado, C., & Bujeiro, R. (2009). *Blue Division Soldier 1941–45: Spanish Volunteer on the Eastern Front.* Oxford: Osprey Publishing.

Katsiaounis, R. (2000). *I Diaskeptiki 1946–1948* [Η Διασκεπτική 1946–1948]. Nicosia: Scientific Research Centre.

Katsourides, Y. (2013a). Determinants of Extreme Right Reappearance in Cyprus: The National Popular Front (ELAM), Golden Dawn's Sister Party. *South European Society and Politics, 18*(4), 567–589.

Katsourides, Y. (2013b). Nationalism, Anti-colonialism and the Crystallisation of Greek Cypriot Nationalist Party Politics. *Common Wealth and Comparative Politics, 51*(4), 503–523.

Margaritis, G. (2001). *History of the Greek Civil War 1946–1949* [Ιστορία του Ελληνικού Εμφυλίου Πολέμου 1946–1949]. Athens: Vivliorama.

Marketos, S. (2006). *How I Kissed Mussolini: The First Steps of Greek Fascism* [Πώς φίλησα τον Μουσσολίνι. Τα πρώτα βήματα του ελληνικού φασισμού]. Athens: Vivliorama.

Marketos, S. (2009). Η ελληνική άκρα δεξιά τη δεκαετία του 1940 [The Greek Far Right in the '40s]. In C. Chatziosif (Ed.), *ΙστορίατηςΕλλάδαςτου 20ούαιώνα: Ανασυγκρότηση, Εμφύλιος, Παλινόρθωση 1945–1952* [History of Greece in the 20th Century: Reformation, Civil War, Restoration 1945–1952] (Vol. D2, pp. 1–66). Athens: Vivliorama.

Mazower, M. (1994). *In Hitler's Greece* [Στην Ελλάδα του Χίτλερ]. Athens: Alexandreia.

Mudde, C. (1996). The War of Words Defining the Extreme Right Party Family. *West European Politics, 19*(2), 225–248.

Nikolakopoulos, I. (2005). Η Τραγική Πορεία προς τον Εμφύλιο Πόλεμο [The Tragic March Towards the Civil War]. In C. Karagiorgis (Ed.), *Δημοκράτες χωρίς Δημοκρατία-Τα μοιραία χρόνια 1946–47* [Democrats Without Democracy. The Fatal Years] (pp. 11–23). Athens: Proskinio.

Papageorgiou, S. (2004). *Grivas and the X Organization: The Lost Archive* [Ο Γρίβας και η «Χ», Το χαμένο αρχείο]. Athens: Nea Thesis.

Passmore, K. (2002). *Fascism. A Very Short Introduction.* Oxford: Oxford University Press.

Paxton, R. (2007). *The Anatomy of Fascism.* New York: Knopf Doubleday Publishing Group.

Rallis, G. (1993). *Looking Back* [Κοιτάζοντας πίσω] (Vol. 301). Athens: Ermeias.

Stevens, J. (1982). On Present Conditions in Central Greece. In L. Baerentzen (Ed.), *British Reports on Greece 1943–44* (p. 5). Copenhagen: Museum Tusculanum.

Weiss, J. (1977). *Conservatism in Europe 1770–1945. Traditionalism, Reaction and Counter-Revolution.* London: Thames and Hudson.

Woodhouse, C. M. (1948). *Apple of Discord.* London: William B Oneill.

Woodhouse, C. M. (2002). *The Struggle for Greece, 1941–1949.* London: Hurst Publishers.

Archival material

Y.D.I.A. Diplomatic and Historical Archives of the Greek Ministry of Foreign Affairs, 88/1, 1948.

Newspapers

Efimeris 3/10/1948.

Efimeris ton Chiton 8/07/1945, 24/11/1946, 2/02/1948a, 23/02/1948b, 1/03/1948c, 20/12/1948d, 1/08/1949.

Eleftheria 12/02/1945.

CHAPTER 8

Failed Reunification Attempts in Cyprus: Makarios and *Bu Memleket Bizim*

Şevki Kıralp

INTRODUCTION

According to John Breuilly (1993), *nationalism* is a way of emphasizing an entity's interests over all others. Inherently, while Greek and Turkish Cypriots embrace nationalism as a form of ethnocentric attachment to their ethnic group, they will likely neglect the other community's needs and interests. Ethnic nationalism, as well as lack of mutual empathy and trust between the two communities, appears to be a key factor inhibiting the island's reunification. As this chapter argues, no attempt to reunify Cyprus is likely to achieve its goal until it is supported by both communities. It is a matter of fact that the Greek Cypriot community has for centuries been economically and numerically superior to its Turkish Cypriot counterpart. The Turkish Cypriot community has been supported by Turkey since the mid-1950s; however, there currently exists a sort of balance of power between the two sides. Neither side appears to be capable of imposing policies on the other, so neither side can reunify the island while neglecting the opinions of the other side.

Ş. Kıralp (✉)
Near East University, Nicosia, northern Cyprus
URL: https://neu.edu.tr

© The Author(s) 2018
T. Kyritsi and N. Christofis (eds.), *Cypriot Nationalisms in Context*,
https://doi.org/10.1007/978-3-319-97804-8_8

155

Consensus and collective action from the two communities is clearly needed to reunify Cyprus. In addition, even if the Cyprus conflict has largely been a contest between Turkish and Greek nationalisms, it can hardly be denied that the way we generally understand the *bicommunality* of Cyprus evokes an alleged "priority" of the two communities over the other ethnic groups (e.g., Armenians, Latins, and Maronites). Multiculturalism may then offer a better methodology compared to bicommunality when encountering ethnic nationalism in Cyprus. Ironically, though, just as ethnic nationalism apparently overshadows bicommunality in Cyprus, the bicommunality in turn overshadows multiculturalism. Throughout the history of Cyprus, the understanding of "island patriotism" and respecting the multicultural structure, integrity, sovereignty, and independence of Cypriot society has been challenged by the ethnic nationalisms that have prevailed in both communities in various forms (Loizides 2007). These ethnic nationalisms therefore present obstacles to achieving bicommunality and multiculturalism on the island.

The "divide-and-rule" policies of British colonialism and NATO imperialism, as well as the pre-independence and post-independence ethnic nationalisms, have been among the main factors dividing the two communities and damaging their peaceful coexistence (Mallinson 2010). For over fifty years, the two communities have been physically separated from each other. The two sides have since failed to reach a settlement and reunite the island. The Greek Cypriot leader Makarios and the Turkish Cypriot platform *Bu Memleket Bizim* (This Country Is Ours) have been among the political actors aiming for the reunification of the island. They both failed to gain support from the other community, however, so these actors' efforts failed to achieve their desired goals.

NATIONALISM IN CYPRUS: *ENOSIS* AND *TAKSIM*

When the Greek nation-state was founded in 1827, according to the *Megali Idea* (the Great Idea—the main inspiration behind Greek nationalism), the mainland Greeks sought to liberate all ethnic Greek peoples from the Ottomans and integrate such territories into Greece (Kızılyürek 2002; Peristianis 2008). In short, Greek nationalism in Cyprus emerged much earlier than its Turkish counterpart. In 1878, Cyprus became a British protectorate, and in response to the Ottoman alliance with Germany in World War I, the British annexed Cyprus in 1914. As part of the Treaty of Lausanne, the newly established Republic of Turkey gave up its claim to Cyprus, which later became a British crown colony in 1925 (Clogg 1980; Hale 2000, p. 45; Demirözü 2007; Ker-Lindsay 2011, p. 13). While the Greek and Turkish governments avoided conflict with the British over the Cyprus issue, Greek Cypriots launched a massive mobilization to unite Cyprus with Greece in 1931. Greek Prime Minister Eleftherios Venizelos condemned the Greek Cypriot mobilization (Kızılyürek 2002, p. 85). Likewise, the Turkish government assured British officials that if Turkish Cypriots were to mobilize in such a manner, it would be interpreted as "a challenge against the Kemalism[1] itself" (Kızılyürek 2002, p. 44).

Following World War II, Greece suffered from a civil war between communists and nationalists (1947–1949). While the western alliance supported the Greek nationalists fully, the eastern socialist states failed to back the communists effectively (Howard 2001, p. 128; Gaddis 2005, p. 22). In Cyprus, the communist Progressive Party of Working People (*Ανορθωτικό Κόμμα Εργαζόμενου Λαού*—AKEL) and the Orthodox Church were the most dominant actors in Greek Cypriot politics. The church depended upon the victory of nationalists, while AKEL was reliant on the success of the communists (Drousiotis 2002, pp. 3–8). The suffocation of Greek communism weakened AKEL's position and contributed toward the leading role that the Orthodox Church played on the *pro-enosis* front. In 1950, AKEL and the church organized a plebiscite on the question of *enosis*. Some 95% of Greek Cypriot voters voted in favor of it. Furthermore, Makarios, one of the most important figures in Cypriot history, became the Archbishop of the Cypriot Church (Peristianis 2008, pp. 159–160). In 1952, Turkey and Greece both became members of the NATO military alliance. In 1953, Greek Prime Minister Alexander Papagos met Anthony Eden, who was then the British Minister of Foreign Affairs, and mentioned his intention to annex Cyprus. Eden refused to negotiate on the *enosis* issue, however (Kızılyürek 2002, p. 102). In 1954, Greece made a formal request to the UN General Assembly to annex Cyprus. While Greece demanded *enosis*, it assured that Turkish Cypriots would be given minority rights. Turkey and Britain both rejected the Greek demand (O'Malley and Craig 2001, p. 12; Fırat 2007, pp. 597–598). In 1955, George Grivas, an experienced Greek Cypriot officer who fought the communists in the Greek Civil War, came to Cyprus and founded EOKA (*Εθνική Οργάνωσις Κυπρίων Αγωνιστών*—National Organization of Cypriot Fighters) and launched a pro-*enosis* struggle against British colonialism (Markides 1977).

Cyprus, however, held a significant geostrategic importance for the UK and NATO, being positioned between Eastern Europe and the Middle East. Furthermore, relinquishing Cyprus to Greece would potentially damage Anglo-Turkish relations and offend Turkey, which was now a fresh member of the western alliance (Holland 1998).

The British played the Turkish card against the pro-Enosis Greek nationalists. The colonial ruler recruited Turkish Cypriots to act as police officers against the EOKA fighters, and it encouraged Turkey to play a more effective role in the Cyprus question. The British offered a partition of Cyprus between Greece and Turkey as a possible solution, and this formula was embraced by Turkey and Turkish Cypriots (Ker-Lindsay 2011, pp. 20–22). Such divide-and-rule policies by the British seriously damaged the interethnic dynamics of the island (Mallinson 2010). The Turkish Cypriot police, which had been recruited by the British, clashed with the EOKA in armed conflicts, and this bloodshed damaged intercommunal relations in Cyprus. In 1957 and 1958, Turkish Cypriots founded the TMT (Türk Mukavemet Teşkilatı/Turkish Resistance Organization) and interethnic violence grew further still, particularly in Nicosia. EOKA and TMT exerted pressure on the left-wing and prevented Greek Cypriot and Turkish Cypriot leftists from joining forces. In 1958, NATO mediation between Greece and Turkey led to them moderating their Cyprus policies. TMT and EOKA then mutually announced a ceasefire (Crawshaw 1978).

In 1959, the Zurich and London treaties were signed. These aimed for the establishment of an independent Cypriot state based on sharing power between the Greek Cypriots (82% of the population) and the Turkish Cypriots (18% of the population). Greece, Turkey, and the UK became guarantor powers responsible for the security and preservation of the constitutional order of the Republic of Cyprus (Ker-Lindsay 2011). The Cypriot Christians (not just Greeks but also Maronites, Armenians, and Latins) were constitutionally involved in the Greek Cypriot community. The Turkish Cypriot community, however, was given the status of equal community based on veto rights provided by the constitution (Markides 1977). The UK, meanwhile, gained two sovereign base areas on the island. Nevertheless, it is reasonable to interpret the Zurich–London treaties as an intra-NATO settlement that was imposed on Greek and Turkish Cypriots. Indeed, Archbishop Makarios was very reluctant to sign the agreements. In addition to the constitution conceived by Britain, Turkey, and Greece, the Treaty of Guarantee and the

Treaty of Alliance restricted Cyprus's sovereignty and greatly dissatisfied Greek Cypriots (Hale 2000, pp. 132–135; Dodd 2010, pp. 20–40). In 1960, Archbishop Makarios became President of the new republic, while Turkish Cypriot leader Dr. Fazıl Küçük became Vice-President. In September 1961, Makarios went to the Belgrade Conference and made Cyprus a member of the Non-Aligned Movement (NAM) (Mallinson 2010). The aim of Makarios was to prepare an international background that would enable him to abolish, or at least limit, the Turkish Cypriot veto rights in future. Küçük was well aware of this, yet he did not exercise his veto over the non-aligned foreign policy. Küçük believed membership in NAM would raise suspicions over Makarios in NATO and perhaps enable Turkey to intervene more in Cypriot politics on behalf of Turkish Cypriots (Clerides 1989, pp. 124–125). In the new Cypriot state, the Turkish Cypriot contribution to the GDP (Gross Domestic Product) of Cyprus was relatively small when compared to that of Greek Cypriots. In September 1963, the Ministry of Finance declared that annual taxes raised from Turkish Cypriots amounted to only 8% of those raised from Greek Cypriots (PIO 1963). Greek Cypriot political leaders, particularly Minister of Interior Polycarpos Georgadjis, claimed on some occasions that "all the privileges of the state [were] enjoyed by the Turks" (Drousiotis 2005, p. 15).

In November 1963, President Makarios requested a set of constitutional amendments that would limit the Turkish Cypriots' veto rights. Turkish Cypriot representatives promptly rejected the proposal and abandoned their seats in the executive and legislative branches (Ker-Lindsay 2011, pp. 30–32). Interethnic violence subsequently emerged. Turkish Cypriot civil servants left their jobs, while the TMT formed enclave regions as a way of protecting the Turkish Cypriot population from armed Greek Cypriot groups. These ghettos also helped prepared the background for the federalization (OR partition) of the island, however. During 1963 and 1964, Cyprus suffered from interethnic violence, and the two communities became physically separated from each other (Kızılyürek 2005). One could claim, however, that the Greek Cypriots' attempts at amending the constitution were aimed at establishing a majoritarian democracy, thus rendering the Turkish Cypriot community a minority within the state by ending its status as an equal to the Greek Cypriot majority (Clerides 1989).

Greece and Turkey came to the brink of war. The USA wanted to dissolve the Republic of Cyprus and allow Britain, Greece, and Turkey to share control of the island. Turkey was offered a military base in Karpasia, leaving the rest of the island to Greece based on the Acheson Plan.[2] Makarios refused to make territorial concessions to Turkey, however, and demanded the preservation of the independence and integrity of Cyprus (Hart 1990, p. 19). In 1964, based on an agreement between Nicosia and Athens, Greece deployed a division of troops to Cyprus. Makarios soon realized, however, that these troops were in fact there to oust the Cypriot government should an intra-NATO solution based on a form of partition (taksim) or "double-*enosis*" be found (O'Malley and Craig 2001). UN peacekeeping forces were also sent to Cyprus. In 1964 and 1965, Makarios enjoyed considerable support from the NAM and third-world countries in the UN, so he managed to preserve Cyprus's independence (Mallinson 2010, pp. 139–141). Furthermore, the Soviet Union had declared its support for Makarios in defending and preserving the integrity of Cyprus (Hale 2000, p. 156). In April 1965, Derviş Ali Kavazoğlu, a Turkish Cypriot member of AKEL's executive committee, and Costas Misiaoulis, a Greek Cypriot member of PEO (Παγκύπρια Εργατική Ομοσπονδία/Pancyprian Federation of Labor) were victims of an assassination. Both men had supported an independent and united Cyprus, and they were well known for their anti-*enosis* and anti-partition stances (Vanezos 2009, pp. 33–37).

As announced in June 1966 by Minister of Commerce and Industry Andreas Araouzos, due to preferential Commonwealth trade, Greek Cypriots enjoyed significant economic growth (PIO 1966). The Greek Cypriot community, including President Makarios, now realized that they could jeopardize their living standards if they were to unite with Greece (Papandreou 2006, p. 223). On April 21, 1967, the Greek military seized power in Athens. In November 1967, Greek Cypriot troops attacked the Turkish Cypriot village of Kophinou. Turkey requested that the Greek junta recall the Greek division (that had been deployed in 1964), as well as General George Grivas, the commander-in-chief of the Greek Cypriot army. The colonels of the junta met these demands. In January 1968, President Makarios declared that he would no longer follow *enosis* policies, claiming it was simply not "feasible" (Kızılyürek 2005). By this point, hundreds of people had lost their lives to the violence, tens of thousands of Turkish Cypriots had abandoned their houses and moved to enclave regions, and the two communities had become separated from each other.

MAKARIOS' ATTEMPTS TO REUNITE CYPRUS: 1968–1974

In January 1968, Makarios made a historically important speech where he mentioned his desire to reach a peaceful settlement with the Turkish Cypriots. In his speech, Makarios underlined that for him, the Turks of Cyprus were "equal citizens" (PIO 1968). This indicated that he had no intention of limiting the individual rights of Turkish Cypriots but rather just their communal veto right. This would render Cyprus an island ruled by the prevailing political will, namely that of the Greek Cypriot population. In the February elections, Takis Evdokas, a pro-*enosis* candidate gained no more than 5% of Greek Cypriot votes, while Makarios was reelected with over 95% of the vote (Kızılyürek 2005). Makarios removed the police barricades and reassured Turkish Cypriots of their freedom to travel. He allocated funds from the government's budget and repaired a significant number of Turkish Cypriot homes. He invited the Turkish Cypriots to abandon the enclaves and return to their homes (PIO 1969). AKEL, EDEK (the United Democratic Central Union), *Eniaion Komma* (the United Party), and the vast majority of Greek Cypriots supported Makarios's pro-independence policies (Markides 1977). Later in the year, intercommunal talks began. The Turkish Cypriot side agreed to diminish their veto rights, but in return, prompted by Turkey, the Turkish Cypriot representative, Rauf Denktaş, asked for autonomy in local administration. Makarios rejected the Turkish Cypriot proposals and until 1974, the talks were often deadlocked due to disagreement on the local administration issue (Clerides 1989).

Without a resolution to the Cyprus question, Turkish Cypriots did not find it secure enough to dissolve the enclaves and return to the homes they left in 1963–1964. Their living standards therefore continued to be low. In 1969, the National Front, an anti-Makarios and anti-communist terrorist organization, was founded. The terrorists' aim was to force Makarios to suppress AKEL and return to pro-*enosis* policies (Kızılyürek 2005). On March 8, 1970, the terrorists made an attempt on Makarios' life. The Cypriot police captured the would-be assassins, however. During the investigation process, the police gathered evidence implicating Polycarpos Georgadjis, the former Minister of Interior, as the architect of the assassination attempt. On March 15, 1970, Georgadjis was killed while trying to leave Cyprus. According to Clerides, the former minister was killed by his associates (certain Greek officers serving in the National Guard). By doing this, the Greek officers had silenced Georgadjis and prevented their role in the assassination attempt from being uncovered (Clerides 1989, pp. 361–372).

In 1971, intercommunal talks were still deadlocked due to disagreements over local administration. Colonel George Papadopoulos, the leader of the ruling Greek junta, wanted to enjoy good relations with Turkey and NATO. He therefore put pressure on Makarios to accept the Turkish Cypriot proposals. Makarios refused to concede to interference from Athens (Kranidiotis 1985, pp. 341–344), and he articulated his dissatisfaction with Greece and Turkey's manipulations, as well as the stance of the Turkish Cypriots. On October 8, 1971, he made the following statement:

> The negotiator on behalf of the Turkish Cypriot community is Mr. Denktaş, but as he empathetically stated, he accepts Ankara's directives as if they came out of the Koran. The position of Greek Cypriot side, which Mr. Clerides represents, is different on this point. We co-operate with Athens, but we do not always accept their instructions as if they came out of the Bible. (PIO 1971)

In late 1971, Grivas secretly returned to Cyprus and organized the EOKA B terrorist organization. Grivas wanted to force Makarios to resign as president and pave the way for pro-Enosis policies. Makarios, and his supporters, distrusted the Greek military in Cyprus, so he imported heavy and light machineguns from Czechoslovakia. When the guns were imported in February 1972, the Greek junta believed that Makarios would distribute them to AKEL and EDEK members. Papadopoulos therefore asked Makarios to submit the guns to either the army or the UN peacekeeping forces. When he refused to do so, the junta demanded that Makarios resign. Makarios managed to alert the US government, however. Clerides visited the US Embassy in Cyprus, and, Henry Tasca, the US Ambassador to Greece, immediately met with Papadopoulos. The American diplomat asked the junta to withdraw its demands for Makarios' resignation (Clerides 1990, pp. 124–129). On February 16, 1972, around three thousand Greek Cypriots demonstrated near the presidential palace, protesting the junta's interference in Cypriot politics. Makarios made a speech where he said, "Cypriots must have the final word on their future" (*Agon* 1972).

Makarios managed to gain the support of Greek Cypriots for his pro-independence policies. However, he did not try to gain support and trust from Turkish Cypriots. The lack of consensus between the two communities forced Turkish Cypriots to remain in the enclaves. Additionally, the extreme nationalists in Greece and Cyprus accused Makarios and the Greek Cypriot left of abandoning the national desire for Hellenism (Uslu 2003, p. 107). The ideological conflict between the anti-Makarios and pro-Makarios segments were often reflected in the Greek and Greek Cypriot press. In Greece in 1973, Brigadier Dimitrios Ioannidis ousted the Papadopoulos government and claimed power in Athens. Following the death of Grivas in January 1974, he granted direct support to EOKA B and its Greek collaborators within the Cypriot army. Makarios realized that an Athens-sponsored front was being established against him. On July 2, 1974, he wrote a letter to the junta asking for the removal of Greek officers from the island. He underlined that he was "not the appointed prefect or locum tenens of the Greek Government in Cyprus, but an elected leader of a large section of Hellenism" (Miller 2009). Makarios made it clear that he did not consider it his national duty to succumb to the junta's political manipulations. He also released the letter to the press. Essentially, he wanted to bolster the Cyprus-centered Hellenism, so it would outweigh the Athens-centered Hellenism for Greek Cypriots. While it is evident that he was ready to struggle for a Cyprus ruled by Cypriots by resisting the Greek junta, he did not find any formula that enabled him to enlist the support of the Turkish community in Cyprus (Kıralp 2014).

On July 15, the Cypriot army, encouraged by Ioannidis, attacked the Presidential Palace, and the Greek officers in the Cypriot army seized power. Until July 20, no harm was visited upon Turkish Cypriots. The army and EOKA B instead went after the supporters of Makarios, AKEL, and EDEK, and the ensuing armed clashes caused great causalities (Clerides 1990). During that period, in the eyes of the Greek people who mostly opposed the junta, Makarios was the last person standing against the military regime in Greece. He had already grown into a hero and become a symbol of resistance against the junta. This popularity was seen as a danger by the junta elite, prompting them to oust him (Markides 1977). One could speculate that the junta expected the US government to support its military action against the Cypriot government by preventing a Turkish response, since Makarios and the Cypriot leftists were generally disliked by the western alliance (see Fouskas 2001;

O'Malley and Craig 2001; Uslu 2003). From the Greek-sponsored coup until the subsequent Turkish intervention, the violence in Cyprus had an intra-Hellenic rather than an interethnic character.

In response to the junta's military action, on July 20, 1974, the Turkish army launched its own military campaign in Cyprus. When analyzing the Turkish foreign policy for Cyprus, the first thing to consider is the geostrategic importance of the island. Most islands in the Aegean Sea were taken over by Greece, and Turkey faced some security weaknesses. Since the 1950s, Ankara had tried to impede *enosis* and avoid any geostrategic weakness that could threaten Turkey's southern coast. One could hardly claim that Turkey had good relations with Makarios, but in Turkish eyes, Sampson was the very symbol of *enosis*, and his regime could endanger Ankara's security plans. With the Greek junta's 1974 intervention, Turkey found the justification for its own military action. While the northern portion of the island would be very useful for safeguarding Turkey's southern coast, Turkey's sympathy toward Turkish Cypriots was also a factor motivating its intervention in Cyprus (Fırat 2007).

In 1973, following the outbreak of the Arab–Israeli war, the US government asked the British to allow its armed forces to use the British sovereign bases in Cyprus. The UK government (as well as Makarios) refused to participate in the war and did not grant this request (Fouskas 2001). This led the US government to reconsider its security policies for the Middle East. First, Cyprus could hardly be regarded as an effective NATO base because of the British stance. Second, Cyprus was led by a non-aligned leader, so the island was not under NATO influence. Indeed, the Makarios government, supported by AKEL, had the sympathy of the Soviet Union and the NAM. It is accepted fact that the USA knew in advance not just about the Greek intervention but also about the Turkish one. Both interventions were hardly contradictory to the US interests, however, because they would likely maximize NATO control over the island (O'Malley and Craig 2001). With these military actions, the hegemony of NATO over the eastern Mediterranean increased.

In the summer of 1974, Cyprus suffered from the Greek and Turkish interventions. Thousands of people lost their lives to the violence.[3] Both communities suffered from atrocities, and around 160,000 Greek Cypriots and 60,000 Turkish Cypriots consequently became refugees (O'Malley and Craig 2001, p. 221).[4] A de facto partition of Cyprus had been realized. Greek Cypriots were clustered in the south, with Turkish

Cypriots in the north. Makarios had failed to reunite Cyprus and pre-serve the integrity and sovereignty of his state, mostly because he had failed to find a consensus with the Turkish Cypriot community.

BU MEMLEKET BIZIM AND ATTEMPTS TO REUNITE CYPRUS: 1996–2004

In the post-1974 era, the vast majority of Turkish Cypriots expressed increasing support and loyalty to the Ankara-centered nationalism. They deemed Turkey their savior after living for 11 years (1963–1974) in enclaves, isolated from Cypriot politics and many aspects of eco-nomic life. During this time, Turkish Cypriot living standards signifi-cantly increased. Tens of thousands of people also came to Cyprus from Turkey, and this greatly dissatisfied the Greek Cypriot side. The Turkish Cypriot left's rise to power was impeded several times by Ankara's inter-ventions. Nevertheless, opposing Turkey's position in Cypriot politics and supporting the reunification of Cyprus hardly seemed attractive to most Turkish Cypriots (Hasgüler 2007). The regime led by Rauf Denktaş tended to label any political behavior supporting island patri-otism as "treason to Turkism". The federative solution was only on the political agenda of a few minority parties, such as the CTP (Republican Turkish Party) and TKP (Communal Liberation Party), as well as several non-governmental organizations (Kızılyürek 2005, p.255).

In the 1990s, however, two significant events changed public opin-ion. In 1992, due to competition for the leadership of the right, the UBP (National Unity Party) was divided in two. While Dervish Eroğlu and his supporters remained in the UBP, the supporters of Denktaş, including his son Serdar Denktaş, went on to found the Democratic Party (*Demokrat Parti*, DP). From then until the so-called *Annan Era*, the CTP became a partner in a DP-centered coalition, while the TKP became a partner in a UBP-centered coalition.[5] This fragmentation of the right enabled the left to rise to power, at least through coalitions (Kızılyürek 2005). In 1996, Kutlu Adalı, an anti-Denktaş journalist, was the victim of an unsolved murder. This led the Turkish Cypriot commu-nity to question the regime in northern Cyprus (Demetriou and Vlachos 2007).

In the late 1990s, Mustafa Akıncı, the leader of the TKP, proposed a resolution draft that would incorporate the Turkish Cypriot police forces into elected Turkish Cypriot authorities' control rather than the army's. The Commander-in-Chief of the Turkish Cypriot armed forces, who was a Turkish General, quickly condemned the proposal, leading to a political conflict between the Turkish Cypriot left and the army (*Milliyet* 2000). A number of left-wing NGOs organized demonstrations protesting against Denktaş, the army, and Ankara. Meanwhile, the journalists of the anti-Denktaş newspaper *Avrupa* (Europe) were arrested and accused of espionage. While Denktaş sided with the army and maintained his pro-Ankara political line, the entire anti-Denktaş opposition had joined forces in establishing the platform *Bu Memleket Bizim* (This Country is Ours). This comprised some 41 organizations, including left-wing political parties and left-leaning and liberal-democrat NGOs. In a short time, the platform organized mass rallies and protested against the incarceration of the journalists. The slogan "Denktaş, take the General with you and go away!" indicated the profound dissatisfaction of the Turkish Cypriot masses with their political system (Kızılyürek 2005; Demetriou and Vlachos 2007).

In the early 2000s, due to the economic crisis and the bankruptcy of banks in the north, the living standards of thousands of Turkish Cypriots were sharply diminished. This caused thousands of people to protest Denktaş near his palace. In Turkish Cypriots' understanding of domestic politics, the major source of the dissatisfaction was the UBP and Denktaş because their policies had led to corruption and social injustice (Kızılyürek 2005). While the streets were filled with demonstrations against him, Denktaş was invited by UN Secretary General Kofi Annan to widen and accelerate intercommunal talks. He was very reluctant to return to the negotiation process, and he was encouraged by Ankara to reject Annan's invitation. The stances of Denktaş and Turkey had triggered a growth in Cyprus-centered patriotism among Turkish Cypriots, however, and the majority of people began advocating the federal solution. In 2001, the intercommunal talks were enlarged. Most significantly, though, Cyprus's EU accession became a certainty in 2002 (Demetriou and Vlachos 2007).

In 2002, the AKP (*Adalet ve Kalkınma Partisi*—Justice and Development Party) came into power in Turkey. The AKP government positioned good relations with the EU as a high-priority foreign policy goal. They therefore dealt with the Cyprus question in a different manner than former Turkish governments had. Denktaş received significantly less Turkish support with the AKP's rise to power (Balcı 2010).

In 2002 and 2003, tens of thousands of Turkish Cypriots participated in mass rallies advocating EU accession and reunification of the island. In that period, however, the nationalists in Turkey had united against the AKP and its pro-federation approach to Cyprus. Their fundamental attitudes toward the Cyprus issue were based on the traditional pro-partition line. Denktaş tried to steer the AKP back to the traditional line and organized various visits to different cities in Turkey. He was supported by nationalists in Turkey, but he failed to gain support from the Turkish government. Moreover, Turkish Cypriot public opinion was directed sharply against his partitionist policies (Kızılyürek 2005). In that period, the political system in the north seemed unrepresentative of most Turkish Cypriots (Pericleous 2009). The Turkish Cypriot community was prevented from traveling, because the passports issued by the Turkish Cypriot authorities were not recognized overseas, and Denktaş prohibited people from obtaining Cypriot passports. In 2003, mostly due to public dissatisfaction, Denktaş was forced into a political maneuver where he allowed Turkish Cypriots to freely apply for passports from the Republic of Cyprus. The checkpoints were opened and the pro-federation CTP significantly increased its share of the vote (Hasgüler 2007; Demetriou and Vlachos 2007). For the first time in Turkish Cypriot politics, a left-centered coalition had been established.

In that period, the pro-Denktaş nationalists in Turkey and Turkish Cypriot community relied on their traditional nationalist, anti-federalist stance, accusing *Bu Memleket Bizim* of "treason".[6] The ideological conflicts between the pro-Annan and anti-Annan segments in Turkey and northern Cyprus were reflected in the Turkish and Turkish Cypriot press. In 2004, the Annan Plan for the federal reunification of Cyprus was put to the vote in a referendum. The Turkish Cypriot Left was optimistic because AKEL was a coalition partner of the Papadopoulos government. However, Papadopoulos, DIKO (the Democratic Party), and EDEK were greatly dissatisfied with the plan. The Treaty of Guarantees would not be abolished, the number of Turkish citizens in Cyprus that would be given Cypriot citizenship was unclear, and a significant percentage of Greek Cypriot refugees would not be allowed to return to their former homes in the north (Mavratsas 2010). Papadopoulos was well known for his anti-federal political line, and DIKO and EDEK also supported this. Moreover, Papadopoulos blackmailed AKEL by threatening to terminate AKEL's partnership in the coalition unless the party took a position against the Annan Plan (Kızılyürek 2014, pp. 118–119). Moreover,

Papadopoulos did not refrain from describing the federative solution proposed by Kofi Annan as a "plan of partition".[7] In his historical speech, he invited Greek Cypriots to "say a powerful no" to the Annan Plan. In April 2004, 75% of Greek Cypriots voted against the plan, while 65% of Turkish Cypriots voted in favor of it. The Annan Plan failed to reunite Cyprus, and Turkish Cypriots were bitterly disappointed. Their massive mobilization was over, and the attempts of *Bu Memleket Bizim* to reunite Cyprus had ultimately failed (Demetriou and Vlachos 2007).

CONCLUSION

This chapter analyzed two processes that failed to reunite Cyprus. The first was led by President Makarios, while the second was based on a Turkish Cypriot mobilization led by *Bu Memleket Bizim*. While Makarios wanted to prevent the Greek junta from intervening in Cypriot politics and keep Cyprus independent, he also wanted to render Turkish Cypriots a "privileged minority", rather than an equal partner, in an island state dominated by the Greek Cypriots. He failed to achieve his goals because he lacked support from the Turkish Cypriot community. *Bu Memleket Bizim*, meanwhile, aimed to establish a federal partnership between the two communities in Cyprus and reunite the island. They refused to follow the partitionist policies of Denktaş and stood against Turkey's interventions in Turkish Cypriot politics. When the AKP came into power, the partitionist policies of Turkey were apparently abandoned. The efforts made by Makarios and *Bu Memleket Bizim* were both accused of abandoning the national cause by the nationalists of Cyprus. Both initiatives wanted a Cyprus ruled by Cypriots, but there were external interventions in both cases. In 1974, both the Greek junta and Turkey exercised their military power to reshape Cyprus. The US government tolerated these in order to promote western interests in the eastern Mediterranean. In 2004, the AKP embraced the pro-federation mobilization of *Bu Memleket Bizim* and encouraged Turkish Cypriots to vote for the Annan plan, mostly because they were trying to transform the foreign and domestic policies of Turkey. On the other hand, anti-federalist nationalists in Turkey also intervened by supporting Denktaş. The Makarios and *Bu Memleket Bizim* cases highlight that the chasm separating the two communities is unlikely to be bridged until both sides can get behind a common goal.

In the post-Annan era, intercommunal talks continue. The Greek Cypriot side demands the abrogation of external guarantees, while the Turkish Cypriot side favors their maintenance. Security has always been an issue dividing the two communities. Greek Cypriots do not feel secure with Turkish guarantees, while Turkish Cypriots feel insecure without them. Currently, from the perspective of the two communities, the Cyprus question is perceived as a question of whether to be "with or without" Turkey. Turkish Cypriots conceive these guarantees as a safeguard against any attempt to class them as a simple minority again. In turn, Greek Cypriots feel the guarantees would give Turkey an ever-lasting trump card to play when interfering in Cypriot politics. What is more, some emerging factors are shaping the political agenda in Cyprus. Among these factors, there are disputes about hydrocarbon reserves and continental shelves; small-but-effective, extreme-nationalist circles on both sides; and the economic, technological and cultural "Turkification" of the north, as well as the long but unproductive history of negotiations over federalism.

Notes

1. Kemalism was the central ideology of the Turkish Republic, as established by Mustafa Kemal Ataturk. See Christofis in this volume.
2. The Acheson Plan was proposed by experienced US diplomat Dean Acheson. According to the plan, the island would be divided in three. Britain would keep its bases, Turkey would gain a sovereign base area, and the remainder of the island would be incorporated into Greece. Turkish Cypriots would be provided with minority rights and local autonomy in some Greek-ruled regions. However, Greece and Turkey could not come to an agreement on Turkish Cypriot rights and the territorial adjustment. Additionally, Makarios strongly objected to the plan. For further details, see O'Malley and Craig (2001).
3. Due to the violence of 1963–1964 and 1974, around 2000 Cypriots were classed as "missing." These "missing" persons comprised around 1500 Greek Cypriots and 500 Turkish Cypriots (CMP 2014). It is also beneficial to note that in 1963–1967, the number of Turkish Cypriot casualties was greater than that of Greek Cypriot casualties. In 1974, however, the number of Greek Cypriot casualties was greater than that of Turkish Cypriot casualties.
4. It is critical to stress that Greek Cypriots suffered more than the Turkish Cypriots from the housing problems caused by the de facto partition.

The northern part of the island hosted many Greek Cypriot properties capable of fulfilling the accommodation needs of Turkish Cypriots. In contrast, southern Cyprus was already full of habitants, yet it needed to house another 160,000 people who had essentially abandoned their houses in the north to go to the south. This issue of property is one of the most difficult aspects of the Cyprus question.

5. In 2002, UN Secretary General Kofi Annan prepared a framework aimed at a federal reunification of Cyprus. In Turkish Cypriot politics, the term "Annan Era" generally refers to the process commencing in 2002 and ending in 2004 with the referendum held in both the island's communities.

6. For instance, Turkish columnist Necati Özfatura used the term "treason" when criticizing the pro-federation attitudes of Turkish Cypriots in his article published in the *Türkiye* (Turkey) newspaper on January 3, 2004.

7. In the speeches of the anti-federal leaders in both communities, the public is misled and false perceptions about federalism are created. Greek Cypriot anti-federal figures tend to describe federalism as a partition or two separate states. In contrast, Turkish Cypriot anti-federal figures label federalism as becoming a minority under Greek Cypriot rule. Federalism has nothing to do with either of these views, however (see Kızılyürek 2005). In reality, federalism is a regime for single sovereignty based on sharing power between the devolved regions. While these enjoy a degree of autonomy in their internal affairs, they still act as a united entity in security, economic, and foreign policies (see Heywood 2000).

References

Balcı, A. (2010). 1990 Sonrası Türk Dış Politikası Üzerine Bazı Notlar: Avrupa Birliği ve Kıbrıs Örneği [Some Notes on Post-1990 Turkish Foreign Policy: EU and the Cyprus Example]. In C. Yenigün & E. Efegil (Eds.), *Türkiye'nin Değişen Dış Politikası* [The Changing Turkish Foreign Policy] (pp. 87–99). İstanbul: Nobel Ya-yınları.

Breuilly, J. (1993). *Nationalism and State*. Manchester: Manchester University Press.

Clerides, G. (1989–1992). *My Deposition* (Vol. I–IV). Nicosia: Alithia.

Clogg, R. (1980). *A Short History of Modern Greece*. Cambridge: Cambridge University Press.

Crawshaw, N. (1978). *The Cyprus Revolt: The Origins, Development and Aftermath of an International Dispute*. London: William Clowes.

Demirözü, D. (2007). *Savaştan Barışa Giden Yol: Atatürk-Venizelos Dönemi Türkiye-Yunanistan İlişkileri* [The Road from the War to the Peace: Turkey-Greece Relations in Ataturk-Venizelos Era]. Istanbul: İletişim.

Demetriou, T., & Vlachos, S. (2007). *Προδομένη Εξέγερση* [The betrayed rebellion]. Nicosia: Sosialistiki Ekfrasi.

Dodd, C. (2010). *The History and Politics of the Cyprus Conflict*. Basingstoke: Palgrave Macmillan/Springer.

Drousiotis, M. (2002). *Cyprus 1974: The Greek Coup and the Turkish Invasion*. Nicosia: Hellenic Distribution Agency.

Drousiotis, M. (2005). *Η Πρώτη Διχοτόμηση: Κύπρος, 1963–1964* [The First Partition: Cyprus 1963–1964]. Nicosia: Alfadi.

Fırat, M. (2007). 1960–1980: Göreli Özerklik-3 Yunanistanla İlişkiler [1960–1980: Subjective Non-alignment, Relations with Greece]. In B. Oran (Ed.), *Türk Dış Politikası: Kurtuluş Savaşından Bugüne Olgular, Belgeler, Yorumlar 1919–1980* [Turkish Foreign Policy: From the Struggle of Independence Till the Present Date, Phenomena, Documents and Comments 1919–1980] (Vol. I, pp. 716–768). İstanbul: İletişim.

Fouskas, V. (2001). Reflections on the Cyprus Issue and the Turkish Invasions of 1974. *Mediterranean Quarterly, 12*(3), 98–127.

Gaddis, J. L. (2005). *The Cold War: A New History*. London: Penguin.

Hale, W. M. (2000). *Turkish Foreign Policy: 1774–2000*. London: Frank Cass.

Hart, P. T. (1990). *Two Nato Allies at the Threshold of War: Cyprus, A Firsthand Account of Crisis Management, 1965–1968*. London: Duke University Press.

Hasgüler, M. (2007). *Kıbrıs'ta Enosis ve Taksim Politikalarının Sonu* [The End of the Politics of Enosis and Partition in Cyprus]. Istanbul: Alfa.

Heywood, A. (2000). *Key Concepts in Politics*. London: Macmillan.

Holland, R. (1998). *Britain and the Revolt in Cyprus, 1954–1959*. New York: Oxford University Press.

Howard, D. A. (2001). *The History of Turkey*. Westport: Greenwood.

Ker-Lindsay, J. (2011). *The Cyprus Problem: What Everyone Needs to Know*. New York: Oxford University Press.

Kıralp, Ş. (2014). *National Identity and Elite Interests: Makarios and Greek Cypriot Nationalism* (1967–1974). Ph.D. dissertation, Keele University.

Kızılyürek, N. (2002). *Milliyetçilik Kıskacında Kıbrıs* [Cyprus Ablocated by Nationalism]. Istanbul: İletişim Yayınları (in Turkish).

Kızılyürek, N. (2005). *Birleşik Kıbrıs Cumhuriyeti: Doğmamış Bir Devletin Tarihi* [United Republic of Cyprus: The History of an Unborn State]. Istanbul: İletişim.

Kızılyürek, N. (2014). *Yorgos Vasiliu: Düne ve Yarına Dair Düşünceler* [George Vasiliou: Ideas on the Past and the Future] (Ş. Kıralp & N. Kızılyürek, Trans.). Limassol: Heterotopia.

Kranidiotis, G. (1985). *Ανοχύρωτη Πολιτεία: Κύπρος 1960–1974* [The Unfortified State: Cyprus 1960–1974]. Athens: Estia.

Loizides, N. (2007). Ethnic Nationalism and Adaptation in Cyprus. *International Studies Perspectives, 8*(2), 172–189.

Mallinson, W. (2010). *A Modern History of Cyprus.* New York: I.B.Tauris.

Markides, K. (1977). *The Rise and the Fall of the Cyprus Republic.* Yale: Yale University Press.

Mavratsas, C. (2010). The Referendum of 24 April 2004: A Resounding Victory for Greek Cypriot Nationalism. In A. Aktar, N. Kızılyürek, & U. Özkırımlı (Eds.), *Nationalism in the Troubled Triangle: Cyprus, Greece and Turkey.* Basingstoke: Palgrave Macmillan.

Miller, J. E. (2009). *The United States and the Making of Greece: History and Power, 1950–1974.* Chapel Hill, NC: University of North Carolina Press.

O'Malley, B., & Craig, I. (2001). *The Cyprus Conspiracy: America, Espionage and The Turkish Invasion.* New York: I.B. Tauris.

Papandreou, A. (2006). *Η Δημοκρατία στο Απόσπασμα* [The Democracy at Gunpoint]. Athens: Livani.

Pericleous, C. (2009). *Cyprus Referendum: A Divided Island and the Challenge of the Annan Plan.* New York: I.B.Tauris.

Peristianis, N. (2008). *Nation, Nationalism, State, and National Identity in Cyprus* (Doctoral dissertation). Middlesex University.

Uslu, N. (2003). *The Cyprus Question as an Issue of Turkish Foreign Policy and Turkish-American Relations: 1959–2003.* New York: Nova Publishers.

Vanezos, H. (2009). *Derviş Ali Kavazoğlu* (S. Baran, Trans.). Nicosia: Galeri Kültür Yayınları.

Archival Material Accesed Through Press and Information Office Databases

PIO. (1963). *Statement by the Ministry of Finance* [Press Release]. 12 September 1963. Available at: http://www.piopressreleases.com.cy/easyconsole.cfm/page/search. Accessed 12 Sept 2014.

PIO. (1966, June 15). *Address of Commonwealth Trade Ministers' Conference by Mr. A. Araouzos* [Press Release]. [Online] Available at: http://www.piopress-releases.com.cy/easyconsole.cfm/page/search. Accessed 12 Sept 2014.

PIO. (1968, January 12). *The President's Statement* [Press Release]. [Online] Available at: http://www.piopressreleases.com.cy/easyconsole.cfm/page/search. Accessed 12 Sept 2014.

PIO. (1969, July 1). *Facilities Granted to Turkish Cypriots* [Press Release]. [Online] Available at: http://www.piopressreleases.com.cy/easyconsole.cfm/page/search. Accessed 12 Sept 2014.

PIO. (1971, October 8). *Interview by His Beatitude the President of Republic of Cyprus Archbishop Makarios to Mr. Djelalettin Chetin, Correspondent of the Turkish Newspaper 'Hurriyet'* [Press Release]. [Online] Available at: http://www.piopressreleases.com.cy/easyconsole.cfm/page/search. Accessed 12 Sept 2014.

Newspapers

Agon, 17/02/1972.
Milliyet, 25/07/2000.
Türkiye, 3/01/2004.

Website

Committe on Missing Persons in Cyprus. (2014). *Home Page*. Available at: http://www.cmp-cyprus.org/. Accessed 8 Oct 2014.

PART III

National Identity and the Development of Prejudice

Between Nationalist Absorption and Subsumption: Reflecting on the Armenian Cypriot Experience

Sossie Kasbarian

INTRODUCTION

The Armenian community is one of the three recognized national minorities of Cyprus, together with the Maronites and the Latins (Roman Catholics), identified in the 1960 constitution (Article 2 and 3) as "religious communities" and considered part of the state fabric. In the broad context of dominant opposing nationalisms—Turkish and Greek—a minority position can theoretically act as a challenge to exclusionary narratives. Minorities can test and interrogate the nuances and limits of "imagined communities" and illustrate life on the margins— necessarily liminal, pragmatic and adaptable. In the landscape of co-dependent Greek and Turkish nationalisms, the Armenians (and other minorities) can be assumed to represent an "other" way of being Cypriot.

The Armenian "Other" in the Cypriot story can act like George Simmel's "stranger" who "learns the art of adaptation more searchingly,

S. Kasbarian (✉)
Division of History and Politics, University of Stirling, Stirling, UK

© The Author(s) 2018   177
T. Kyritsi and N. Christofis (eds.), *Cypriot Nationalisms in Context*,
https://doi.org/10.1007/978-3-319-97804-8_9

if more painfully, than people who feel entitled to belong, at peace with their surrounding" (Sennett 2009). The stranger, by his very act of entering a society, holds up a mirror to it, revealing its nature, its nuances, and workings, with an insight that only an outsider can. Simmel's concept of the stranger is particularly fitting to the Armenians as intimate Others in Cypriot society—combining the apparently contradictory qualities of being both close and distant. By being both an outsider and embedded in the locale, the stranger is valued for his objectivity and broader perspective: "his position in this group is determined, essentially, by the fact that he has not belonged to it from the beginning, that he imports qualities into it, which do not and cannot stem from the group itself" (Simmel in Wolff 1950, p. 402). The "unity of nearness and remoteness" embodied by the stranger in a society means that "his position as a full-fledged member involves both being outside it and confronting it". Simmel's concept of the Stranger in a society—"not the wanderer who comes today and goes tomorrow but rather... the person who comes today and stays tomorrow" (Simmel 1950, p. 402) holds a number of characteristics that potentially pertain to the case of the Armenians in Cyprus. Firstly, the stranger is someone who is a member of the society but is not historically attached to it, maintaining "social distance" and holding a cosmopolitan worldview. He/She brings a more objective perspective and can act as a kind of mediator with other places, ways, and philosophies. In short, the stranger in this reading has huge value by being oriented elsewhere, while increasingly embedded in the locale, and maintaining networks, connections, and ways of thinking and doing that are different from the prevailing mainstream culture (Rogers 1999).

This chapter contextualizes the Armenian community in Cyprus amid the various tensions and visions of the Cypriot nation as espoused by different state, community and regional actors. The chapter incorporates the findings of field research carried out by the author from 2002 up to January 2017. It aims to assess the (symbolic) role that minorities in Cyprus have played and potentially can play in a more inclusive expansive vision of the nation. The chapter seeks to address how the Armenian Cypriot community has been politically co-opted into Greek Cypriot nationalism, while exercising a significant degree of autonomy in cultural and social matters. It makes the argument that the Armenians in Cyprus have been absorbed by the Greek Cypriot nation politically speaking, in that their difference in experience and particularities are glossed over or ignored, absorbed into Greek Cypriot nationalisms. In contrast, socially and culturally, the Armenian community in Cyprus has been successful in maintaining and negotiating a distinct identity in Cyprus, subsumed under a more inclusive multi-cultural vision of the nation. Absorption signifies no longer having a separate voice or agency, i.e. full incorporation into something hegemonic. Subsumption, in contrast, means maintaining a distinct identity while being contained as part of a wider group. The choice of absorption and subsumption as concepts, as opposed to the more traditional categories of assimilation and integration, is a deliberate attempt to go beyond linear and out-dated understandings of sociological processes and state policies. Both concepts are based on an intrinsic fluidity which recognizes that (national) identities are dynamic, evolving and non-essentialist.

SITUATING THE ARMENIAN COMMUNITY IN THE CYPRIOT STATE AND SOCIETY

Cyprus has been an Armenian home since the sixth century,[1] the history of Armenians and Cyprus overlapping at times. Despite its small size, the Armenian community in Cyprus has both durability and historical and cultural importance. At its peak in the early 1950s, there were 7000 Armenians in Cyprus but many left after the EOKA (Εθνική Οργάνωσις Κυπρίων Αγωνιστών/National Organization of Cypriot Fighters) nationalist uprising and struggle for independence. The Cyprus Press and Information Office (PIO) Web site states that there are "about 3500" Armenians currently residing on the island but does not distinguish between Cypriot and other Armenians.[2] 2016 figures put the Armenian component of the Greek Cypriot community at 0.4%.[3]

The island has had a steady Armenian presence for centuries, as well as serving as a temporary home of varying duration for more recent waves of exiled, displaced, migrant and refugee Armenians. The contemporary community is in majority composed of the descendants of the survivors of the 1915 genocide carried out by the Ottoman state, a large wave of arrivals who, in time, merged with the existing local Armenian community. Armenian community life has always been strong in the cities of Nicosia, Larnaca, and Limassol. More recently, a new community composed of Armenians from Armenia and Russia has sprung up in Paphos.

As elegantly elucidated by Susan Pattie (1997), the Armenians, following the collective trauma of the genocide, (re)constructed community in Cyprus, sustained by their "faith in (their) history", culture and identity. Arguably this practiced self-belief has nourished the Armenian community, bound together by the transmitted memories of the tragedies that led to their arrival in Cyprus. All over the region, post-1915, Armenian communities were slowly (re)built as sites of survival, resistance, and resilience (Migliorino 2008). Despite the typical and inevitable discrimination and difficulties, the Armenian refugees were successful in reconstituting and reconfiguring their existences in Cyprus as sanctuary, and safeguarding the ensuing generations who experienced Cyprus as home.

Despite the genocide being fresh in their memory, many Armenian refugees settled in Turkish neighborhoods, making a distinction between the Turks they had fled from and the Cypriot Turks. The common Turkish language was also a deciding factor for settling close by in terms of jobs and fitting in (Pattie 2009). Many Armenians and Turks have fond memories of these times (An 2009) and some friendships were renewed after the borders opened[4] in 2003.[5] Armenians grew to be integrated into both the Greek and Turkish Cypriot communities through social and business connections. In fact, many Armenians, by virtue of living alongside both Greek and Turkish Cypriots pre-1960 can empathize with the personal experiences and struggles of both sets of neighbors and friends. The escalating nationalism of both sides was not something that Armenians could subscribe to. Having survived massacre along ethno-religious-national lines they had come to value the stability of living under British rule in Cyprus.

The British colonial period reframed the religious-based Ottoman identities into ethnic identities which were bolstered by increasing nationalism on both sides. The Greek Cypriot desire for *enosis* (union with Greece) enflamed Turkish Cypriot desire for *taksim* (partition). The 1960 constitution which established an independent Cypriot state recognized only two national communities—the Greek Cypriot (82% of the population) and the Turkish Cypriot (18% of the population)—thereby casting aside the historical rich diversity of Cypriot life—from the Jewish to the Linobambaki.[6] The three recognized minorities—deemed "religious communities"[7]—were given the "choice" of deciding which national community they wished to join. This act of symbolic violence effectively erased the possibility of the minorities as Cypriots being equal citizens—the only way of being part of the state was to be swallowed into one of the two dominant communities. In the words of Constantinou (2007, p. 248), "the most disturbing thing about being a Cypriot is that one can only be a Greek or a Turkish Cypriot"; any other option is a "constitutional impossibility". The negation of identities of all but Greeks and Turks by the Constitution was arguably the seal of the ethno-nationalism that has prevailed since. As Constantinou (2009) has definitively argued, the 1960 Constitution of Cyprus deemed all ethnicity in Cyprus apart from Greek and Turkish as "surplus" and therefore "expendable". The ensuing ethnic homogenization project of the Cypriot state meant that other identities had to be dissolved in an increasing polarization along binary lines. The result has been a hegemonic imagining of the Cypriot state as bi-communal, fixed and static along quasi-primordial lines.

Nationalist aspirations and conflict continued, with a sharp rise in 1963 when the Turkish Cypriots were driven from their homes and forced into armed enclaves under Turkish Cypriot control. The conflict took a decisive turn when EOKA B with the Greek junta led a coup against the president of Cyprus, Archbishop Makarios III, on July 15, 1974, and the Turkish state invaded five days later. Greek Cypriots fled to the south and Turkish Cypriots to the north which came under Turkish occupation. In practice, the 1974 division of the island resulted in the two national communities being profoundly estranged from each other for over three decades and its legacy is a deep and apparently irreconcilable fracture. Successive governments, international initiatives and advocacies have had little success in any meaningful and substantive rapprochement such that partition now seems inevitable. In fact, successive administrations have bolstered the myth of two opposed, homogenous and monocultural national communities in Cyprus (Bryant 2004) supported by state education (Varnava 2009; Papadakis 2008) and media.

Despite the prevailing myth of homogeneity at the level of the state, contemporary Cypriot society has become increasingly multi-cultural. Armenian life in Cyprus must be situated in the realities of Cypriot society—and a polity that has not adapted to that. Cypriot politics and narratives are still framed in the binary—Turkish and Greek Cypriot nationalist narratives—unable or unwilling to properly engage with how society has changed. Up to 20% of the island's current population are immigrants—representing a remarkable diversity of residents, each negotiating their own trajectories in a multilayered and vibrant society. Political leaders and energies have been so focused on the ossified "Cyprus Question" that all other political matters have been given secondary attention at best. Cyprus is an example of a stagnant political scene—set in the long shadow of a frozen conflict which has framed and defined Cypriot society, but is at odds with its realities on the ground. This hegemonic framework is at best an anachronistic portrayal of a society that has been penetrated by global and regional economic, social and political forces—the effects of which are blindingly obvious given the tiny size of the island. Rather than the ubiquitous description as a "divided island", Cyprus has recently been reconceived as a "multi-diasporic space" and a "spatial laboratory for the study of migration and diaspora" (Teerling and King 2011, p. 2) among other interpretations—all reflecting the lived realities of Cypriot society, in contrast to the stagnant state.

From their arrival, as desperate and ravaged refugees, this disparate group of Ottoman Armenians was gradually transformed into a cohesive and thriving Cypriot community (Pattie 2009). Differentiations and variations within the community have been the norm, strengthened by subsequent waves of arrivals. Prior to Cypriot independence, the community was joined by immigrants from Palestine (1947–1949) and Egypt (1956–1957). The 1970s and 1980s saw the influx of Lebanese, Iraqi and Iranian Armenians into the community, fleeing the troubles in their home countries. Despite differences, there was enough (cultural and social) resonance between the distinct groups such that they were integrated into the Cypriot community for periods ranging from a few weeks to many years before they continued their journeys either back to their originating countries or onto new destinations in the west; some of them ended up staying and settling in Cyprus. The latest additions to the community have been Armenians from Armenia and other parts of the former Soviet Union, as part of an emigration wave picking up momentum since 2000. The present-day internal distinction drawn between *Gyprahays* (Armenian Cypriots) and *Hayastanis* (Armenians from Armenia[8]) is the latest phase of the diasporan tradition of distinguishing and dividing among themselves.[9] The "clash" between them is the current version of encounters between resident and new arrival, and the different experiences and visions of the (trans)nation and community that they represent. For these reasons, many *Hayastanis* have tended to stick to their own group, their extended group (the wider ex-Soviet Russian-speaking group of immigrants) or ultimately blend into an increasingly multi-cultural Cypriot society (Kasbarian 2009a).

In practice, Cypriot culture is based on everyday urban conviviality (Gilroy 2004)—shared and overlapping social interactions that embody a lived multi-culturalism. Difference and diversity are acknowledged but are not a barrier; identities are always evolving and fluid; and all members feel a sense of belonging. Conviviality is based on shared experiences and a shared sense of belonging to an inclusive if contested nation. In the Armenian case therefore, the conviviality is based on being Cypriot, alongside Greek (and other) Cypriots. The conceptual limitations and boundaries of a convivial culture are very much in the shadow of being in a frozen post-conflict situation where conviviality may have been the norm in the past, but is very much limited to the parameters of the Greek and Turkish sides respectively. There are few sites and spaces where a wider Cypriot identity which incorporates Greek and Turkish and other identities prevail.[10]

THE ARMENIAN TRANSNATION

Being part of a worldwide diaspora adds another dimension to the Armenian community in Cyprus. The contemporary Armenian diaspora is spread throughout the world, with its core composed of descendants of the survivors of the Ottoman atrocities and genocide (1881–1922). Until the 1970s the Armenian communities in the Middle East were regarded as the diasporic epicenter. These were predominantly composed of genocide survivors who took refuge in the Levant states, and merged with preexisting Armenian communities throughout the region. The steady decline of the Middle East communities and the rise of communities in North America and Europe reflect global emigration patterns. The transnational communities, through organized as well as informal activities, maintain active links with one another as facilitated through modern communications. Simultaneously, the independence of the Republic of Armenia in 1991 (to which most western diasporans[11] have no historic roots) has contributed to an increasing rootedness of diasporans in their respective "host" states and a more engaged civic participation, alongside a broader orientation toward Armenia (Kasbarian 2006) as a symbolic homeland of the transnation.[12]

For the Armenian diaspora, the Cypriot community is regarded as a kind of bridge between East and West, as well as being within easy reach of the modern day "step-homeland",[13] the Republic of Armenia. Being part of an established and active transnation also lends the Cypriot

Armenian community another (wider) dimension of national identity and consciousness, and provides a source of strength and validation. The community, both on the individual and on institutional level, is actively connected to global Armenian networks and engaged in transnational activities and communications. In recent years, being diasporic has been interpreted as an empowering experience rather than a tragic aberration. In the academy, the prevailing interpretation of being diasporic is one that fits an increasingly deterritorialized world, the norm being identities that are multiple, fluid and adaptable (Kasbarian 2006, 2013). In the Armenian community in Cyprus this layer is found in the multiple family and friendship networks and connections that people actively maintain, as well as in their economic and social connections to other Armenian communities and to Armenia. The consciousness of being part of a nation beyond Cyprus, a diaspora that is globally dispersed but actually quite well organized, is now, over one hundred years after the genocide that gave rise to the modern diaspora, and with the means and tools of globalization having penetrated every household, a validating and enriching experience. For young Cypriot Armenians, being Armenian or part Armenian is no longer something they prefer to keep private (Kasbarian 2006, 2013) for fear of ridicule, questioning or prejudice, because dual or multiple identities are more commonplace.

For a small minority in the community, Armenia has been reconceptualized as a potential (second) home in so far as they have bought property there, done business there, and spent substantial time there. However, for the overwhelming majority of the community, Armenia is a tourist destination and a hub where they can meet with other diasporans at pan-Armenian gatherings and events (Kasbarian 2016). Visiting Armenia is seen as an important rite of passage for those young diasporans who have attended community clubs and schools, facilitated through initiatives like "Ari Doun" ("Come Home") led by the Armenian Ministry of the Diaspora.[14] The independence of Armenia made it accessible to the diaspora, and has led to diasporans getting to know the "step-homeland", and recognizing that they are in fact home in their locales. This partially explains the very small numbers of diasporans moving to Armenia (Kasbarian 2016), along with the fact that it is a developing post-Soviet country. Cypriot Armenians for the most part maintain a touristic/heritage interest in Armenia, with some pursuing business and investment as well. Young Cypriots who have been hit by the recent economic crisis, resulting in rising youth unemployment and very low salaries, rarely consider Armenia as a possible career move, preferring to take posts in the Far East, Middle East or where possible, Europe. It would appear that economic realities are far stronger a pull than any nationalism. This is reinforced by the fact that Armenia is basically an unknown country for Armenian diasporan youth who may not share the proverbial diasporan sentimentality of their (grand)parents, and struggle with the Eastern Armenian language, and decades of a strong Soviet/Russian cultural influence. In conclusion, being diasporan in Cyprus has two seemingly contradictory effects—on the one hand, it adds an additional layer of identity, orientation and interest; on the other, it reinforces the sense of being more rooted in Cyprus, and being more Cypriot. These two tendencies coexist harmoniously and are relatively unproblematized in the present historical moment.

Armenia and Cyprus also have substantial political ties and cordial relations. The community, and in particular the Parliamentary representative of the Armenian community, Mr. Vartkes Mahdessian, has been instrumental in this regard, frequently mediating and playing a supportive role on state visits, cultural activities, and exchanges.[15] The Representative has played an active role in promoting closer ties between the two countries, between the community and Armenia, and in promoting the interests of the community to the state. He was honored with a medal of the Republic of Armenia National Assembly in 2015 for all his activities. The Representative is an increasingly important role in the age of social media in playing a visible role in advocating for the community, speaking for their interests and lobbying for their causes.[16]

Contemporary Community—Contextualizing Struggles and Challenges

In terms of the state, there are two related issues that are of utmost concern to the community. The first is the need to rectify the categorization of the Armenians as being a "religious community"[17] (see above) in the 1960 Constitution. As discussed, this has cost the minorities dearly in terms of denying their Cypriotness as Maronites, Armenians and so on. It has also had the effect of making minorities in the eyes of nationalist society, not "real Cypriots" but second-class citizens who have been (magnanimously) absorbed into the Greek Cypriot polity. The Armenian Representative has been leading a campaign to rename the Armenian "religious group" as the "Armenian community".[18] The related issue of concern for the three minorities is that even though each group elects a member of parliament to represent the group's interests, these three MPs have no real power (no vote or right to submit a bill etc.), and are mostly a symbolic presence in parliament, reduced to lobbying and contributing only when invited to do so. These two issues, although present since the inception of the Republic, have taken on a new urgency in light of the most recent round of peace talks (and proposed changes to the constitution)[19] and also reflect the minorities' new confidence in being part of the state fabric. Politically speaking, the Armenian community is disempowered, defined by the Greek Cypriot legal framework, absorbed into the Greek Cypriot polity and forced to accept the Greek Cypriot agenda.

In contrast, the community enjoys a distinct and active social and cultural life, which constitutes a distinct part of the mainstream Cypriot scene as well as overlapping with it on occasions. The Cypriot community, like much of the western diaspora is "institutionally saturated" (Tölölyan 2000, p. 130). The dense and active network of sports clubs, organizations, churches, community groups, schools, media outlets, arts and cultural associations defy the small size of the community (Pattie 1997). The sheer volume of organization and activity also reflects the fact that this is not a cohesive community, but contains both historical and current divergence, debates and disagreement, along the lines of orientations, political leanings and priorities. This contentious element to the community (shared by most other Armenian diasporic communities) rather than being seen as a weakening factor, can be viewed as one that fuels it, keeping discussion and difference at the heart of the perennial question of who represents a diaspora (community). Indeed the 2015 centenary of the genocide revealed the Armenian diaspora to be a very broad church, and ultimately an inclusive one, despite tensions and battles within (Kasbarian 2018).

A major problem that the community shares with much of the western diaspora is the decline of western Armenian. In Cyprus this has been exacerbated by the closure of the only Armenian secondary school, the Melkonian Education Institute in 2006. This unique (boarding) school was established by the Melkonian brothers (tobacco traders from Egypt) in 1926, to house and educate the orphans from the genocide. As such it is a significant heritage site for the Armenian Cypriot community, the diaspora at large and for the Cypriot state. Its closure led to a public outcry and transnational furor (Kasbarian 2009b), and has ended up in a stalemate, with no development and no decisions, despite many efforts. Although the student body of the school in recent years had not included many Armenian Cypriots, this now leaves them no choice but to go on to a state (Greek) school or if they have the means, a private (English medium) school. The loss of the Melkonian Institute was a serious blow to the community also in terms of cultural and social life, as well as being a loss of status within the diaspora.

The problem of maintaining the western Armenian language in Cyprus extends beyond the Melkonian Institute, with language teachers for the primary schools now having to be recruited from elsewhere (most commonly, Lebanon). Western Armenian (the language of the western diaspora) is considered an endangered language by UNESCO and organizations like the Gulbenkian Foundation have made it a priority to tackle it.[20] The western Armenian language is recognized and protected by the Cypriot government as a "minority language" according to the guidelines of the European Charter for Regional or Minority Languages. The latter have pointed out the shortcomings of the state in terms of minority languages repeatedly,[21] and crucially stated that "more awareness needs to be raised among the majority about Cyprus' regional or minority languages as an integral part of the country's cultural heritage".[22] One success story is that Armenian language classes have been available at the University of Cyprus since 2010, catering mainly to non-Armenian spouses or those with some Armenian descent.

The contemporary Armenian experience in Cyprus reflects the challenges and struggles of the populace at large. The current economic crisis, rising unemployment, and youth brain drain are themes within the community as much as society at large. The community is multi-layered and multi-oriented, a fact mirrored in a wider society that is in practice neither monolithic nor homogenous on the ground. What is clear is that the younger generations are increasingly rooted in Cyprus and fully owning their Cypriot identity. This is reflected in the fact that the Greek language is their language of socialization, in contrast to previous generations where it was their third or even fourth language. One could make the assumption that the more multi-cultural Cypriot society has become, the more at home and confident minorities like Armenians have felt. However, there is not necessarily this correlation as minorities can be as exclusionary as majorities, and vigilant about protecting and policing their boundaries with others. The Armenian community faces the additional impact of Armenian immigration—mostly Armenians from Armenia and the former Soviet Union. Some of the latter have been less than stellar in their conduct, and are considered to have sullied the good reputation of Armenians in Cyprus. For these and other reasons (Kasbarian 2009a) Armenian Cypriots are sometimes wary of embracing their "brethren", some of whom have been involved in crime and brought bad publicity on to a community which has always prided itself on an exemplary public image.

Public Image and Private Pain

In the past two decades, the Armenian community in Cyprus has been actively engaged in being more visible in the state. This coincides with their feelings of security within the state, coupled with the shift in diasporic identity from one of exilic weakness to one of transnational resourcefulness (Kasbarian 2009a, 2015). This increase in visibility is aided by social media; increased communications and connections, both within the community and with other Cypriots; as well as more active participation in the state. The great majority of Armenians are rooted in Cyprus, and are invested in the future of the island as much as other Cypriots. There has therefore been more effort to represent themselves (as a community), to be increasingly vocal when given platform, and to be more involved in national projects and initiatives. While this has always been the case at the individual level, the core community, as an imagined and material political construct, has moved from being somewhat protective and reserved to being more porous and open. This is partially due to the escalating numbers of exogamy and a new generation that is likely to have multiple identities of which Armenian is just one. Traditional community structures like the schools and youth groups are struggling to keep up with this change, in the same way that Cypriot state schools are challenged by the sharp increase of pupils from mixed ethnic and linguistic backgrounds (Theodorou and Symeou 2013).

This increased visibility is also aided and sometimes led by the state as part of its own political agenda. One of the recent means to raise the profile of the Armenian community is the publication of a number of noteworthy items by the state media, with the cooperation and support of the Armenian community, and in particular the Representative's office. "The Armenians of Cyprus"[23] is an informative 40-page booklet published by the PIO in 2016 as part of their series on the "Cyprus Religious Groups", distributed free of charge and also available online. This visibility extends to the Cypriot urban landscape which already testifies to a long and rich Armenian historic presence. The centenary of the genocide in 2015 resulted in a number of new urban initiatives, most recently (November 2016) the naming of the "Armenian Genocide Park" in Paphos, dedicated to the memory of the genocide victims, and complete with a *Khachkar*[24] specially flown over from Armenia.[25] Placing the Armenian experience in the public arena not only honors Armenian Cypriots but also integrates the Armenian story with the Cypriot one— making the Armenian Cypriot experience part of the wider Cypriot identity—thereby challenging ethno-nationalist narratives which see them as outsiders. In these small symbolic ways, the Armenians, while politically co-opted into the Greek Cypriot package, are validated as a distinct identity with their own Cypriot trajectory.

As part of the genocide centenary program, the Armenian Representative initiated the publication of a compilation of Cypriot press archives reporting on the genocide (and preceding massacres).[26] This bilingual (Greek and English) book is both an impressive resource, and a moving testimony to the Armenian Cypriot community and the diaspora at large, as "the living evidence of the Armenian genocide and its consequences".[27] The Office of the Armenian Representative has obviously prioritized raising the profile of Armenians in Cyprus through educational and cultural production.[28]

The Office has also been at the helm of a number of initiatives regarding Armenian life in the northern occupied territories which were brought to a halt in 1974. Since 2007 the annual pilgrimage to St. Makar monastery (known as Magaravank in Armenians, an important spiritual site for Armenians at least since 1425) was revived. The Armenian Church of Sourp Asdvadvadzin (and its precincts) on Victoria Street, (northern) Nicosia was desecrated and left in ruins after 1974. It was restored by the United Nations Development Programme— Action for Cooperation & Trust in Cyprus (UNDP-ACT), with the sponsorship of USAID, and won a European Nostra Award[29] in 2015. The First Mass since 1964 was held on 11 May 2013, and the church reconsecrated, with three annual masses now permitted. Visiting Armenian sites such as these on "the other side" is not easy and needs to be arranged through official channels, accompanied by Turkish military.

A crucial actor in the "imagining" of the community (Anderson 1983) has been the media outlet *Gibrahayer*[30] (Cypriot Armenians). What started out as an email database of a close circle in 1999 by creator

Simon Aynedjian, now has 32,000 subscribers to the (free electronic) newsletter and over 21,000 followers on the Facebook site.[31] *Gibrahayer* is well-known as a huge success story within the diaspora, elevating the Cypriot community to a status that far belies its small size. Its success must be attributed to its creator and editor who still runs it mostly by himself and on a voluntary basis.

Gibrahayer's importance is threefold. Firstly, it is a self-representation of the community and chronicles their activities, functions, debates, concerns, and discussions. Secondly, it portrays the community to those outside the community (the vast number of followers) constructing a distinct image and brand. Thirdly, *Gibrahayer* serves as a connector, of the community, the state, the diaspora, Armenia and beyond. The vision of the community as imagined by *Gibrahayer* has a clear local core and leadership, with clear infrastructure and organization, but its remit, concerns, and interactions are far and wide. The large numbers of Greek and Turkish Cypriot subscribers means that the community is embedded in national issues. Gibrahayer has also taken a pro-dialogue, pro-Cypriot stance, supporting and publicizing bi-communal projects and initiatives. *Gibrahayer*'s creator ascribes its wide appeal to one important decision in 1999—to publish in English, despite some criticism from the community. This has ensured its global appeal—currently the largest number of subscribers is based in the USA, followed by Cyprus, then the UK.[32]

There is discernible a common narrative thread running through the public image of the Armenian community in Cyprus. This usually includes the following themes—the long history of Armenian presence on the island; the genocide which is the common point of origin for most of the present community; the shared suffering at the hands of "the Turk"; the community's integration in Cyprus and their social, economic and cultural contribution. This "master narrative" is evident in state media and discourse but also in community forums. The latter has a twofold effect: firstly, of reinforcing the narrative upon the community as an act of self-validation, and secondly, presenting it to external audiences. There is thus a familiar performative element at most public events—performing this narrative to state officials, other Cypriots and outsiders, as well as acting as a unifying cohesive mantra to the community (who have internalized their subaltern status). The small size of the community has meant that despite feeling more secure in their status in Cyprus, they still have to be cautious and tread carefully in a politicized environment. Thus, stressing the themes above in a clear narrative has an affirming quality, and sits beside the dominant Greek Cypriot nationalist narrative nicely. This narrative molds the Armenian outsider into an image that is palatable to the nationalist, and supports the dominant nationalist discourse.

Despite the "shared suffering" narrative, perhaps the most important divergence with the majority Greek Cypriot community is the Armenian Cypriot experience of loss. The majority of Armenians lived in what became the Turkish Cypriot administered part of Nicosia in 1960, and following the conflicts between Greek and Turkish Cypriots from 1963 onwards, they were forced to leave their homes and seek refuge in the Greek Cypriot administered sector. This displacement and loss has never been fully acknowledged or articulated by the Cypriot state or society at large. The state drew a distinction between those displaced in 1963 (most Armenians) as *tourkoplikti* (struck by the Turks) and the majority Greek Cypriots who became displaced in 1974 and were officially considered refugees, or *prosfiyes*. Demetriou (2014) in a groundbreaking article analyses how this distinction has created and reinforced the perceived difference between the dominant group and the minority Armenians, and their respective losses, thereby positioning the Armenian experience as somehow lesser than the Greek experience. That these losses are rarely registered or discussed outside the private realm is a source of pain for many Armenians who feel relegated to second-class citizens whose loss is not (worth) the same as the 1974 losses. It is also an act of exclusion and negation that seeks to frame the Cyprus conflict along a simplistic binary of Greek and Turkish and paves the way for the Greek Cypriot monopoly of a narrative of victimhood. Demetriou says that "post 1960s, displaced Armenians have had to tread a fine balance between identification with Greek Cypriots and the marginalization within that community" (p. 171). This act of nationalist violence can be seen as a silencing of the distinct experience of the Armenians of Cyprus. More broadly, this act of belittling or sidelining the experience of loss and displacement in 1963 is an act of violence in itself, and one that continues to hurt. This violence can be viewed as a silencing of the distinct experience of the Armenians of Cyprus and their co-option into an undifferentiated hegemonic Greek Cypriot narrative of victimhood, in response to Turkish aggression. By being classified as Greek Cypriots since 1960, the minority experiences have suffered an act of violence (however intentioned) which has on the one hand given them security with regard to the Cypriot state, and on the other subsumed them into the Greek Cypriot polity, thereby silencing or at the very least marginalizing their own experiences and trajectories.[33]

In the latest round of peace talks in 2017, the Armenian Representative brought together different community leaders and put together a proposal articulating the Armenian position—along with a list of the Armenian properties on the Turkish side—which was sent to all the different political players. Unfortunately, the negotiations have come to nothing and now partition looks inevitable for the island. What voice the Armenian community will have, especially in regard to the properties on the Turkish side is unclear, but the situation looks far from reassuring.

CONCLUDING THOUGHTS

The Armenian experience is another dimension in the fabric of the Cypriot nation, a distinct identity that maintains its integrity while being subsumed into a larger landscape. As discussed, the Armenians, while recognized as being a minority, have been politically absorbed into the Greek Cypriot polity, their distinct concerns and trajectories (re)interpreted by the dominant nationalist state narrative. In contrast, the Armenians are subsumed culturally and socially into an increasingly multi-cultural Cypriot society. By being recognized as distinct, by having a dense organized infrastructure, and by virtue of being part of a well-established diaspora, the community exercises an active cultural and social identity. The Armenian Cypriot story is an interesting case of negotiating difference and commonality, distance and connection, in a meaningful way.

While mainstream contemporary political debates on "outsiders" (refugees, asylum seekers, economic migrants, the displaced and stateless) are imbued with negativity, the marginal, liminal newcomer in Simmel's concept is one that offers opportunity and potential—both to the society at large and conceptually, in the study of societies marked by nationalist conflict, like Cyprus. The outsider who is in fact inside can offer understanding and insight about a society, both from his/her perspective, but also in terms of how the society treats him/her. Minorities in a nation are the conceptual sites in which we can meaningfully grapple with what kind of nation or society we are and want to be. In a global context where the refugee crisis has fueled a bitter and polarized politics, it is imperative to critically re-examine the lived conviviality of older communities that have turned "strangers" into friends and extended family.

Notes

1. George Hill's history of Cyprus contains many references to the Armenian presence starting from the end of the sixth century (see Hill 1949).
2. www.moi.gov.cy/moi/pio/pio.nsf/All/DBF419D7DF6CC18EC2256F CE00331E37?OpenDocument.
3. The full figures are: Greek Cypriot community 706,800 or 74.6%; Turkish Cypriot community 92,200 or 9.8%; foreign residents 148,000 or 15.6%; the religious groups which belong to the Greek Cypriot community constituted: Armenians: 0.4% of the Greek Cypriot community; Maronites: 0.7% of the Greek Cypriot community; Latins: 0.1% of the Greek Cypriot community. Republic of Cyprus Demographic Report Statistics, 2016, http://www.mof.gov.cy/mof/cystat/statistics.nsf/All/ 6C25304C1E70C304C2257833003432B3/$file/DEMOGRAPHIC_ REPORT-2016-271117.pdf?OpenElement.
4. From the 1974 division of the island it was not possible for ordinary citizens to cross from one "side" to the "other", the borders being heavily militarized. On 23 April 2003, the Turkish Cypriot leadership made the surprise move of relaxing the borders, ushering in a brief period of hope and excitement among Cypriots. See Demetriou (2007).
5. See also a recent documentary *Birlikte* (Together) Memories of the Armenian Cypriots made by Asi Productions, https://www.youtube. com/watch?v=3TyOeUoRn7Q.
6. The Linobambaki (meaning those of cotton and linen) were a Crypto-Christian group (with Catholic origins), who combined both Islamic and Christian practices and identities, to avoid persecution during the Ottoman period.
7. The misnomer that the three state minorities are "religious communities" as defined by the Constitution has been a point of dispute both internally and internationally: European institutions like the Advisory Committee on the Framework Convention for the Protection of National Minorities regularly express concern about it.
8. The initial wave of Hayastansis was actually Cypriot returnees who emigrated to Armenia in the 1960s. Subsequent waves are part of the substantial numbers of economic migrants from the former Soviet Union who have found their way to Cyprus in the hope of a better future.
9. Pattie (1997, pp. 88–103) explores the tensions between *deghatsis*, the established Armenian community, and the *kaghtagans* (refugees) from the late nineteenth to the mid-twentieth century, revealing that there was little mixing and very few intermarriages between the two groups for about twenty years.
10. The most successful of these are the buffer-zone based Home for Cooperation, http://www.home4cooperation.info/what-is-the-h4c and the Association for Historical Dialogue and Research, http://www.ahdr. info/home.php.

11. "Western diasporans" refers specifically to the descendants of those Armenians who hail from present-day Eastern Turkey. They are clearly distinguishable from the post-Soviet wave of Armenians from the Republic and the former Soviet Union who constitute a distinct 'new' diaspora and are known as eastern diasporans.

12. Tölölyan (2000, pp. 107–135) uses the term "transnation" to mean "all diasporic communities and the homeland; the nation-state remains important, but the permanence of dispersion is fully acknowledged and the institutions of connectedness, of which the state is one, become paramount".

13. My concept of a "step-homeland" encapsulates a situation where two entities that are not related by descent are forced into a familial relationship by external forces; that is, it is not a naturally occurring relationship but one that is forged through circumstances. The sense of step-ness also carries with it connotations of difficulty and a need for adjustment by both parties. See Kasbarian (2016).

14. Since 2009, graduates of the Nareg primary schools in Cyprus go on a two-week trip to Armenia, sponsored and arranged by the Armenian Representative Vartkes Mahdessian as part of the "Ari Doun 2017" programme, http://www.intellinews.com/ yerevan-calls-on-diaspora-to-help-rebuild-armenia-118055/.

15. Interview with the Armenian Representative, Mr. Vartkes Mahdessian, Nicosia, 15 September 2017.

16. See for example, https://www.facebook.com/Vartkes-Mahdessian-Armenian-MP-in-the-Cyprus-Parliament-135603569846256/.

17. This is even more of a misnomer in the Armenian case as Armenians belong to the full spectrum of Christian churches and denominations, although the majority are Armenian Apostolic (Orthodox).

18. http://cyprus-mail.com/2017/06/26/armenians-like-officially-designated-community/.

19. http://www.cna.org.cy/webnews.aspx?a=6610d6d63c3945a89c1ee-910e6271c5d.

20. https://gulbenkian.pt/armenian-communities/priorities-and-activities/language-and-culture/.

21. Application of the European Charter for Regional or Minority Languages Biennial Report by the Secretary General of the Council of Europe to the Parliamentary Assembly, Doc. 13436 (3 March 2014), https://www.coe.int/t/dg4/education/minlang/sgreports/SGReport2013_en.pdf "The Cypriot authorities continue to have a positive attitude toward the needs and wishes of the speakers of the regional or minority languages. However, a more structured approach targeting specifically the Armenian and the Cypriot Maronite Arabic languages is necessary. … but there is an

obvious need for a presence on television for both Armenian and Cypriot Maronite Arabic. While Armenian education at preschool and primary school level is satisfactory, secondary education remains in a delicate position, and teacher training in Armenian is still not available".

22. Application of the European Charter for Regional or Minority Languages Biennial Report by the Secretary General of the Council of Europe to the Parliamentary Assembly, Doc. 13436 (3 March 2014), https://www.coe.int/t/dg4/education/minlang/sgreports/SGReport2013_en.pdf.

23. The Armenians of Cyprus. PIO 273/2016 (text by Alexander-Michael Hadjilyra), http://www.publications.gov.cy/moi/pio/publications.nsf/All/A53114877AECA553C2257B7B0028F716/$file/Armenians%20book%202016%20ENGLISH%20WEB1.pdf.

24. A *Khachkar* is a "stone-cross", a cross (an accompanying ornamentation) carved into stone, popular in medieval Armenia, and an art revived in the twentieth century.

25. https://m.facebook.com/Gibrahayer/posts/1230239497019022, 30 November 2016.

26. *The Armenian Genocide through the Cypriot Press 1914–1923 with reference to earlier massacres*. 2016, Nicosia Cyprus. Cassoulides Masterprinters. See also Shiakali (2016).

27. "A Message from the Community", Vartkes Mahdessian, Representative of the Armenian Community, p. 10.

28. See also a DVD on "The Armenians in Cyprus" sponsored by the Ministry of Education and Culture, and produce on the Representative's Office, 2011.

29. http://www.europanostra.org/armenian-church-monastery-nicosia-project-gives-hope-communities-cyprus/.

30. http://www.gibrahayer.com/.

31. Telephone interview with Simon Aynedjian, 4 January 2018.

32. Armenia comes 20th on the list. Email correspondence with Simon Aynedjian, 4 January 2018.

33. This lack of critical differentiation extends to other minority experiences, counted as part of the Greek Cypriot community since 1960. The Maronite experience for example is also distinct. Most Maronites were displaced in 1974 from their villages in Karpasia but some chose to stay in the "enclaves", some of whom "choosing" to move after the establishment of the unrecognized "Turkish Republic of northern Cyprus" ("TRNC") in 1983. Maronites have always had access to their properties "on the other side" and many of them have repossessed them since the borders opened in 2003. Due to their relative ease of access to "the other side", sealed off from 1974 to 2003 for other Cypriots, the Maronites have been viewed with a degree of suspicion by both Greek and Turkish Cypriot communities, with little understanding.

REFERENCES

An, A. (2009). The Socio-cultural Relationship of the Armenian and Turkish Cypriots. In A. Varnava, N. Coureas, & M. Elia (Eds.), *The Minorities of Cyprus: Development Patterns and the Identity of the Internal-Exclusion* (pp. 282–298). Newcastle-upon-Tyne: Cambridge Scholars Publishing.

Anderson, B. (1983). *Imagined Communities.* London: Verso.

Bryant, R. (2004). *Imagining the Modern: The Cultures of Nationalism in Cyprus.* London: I.B. Tauris.

Constantinou, C. (2007). Aporias of Identity: Bicommunalism, Hybridity and the Cyprus Problem. *Cooperation and Conflict, 42*(3), 247–270.

Constantinou, C. (2009). Cyprus, Minority Politics and Surplus Ethnicity. In A. Varnava, N. Coureas, & M. Elia (Eds.), *The Minorities of Cyprus: Development Patterns and the Identity of the Internal-Exclusion* (pp. 361–372). Newcastle-upon-Tyne: Cambridge Scholars Publishing.

Demetriou, O. (2007). To Cross or Not to Cross? Subjectivization and the Absent State in Cyprus. *Journal of the Royal Anthropological Institute, 13*(4), 987–1006.

Demetriou, O. (2014). 'Struck by the Turks': Reflections on Armenian Refugeehood in Cyprus. *Patterns of Prejudice, 48*(2), 167–181.

Gilroy, P. (2004). *After Empire: Melancholia or Convivial Culture?* London and New York: Routledge.

Hill, G. (1949). *A History of Cyprus* (4 Vols.). Cambridge: Cambridge University Press.

Kasbarian, S. (2006). *Rooted and Routed: The Contemporary Armenian Community in Cyprus and Lebanon.* Ph.D. dissertation, School of Oriental and African Studies, London.

Kasbarian, S. (2009a). The Armenian Community in Cyprus at the Beginning of the 21st Century: From Insecurity to Integration. In A. Varnava, N. Coureas, & M. Elia (Eds.), *The Minorities of Cyprus: Development Patterns and the Identity of the Internal-Exclusion* (pp. 175–191). Newcastle-upon-Tyne: Cambridge Scholars Publishing.

Kasbarian, S. (2009b). Whose Space, Whose Interests? Clashes Within Armenian Diasporic Civil Society. *The Armenian Review, 51*(1–4), 81–109.

Kasbarian, S. (2013). Diasporic Voices from the Peripheries—Armenian Experiences on the Margins of Community in Cyprus and Lebanon. *The Cyprus Review, 25*(1), 81–110.

Kasbarian, S. (2015). The 'Others' Within: The Armenians in Cyprus. In A. Gorman & S. Kasbarian (Eds.), *Diasporas of the Modern Middle East: Contextualising Community* (pp. 241–273). Edinburgh: Edinburgh University Press.

Kasbarian, S. (2016). The Myth and Reality of 'Return'—Diaspora in the Homeland. *Diaspora—A Journal of Transnational Studies, 18*(3), 358–381.

Kasbarian, S. (2018). The Politics of Memory and Activism: Armenian Diasporic Reflections on 2015. *Nationalities Papers, 46*(1), 123–143.

Migliorino, N. (2008). *(Re)Constructing Armenia in Lebanon and Syria: Ethnocultural Diversity and the State in the Aftermath of a Refugee Crisis*. Oxford and New York: Berghahn.

Papadakis, Y. (2008). Narrative, Memory and History Education in Divided Cyprus: A Comparison of Schoolbooks on the "History of Cyprus". *History and Memory*, *20*(2), 128–148.

Pattie, S. P. (1997). *Faith in History: Armenians Rebuilding Community*. Washington and London: Smithsonian Institution Press.

Pattie, S. P. (2009). New Life in an Old Community. In A. Varnava, N. Coureas, & M. Elia (Eds.), *The Minorities of Cyprus: Development Patterns and the Identity of the Internal-Exclusion* (pp. 160–174). Newcastle-upon-Tyne: Cambridge Scholars Publishing.

Rogers, E. M. (1999). Georg Simmel's Concept of the Stranger and Intercultural Communication Research. *Communication Theory, 9*(1), 58–74.

Sennett, R. (2009). *The Craftsman*. London: Penguin.

Shiakali, A. (2016). Οι Αρμένιοι της Κύπρου [Armenians of Cyprus]. *Φιλελεύθερος* [Phileleftheros].

Simmel, G. (1950). The Stranger. In K. Wolff (Trans.), *The Sociology of Georg Simmel* (pp. 402–408). New York: Free Press.

Teerling, J., & King, R. (2011). *Cyprus as a Multi-diasporic Space* (Working Paper No. 67). Sussex Centre for Migration Research, University of Sussex.

The Armenian Genocide Through the Cypriot Press 1914–1923 with Reference to Earlier Massacres. (2016). Nicosia: Cassoulides Masterprinters.

The Armenians of Cyprus (Cyprus Religious Groups), Press and Information Office Cyprus.

Theodorou, E., & Symeou, L. (2013). Experiencing the Same but Differently: Indigenous Minority and Immigrant Children's Experiences in Cyprus. *British Journal of Sociology of Education, 34*(3), 354–372.

Tölölyan, K. (2000). Elites and Institutions in the Armenian Transnation. *Diaspora: A Journal of Transnational Studies, 9*(1), 107–135.

Trimikliniotis, N., & Demetriou, C. (2012). Cyprus. In R. Zapta-Barrero & A. Triandafyllidou (Eds.), *Addressing Tolerance and Diversity Discourse in Europe* (pp. 275–293). Barcelona: CIDOB: Barcelona Centre for International Affairs.

Varnava, A. (2009). The Minorities of Cyprus in the *History of Cyprus* Textbook for Lyceum Students: A Critique. In A. Varnava, N. Coureas, & M. Elia (Eds.), *The Minorities of Cyprus: Development Patterns and the Identity of the Internal-Exclusion* (pp. 299–313). Newcastle-upon-Tyne: Cambridge Scholars Publishing.

Varnava, A., Coureas, N., & Elia, M. (Eds.). (2009). *The Minorities of Cyprus: Development Patterns and the Identity of the Internal-Exclusion*. Newcastle-upon-Tyne: Cambridge Scholars Publishing.

CHAPTER 10

Turkish Migration into the North of Cyprus and the (Re)Construction of Turkish Cypriot Identity in the Turkish Cypriot Press (1995–2013)

Mustafa Çıraklı

INTRODUCTION

The lingering of the Cyprus conflict between the two main communities of the island has significant implications for the identity politics of the island (Papadakis 2003; Psaltis 2012). In this regard, identity narratives of both the Greek Cypriot and Turkish Cypriot communities rely on representations of the past which reify a certain victimhood and "national struggle for survival". At the same time, given the history of Greek Cypriot aspirations for union with Greece (*enosis*) and the existence of an unrecognized state in the form of the "Turkish Republic of northern Cyprus" ("TRNC") with a strong relationship with Turkey—both on premises of ethnic-kinship and also on grounds for supporting the Turkish Cypriot "national cause" (as the "protector")—there exists a certain "motherland nationalism" premised on primary loyalty to

M. Çıraklı (✉)
Near East University, Nicosia, northern Cyprus
URL: https://neu.edu.tr

© The Author(s) 2018
T. Kyritsi and N. Christofis (eds.), *Cypriot Nationalisms in Context*,
https://doi.org/10.1007/978-3-319-97804-8_10

199

"mainlands" and identification as Greek or Turkish (Psaltis and Cakal 2016). There are also various subversive discourses, often associated with leftist political orientations that aim to resist these superordinate forms of identification with the so-called motherlands and the official narratives of victimhood, promoting instead a Cypriot identity drawing on the local Cypriot traditions and cultural similarity between the Greek and Turkish Cypriots (Loizides 2007).

Another important dimension of the Cyprus issue implicated in identity politics, nonetheless, is the presence of individuals of Turkish origin who have moved to Cyprus from Turkey since 1974. While the Greek Cypriot views on the issue are relatively well-known, the Turkish Cypriot positions and perceptions on Turkish immigrants/settlers[1]—though an important source of contestation (Hatay 2005; Navaro-Yashin 2006; Loizides 2011; Psaltis and Cakal 2016)—remain relatively under-researched. As Psaltis and Cakal (2016) too have underlined, while the Turkish influx since 1974 created an opportunity for interaction between mainland Turks and Turkish Cypriots, Turkey's continued interference in the Turkish Cypriot affairs meant that the settlers/immigrants are perceived as a threat to the cohesion of the Turkish Cypriot community and with many fearing that ever-increasing numbers of immigrants/settlers from Turkey dilute the "Cypriot" character of their identity as well as their community's autonomy.

Accordingly, the chapter provides an account of the ways in which the twin issues of immigration from Turkey and the citizenship status of Turkish settlers were framed within competing discourses on identity in the Turkish Cypriot newspapers which represent key sites of nationalism and identity (re)construction. To that end, the chapter begins by providing a brief overview of the Turkish Cypriot newspapers and their enduring relationship to nationalism and the Cyprus problem. This is followed by a qualitative analysis of a selection of news reports and columns significant to the immigration debate. In order to gain a good understanding of the nature of this environment, the analysis concentrates less on the linguistic (de)construction of particular texts than on the change and continuity in the articulation of core concepts that have been important to particular discourses on immigration, Turkish settlers, and identity. The framing of the populations from Turkey in relation to national identity in the Turkish Cypriot community is analyzed diachronically across two distinct time periods distinguished by Cyprus's accession into the EU, i.e. pre-2004 and post-2004 era respectively. This is followed by a summarizing account which further evaluates the interplay between various framings of immigration, the Turkish settlers and the competing narratives on national identity.

NATIONALISM AND THE TURKISH CYPRIOT MEDIA

The news media are often considered an integral part of a political system, informing, prioritizing and framing events, thus shaping the opinions and society itself (Fairclough 2001; Wodak et al. 2009). Cyprus, and the northern part of the island more specifically, is no exception to this. Discourses articulated in the Turkish Cypriot media, moreover, mirror the mainstream narratives that dominate the political field, which is those preferred by politicians and the political parties. This overriding feature of the media in northern Cyprus as a conduit of political discourse is captured well by the "polarized pluralist model" developed by Hallin and Mancini (2004; see also Papathanassopoulos 2007). In their influential work on media systems across Europe, the authors highlight the main characteristics of this model as consisting of a politically oriented press, high political resonance in journalism, prevalence of the State as an owner and regulator and a high degree of ideological diversity and conflict that is "atypical in a Mediterranean society with a strong role for the state and the political parties" (2004, pp. 68–73).

In this regard, newspapers in northern Cyprus are placed at the heart of the (re)production of the Cyprus conflict, either promoting the status quo to signify Turkishness based on independent statehood and suspicion toward the Greek Cypriot community—or, to the contrary, an oppositional discourse contesting the secessionist, nationalist notion of the political community marked by independent statehood and belonging, premised on Cypriotness. In this context, the media is part of a complex public sphere that forms and redefines collective identity. Indeed, the Turkish Cypriot media (but also its Greek Cypriot counterpart in the south (See Avraamidou and Kyriakides 2015; Christophorou 2010; Christophorou et al. 2010), is enmeshed in pervasive contemporary political economic, social and cultural dynamics marked by the ongoing conflict.

Though implicated in it, the enduring relationship of the Turkish Cypriot newspapers with the Cyprus problem predates the outbreak of the bi-communal violence of the mid-1950s and 1960s and that of the inter-communal fighting which served as a prelude to the de facto partition of the island in 1974. In fact, from their inception toward the end of the nineteenth century, the early Turkish Cypriot newspapers were not only critical opponents of Greek Cypriot demands for *enosis* but were critical in promoting nationalist ideals based on Turkishness. As Nevzat (2005) has shown, in the repressive years of the British colonial administration (1931–1960), the Turkish language newspapers became major platforms for the dissemination of opinion and nationalist propaganda. The emergence of party politics in the early 1970s was another important factor which further politicized the newspapers with the entering of political parties on the scene. One direct outcome of party politics was the setting up of newspapers as party mouthpieces. But a more indirect impact here also relates to a certain opening-up of Turkish Cypriot politics during this period that had previously been inhibited by the unique conditions of the siege—the period during which significant numbers of Turkish Cypriots lived in ethnic enclaves (see Bryant and Hatay 2011). Though not entirely free from the authoritarian grip of the nationalist leadership, the emerging of new political parties which represented—to some degree—diverse agendas and a broad spectrum of opinions also led to a certain diversification of editorial policies of the Turkish Cypriot newspapers from then onwards.

More recently, there has been a further improving of the political climate when the moderate Republican Turkish Party (*Cumhuriyetçi Türk Partisi*, CTP) was elected into office in 2003 which saw the government working together with the "Turkish Cypriot Journalists Association" (*Kıbrıs Türk Gazeteciler Birliği*) to ease the previous restrictions on freedom of access, movement, and coverage (Kahvecioğlu 2008). The improving of press freedoms but also a number of other developments further elaborated below, have in the last decade allowed for an active independent media landscape, regarded as "free" by the latest Freedom House report (2017) with both leftist and rightist newspapers, (some openly critical of the establishment) able to report on highly controversial issues (including the role of the Turkish army) that was once considered "taboo".

The *Yenidüzen* (New Order), for instance, began circulating in 1975 as the mouthpiece for the leftist CTP and has consistently promoted a bi-zonal, bi-communal federation. The *Afrika* (2000) too promotes the reunification of Cyprus but one resulting from a return to the 1960 constitutional order and is also the only Turkish Cypriot daily newspaper that explicitly describes Turkey as an "occupier". The *Kıbrıs* (Cyprus), on the other hand, with the highest circulation in the "TRNC" shifted its position in relation to the Cyprus problem to a moderate, pro-solution and pro-EU stance. The *Halkın Sesi* (Voice of the People) is a center-right newspaper and the longest-surviving Turkish Cypriot daily, having begun publication in 1942. The newspaper played a key role in the promotion of Turkish nationalism and has been a consistent supporter of nationalist policies. *Yeni Volkan* (New Volcano) is on the extreme right of the political spectrum, a highly nationalistic newspaper favoring the *status quo* (or a "two-state solution") and ever closer ties with Turkey.[2]

The apparent diversity and differing ideological standpoints notwithstanding, the role of the State and its intervention in the functioning of news reporting through its centralized news agency, the *Türk Ajansı Kıbrıs* (Turkish Agency Cyprus, TAK) is an important dimension of news reporting which mediates further the relationship between the media and politics in northern Cyprus. The Agency, since its founding in 1975, has served as the primary source of information, enabling the state to disseminate news often reflecting its priorities and political bias. According to Azgin and Baillie (2011, p. 693), TAK's position results from the unique political economy of the Cypriot media, where, among others, "relatively small newspapers cannot ... afford the luxury of independent, investigative journalism". In effect, this has meant that newspapers in the north tend to report heavily on what has been selected from among the press releases provided by the TAK, resulting in a certain uniformity of news across media outlets "with minor changes often made 'in-house' by editing the text or the headline of the agency stories".[3] In this context, the views articulated in commentaries can be considered valuable sites to observe more explicit frames in relation to settlers, immigration, and identity-related discourses. It is also important to note, as Azgin and Baillie (2011, p. 692) have suggested previously, that in the Turkish Cypriot news media (but also to some extent, in the Republic of Cyprus), political columnists play the dual roles of "opinion leader" and "ideological indicator". For this reason, the analysis below focuses on a selection of "hard news" as well as newspaper columns to examine the ways in which various framings of the settlers by the newspapers and their columnists have informed the debate on identity in the Turkish Cypriot community.

MEDIA DISCOURSES ON IMMIGRATION ON THE EVE
OF ANTICIPATED EUROPEAN INTEGRATION

In the aftermath of the de facto partition, the Turkish Cypriot leadership continued to emphasize the "existential threat" imposed by the Greek Cypriot aspirations for *enosis*, and that any form of internal dissent would harm the "national cause" of Turkish Cypriot "survival" on the island (*Zaman* 1975). As such, the opposition newspapers came under heavy attack with such accusations and often labeled as "traitors" when they appeared to take a critical line over the government's handling of domestic problems, or on the broader issues of the Cyprus problem and bilateral relations with Turkey (see, for example, *Bozkurt* 1975; *Zaman* 1976; *Birlik* 1988).

It was precisely within the context of this contestation that identity became a central cleavage of Turkish Cypriot politics, rendering the newspapers a key site where two competing visions of national/collective identity strived for hegemony. While the nationalist, establishment newspapers such as the *Halkın Sesi* and the *Birlik* (Unity) promoted the Turkishness discourse which construed the Turkish Cypriot community as part of the "greater Turkish nation" and the Greek Cypriots as the threatening "other", the newspapers of the leftist opposition such as the *Yenidüzen* and the *Ortam* (Ethos) increasingly critical of the leadership's handling of domestic problems as well as what they saw as its intransigence stance in Cyprus negotiations under the guise of Turkish nationalism, began promoting an alternative notion of identity, emphasizing the distinct "Cypriot" character. The ongoing migration from Turkey, in this connection, would serve as a key reference for these competing identity discourses aimed at constructing distinct "imagined communities".

A critical development here was the leadership change within the leftist CTP which saw Özker Özgür becoming the leader of the party in 1976. Under Özgür, the CTP was the first to take the center-stage in voicing radical views on Turkish immigrants and their naturalization as "TRNC" citizens by the Turkish Cypriot leadership. The CTP's arguments, during this time, explicitly linked immigration from Turkey and the citizenship status of Turkish settlers onto wider debates on identity, societal security, and political autonomy. The seismic shift in the political discourse that occurred during this time in relation to immigration further exasperated the ongoing polarization of the media landscape but also intensified the latter's focus on immigration-related issues.

One of the most prominent features of the leftist media narratives on immigration during this time was the production and amplification of a discourse of fear with reference to the scenarios of disorder, loss of sovereignty and political subjugation. Within it, the Turkish settlers/migrants who first began to arrive as part of a "facilitated settlement programme" (Hatay 2005) were frequently presented as "troublemakers", "unassimilable persons" undermining cohesion and cultural authenticity, and as "cheap labor" taking jobs away from the native Turkish Cypriots. These nativist anxieties also helped promote the view that immigration from Turkey was harming the identity of the community by undermining the demographic equilibrium and diluting its autonomy through large-scale granting of citizenships, giving settlers the right to vote in the local and national elections. In fact, Turkish immigrants cum settlers would soon become the new "enemy", in much the same way the nationalist newspapers had often portrayed the Greek Cypriots. Throughout the 1970s and 1980s numerous news stories and commentaries constructed along this identitarian axis associated migration with unemployment, crime, urban deterioration, loss of autonomy, and a certain clash of civilization related to the perceived cultural differences and the supposed inability of the settlers to assimilate into the Turkish Cypriot society (*Ortam* 1985; *Yenidüzen* 1986a, b).

A key proponent of this nativist view was Kutlu Adalı who argued that the very "Cypriot" character of the Turkish Cypriot community was under imminent threat by the influx of Turkish immigrants and their large-scale naturalization. Only weeks before his tragic murder,[4] Adalı would deliver the following observation:

[I]t is claimed that the Turkish government sends trillions of lira each year, which goes straight into Turkish Cypriot pockets [...] It's true that this was the case at the beginning [...] in the period between 1960-64 and 1964-74. During that time, Turkish Cypriots lived on bare subsistence and sustained their [national] struggle with [financial] support from Turkey. But, even though we lived on handouts [...] we were nonetheless a clean, pure, demographically undisturbed and uninflated community of around 100-120 thousand people [...] After 1974 [however] Ankara made sure that the 'door' was fully open to all Turkish nationals. Our country was suddenly swamped [...] So all that [financial] help from Turkey was rationed [...] Those trillions of lira which Turkey had channelled into Cyprus in the past 22 years hasn't only fed Turkish Cypriots but also thousands of Anatolian people transferred from Turkey [...] What's more, while Turkish Cypriots emigrated elsewhere, the number of Turkish nationals transferred from Anatolia has grown considerably; [they are now] the dominant [ethnic] group, controlling almost all aspects of life. There are now hundreds of [settlers], employed at all levels of the public sector. Half of the police force [...] is of Turkish origin. It is now impossible for the 100-120,000 Turkish Cypriots to control their own affairs here. [We] no longer have the numerical strength to elect [our] own MPs. If there was a referendum vote tomorrow [on Cyprus's reunification], Turkish Cypriots wouldn't be able to get an outcome reflecting their decision. (*Yenidüzen* 1996)

By the end of the 1990s and with Cyprus's EU accession now imminent, fierce discussions regarding the future of Cyprus then began to spill over the issue of immigration. The stark warning Kutlu Adalı gave before his murder in relation to the influence of settler constituency on the political outlook of the Turkish Cypriot community, more precisely that "the settler votes would be pivotal in a possible referendum" (*Yenidüzen* 1996) would resonate deeply ahead of the looming referendum on Cyprus's reunification on the eve of its EU accession.

The controversy first blew up in the run-up to the December 2003 legislative elections. At the heart of the citizenship dispute during this time was the fear on the part of the Turkish Cypriot opposition that their chances of ousting the nationalist leadership at December's elections were being undermined by the large-scale granting of citizenship rights to Turkish immigrants. In other words, Turkish settlers who had been given citizenship by the rightist UBP (Nationalist Unity Party) and the center-right DP (Democratic Party) coalition government, the opposition feared, would oppose the "Annan Plan" and torpedo Turkish Cypriot prospects of joining the EU. To this end, the opposition parties set in motion a "citizenship-stripping" battle by applying for a Supreme Court order to overturn 1600 citizenships granted since the last local elections held in June 2002.

While the citizenship suits and subsequent protests were extensively covered by all newspapers (*Kıbrıs* 2003b, c, d; *Halkın Sesi* 2003; *Afrika* 2003), some newspapers also sensationalized on the reports of "long queues", Turkish immigrants "swamping the hospitals (for health certificates required for citizenship applications)" and "violent brawls breaking out" at various government departments describing the scenes as a "disgrace" (*Kıbrıs* 2003a). The *Kıbrıs* newspaper, that began to shift during this time toward a moderate standpoint, also took a more critical stance in its reporting on the citizenship case brought forward by the leftist opposition BDH (Peace and Democracy Movement) headed by Mustafa Akıncı, charging government officials or "those in favor of the status quo" with "treachery", by effectively "betraying the political will of the Turkish Cypriot community" through the granting of illegal citizenships (*Kıbrıs* 2003b).

The *Yenidüzen* newspaper also lashed out on the Turkish Cypriot authorities for the large-scale granting of citizenships ahead of the elections, suggesting that the "arbitrary" naturalizations were a direct policy of "electoral manipulation" which reflected the "panic" at the level of the UBP-DP coalition government. The newspaper also used a picture on its front page comparing the long queues outside immigration and citizenship offices in the north and the south, with Turkish immigrants and Turkish Cypriots waiting to acquire passports and identity documents of the Republic and the "TRNC" respectively, which visually symbolized—according to the newspaper—"the status quo", that is the unresolved Cyprus Question.

Rather remarkably, however, the issue became muted on the eve of the actual elections. This can be explained by the fact that all granting of citizenships was halted following the end of the official campaign period. It can also be suggested that virtually all parties, including those critical of fresh citizenships, tried to appeal to the "settler vote" to secure seats (*Kıbrıs* 2004). To that end, even the *Yenidüzen*, known for its close ties to the CTP, toned down its reporting on the issue—focusing instead on the "clandestine scaremongering tactics" of the hardliners to provoke the Turkish settlers/immigrants against the Annan Plan to sabotage the reunification of Cyprus.

Although there are no reliable figures on the numbers of naturalized settlers with "TRNC" citizenship to establish with certainty the extent of their influence on the outcome of the elections in 2003, the poll results at the end of the race nonetheless showed that many had indeed supported the pro-EU, pro-reunification parties.[5] The CTP emerged as the first party winning nineteen seats and, together with the BDH, the opposition secured twenty-five seats. The right-wing parties collectively won the remainder twenty-five seats. On the negotiations front, talks were once again resumed in Nicosia and the Turkish Cypriot press geared toward the peace process which culminated in the submission of the infamous Annan Plan to simultaneous referenda in May 2004.

The Framing of Turkish Migrants/Settlers in the Post-2004 Period

While the so-called Annan Plan Referendum failed to secure a deal before the whole of Cyprus was admitted into the EU in May 2004, there was still considerable optimism in the northern part of the island that the Turkish Cypriot commitment to reunification and EU membership would ease the community's ostracization and that the international actors would act to bring the Turkish Cypriot community "in from the cold" (*Halkın Sesi* 2004a, b, c, d; *Yenidüzen* 2004a, b, c; *Kıbrıs* 2005a, b). More importantly, the "settler issue" in the immediate aftermath of the referendum was largely downplayed and found substantial coverage only in the years following the referendum and primarily in the context of the new round of negotiations with the election of the moderate Demetris Christofias as the new President of the Republic in 2008. The focus during this time was on the citizenship status of Turkish settlers in a future deal and the newspapers reported widely on the issue by publishing a number of statements made by Turkish Cypriot leadership in relation to the dispute with Christofias. The *Kıbrıs* newspaper in particular, provided extensive coverage of the political discussions that took place in the southern part of the island on the settler issue (often using reports from the Greek Cypriot media outlets; 2008a, b, c), and sometimes with headlines portraying an intolerant, uncompromising stance (2009) going as far as charging the Greek Cypriot politicians with "racism" (2010a).

Yet, a number of developments toward the end of the decade, in relation to the ongoing Cyprus problem, but also in the context of bilateral relations with Turkey would once again place immigration-related anxieties on top of the public and political agendas of the Turkish Cypriot community. The legislative elections held in 2009 reflected the overall dissatisfaction with the domestic policies of the CTP but also a clear disillusionment with such promises of international and European integration. An important outcome of this disappointment in this sense was a reconfiguration of the partisan identity discourses organized once again around the ongoing migration from Turkey and the naturalization of Turkish immigrants. This was foretold in the context of the fierce debates during and following the introduction of an amnesty by the Turkish Cypriot authorities in 2008 to register unauthorized migrant workers (*Kıbrıs* 2008d, e, 2009, see also below).

When the nationalist UBP returned to the office the following year, the controversy would escalate further. The *Afrika* newspaper during this time was particularly vocal in its criticism of the UBP government's citizenship policy. In one particular headline, the newspaper claimed that the demographic outlook of the northern part of the island was undergoing a complete overhaul and that the process of "Turkification" was in full swing following the election of Derviş Eroğlu as the new Turkish Cypriot leader (*Afrika* 2010a). Its editorial also argued that Turkish Cypriots were now a minority largely thanks to the opposition who had now embraced the settlers as the "new Cypriots" and sponsored their citizenship rights (ibid.). A population census which was held in 2011, was described by *Afrika* as a "sham", with the paper also leading calls for civil disobedience and minimum cooperation with the authorities leading the census (*Afrika* 2011b).

In one particularly fierce article, published the day after the census, Şener Levent, a senior *Afrika* columnist mocked the authorities by telling them to "count him out" (*Afrika* 2011c). More specifically, the article amplified the settlers' supposed cultural distinctness in relation to the "Cypriot culture" with reference to a number of famous Turkish Cypriot personalities, thus construing a distinction between the "natives" and the "settlers" and ultimately suggesting that the authorities "don't bother counting the natives" (ibid.). Not surprisingly, following the announcement of the results, the census was dismissed as "unreliable" (*Afrika* 2011d) and the same columnist would later claim that it was only a "cover-up" since Turkey would never reveal "the true extent of the population transfer it has carried out since 1974" (*Afrika* 2011e).

The so-called Survival Rallies organized during this time by a group of trade unions and opposition parties—largely in reaction to austerity measures orchestrated by Turkey—were key to bring further media attention onto the issue (*Kıbrıs* 2010a, b). In its coverage of the second rally in March 2011, the *Kıbrıs* newspaper, which had limited its attention on the status of settlers in the context of the Cyprus talks in the post-referendum period, began to highlight the ongoing controversy surrounding the issue (2011a). Citing previous census data, the paper claimed that the number of people on the electoral roll had grown twofold between 1976 and 2005 and that "no one knows of the precise immigration figures" (2011b). During this time, heated parliamentary debates on citizenship and a further amnesty for illegal migrants in 2011, which ensued in the context of the rallies, newspapers continued to report on parties' and civil society's positions—official responses were also extensively reported by the *Kıbrıs* and to a lesser extent by the *Afrika* (*Kıbrıs* 2011c, d, e, f, g; *Afrika* 2011a). Following the victory of the CTP in the 2013 legislative elections and with a pledge to introduce stricter criteria for the granting of new citizenships,[6] the debate would lessen in intensity though the newspapers continued to report on the issue, focusing in particular on the reaction from the immigrant civil society organizations (*Kıbrıs* 2013).

A key issue which brought the "settler issue" under spotlight once again was the austerity measures formulated by Ankara. Envisaging the austerity measures, the latest financial protocol with Ankara was signed in December 2012 and included a drastic reduction in the size of the public sector, but also the privatization of key Turkish Cypriot assets including electricity, telecommunications, and harbors.[7] The Turkish Cypriot opposition, including several trade unions opposed the protocol from the outset and claimed that it was a mere pretext to facilitate the transfer of strategic state-owned assets onto Ankara's control, more particularly to those with close ties to the ruling AKP (*Afrika* 2010b, c, d; *Kıbrıs* 2010a). More importantly, such austerity measures were tied to prevalent fears related to loss of identity. In this sense, privatization of public assets was seen as threatening Turkish Cypriot autonomy by further consolidating Ankara's control in its domestic affairs.

These anxieties were employed by the Cypriotness discourse which conceived and emphasized identity once again within an explicitly securitized framework. In other words, Turkish Cypriot identity was defined here in existential terms as the fundamental stumbling block of the political community and with reference to its precarious autonomy that was threatened by Turkey through a double whammy of austerity/privatization policies and the large-scale naturalization of Turkish nationals (*Afrika* 2012a). While the fierce debates on the austerity measures were reported widely by all newspapers in news form, the frames that were employed in representing "the settler issue" were articulated predominantly in the editorials and in the views of the columnists.

A particularly outspoken critic of the "occupation regime" but also the presence of populations from Turkey, the *Afrika* newspaper criticized the "Survival Rallies" for not taking an explicit stance on "Turkey's occupation of northern Cyprus" (2012a, b, c). Nonetheless, the paper's narrative still tied the austerity measures and the privatization plans to the issues of identity and citizenship, arguing that the new privatizations would deliver the "fatal blow" to the Turkish Cypriot community (*Afrika* 2013b). Taking a step further, an article published in the *Afrika* newspaper claimed that as a result of the numerical superiority of the settler constituency, all MPs in the future would be of Turkish origin (*Afrika* 2012d).

For Ali Kişmir, another *Afrika* columnist, large-scale naturalizations, granting of residency rights and allowing large numbers of settlers/immigrants to stay in the north not only undermined the Turkish Cypriot identity but imposed a significant socio-economic burden on the community. The line of argument introduced here, in relation to resource distribution is particularly telling. In this narrative, the settlers were portrayed as "debilitating people", standing outside of the natives, utilizing the unjust gains provided by the system.

By construing the settlers as backward in socio-economic terms, an axis is established here placing settlers between the two extreme categories of "land grabbers" with reference to Greek Cypriot properties or "scroungers", emphasizing in either case that they have benefitted unjustly from the status quo, given tremendous advantages and benefits on the one hand, or as a drain on scarce sources on the other. The latter was further emphasized in the context of austerity and privatization policies in which immigrants/settlers were blamed for imposing a high burden on the state's distributive capacities. Indeed, such views were articulated in an article published on the newspaper on the planned privatization of the "public electricity authority" (KIBTEK) in which the large numbers of immigrants/settlers were blamed for the shortfall in the electricity production, ultimately suggesting that the price hikes and privatization plans were designed from the outset to sustain an artificially bloated and unnecessarily large population of immigrants/settlers (*Afrika* 2013c). Echoing similar views to Kutlu Adalı cited above, the article also asserted that the financial assistance from Turkey was targeted primarily "toward its own people", hence insufficient to benefit the "native" Turkish Cypriots (*Afrika* 2013c).

The daily *Yenidüzen* too has been a consistent critic of Turkish migration into northern Cyprus and the naturalization of large numbers of Turkish immigrants. Though the paper differed significantly from its rival *Afrika*, in its negation of using the "occupier" label against Turkey, it nonetheless promoted an assertive rhetoric on autonomy which called for less interference from Ankara in Turkish Cypriot affairs. On the settler issue too, the paper featured regular columns on the issues of identity, immigration, and citizenship but charging its criticism toward the right-wing parties in Nicosia and not toward Ankara. Indeed, as Sami Özuslu, one high-profile columnist of the daily put it:

> The citizenship issue in northern Cyprus can be traced back to the Cyprus Problem. We were trying to prove that we were not a "minority" against the Greek Cypriots so [they] followed a deliberate policy of increasing the Turkish population on the island ... The biggest wave was following the war in 1974. Families from Anatolia were encouraged to settle in Cyprus. In the later years, the biggest explosion happened toward the end of the 1980s. During the Özal administration in Turkey, entry with ID cards created a new rush. Immigration or population transfer are not the same as citizenship. But the right-wing governments [in Cyprus] and the clique in charge of the "Cyprus affairs" [in Turkey] made sure that the numbers were boosted also on paper. UBP was the main actor which created the sloppy, lax citizenship regime. (*Yenidüzen* 2013c)

In another article, praising the tighter citizenship laws introduced a year later by the CTP government, the columnist would claim once again that UBP was the main culprit and CTP had always been the party to "apply the brakes" on new citizenships:

> Citizenship policy exemplifies the ideological divide between the two mass parties positioned on the opposite ends of the political spectrum. On the one hand, there is the UBP with its remnant of the 1950s, "head-counting" population policy, guided by the "Turk comes, another Turk goes" practice; on the other hand, there is the CTP which approaches the issue of population transfer from a humanitarian but also legalistic and identity perspective ... The Turkish Cypriot community can no longer bear the burden of 'citizenship' created mostly by the UBP. (*Yenidüzen* 2014)

A similar view was also promoted by another senior columnist and chief editor of the *Yenidüzen* newspaper, Cenk Mutluyakalı. An outspoken critic of the granting of new citizenships to Turkish migrants, Mutluyakalı regularly framed the issue with an existential understanding of autonomy in which naturalization of Turkish migrants was construed a threat to the "political will" of the Turkish Cypriot community. In this understanding, the granting of citizenship rights to Turkish nationals is seen as part of a bigger project to maintain right-wing governments and subsequently to consolidate Ankara's grip over the Turkish

Cypriot community. An interesting feature of this leftist narrative is the distinction it introduces between protecting the rights of the Turkish migrant workers and their children, on the one hand, and obtaining of citizenship rights on the other. This was illustrated in the following argument put forward by Mutluyakalı:

> No one should ignore the bureaucratic discrimination they face [in obtaining work permits], their exploitation [at the hands of illegal "gangmasters"] or denial of their human rights ... they can be granted long-term work permits, residency rights and further easing in setting up their own businesses; granting them citizenship rights [however], is an entirely different matter, a different politics ... and if it's part of a grander operation[sic] to manipulate the political will ... that's when we have to say enough is enough. (*Yenidüzen* 2013a)

A similar concern was also expressed by the same journalist in relation to the unique political context marked by the Cyprus Question, in that "[northern Cyprus] is not like any other country, [the total number of settlers] those that have been naturalized through the Cabinet and the ones that have been transferred now outnumber the natural-born citizens [...] we have to draw a line, [with certain exceptions] all fresh naturalizations should be terminated indefinitely (*Yenidüzen* 2013b)".

Notwithstanding the consistent commitment the leftist newspapers *Afrika* and the *Yenidüzen* displayed to the "immigration threat" narrative, other outlets are divided on the issue and their columnists represent diverse viewpoints. The *Kıbrıs* newspaper is a good example here. An influential daily, the newspaper's editorial policy has also undergone the most profound change during the Annan Plan years from a nationalist to a moderate, pro-EU stance. The newspaper, nonetheless, maintained a balanced and neutral position on the settler issue, allowing a good range of views to be expressed in its columns. In this context, the *Kıbrıs* columnists articulated diverse viewpoints on immigration and citizenship—divided along competing discourses on Turkish Cypriot identity.

According to Hasan Hastürer, the socio-cultural changes that had taken place in the northern part of the island since the partition, did not reflect a positive transformation, "something that the Turkish Cypriots themselves have undertaken" and that with the constant undermining of those cultural values, it was inevitable the community "will soon be snubbed [by the newcomers] on their own land" (*Kıbrıs* 2014). Another column written by the same author, in the context of the ongoing peace negotiations was even more alarming. In it, the columnist predicted that failure to reach a deal in current talks would result in a "population boom" in the north through new wave of naturalizations (*Kıbrıs* 2016). More specifically, the commentary claimed that the new naturalizations would almost inevitably be imposed from Turkey, using "labour market shortages" and "economic growth" as pretexts and that no Turkish Cypriot government would be able to resist pressure from Ankara to pave the way for fresh citizenships. Should the Cyprus problem linger beyond 2017, the article also projected that the population of the north, over the next several decades would surpass that of the Republic.

As indicated above, however, another high-profile columnist of the same newspaper consistently promoted a nationalist understanding of identity, premised on Turkishness. Indeed, what is at the heart of the identity crisis, for the prominent columnists of the newspaper, such as Ahmet Tolgay, is a "rejection of Turkish identity" and "a peculiar form of racism unique to the Turkish Cypriot community" (*Kıbrıs* 2015a). As the columnist would elaborate further in a particularly telling oped on Cypriotness:

> As for the so-called "Greek-speaking" and "Turkish-speaking Cypriots". This is a utopic idea, forged in order to create a "Cypriot race". It is a dangerous virus that is being spread by the Greek imperialist propaganda. It is very clear that those living in the south [Greek Cypriots] never act in the spirit of Cypriotness. They are guided by the spirit of Hellenism. Yet they expect from us, in fact they insist, that we cut off our ties with our roots, our history, our ethnic values, tradition and culture and with [our motherland] Turkey. The [so-called intellectuals among us] are trotting along a path to destroy the 445-year-old Turkish culture in Cyprus. (*Kıbrıs* 2015b)

Perhaps more remarkably, the columnist's views on Turkish settlers also tied the issue onto an insular understanding of human rights further propped up with neo-liberal undertones. To that end, and in relation to the immigration reform planned by the CTP-DP coalition government, the columnist wrote:

> These [systematic] blows to our economy are also devoid of any human rights concerns. The flight of thousands of Turkish origin migrants, those that form the backbone of our human capital — and the labor crisis [their return back to Turkey] has triggered — is repeatedly ignored. Those who

didn't leave voluntarily are now being forced to leave through this cynical immigration ploy. There are numerous associations representing sectoral interests but we lack an organization to resist such gross undermining of human rights. (*Kıbrıs* 2015c)

A sharp Turkishness rhetoric, framing the settler issue in essentialist, ethno-nationalist terms, was also found in the columns of the *Halkın Sesi* newspaper. In this regard, the presence of Turkish immigrants and their naturalization were viewed within an explicitly nationalist framework characterized by the much-cherished Turkish Cypriot relationship with Turkey and on the basis of ethnic-kinship. Perhaps more remarkably and largely due to the editorial legacy of the newspaper promoting a nationalist stance on the Cyprus conflict, the views expressed in its columns on issues relating to citizenship and immigration also tended to frame the presence of settlers more explicitly within the context of the ongoing negotiations.

In this sense, "boosting the numbers" through new citizenships to ensure a numerically stronger Turkish Cypriot community was considered a "crucial policy" in order to secure better consociational returns on the negotiating table, but also to "undermine Greek Cypriot negotiating position which claims sole ownership of the whole island based on their numerical superiority ... offering, in turn, mere minority rights for the Turkish Cypriot community" (*Halkın Sesi* 2015). A number of economic arguments were also echoed in this vein that "larger population which can facilitate economic growth but also to generate more tax revenue in order to ensure the sustainability of the 'pensions fund' and to stop the worrying demise of state-run industries" (*Halkın Sesi* 2012).

CONCLUSION

Almost forty years after their first arrival following the de facto partition of the island, the presence of populations from Turkey (and their descendants) continues to underpin identity narratives on both sides of the island. As the analysis above has shown, the narratives utilized by Turkish Cypriot newspapers and their columnists in framing the presence of populations from Turkey are shaped by the prevailing, rival discourses of Turkishness and Cypriotness aimed at creating distinct "imagined communities". A number of developments, most notably the prospects of EU accession had an important effect in the representation of the "settler issue" particularly within the Cypriotness discourse as a certain "challenge"—with reference to the precarious nature of the community's autonomy—which threatened Turkish Cypriot desires for change. While such anxieties were temporarily muted in the post-referendum period, during which headlines were dominated by expectations of being welcomed in by the international community, the settler issue continued to lurk in the background and became a bone of contention once again in the context of Ankara's recent austerity agenda. The glaring absence of a paradigmatic change in terms of how the settler issue has been presented in the Turkish Cypriot newspapers, and the persistence of traditional, existentialist anxieties, can be explained by the structural and historical features of the settler issue—most notably its linkage to the bilateral relations with Turkey as well as the contingent nature of the "window of opportunity" represented by EU membership that was made available. Such features are inextricably linked to the pervasiveness of the unresolved Cyprus Problem with important implications for the construction of inclusive identities. Indeed, the need to promote inclusiveness has largely been ignored as the issue was framed in the over-imposing context of the Cyprus Question. Against this background, and considering too that the viability of any solution to the conflict will also depend on its ability to address these issues, there is no doubt that identity-related debates around migration from Turkey will continue to shape the contours of the island's politics for the foreseeable future.

Notes

1. It is an analytically futile attempt to maintain a neat distinction between settlers and immigrants in the context of a frozen conflict as any such attempt carry the potential of disavowing the past injustice and simultaneously distorting the diverse and subjected nature of migration into a territory even though the sovereignty of the territory in question is disputed. To this end, the study retains both categories i.e. "immigrant" and "settler" with the latter generally designated for the Turkish nationals holding "TRNC" citizenship. Though imperfect, this categorization should not detract from the fact that the primarily focus of the investigation will be the ongoing competition between different ideas about the nature of the migration and the presence of populations from Turkey.

2. Only the *Yenidüzen, Afrika, Kıbrıs* and *Halkın Sesi* were examined in this study.

3. According to Kahvecioğlu (2008), TAK produced bulletins account for as much as 85% of the content that appear in the Turkish Cypriot newspapers.

4. Before his murder, Adalı took up the issue of an alleged armed raid to a *St. Barnabas* monastery which involved the Turkish Cypriot Civilian Defense Organization (*Kıbrıs Türk SIvil Savunma Teşkilati*) and the head of that organization, a Turkish army officer named Galip Mendi. It is widely believed that this led to his murder. In addition, there are many indicators which have surfaced since that links the murder to other extrajudicial killings, kidnappings, bombings and criminal activities carried out by the *Gladio* in Turkey. Indeed, a series of trials in the 1990s launched in the aftermath of the so-called "Susurluk Scandal" linked several of the names with Cyprus and the issues Adalı was writing about as part of the picture.

5. For some estimates see *Kathimerini* (2003); this was suggested earlier by the Chairman of the "TRNC Immigrants' Association" in an interview with the *Cyprus Weekly* (2003).

6. The bill was created in 2015 and restricted the length of the work permits to a maximum of three years following which the permit holder would be required to stay abroad for a minimum period of 90 days before becoming eligible to reapply. But with a change in government before a vote could take place, it was never ratified.

7. The Protocol stipulated that the Turkish Cypriot government had agreed to implement the bilateral economic programme entitled "Towards a Sustainable Economy 2013–2015" in order to reduce its balance deficit to 315 ml Turkish Lira (TL); controversial policy measures included the privatization of the harbors and the electricity authority (Articles 5.2.4.2.1 and 5.2.5.2 respectively) and market liberalization in telecommunications; (5.2.4.2.3), in "TRNC" Prime Minister's Office (2013).

References

Avraamidou, M., & Kyriakides, C. (2015). Media Nationalism and the Negotiation of Inter-ethnic Peace in Cyprus. *Global Media Journal: Mediterranean Edition, 10*(2), 1–21.

Azgin, B., & Baillie, M. (2011). Disturbing the Peace: Gender, Journalism and the Cypriot Press. *Journalism Studies, 12*(5), 689–704.

Bryant, R., & Hatay, M. (2011). Guns and Guitars: Simulating Sovereignty in a State of Siege. *American Ethnologist, 28*(4), 631–649.

Christophorou, C. (2010). Greek Cypriot Media Development and Politics. *The Cyprus Review, 22*(2), 235–245.

Christophorou, C., Sahin, S., & Pavlou, S. (2010). *Media Narratives, Politics and the Cyprus Problem* (PRIO Report 1-2010). Available online at http://eprints.lincoln.ac.uk/7679/1/Media_Narratives,_Politics_and_the_Cyprus_Problem.pdf. Last accessed 5 July 2016.

Cyprus Weekly. (2003, August 8). Settlers Will Vote Against Denktash.

218   M. ÇIRAKLI

Fairclough, N. (2001). *Language and Power* (2nd Ed.). Harlow, London: Pearson.

Freedom House. (2017). *Report on Cyprus*. Available online at https://freedomhouse.org/report/freedom-world/2017/cyprus. Last accessed 30 Aug 2017.

Hallin, D. C., & Mancini, P. (2004). *Comparing Media Systems: Three Models of Media and Politics*. Cambridge: Cambridge University Press.

Hatay, M. (2005). *Beyond Numbers: An Inquiry into the Political Integration of Turkish 'Settlers' in northern Cyprus* (PRIO, Report 4/2005). Available online at https://www.prio.org/Programmes/Extensions/PRIO-Cyprus-Center/Publications/. Last accessed 20 Aug 2016.

Kahvecioğlu, H. (2008). *Country Report—Cyprus. Association of European Journalists*. Full report available online at http://www.aej-uk.org/survey.htm. Last accessed 30 Aug 2016.

Kathimerini. (2003, October 24). 54,000 Settlers in Cyprus Poll.

Loizides, N. (2007). Ethnic Nationalism and Adaptation in Cyprus. *International Studies Perspectives, 8*(2), 172–189.

Loizides, N. (2011). Contested Migration and Settler Politics in Cyprus. *Political Geography, 30*, 391–401.

Navaro-Yashin, Y. (2006). De-ethnicizing the Ethnography of Cyprus: Political and Social Conflict between Turkish Cypriots and Settlers from Turkey. In Y. Papadakis, N. Peristianis, & G. Welz (Eds.), *Divided Cyprus: Modernity, History, and an Island in Conflict* (pp. 84–99). Bloomington, IN: Indiana University Press.

Nevzat, A. (2005). *Nationalism Amongst the Turks of Cyprus: The First Wave*. Oulu: University of Oulu.

Papadakis, Y. (2003). Nation, Narrative and Commemoration: Political Ritual in Divided Cyprus. *History and Anthropology, 14*(3), 253–270.

Papathanassopoulos, S. (2007). The Mediterranean/Polarized Pluralist Media Model Countries: Introduction. In G. Terzis (Ed.), *European Media Governance: National and Regional Dimensions*. Bristol: Intellect Books.

Psaltis, C. (2012). Culture and Social Representations: A Continuing Dialogue in Search for Heterogeneity in Social Developmental Psychology. *Culture & Psychology, 18*, 375–390.

Psaltis, C., & Cakal, H. (2016). Social Identity in a Divided Cyprus. In S. McKeown, et al. (Eds.), *Understanding Peace and Conflict Through Social Identity Theory* (pp. 229–244). New York: Springer.

TRNC Prime Minister's Office. (2013). *Ekonomik Program 2013–2015*. Full text available online at: http://www.kktcbasbakanlik.org/Portals/1031/EKONOMIK_PROGRAM-2013-15.pdf. Last accessed 22 Sept 2014.

Wodak, R., et al. (2009). *The Discursive Construction of National Identity*. Edinburgh: Edinburgh University Press.

Newspapers

Afrika 9/07/2000, 13/03/2003, 30/04/2010a, 1/07/2010b, 5/07/2010c, 30/07/2010d, 29/07/2011a, 26/11/2011b, 29/11/2011c, 10/12/2011d, 12/12/2011e, 31/01/2012a, 4/02/2012b, 27/03/2012c, 5/07/2012d, 6/01/2013a, 23/03/2013b, 21/11/2013c.

Birlik 14/1/1988.

Bozkurt 31/8/1975.

Halkın Sesi 10/10/2003, 19/05/2004a, 17/06/2004b, 18/06/2004c, 20/06/2004d, 19/06/2012, 13/02/2015.

Kıbrıs 8/10/2003a, 10/10/2003b, 15/10/2003c, 4/11/2003d, 7/04/2004, 7/10/2005a, 9/10/2005b, 4/05/2008a, 15/05/2008b, 25/05/2008c, 17/09/2008d, 13/11/2008e, 8/03/2009, 15/10/2010a, 16/10/2010b, 3/03/2011a, 4/03/2011b, 12/03/2011c, 24/03/2011d, 1/04/2011e, 3/05/2011f, 4/06/2011 g, 24–30/10/2013, 21/12/2014, 04/09/2015a, 17/09/2015b, 30/12/2015c, 22/04/2016.

Ortam 29/5/1985.

Yenidüzen 20/01/1986a, 10/02/1986b, 2/04/1996, 28/04/2004a, 10/05/2004b, 21/05/2004c, 19/04/2013a, 26/05/2013b, 26/09/2013c, 24/07/2014.

Zaman 19/9/1975, 28/6/1976.

CHAPTER 11

The Development of Prejudice in Children: The Case of Cyprus

Maria Ioannou and Angelos P. Kassianos

INTRODUCTION

In this chapter, we discuss the concept of prejudice, broadly defined as a generalized antipathy toward a social group (Allport 1954), and how it develops in children through the lens of different developmental theories. We use these theoretical foundations to examine the case of Cyprus in relation to prejudice development among Greek and Turkish Cypriot children. In the first part of the chapter, we discuss concepts adjacent to prejudice such as category awareness, identification with one's own category, preference for one's own social group, and discrimination against other social groups, and we present the key social psychological theories of prejudice development in children. The second part of the chapter is devoted to presenting the case of Cyprus as a context of ethnic conflict and inter-ethnic prejudice. We review the main studies aiming to track the onset as well as the nature of prejudice among Greek and Turkish Cypriot children and critically discuss these studies while highlighting the specificities of the Cypriot sociopolitical context. In the last part of the

M. Ioannou (✉)
University College Groningen, Groningen, The Netherlands

A. P. Kassianos
University College London, London, UK

© The Author(s) 2018
T. Kyritsi and N. Christofis (eds.), *Cypriot Nationalisms in Context*,
https://doi.org/10.1007/978-3-319-97804-8_11

221

chapter, we discuss how existing theories of prejudice development can not only inform the case of Cyprus but can also be informed by it. We conclude by offering a set of recommendations about addressing prejudice in childhood through research and education.

Development of Prejudice in Children

Children begin to behave as social actors, meaning that they begin to be aware of social categories and to identify themselves as members of a social category, from as early as three to five years old (Clark and Clark 1947; Piaget and Weil 1951). Category awareness and identification with selected categories go hand in hand with the subsequent formation of concepts, beliefs, attitudes, and behaviors toward groups outside one's own.

Brown (2010) in a comprehensive report on the development of prejudice in children, offers a distinction between (a) children's awareness of social categories; (b) their choice of categories with which they identify and express preference for; and (c) their full-blown intergroup attitudes and behavior. Even though these stages are, at least from a certain age onwards, interlinked, this distinction is helpful in terms of understanding how prejudice transforms from a mere preference for (or bias toward) one's own group, the ingroup (ingroup preference) to the outward discrimination against other, typically adversarial, groups, that are construed as outgroups (outgroup derogation).

Age, gender, and ethnicity are the most dominant categories during the first years of children's lives. In a classic study, Clark and Clark (1947) presented white and colored children with two or more dolls, one of them of white color and another one of brown color, and asked them to point to the one that looked more like a white or a colored child. The findings of their study showed that 75% of the children at the age of three correctly pointed at their own ethnicity's doll and this elevated to 90% at the age of five.

Studies show that ethnicity is the most prevalent source of categorization in young children, which speaks to the centrality of ethnicity as a category of reference. When Brown and Yee (1988) for example, presented pictures representing different ethnicity, gender, and age groups to children, they found that children at the age of three made no distinctions between these photographs but by the age of five, ethnicity emerged as a criterion for categorization. This illustrates that the five-year-olds were better at grouping pictures based on ethnicity rather than based on gender and age.

Awareness of own country and knowledge about other countries are recorded at about 5 years of age, which is when children start to classify themselves as members of their own national group (Piaget and Weil 1951). By mid-childhood (ages eight to nine), children's knowledge of the people who belong to their own group expands considerably. By age ten, if not earlier, children have knowledge of the main stereotypical traits that are attributed to members of their own national group (Piaget and Weil 1951).

Apart from being aware of the existence of categories, young children also show a preference for their own group. In a study by Tajfel et al. (1972), for example, Scottish, English and Israeli children were asked to categorize a set of photographs into two categories (English and Scottish or Oriental and European) and rate how much they liked the look of the individuals portrayed in the photos. The results showed a clear preference for one's own nationality. Other studies conducted in Israel (Bar-Tal 1996; Teichman et al. 2007), Australia (Nesdale 1999) and Great Britain (Bennett et al. 1998), confirm that strong ingroup identification *and* ingroup preference emerge in early childhood.

Ingroup preference goes hand in hand with a liking of the ingroup (and its members), which, as will be discussed next, can give way to a comparison with outgroups and can culminate to intergroup bias and outgroup derogation. Intergroup bias refers to a clear preference of the ingroup in comparison to outgroups (Hewstone et al. 2002) and it typically takes the form of liking the ingroup more than the outgroup (Brewer 2001). Under some circumstances, ingroup liking can be accompanied by outgroup derogation, that is having negative attitudes and actively discriminating against an outgroup, as opposed to just liking it less than one's own group (Hewstone et al. 2002).

While category awareness and initial identification may be regarded as universal processes (taking place invariably across individuals and contexts), the degree to which children identify with their chosen categories and the extent to which mere ingroup preference is also accompanied by negative outgroup attitudes and discrimination, is more likely to be affected by contextual factors. Such factors include the presence of conflict between two social groups or being raised in an environment where one is exposed and thereby influenced by the attitudes held by family and peers, or communicated via formal schooling and the media.

Psychological theories of prejudice development in children differ in the emphasis they place on contextual factors affecting prejudice development. A presentation of the main social psychological theories of prejudice development in children follows.

SOCIAL PSYCHOLOGICAL THEORIES OF PREJUDICE DEVELOPMENT IN CHILDREN

Sociocognitive Theory of Development

Until recently, the most influential theories of prejudice development adopted a social cognition approach to prejudice development, which largely draws from the cognitive-developmental theory of Jean Piaget. Inspired by Piaget's work, Aboud (1988) formulated the *Sociocognitive theory of development* via which she proposed that the stage of cognitive development is the main determinant of children's attitudes and behaviors toward outgroup members. According to this theory, at earlier cognitive stages younger children are more egocentric and tend to overestimate categorization. This leads them to conceptualize their social environment using distinct categories whose differences are exaggerated. Aboud (1988) contends that there is a decline in the expression of prejudice after the age of seven, which coincides with a shift to more advanced stages of cognitive development. At this age, children can understand that members of different social groups like Blacks [sic] and Whites can be both good and bad. In older ages, when their cognitive system matures, children are able to recognize similarities across groups and differences within their own group while being more capable to empathize and to take other people's and groups' perspectives into account. Additionally, older children stop to focus merely on group-differences, and they develop the ability to make social judgments also on the basis of individual characteristics.

While the findings of a number of studies provide support to the developmental predictions of this theory (e.g., Bar-Tal 1996; Doyle and Aboud 1995), the critiques of the Sociocognitive theory point out that it underestimates or does not take into account the role of the context in the formation and evolvement of cognitive processes (Verkuyten 2004; Verkuyten and Thijs 2001). We present next approaches or theories that acknowledge the role of social context in prejudice development and attempted to factor it in their theorizing.

Social Learning Approach

The *social learning approach*, influenced by Albert Bandura's social learning theory, contends that humans may come with a propensity to prejudge, stereotype, and discriminate, but they are also brought up in an environment which influences the content of their social images. According to this approach, children are influenced by their social surroundings (e.g., peers, family, media, and school) in forming an image about their own groups as well as about other groups. For example, Gordon Allport (1954) in his seminal book *The Nature of Prejudice* suggested that children first tend to copy and then internalize what they are exposed to in their environment. Along with this proposition comes the prediction that prejudice increases with age, when children start to internalize others' attitudes. This prediction is in direct opposition to the sociocognitive theory's prediction that prejudice declines in older ages because of cognitive maturity.

Social Identity Theory of Development (SIDT)

The SIDT, developed by Nesdale (1999) draws primarily on the Social Identity Theory of Tajfel and Turner (1979). At the heart of the account of the Social Identity Theory is that intergroup attitudes that are a product of individuals' identification with a social category (ingroup) and that the *strength of identification* with their ingroup will dictate the nature of the relationship with other social groups (outgroups). Children, like adolescents and adults, have a fundamental need to belong that motivates them to become members of different social groups (Nesdale 1999). Belonging to a particular social group relates directly to children's sense of self-worth and therefore the ingroup's social standing largely determines their self-esteem. To maintain positive self-esteem or enhance self-esteem, children develop the need to belong to high-standing/successful social groups. To achieve a positive image for the ingroup, individuals either favor their ingroup and/or derogate against outgroups that are in direct competition with their own group. Nesdale (1999) and Nesdale and Brown (2004) argue that in more competitive contexts and when under threat (from outgroups), identification with ingroup is even stronger, and the likelihood of outward discrimination against outgroups, as opposed to mere ingroup preference, is even larger.

Finally, according to SIDT, the developmental course of prejudice in children can be divided into four stages: (a) the undifferentiated stage during which social category cues are not salient (two–three years of age); (b) the ethnic awareness stage during which children become aware of their ingroup and identify with it. Since ethnicity is one of the most salient markers of group categorization, awareness of and identification with own ethnic group is observed early on (three–five years of age); (c) the ethnic preference stage at which children demonstrate preference for their ingroup without any particular outgroup focus (six–seven years of age); (d) ethnic prejudice stage where a shift from ingroup preference to outgroup derogation can be observed (ages of seven and above). For outgroup derogation to occur in the latter stage, certain conditions need to be met, like for example ethnic constancy (the understanding that one's identity is unchangeable) and presence of competition, confliction, and threat from other groups.

Societal-Social-Cognitive-Motivational Theory (SSCMT)

Barrett (2007) and Barrett and Davis (2008) developed a more comprehensive model that strives to take into account all the possible factors which impact children's attitudes toward other groups. This led to the formation of the Societal-social-cognitive-motivational theory (SSCMT), which draws largely from all of the aforementioned theories. The SSCMT is in agreement with the social learning approach, as to the claim that all children grow up and socialize in unique societal environments, which are shaped by historical, geographical, economic, and other circumstances. These circumstances shape the relationships between the children's ingroup and relevant outgroups. The children become aware, and in the long run they become bearers, of these intergroup norms as these are communicated to them primarily by their parents and by their teachers via a number of ways including oral histories, school textbooks, and mass media.

In agreement with the sociocognitive theory and the Social Identity Theory, Barrett (2007) and Barrett and Davis (2008) argue that which information the children are going to attend to will be influenced by the children's personal characteristics, as for example the level of identification with their ingroup, level of cognitive development, and other motivational and affective processes like their ability for empathy and perspective taking.

The Case of Cyprus

Years of turmoil between the Greek and Turkish Cypriot communities in Cyprus culminated in a coup d'état backed up by the Greek military in 1974 and a Turkish military operation days later. These interventions led to the geographical division of the island across ethnic lines. In practice, this meant a complete physical separation of the two communities and their social, emotional, and political alienation (Zembylas et al. 2011). The division prevented any form of contact between the two communities who became increasingly estranged. This non-communication provided fertile ground for the cultivation of different social representations within the two communities particularly with regards to *the Cyprus Question* and the country's history (Makriyianni and Psaltis 2007; Psaltis 2011). Education has been one of the mediums used to propagate each side's narrative (Mertan 2011).

According to the narrative that is promoted especially by formal education, in the Greek Cypriot community, Turks are the enemy for they invaded and occupied a section of the island and because they prevent peace from prevailing (Papadakis 2008). Spyrou (2002) conducted ethnographic fieldwork in Greek Cypriot schools where he asked primary school children to name a group of people who are very different from them. The vast majority of the children mentioned the Turks. When the researcher asked them to write down the opposites of a number of words, including the word "Turks", the most frequent responses were "Cypriots" (equated with "Greek Cypriots"), "Greeks", "[Christian] Orthodox", and "good" (p. 264). Furthermore, the children described Turks with the use of very negative adjectives such as "barbarians", "heartless", "dirty", "illiterate", "rapists", and "murderers" (p. 264).

Turkish Cypriots, on the other hand, are perceived by most Greek Cypriot children as victims and sufferers, much like Greek Cypriots, because of Turkey's offensive policies (Spyrou 2002). As Spyrou concluded, children see Turkish Cypriots as "different kinds of people" (p. 266) in comparison to mainland Turks and they are not perceived as the real problem in Cyprus. Another set of findings of this study showed that the categories "Turks" and "Turkish Cypriots" were not in reality independent of each other and were rather fluid in terms of their content. For example, Greek Cypriot children classified Rauf Denktaş, the Turkish Cypriot leader at the time, as a Turk (even though he was Turkish Cypriot), precisely because he was seen as "evil" just like the

"Turkish occupiers" (Spyrou 2002, p. 266). As other studies showed, the distinction between "Turks" and "Turkish Cypriots" is, in fact, rarely made (Zembylas and Bekerman 2008). Often the word *they* is used by Greek Cypriots to describe everyone living on the other side of the divide (Zembylas and Bekerman 2008).

The mainstream historical narrative in the Turkish Cypriot side is one in which Turkish Cypriots are construed as victims who managed, however, with the help of motherland Turkey to endure the perpetual siege of Greek Cypriots (Lacher and Kaymak 2005). For Turkish Cypriots, Greek Cypriots and not Greeks are the main enemy. Mertan (2011) describes that in school, Turkish Cypriot children are in various ways asked to show their allegiance to Turkey and its symbols while at the same time the derogation and alienation of the "other" is also put forward. She provides as an example of that the increase of the popularity of the Turkish word "Gavur" (infidel), a word used by Muslims to define the non-Muslim adversarial groups, to describe Greek Cypriots.

Ingroup Identification and Prejudice Development Among Greek and Turkish Cypriot Children

The only systematic studies that tracked the development of prejudice in children in Cyprus, were conducted by Stavrinides and Georgiou (2011), in the Greek Cypriot community and Mertan (2011), in the Turkish Cypriot community. These studies were part of a multi-country project aiming at measuring the development of ethnic identification and prejudice in children aged between seven and eleven years.

One of the main goals of the project was to test the contradicting predictions of the different theories of prejudice development in children, presented earlier in this chapter. Specifically, the project sought out to provide answers to questions such as: (1) are ethnic/national identification and prejudice increasing with age as the Social Identity Development Theory would predict or do they decrease with age as the sociocognitive theory would predict?; (2) is there an association between ethnic/national identification and ingroup preference and/or outgroup derogation as the Social Identity Development Theory would predict?; and (3) in high-conflict contexts where there is perceived threat from the outgroup, is ingroup preference coupled with outgroup derogation as the Social Identity Development Theory would predict?

The countries participating in the project were either countries that recently faced or are still facing armed intergroup conflict: Cyprus (Greek Cypriots and Turkish Cypriots), Israel (Jews and Palestinians), Bosnia-Herzegovina (Bosniaks and Serbs), Northern Ireland (Protestant and Catholics) and the Basque country (Basque and Spanish), or countries that did not experience violent conflict in the recent past: England and the Netherlands.

Stavrinides and Georgiou (2011) and Mertan (2011) used similar methodologies but utilized two different samples, Greek Cypriot children and Turkish Cypriot children, respectively. Their sample consisted of almost equal numbers of boys and girls and was divided into two age groups; the younger age group whose mean age was about seven years in both samples and the older age group whose mean age was about ten years for the Greek Cypriot sample and eleven years for the Turkish Cypriot sample. The sample size of each age group was for Greek Cypriots: younger group ($n=18$), older group ($n=57$), and for Turkish Cypriots: younger group ($n=39$), older group ($n=32$).

Both studies measured: (i) identification with national identity (i.e., Greek or Turkish Cypriot identity accordingly) (e.g., importance of identity, degree of identification, affect toward identity); (ii) attribution of positive (e.g., clean, friendly, clever, happy) and negative (e.g., dirty, unfriendly, lazy, dishonest) traits to the ingroup, the target outgroup (Turkish Cypriots for Greek Cypriots and Greek Cypriots for Turkish Cypriots), as well as to neutral outgroups (Irish and Dutch); and (iii) feelings of like/dislike toward the ingroup, the target outgroup, and the neutral groups.

Ingroup favoritism was operationalized as ascribing more positive traits to the ingroup than to the target or neutral outgroups and reporting more liking of the ingroup in comparison to the target and neutral outgroups. *Outgroup derogation* was operationalized as ascribing more negative traits to outgroups than to ingroup and reporting more feelings of dislike toward outgroups in comparison to ingroup. The two studies sought to investigate whether: (1) the degree of: (i) identification with Greek or Turkish Cypriot identity; (ii) ingroup favoritism; and (iii) outgroup derogation, differed by age and gender; and (2) identification with Greek or Turkish Cypriot identity correlated with ingroup favoritism and outgroup derogation.

The results for Turkish Cypriot children showed clear evidence of ingroup favoritism as well as of outgroup derogation across age and gender categories. Turkish Cypriot children, regardless of their age or gender, exhibited ingroup favoritism by attributing more positive traits to their ingroup than to all outgroups (Greek Cypriots, Dutch and Irish), and they also attributed more negative traits to Greek Cypriots (but not to Dutch and Irish) than to their ingroup (outgroup derogation). Outgroup derogation, therefore, was only expressed toward the target outgroup: Greek Cypriots. Turkish Cypriot children also reported liking their own group more than the two neutral outgroups and Greek Cypriots. They furthermore ranked Greek Cypriots as the least liked group of all outgroups.

Identification with the Turkish Cypriot identity was at very high levels in the Turkish Cypriot sample, but it did not differ by age group. The degree of identification, however, differed by gender: girls reported higher identification with the Turkish Cypriot identity than boys. Finally, identification with the Turkish Cypriot identity was found to correlate with ingroup favoritism but not with outgroup derogation. Stronger identification with the Turkish Cypriot identity was linked to more liking of the ingroup but was not accompanied by a greater dislike for outgroups.

The results for Greek Cypriot children regarding ingroup preference and outgroup derogation were similar to the ones of Turkish Cypriot children. Greek Cypriot children showed clear ingroup preference as the ingroup was attributed the highest number of positive traits and was liked the most, whereas the outgroups (Dutch, Irish and Turkish Cypriots) were liked less and were attributed more negative traits. The discrepancy between ingroup and outgroup was even greater for the target outgroup (Turkish Cypriots). Contrary to Turkish Cypriot children for whom there was no age or gender difference in ingroup preference or outgroup derogation, older Greek Cypriot children reported less liking for all outgroups than younger children. Similarly to the results of the Turkish Cypriot sample, on the other hand, Greek Cypriot girls were found to identify with Greek Cypriot identity more strongly than boys. Lastly, there was no association between identification with Greek Cypriot identity and ingroup preference or outgroup derogation in the Greek Cypriot sample.

The results of the two studies combined showed that both Greek and Turkish Cypriot children exhibited a clear preference for their own group which was also accompanied by active outgroup dislike toward the ingroup's target outgroup, namely Greek Cypriots for Turkish Cypriots, and Turkish Cypriots for Greek Cypriots. This finding suggests that prejudice, taking the form of both ingroup preference *and* outgroup derogation, is already present at the age of seven, in both Greek and Turkish Cypriot children. Children in both communities also distinguished between neutral groups and the target outgroup: whereas they demonstrated intergroup bias that took the form of ingroup preference between their ingroup and all other outgroups, when it came down to outgroup derogation, this was observed only for the target outgroups.

Another important finding is that neither ingroup preference nor outgroup derogation declined with age as the sociocognitive theory would predict. That means that the cognitive advancement, which comes with age and allows children to think in more refined and less reified terms about intergroup relations, does not affect the way children feel about outgroups in the Cypriot context. If anything, it was the younger and not the older children who showed more positive attitudes toward Turkish Cypriots in the Greek Cypriot community, by comparison to their older counterparts.

Possible explanations for this latter finding is that older Greek Cypriot children have had more exposure to negative ingroup norms toward the outgroup or that that older children spent more time in formal schooling, which means that they are also more likely to have been influenced by nationalistic education. Of course, these should also stand true for (older) Turkish Cypriot children as well. However, older Turkish Cypriot children were not found to be more prejudiced than their younger counterparts in the reported study.

The absence in the Turkish Cypriot sample of an age effect similar to the one observed in the Greek Cypriot sample could be attributed to the changes that took place in history textbooks since 2003 in the Turkish Cypriot community, which was three years before these data were collected. The new history textbooks, according to Mertan (2011) provide a more balanced account of historical events, and as such, they do not directly aim at strengthening the Turkish Cypriot identity and at nurturing hostility against the other community (Papadakis 2008). The absence of more studies akin to the ones of Mertan (2011) and Stavrinides and Georgiou (2011) does not allow us to further corroborate or reject any of these potential explanations of the findings. Furthermore, there is no published study known to us that tracked the changes in the attitudes of

Turkish Cypriot students toward the Greek Cypriot community before and after the adoption of the new textbooks.

The results of the two studies also showed that, contrary to the main prediction of the Social Identity Development Theory, identification with the Greek and Turkish Cypriot identities was not found to be associated with more dislike toward the outgroup. There was only some evidence in the Turkish Cypriot community that identification with the Turkish Cypriot identity was correlated positively with positive ingroup attitudes, but not with outgroup derogation. The absence of a relationship between national identification and outgroup derogation is surprising, particularly in a context like Cyprus where intergroup conflict is predominantly based on ethnic memberships.

A problem of the two studies in our view is that they measure identification with the identities "Greek Cypriots" and "Turkish Cypriots" without really knowing what the content of each of these two identities is for the children who participated in the studies. The mere fact that these identities are compound, consisting of two different identities, the subgroup or ethnic identity: "Greek"; "Turkish" and the civic identity "Cypriot", raises the question of which part of the identity each child is mostly identified with.

Finally, an interesting finding of Georgiou and Stavrinides' and Mertan's (2011) studies that was true for both communities was that girls attributed more importance to their Greek or Turkish Cypriot identity than boys of the two communities. Even though higher identification with their national identity, did not lead to a gender effect on ingroup preference and outgroup derogation, this discrepancy between boys and girls in both communities is interesting. When discussing this finding, Mertan contended that girls are more exposed to family narratives from female family members, thus implying that female family members are more likely to reproduce the dominant narrative of their communities, which could lead to a stronger sense of belonging to the community. This contention is backed up by recent findings from nation-wide surveys showing women in both communities to be less ready and willing to reconcile with the other community. Greek Cypriot women and to a lesser extent Turkish Cypriot women in comparison to men of their respective communities, report that they feel more threatened by the other community, that they are more anxious to meet with members of the other community and that they are more likely to want to keep their distances from the other community (UNDP-ACT and

SeeD 2015). This fearful response to the other community that is more prevalent in women than men, is likely to be conveyed to children of the same gender. Stronger identification with the community's identity could be seen as a way to buffer oneself against a feared "other".

This latter point about the possibility of children adopting their parents' attitudes raises the discussion of how the schooling system (and particularly school teachers) can, and in our view do, play a role in shaping children's attitudes. In earlier parts of this chapter, we alluded to the role of formal education in generating and sustaining intergroup prejudice in Cyprus. Schoolteachers are the ones responsible for implementing national educational strategies and the national curriculum, and they are the representatives of the educational system with whom the children have the most frequent contact.

There are studies with Greek Cypriot teachers showing that in their majority they have rather negative feelings toward Turkish Cypriots, and even more importantly, that they find it hard to overcome the fears and anxieties they have toward the other community (Zembylas 2010; Zembylas et al. 2011). In an ethnographic study, Zembylas (2010) evaluated the perception of Turkish-speaking children within Greek Cypriot teachers' discourses. He found that Greek Cypriot teachers espouse ethnocentric views when it comes to Turkish-speaking children. One of the teachers in the study, for example, mentioned that Turkish-speaking children "are children but they are also of Turkish origin" (p. 14). Greek Cypriot teachers furthermore rationalized their negative views using the political situation in Cyprus thus defending the "right" of Greek Cypriots to be racists.

Greek Cypriot teachers were also found to be unprepared and unwilling to adopt reconciliatory policies. Zembylas et al. (2011) examined the reactions of Greek Cypriot teachers to the government's initiative to set the promotion of a culture of peaceful coexistence between Greek Cypriots and Turkish Cypriots, as its central educational objective for the year 2008–2009 (Ministry of Education and Culture 2008, as cited by Zembylas et al. 2011). The initiative emphasized that education should highlight the elements that unite Greek and Turkish Cypriots and that characterize them as one people. Toward that end, teachers were encouraged to "get closer and become acquainted with the cultural expression of the two communities, so that they can transfer it to the students" (Ministry of Education and Culture 2008 as cited by Zembylas et al. 2011, p. 332). There was also a direction for the values of peaceful coexistence to be diffused in all aspects of school life and exchange of visits to and from Turkish Cypriot schools came up as an idea. The latter suggestion was heavily criticized by the main trade union of teachers who issued a formal statement expressing their "strong disagreement regarding the suggestion for visit exchanges between Greek Cypriots and Turkish Cypriots" (Zembylas et al. 2011, p. 332).

In the same study, Zembylas et al. asked participants questions about their attitudes toward reconciliation and their perceptions toward the educational objective. The findings showed that teachers appreciated the importance of cultivating peaceful coexistence but that they felt that they lacked the readiness to implement the new objective while they also had their reservations with regards to its feasibility. More importantly, younger teachers (aged 36 and under; born after the division of the island) were significantly less positive toward the new objective in comparison to the older cohort.

Contrary to Greek Cypriots, Turkish Cypriots have made some decisive steps of progress in eradicating nationalism from education with the most prominent step being the change of history textbooks in 2003 (Mertan 2011; Papadakis 2008). Academics and teachers themselves were key actors in the conception and the implementation of this initiative. Turkish Cypriot teachers often stand in the forefront of reconciliation via their main trade union (KTOS). This goes to say that the dominant views in the schoolteacher communities of the two sides differ and that this too may play a moderating role in whether initial prejudicial beliefs of children in the two communities are sustained through late childhood and adolescence or whether they are mitigated to give room for more reconciliatory views.

DISCUSSION

Our goal in this chapter was twofold: (i) to discuss how prejudice develops in children and the factors determining its course as these were identified by theories of prejudice development, and (ii) to critically examine the studies tracking prejudice among Greek and Turkish Cypriot children and to discuss their findings in light of key characteristics of the Cypriot context. As an outcome of addressing these two subgoals, we develop a set of assertions as well as recommendations as follows: (i) gender vis-a-vis prejudice development, (ii) measuring national identification among Greek and Turkish Cypriot children, and (iii) the role of teachers and ways forward.

Gender and Prejudice Development

There is at least some evidence from studies in Cyprus presented in this chapter suggesting that gender might play a role in prejudice development. In these studies, girls were found to identify more strongly with their ingroup than boys, and this was the case in both communities. While stronger ingroup identification was not found to correlate with higher ingroup preference and/or outgroup derogation in these studies, this could have merely been a result of small sample sizes. There is overwhelming literature in social psychology showing that stronger ingroup identification correlates with stronger ingroup preference and a greater propensity to derogate against outgroups, especially in contexts of conflict (e.g., Nesdale 1999). Gender differences were also detected in older ages in both communities in nation-wide survey. Women by comparison to men were found to be more prejudiced toward the other community and more resistant to the idea of coexistence (UNDP-ACT and SeeD 2015).

These findings suggest that gender is a factor worth taking into account when examining the development of prejudice in children and the differing expressions of prejudice in adults. Yet, gender, as a construct, is absent from theories of prejudice development in children. The developmental processes described by these theories are considered to be invariant across genders; thus no predictions were formulated in the past as to whether gender can moderate the onset as well as the development and the nature of prejudice in children.

There are grounds to believe, however, that boys and girls do develop differently as social actors, especially due to differing environmental influences. To name one example, gendered toys, like guns and soldiers for boys, as opposed to dolls for girls, encourage boys to be more pre-occupied with conflict, combat and war, which could render them more sensitive to the existence of outgroups while also encouraging them to adopt a more offensive (militant) attitude toward them. Girls, on the other hand, are often brought up in an environment where men of their ingroup are there to protect them from threatening outgroupers, namely other men who are "barbarians", "rapists" and "murderers" (Spyrou 2002). Hence, boys are braised for a fight, while girls are more prone to fear the enemy. These differences should be even more prevalent in countries where the threatening outgroup is part of children's everyday reality.

We argue that it is important for theories of prejudice development to pay attention to the factor of gender in order to examine what causes boys and girls, and men and women, to develop different ingroup identification and outgroup behavior patterns. We simultaneously want to flag the importance of attending to the gender divide in Cyprus, so as to both understand the origins of it and to address it.

National Identification of Children

As we discussed earlier, measuring identification with the identity "Greek Cypriot" or "Turkish Cypriot" comes with the challenge of not knowing what the content of each of these two identities is for the children under study. Studies by Christou and Spyrou (2012) and Makriyianni (2006) have shown that while Greek Cypriot children categorize themselves as Cypriots when asked who are included in the category "Cypriot" they respond Greek Cypriots and exclude Turkish Cypriots. These findings suggest that the meaning children attribute to the category "Cypriot" does not correspond to the official use of this category label, that is, an umbrella category which is inclusive of all communities living on the island.

We argue that there are more nuanced ways of measuring strength of identification without ignoring the identity's content. For example, Psaltis (2011), instead of measuring identification with Greek Cypriot and Turkish Cypriot identities, he measured individuals' attitudes toward *motherlands* (Greece and Turkey) and toward the current practice of use of their symbols (i.e., flag, national anthem). Psaltis labeled the adherence to Hellenic/Turkish ideals and symbols and the attachment to the corresponding motherlands as *Helleno/Turco-centrism* and the preference for Cypriot national symbols and the detachment from the motherlands as *Cypriocentrism*. Psaltis (2011), clustered his Greek Cypriot participants based on their responses to these two dimensions. The clustering produced three groups, individuals who were high in Cypriocentrism and low in Hellenocentrism, individuals who were moderate on both dimensions, and individuals who were low on Cypriocentrism and high on Hellenocentrism. He found the latter group to be less trusting toward Turkish Cypriots, less willing to forgive or to take the perspective of the other community, and to have less positive feelings toward them. It was therefore the identification with the Hellenic part of the Greek

Cypriot identity that was found to lead to a negative perception of the outgroup. To our knowledge, studies using this methodology for measuring identity in the two communities with children as participants, have not yet been done.

The Role of Teachers and Ways Forward

Schoolteachers are influential figures in children's lives and are often a primary source of knowledge about a number of topics including the nature and the history of intergroup (bi-communal) relations in Cyprus. Teachers function within the formal schooling system, which, in Cyprus, has traditionally been devoted to preserving and communicating the self-serving official narrative of each community. Yet, while in the Turkish Cypriot community's teachers have played a pivotal role in instigating a revolt against indoctrination and in influencing the decision to produce new, more balanced, history textbooks, Greek Cypriot teachers remained loyal safeguards of an ethnocentric education system. Even when the otherwise nationalistic agenda of the Ministry of Education of the Republic of Cyprus, encouraged teachers to initiate bi-communal contact, for example through school visits, teachers did not comply with the request. On the contrary, they vehemently opposed it (Zembylas et al. 2011).

Zembylas et al.'s (2011) study examining the reasons for which Greek Cypriot teachers opposed the idea of rapprochement at the school level, revealed that their negative stance was partly attributed to low self-efficacy in their abilities to initiate intergroup contact and to become the gateway to the other community for their students. Interestingly, a study carried out in years 2014–2015 by the Research Institute Promitheas, showed that approximately 70% of Greek Cypriot children ($n = 80$) aged twelve to fifteen, reported feeling insecure or uncomfortable with the idea of interacting with members of the Turkish Cypriot community (results reported in Ioannou 2016). The similarity between students' and teachers' results on the dimension of contact self-efficacy is noteworthy and it provides support to the social learning approach to prejudice development, according to which children copy and internalize the attitudes and behaviors of their most influential others.

Overcoming personal and systemic barriers in order to adopt a more open, empathetic, and dialectic stance toward the "other", is by no means an easy task for teachers. To the extent though, that barriers are not crossed due to a lack of knowledge around bi-communal issues and lack of confidence to establish connections with the other side, as Zembylas et al.'s (2011) study suggests, there are ways forward. Fortunately, there are organizations in Cyprus, such as the inter-communal Association for Historical Dialogue and Research (AHDR), which aim at supporting teachers through different professional development programs in developing knowledge needed to address issues revolving around bi-communal relations in Cyprus. As a matter of fact, one of the main goals of AHDR is to provide teachers as well as children with the opportunity to advance their knowledge on how to teach and how to learn history. As history is probably the most contented (by being politically-loaded) subject in Greek and Turkish Cypriot schools, AHDR provides teachers (and pupils) the chance to openly address it. We argue that such initiatives are instrumental in supporting teachers in developing the knowledge, skills, and abilities needed to address sensitive matters around bi-communal relations.

Instead of a Conclusion

We believe it would be an omission to end this chapter on prejudice and its development without at least briefly mentioning the most widely studied and most promising "antidote" to prejudice: intergroup contact. Intergroup contact, defined as the positive interaction between members of different social groups (Allport 1954), has been tested and found to reduce prejudice in a number of contexts (see Pettigrew and Tropp's 2006, meta-analysis), including Cyprus (e.g., Ioannou et al. 2017a; McKewon and Psaltis 2017). Despite the fact that face-to-face contact became possible after the partial lift of the travel restrictions on the island in 2003, study results show that this opportunity was not utilized particularly by Greek Cypriot youth who report consistently very low levels of direct contact (UNDP-ACT and SeeD 2015). According to knowledge from social psychology, face-to-face contact may not be pursued because of psychological barriers, as for example, anxiety for interacting with the outgroup (Stephan and Stephan 1985), that make individuals apprehensive about intergroup encounters. The studies presented earlier in the chapter suggest that the latter is the case at least for Greek Cypriots.

Researchers have proposed that indirect contact, which does not require face-to-face interactions between members of different groups, may provide a means to reap some of the benefits of contact in low-contact settings (Dovidio et al. 2011; Hewstone and Swart 2011). There is evidence supporting the effectiveness of indirect contact in the Cypriot context. Merely witnessing a friend having contact with a Turkish Cypriot procured more positive attitudes and less intergroup anxiety for female Greek Cypriot students (Ioannou et al. 2017a); imagining having a positive interaction with a member of the other community led to more positive attitudes, a reduction of intergroup anxiety, and a greater desire to approach the other community for both Greek and Turkish Cypriot students (e.g., Husnu and Crisp 2010; Ioannou et al. 2017b), positive family story-telling and reading literature portraying friendships between Turkish and Greek Cypriot children led to more positive attitudes and behavioral intentions, more outgroup trust, more forgiveness and a greater support for peace, in Turkish Cypriot children (Husnu et al. 2018).

Intergroup contact is, of course, not panacea; understanding prejudice in children or in adults requires a multi-dimensional and comprehensive approach and addressing prejudice cannot boil down to a single intervention. There is, however, strong evidence that intergroup contact, even in its indirect forms, can be beneficial for intergroup relations in Cyprus. We argue that this evidence should be taken into account by relevant stakeholders including teachers themselves. Given that mixed settings, such as mixed schools, are largely absent in Cyprus, and contact cannot naturally occur, adults, often teachers, are called to be the ones to initiate and facilitate contact. Unless adults, and teachers in particular, become comfortable with the idea of approaching the other community, children in Cyprus will continue to grow up, get educated and socialize in their side of the divide, indifferent to, or intimidated by, the idea of the "other" and therefore unlikely to cross the mental and physical boundaries that nurture prejudice.

References

Aboud, F. E. (1988). *Children and Prejudice*. New York: Blackwell.
Allport, G. W. (1954). *The Nature of Prejudice*. Cambridge, MA: Addison-Wesley.
Barrett, M. (2007). *Children's Knowledge, Beliefs and Feelings About Nations and National Groups*. Hove, East Sussex: Psychology Press.

Barrett, M., & Davis, S. C. (2008). Applying Social Identity and Self-Categorization Theories to Children's Racial, Ethnic, National and State Identifications and Attitudes. In *Handbook of Race, Racism and the Developing Child* (pp. 72–110). Hoboken, NJ: Wiley.

Bar-Tal, D. (1996). Development of Social Categories and Stereotypes in Early Childhood: The Case of 'the Arab' Concept Formation, Stereotype and Attitudes by Jewish Children in Israel. *International Journal of Intercultural Relations, 20*(3), 341–370.

Bennett, M., Lyons, E., Sani, F., & Barrett, M. (1998). Children's Subjective Identification with the Group and In-Group Favoritism. *Developmental Psychology, 34*(5), 902–909.

Brewer, M. B. (2001). Ingroup Identification and Intergroup Conflict: When Does Ingroup Love Become Outgroup Hate? In R. D. Ashmore, L. Jussim, & D. Wilder (Eds.), *Rutgers Series on Self and Social Identity; Vol. 3: Social Identity, Intergroup Conflict, and Conflict Reduction* (pp. 17–41). New York: Oxford University Press.

Brown, R. J. (2010). *Prejudice: Its Social Psychology*. Oxford: Wiley-Blackwell.

Brown, R. J., & Yee, M. D. (1988). *Children's Social Comparisons: Effects of Interpersonal and Intergroup Information upon Children's Self-Evaluations*. Canterbury: University of Kent.

Christou, M., & Spyrou, S. (2012). Border Encounters: How Children Navigate Space and Otherness in an Ethnically Divided Society. *Childhood, 19*(3), 302–316.

Clark, K. B., & Clark, M. P. (1947). Racial Identification and Preference in Negro Children. In E. E. Maccoby, T. M. Newcomb, & E. L. Hartley (Eds.), *Readings in Social Psychology, 86*, 602–611.

Dovidio, J. F., Eller, A., & Hewstone, M. (2011). Improving Intergroup Relations Through Direct, Extended and Other Forms of in Direct Contact. *Group Processes & Intergroup Relations, 14*, 147–160.

Doyle, A. B., & Aboud, F. E. (1995). A Longitudinal Study of White Children's Racial Prejudice as a Social-Cognitive Development. *Merrill-Palmer Quarterly, 41*(2), 209–228.

Hewstone, M., Rubin, M., & Willis, H. (2002). Intergroup Bias. *Annual Review of Psychology, 53*(1), 575–604.

Hewstone, M., & Swart, H. (2011). Fifty-Odd Years of Inter-Group Contact: From Hypothesis to Integrated Theory. *British Journal of Social Psychology, 50*(3), 374–386.

Husnu, S., & Crisp, R. J. (2010). Imagined Intergroup Contact: A New Technique for Encouraging Greater Inter-ethnic Contact in Cyprus. *Peace & Conflict: Journal of Peace Psychology, 16*(1), 97–108.

Husnu, S., Mertan, B., & Cicek, O. (2018). Reducing Turkish Cypriot Children's Prejudice Toward Greek Cypriots: Vicarious and Extended

Intergroup Contact Through Storytelling. *Group Processes & Intergroup Relations, 21*(1), 178–192.

Ioannou, N. (2016). *Indirect Contact with the Turkish Cypriot Community: Evaluating an Intervention.* Ph.D. dissertation, University of Cyprus, Nicosia.

Ioannou, M., Hewstone, M., & Al Ramiah, A. (2017a). An Experimental Comparison of Direct and Indirect Types of Contact. *Journal of Experimental Social Psychology.* https://doi.org/10.1016/j.jesp.2017.11.010.

Ioannou, M., Hewstone, M., & Al Ramiah, A. (2017b). Inducing Similarities and Differences in Imagined Contact: A Mutual Intergroup Differentiation Approach. *Group Processes and Intergroup Relations, 20*(4), 427–446.

Lacher, H., & Kaymak, E. (2005). Transforming Identities: Beyond the Politics of Non-settlement in North Cyprus. *Mediterranean Politics, 10*(2), 147–166.

Makriyianni, C. (2006). *History, Museums and National Identity in a Divided Country: Children's Experience of Museum Education in Cyprus.* Cambridge: University of Cambridge.

Makriyianni, C., & Psaltis, C. (2007). The Teaching of History and Reconciliation. *Cyprus Review, 19*(1), 43–69.

McKeown, S., & Psaltis, C. (2017). Intergroup Contact and the Mediating Role of Intergroup Trust on Outgroup Evaluation and Future Contact Intentions in Cyprus and Northern Ireland. *Peace and Conflict: Journal of Peace Psychology, 23*(4), 392–404.

Mertan, B. (2011). Children's Perception of National Identity and In-Group/Out-Group Attitudes: Turkish-Cypriot School Children. *European Journal of Developmental Psychology, 8*(1), 74–86.

Nesdale, D. (1999). Social Identity and Ethnic Prejudice in Children. In P. Martin & W. Noble (Eds.), *Psychology and Society* (pp. 92–110). Brisbane: Australian Academic Press.

Nesdale, D., & Brown, K. (2004). Children's Attitudes Towards an Atypical Member of an Ethnic In-Group. *International Journal of Behavioral Development, 28*(4), 328–335.

Papadakis, Y. (2008). Narrative, Memory and History Education in Divided Cyprus: A Comparison of Schoolbooks on the History of Cyprus. *History & Memory, 20*(2), 128–148.

Pettigrew, T. F., & Tropp, L. R. (2006). A Meta-Analytic Test of Intergroup Contact Theory. *Journal of Personality and Social Psychology, 90*(5), 751–783.

Piaget, J., & Weil, A. M. (1951). The Development in Children of the Idea of the Homeland and of Relations to Other Countries. *International Social Science Journal, 3*, 561–578.

Psaltis, C. (2011). Intergroup Trust and Contact in Transition: A Social Representations Perspective on the Cyprus Conflict. In I. Markova &

A. Gillespie (Eds.), *Trust and Conflict: Representation, Culture and Dialogue* (pp. 83–104). London: Routledge.

Spyrou, S. (2002). Images of 'the Other': 'The Turk' in Greek Cypriot Children's Imaginations. *Race, Ethnicity and Education, 5*(3), 255–272.

Stavrinides, P., & Georgiou, S. (2011). National Identity and In-Group/Out-Group Attitudes with Greek-Cypriot Children. *European Journal of Developmental Psychology, 8*(1), 87–97.

Stephan, W. G., & Stephan, C. W. (1985). Intergroup Anxiety. *Journal of Social Issues, 41*(3), 157–176.

Tajfel, H., Jahoda, G., Nemeth, C., Rim, Y., & Johnson, N. B. (1972). The Devaluation by Children of Their Own National and Ethnic Group: Two Case Studies. *British Journal of Social and Clinical Psychology, 11*(3), 235–243.

Tajfel, H., & Turner, J. C. (1979). An Integrative Theory of Intergroup Conflict. In W. G. Austin & S. Worchel (Eds.), *The Social Psychology of Intergroup Relations* (pp. 33–47). Monterey, CA: Brooks/Cole.

Teichman, Y., Bar-Tal, D., & Abdolrazeq, Y. (2007). Intergroup Biases in Conflict: Re-examination with Arab Pre-adolescents and Adolescents. *International Journal of Behavioral Development, 31*(5), 423–432.

UNDP-ACT, & SeeD. (2015). *Predicting Peace: The Social Cohesion and Reconciliation Index as a Tool for Conflict Transformation.* Nicosia: UNDP.

Verkuyten, M. (2004). Ethnic Identity and Social Context. In M. Bennett & F. Sani (Eds.), *The Development of the Social Self* (pp. 189–216). New York: Taylor & Francis.

Verkuyten, M., & Thijs, J. (2001). Ethnic and Gender Bias Among Dutch and Turkish Children in Late Childhood: The Role of Social Context. *Infant and Child Development, 10*(4), 203–217.

Zembylas, M. (2010). Greek-Cypriot Teachers' Constructions of Turkish-Speaking Children's Identities: Critical Race Theory and Education in a Conflict-Ridden Society. *Ethnic and Racial Studies, 33*(8), 1372–1391.

Zembylas, M., & Bekerman, Z. (2008). Education and the Dangerous Memories of Historical Trauma: Narratives of Pain, Narratives of Hope. *Curriculum Inquiry, 38*(2), 125–154.

Zembylas, M., Charalambous, C., Charalambous, P., & Kendeou, P. (2011). Promoting Peaceful Coexistence in Conflict-Ridden Cyprus: Teachers' Difficulties and Emotions Towards a New Policy Initiative. *Teaching and Teacher Education, 27*(2), 332–341.

CHAPTER 12

An Appraisal of the Works of Rolandos Katsiaounis: Society, Labor, and Anti-colonialism in Cyprus, 1850s–1950s

Andrekos Varnava

INTRODUCTION[1]

The passing of Rolandos Katsiaounis on June 30, 2014 was deeply saddening and shocking, even though I knew of his illness. Naturally many memories flooded back for me. I had first written to Rolandos when as a Ph.D. candidate I was planning my research trip to Cyprus in 2002. I wrote to him about wanting to visit the State Archive in Cyprus to look for documents on the strategic role of Cyprus during the first five or so decades of British rule (i.e., 1878–1925). In his customary blunt way, Rolandos replied that I would find no documents on this subject there. He was, to my happiness and excitement, wrong and my own personal discovery of this archive would bring us together and result in one thing we had in common beyond being historians, our love of this archive.

A. Varnava (✉)
University of Flinders, Adelaide, SA, Australia

A. Varnava
Honorary Professor in History, De Montfort University, Leicester, UK

© The Author(s) 2018   243
T. Kyritsi and N. Christofis (eds.), *Cypriot Nationalisms in Context*,
https://doi.org/10.1007/978-3-319-97804-8_12

Our next encounter was at one of my first conferences after I had moved to Cyprus in September 2006, "Nationalism in a Troubled Triangle: Cyprus, Greece and Turkey" held at the University of Cyprus from November 10–11, 2006. If memory serves me right Rolandos did not present a paper at the conference, but delivered a scathing attack on one of the presentations that must have lasted almost as long as a regular 20-minute presentation! We finally formally met at another conference, the PRIO Cyprus Centre annual conference, *One Island, Many Histories: Rethinking the Politics of the Past in Cyprus*, from November 21–22, 2008. The meeting was not memorable: he merely acknowledged that he knew who I was and subsequently sat quietly during my talk and asked no questions. Later he would imply to me that for him this was a mark of respect. We met many times after that at the State Archives, and ironically more so when I returned to Australia and visited Cyprus in 2010 and 2012 for research trips. It was on the three occasions when we met at the archives, once before I left for Adelaide in January 2009 and two times (2010 and 2012) after, when Rolandos invited me to his home for lunch and I came to know more of the man behind the historian. This article will critically engage with his main historical works and will be infused with my impressions and recollections of the man, since he wore his heart on his sleeve, along with his politics and passion for his historical work and ideas.

This chapter, however, does not aim to be a trip down memory lane, but a re-evaluation of Katsiaounis' works and especially those which relate to nationalism and more broadly identity. This, in fact, colors almost all his works to one degree or more. After a brief biography of the man and his career, I wish to explore closely his work in a chronological and analytical fashion according to his career, thus starting with his earliest interests in the Cypriots in London for his M.A. and several subsequent publications, then going back in time to the second half of the nineteenth century with his Ph.D. and subsequent monograph on the rise of the Cypriot laboring class, and finally to his last monograph on the post-World War II consultative assembly and related publications. After this, an attempt will be made to discuss his unfinished projects, before an evaluation of his legacy will be attempted.

Born in Famagusta on February 4, 1954, Rolandos was born into the AKEL family. His uncle, Christos Katsiaounis, was among the leaders of the Cypriot Communist Party and a founding member of AKEL and a member of its Central Committee. AKEL ran through Rolandos veins, and he too eventually became a member of the party's Central

Committee. The other personal element so important to understanding Katsiaounis was the displacement of his family in 1974 and his somewhat hardline stance (for an AKEL supporter) on reunification, which saw him support AKEL's "soft no" to the "Annan Plan" in 2004, yet which was tempered by his outspoken revelations about the atrocities committed by both communities during the 1950s, 1960s, and 1970s. Katsiaounis studied at the English School, something he was incredibly proud of, and showed his love for the school by living in an apartment overlooking it. He completed his first degree at Queen Mary College, University of London in 1979, the year I was born, and his M.A. at Birkbeck College, University of London in 1982. He then took a break from academic studies but returned to do his Ph.D. at King's College, University of London in 1996. His M.A. dissertation titled "Ο Εύδωρος Ιωαννίδης και η πολιτική οργάνωση της Κυπριακής Παροικίας του Λονδίνου" (Evdoros Ioannidis and the Political Organisation of the Cypriot Community in London) was his first research into the Cypriot community in London and seems to influence, but was not the basis, for his two articles on the subject published in 1996 and 2000. I can only speculate that Katsiaounis was interested in the London Cypriots because of their role in the Communist Party of Great Britain (CPGB). Many Cypriots in London were genuine communists, fundraised tirelessly, and a number of them such as Michaelakis Economides and Ezekias Papaioannou became active in the "League against Imperialism" and served in the Spanish Civil War (Smith and Varnava 2017). These Cypriot communists were closely affiliated to the Cypriot Communist Party, which was outlawed in 1931 after the mass demonstrations in Cyprus, which led to the burning of Government House, and which advocated Cypriot independence from British rule and not *enosis*—the union of the island to Greece. Katsiaounis, however, was more interested in Evdoros Ioannides, and those other London Cypriots, who became involved with the CPGB only because it supported their anti-colonialism, initial calls for self-government, and after AKEL was formed, *enosis*. For his Ph.D., much the same as I would later do (from my honors thesis) for mine, he went back in time to the nineteenth century and produced a monograph that was quickly published by the Cyprus Research Centre of the Ministry of Education and Culture—where Katsiaounis had fortunately found employment in January 1991.[2] There is no doubt that the book from his Ph.D. *Labour, Society and Politics in Cyprus in the Second Half of the Nineteenth Century*, is his most influential historical work (Katsiaounis 1996b).

This is partly because it is ground-breaking in so many ways, has broader regional and imperial significance, and because his only other book is in Greek and cannot reach the same audience. Katsiaounis was the first to focus on the laboring classes during this period and he opened up this area of study, which in my view still requires much work. It was important that Katsiaounis situated his study of the emerging laboring class within the broader changes to society in Cyprus, within an Ottoman (especially) and British imperial context, and alongside laboring class theories. His next book on the Consultative Assembly dealt with the more studied and controversial British efforts to re-introduce a constitution. This book, although being more about the Greek and to a lesser extent Turkish Cypriot elites, is in some ways an effort to continue the story, albeit several generations later, of the participation of the laboring and middle classes in a mass anti-colonial movement. Following on from this book Katsiaounis was working on a history of AKEL and a history of the Cyprus conflict, neither of which he finished, yet he did produce an interesting article.

CYPRIOTS IN LONDON DURING THE INTER-WAR YEARS

As mentioned above, Katsiaounis wrote his M.A. on the Cypriot community in London, specifically focusing on the career of Evdoros Ioannides, otherwise also known by his pseudonym, Doros Alastos (Ioannides 1937, 1942, 1948; Alastos 1944a, b, 1955, 1960, 1964).[3] Few historians of Cyprus and other scholars who explore the past would know this and indeed it was not until a colleague and I had started to work on the Cypriots of London during the inter-war years that I discovered that Katsiaounis was a pioneer in this area too. Although he was not the first (George and Millerson 1967; Oakley 1987, 1989; Solomos and Woodhams 1995) or the last to write about the Cypriots in London I was not surprised that he had done so, since he had a keen understanding of what was important in the history of Cyprus.

His first article on the subject explored the archiepiscopal question of the 1930s and the role of the Cypriot community in London (Katsiaounis 1996a). Although there are many issues of interest to study in relation to the Cypriots in London, Katsiaounis was most interested in their political activity in relation to happenings in Cyprus. One of the most important political and ecclesiastical issues of the 1930s was the British blocking the return of the Bishops of Kitium and Kyrenia in order for the election of a new archbishop to take place following the death of Archbishop Kyrillos II in 1933. The role of the Cypriots in London was important even if it did not lead anywhere because it showed their desire to involve themselves in colonial affairs. Firstly, it is important to acknowledge that Katsiaounis sets the scene well: with the available Colonial Office records and Cypriot newspapers he utilized he outlines the health and crime problems the community faced in London, as well as the divisions between the right and left, and the organization and aims of the Cypriot Brotherhood. Katsiaounis recognizes that the driving force behind the Cypriot Brotherhood was Dr. Angelos Zemenides, who was assassinated in January 1933. Zemenides belonged to the right-wing (he was an anti-communist), but to a pro-British right. After his death, the Brotherhood split. Soteris Terezopoulos, a leading lawyer of Cypriots and translator for the courts, continued Zemenides' educational work at the Pultney Institute, and his pro-British and pro-Cypriot teachings. Meanwhile, the brotherhood became pro-*enosis* under Archimandrite Michael Constantinides, the pastor at St. Sophia Church, Bayswater, with the involvement of the exiled prominent Cypriot politician Theophanis Theodotou. Nevertheless, they believed that *enosis* could only be achieved with British support. Theodotou was so desperate to return to Cyprus and play a prominent role in Cypriot politics again that he had hatched a plan to convince the British to make Constantinides the archbishop, and thus ingratiate himself with the British colonial authorities in the hope that they would lift his ban on returning to the island. His plan was opposed by the governor of Cyprus, Sir Herbert Richmond Palmer, who was steadfastly opposed to the Cypriot government playing any role in settling the archiepiscopal crisis. In addition, he was adamant that whoever was to become archbishop had to undertake to refrain from politics and restrict himself to religious matters only. Katsiaounis also blames the divisions in the Cypriot community in London and especially the efforts of Terezopoulos, whom he considers to be a Palmer stooge. Terezopoulos, who was also fervently anti-communist, wanted the British authorities to support him in his efforts to encourage Cypriots to learn English and to understand Cypriot history and to therefore think of themselves as Cypriots, in opposition to the Brotherhood, which referred to Cypriots as Greeks. While Katsiaounis would argue that Terezopoulos was trying to undermine the Brotherhood, I would argue that he was trying to present an alternative path for Cyprus and Cypriots. The British decided to exert a greater control over the Brotherhood by having British members appointed to its committee, as well as a greater control over the Cypriots who first arrived in London by appointing Terezopoulos as liaison officer. Katsiaounis did not give enough emphasis to this control, preferring instead to focus on the failure of the initiative. He did not express any support or opposition to the proposal, yet his thoughts on a related matter conveyed to me in private were telling. One time over lunch at his house I revealed that I was keen to investigate the assassination of Antonios Triantafyllides, the son-in-law of Theodotou, which occurred in January 1934. Like his father-in-law, Triantafyllides had been a member of the legislative council and had been a pro-*enosis* supporter; but during the 1931 crisis (leading to the October 1931 riots) some considered him to have betrayed the cause when he started advocating for closer cooperation with the British in order to achieve *enosis* and later in 1933 when he accepted an invitation to join the consultative council. He had of course not changed his support of *enosis*; he had merely changed his opinions on the method by which it was to be achieved, which broadly agreed with the position of the Greek premier, Eleftherios Venizelos. Triantafyllides probably influenced his father-in-law to moderate his pro-*enosis* position (hence the proposal that Constantinides become archbishop), while Theodotou provided the British with interesting information on right-wing elements that may have been involved in the assassination of his son-in-law, again in the hope that he would be allowed to return to his beloved island. Katsiaounis missed these connections (although the Foreign and Commonwealth files had not been released then), while his views on the matter of the Constantinides proposal can be discerned from his comment to me, which was characteristically blunt, that Triantafyllides was simply a traitor—a British lackey. This comment indicated to me that Katsiaounis was able to hide his inner-thoughts and prejudices in his work (although not in the case of Terezopoulos), especially earlier in his career, yet the focus of his work and the questions he sought to shed light on revealing his prejudices.

Indeed his second article on the Cypriots in London focussed on the left-wing Cypriot associations in London and mostly on Evdoros Ioannides and the Committee of Cypriot Autonomy. This indicates that Katsiaounis was interested in left-wing anti-imperialist and, eventually, pro-*enosis* supporters rather than members and supporters of the Communist Party of Cyprus (KKK) who supported Cypriot independence during the inter-war years and opposed *enosis* (Katsiaounis 2000a). In 1937, leading Cypriot elites who were advocating constitutional reform in the island decided to visit London to lobby the British government (Rappas 2014). Katsiaounis claimed that they were emboldened by the formation, in May 1937, of the Committee for Cypriot Autonomy, under Evdoros Ioannides. He had links to the British newspapers, was the London correspondent of *Eleutheria* and had penned the booklet *The Case for Cyprus*. Ioannides and others in the Committee had close ties with several Labour and Communist party parliamentarians. Katsiaounis claimed that the Committee significantly developed the political consciousness of the Cypriot community in London and prosecuted the campaign for self-government for the island. Although there is no doubt, based on Rappas' findings, that the delegation had moved beyond *enosis*, by the 1940s the Committee for Cypriot Autonomy contained many leftists who were pro-*enosis*, such as Ioannides, Ezekias Papaioannou, George Pefkos, Petros Athonas, Panayiotis Paschalis, who were also all members of the CPBG. Indeed it is possible, although Katsiaounis does not make this claim, that they played some role in the formation of AKEL (of which Papaioannou was general-secretary from 1949 onwards for 40 years).

Knowing Katsiaounis, he would have been aware of the FCO files released on the Cypriots in London in 2012. He had, however, moved onto other themes and subjects, which unfortunately remained largely unfinished. Before discussing these, his most important study, emanating from his Ph.D., takes us back to the previous century.

THE RISE OF THE LABORING CLASS DURING THE NINETEENTH CENTURY

Labour, Society and Politics in Cyprus in the Second Half of the Nineteenth Century breaks much ground on various historical themes. Broadly, this was the first book to delve deeply into the labor history of the island. That it does this across both the Ottoman and British empires remains unique and has been useful to many dealing with this period, including myself. It is also unique for being the first to explore the position in society of the lower and middle classes, viewing them as an essential part of the socioeconomic and sociopolitical structure of Cypriot society. His main, overarching, argument was that Cypriot historical developments must be understood beyond racial and ethnic divisions, and must take into account the social divide (Katsiaounis 1996b).

The monograph provides important critical insights into the role of the Church of Cyprus in the economic, political, and social development of the island, a role that is often glorified in the traditional, generalized treatments of Cypriot history as the beacon of Greek national identity in Cyprus. Katsiaounis was one of the first to break this myth in a comprehensive and sustained way, by showing how integral the church was within the Ottoman imperial, political and social hierarchy and how the church wanted to maintain this privileged position under the British, when they immediately asked to be "re-co-opted." The British rejected this as an "Ottoman era vestige," even though co-option was common practice elsewhere and they retained many other Ottoman practices. Katsiaounis also showed that the speech supposedly delivered by a leading prelate to the high commissioner upon his arrival, in which *enosis* was declared as the ultimate goal of the Greek Cypriots under British rule, was nothing short of a myth, thus reinforcing the argument that the church was not the beacon of Greek Cypriot nationalism (Katsiaounis 1996b). Although not the only one (e.g., Bryant 2004), I took these themes even further along in my first book, where, for instance, I linked the behavior of the church during British rule to the policy of British imperial co-option (Varnava 2009), and also in a co-edited volume on the changing meaning of the role of ethnarch since the eighteenth century (Varnava and Michael 2013). Katsiaounis set the tone and others have taken up the challenge to further his findings by using the new evidence as it arises and by applying broader historical and theoretical contexts.

His monograph, of course, has many other interesting insights. He discussed the rise of the laboring class and the development of a middle class as made possible by British colonial modernity grafted onto an island on the Ottoman periphery. He showed how peasants and rural laborers were able to move a rung or two on the social ladder, to obtain work in urban settings in various industries, from building to manufacturing, and in some cases open small businesses. To be sure many industries still revolved around agricultural production, but these were progressively being modernized through the use of new techniques, technology and especially internal and external communications. For him this was the beginning of the real labor class as distinct from the rural laboring class.

THE POST-WORLD WAR II CONSULTATIVE ASSEMBLY

Even before he had published his first book, Katsiaounis had embarked upon research for his second book on the 1940s, with a specific focus on the Consultative Assembly. Driven by the question of whether it was a missed opportunity or not, Katsiaounis first explored the context leading up to the Consultative Assembly.

One of the questions he first wanted to answer was how Anglo-Greek relations as regards to Cyprus changed during the last years of the Second World War and with the start of the Greek Civil War (Katsiaounis 1992). His article (in Greek) discusses the start and escalation of the Greek Civil War and the regency of Archbishop Damaskinos in relation to Greek claims to Cyprus and British rejections of such claims. In this instance, the article was revisiting an old debate (Alexander 1979; Kelling 1988), but one which Katsiaounis' article remade afresh, since others took up the subject after him (Stefanides 1999; Leventis 2002).

The Cyprus Research Centre published his book on the Consultative Assembly in the year 2000. In many ways it was a stark contrast to his first book: published in Greek and therefore appealing only to the Greek reader, it dealt with colonial policy and colonial politics, both as regards the periphery and the metropolis, in ways that his first book had no interest in doing. Nevertheless, although the focus is on the Greek and to a lesser extent Turkish Cypriot elites, there is the feeling that Katsiaounis is picking up the story of his lower and especially middle classes from his first book several generations later as they, in his view, have become politicized (Katsiaounis 2000b).

Katsiaounis makes several important arguments, some of which challenge received wisdom, such as his argument that the Consultative Assembly did not constitute a lost opportunity on what was eventually a dead end road for *enosis*. And this is perhaps part of the problem with this book, that Katsiaounis argues that the mass movement, led by AKEL, was an *enosis* movement, while anybody arguing for close cooperation with the British, must have been working for the British and could not possibly be anti-colonial. This reflects the main difference between AKEL and the Cypriot Communist Party, which had previously rubbished *enosis* only to be replaced by AKEL in order to champion *enosis*. It is true that AKEL argued that *enosis* could be achieved outside Anglo-Greco relations, but there does not appear to have been a mass movement in favor of *enosis* and certainly not a grassroots one.

Katsiaounis claims that the Church led the right-wing movement formed in May 1943 and was therefore elitist, yet the same argument must surely apply to the left-wing movement; both sides presented the solution of *enosis* to the socioeconomic problems facing Cypriots and against the disappointment of British rule, alternatives were rejected. I also do not agree that self-government would have strengthened the *enosis* movement; it may just as well have done the opposite, since with Cypriots more and more in positions of authority and cooperating with each other to bring about good government, it may have strengthened the case for independence. There is no doubt that the Attlee government (endnote) back-pedaled from its initial views to grant Cyprus self-government because of the regional situation, namely the loss of Palestine, yet the Cypriots could not see this—something also lost on Katsiaounis—to show some flexibility and work with the British to obtain a constitution and legislative representation, along the Maltese path.

UNFINISHED WORKS

It was no secret that Katsiaounis was working on two large projects: officially (i.e., for the Cyprus Research Centre) he was working on a history of the Cyprus conflict from about 1950–1974; and secondly, he was working on perhaps his most treasured project, a history of AKEL. In the end, both projects were too big to be tackled together, although Katsiaounis gave both a good shake. His forensic approach to his scholarship found him beavering away in the National Archives of the UK and especially in the State Archives in Nicosia, where he went down rabbit holes and fought to get access to documents he believed it withheld from the public. This also delayed both projects. He did, however, give various presentations, and published an important article that arose from this research, which cut across both projects.

The article, dealing with the politics of the anti-colonial movement, is indeed controversial, but one which needs to be critically engaged with much more than it has been (Katsiaounis 2007). Katsiaounis shows that the anti-colonial movement had both a left-wing and a right-wing element, but that the right-wing was not as genuine. He claimed that the success of AKEL soon after its formation put fear into the right-wing Church inspired nationalism, pushing into an anti-colonial position. There is some truth in this controversial argument, yet it would appear to me to be more complex than this. There were different forms of anti-colonialism in Cyprus and not merely right-wing and left-wing, but pro-*enosis* and anti-*enosis*. The Communist Party of Cyprus was anti-colonial as well as anti-*enosis*, but it then sold itself to *enosis* not because it had judged it to be the popular will of the people, but because it believed that it could neutralize the right. This not only killed off any chance of cooperation with Turkish Cypriots to form one united anti-colonial struggle, but it also meant that the people of Cyprus had no other anti-colonial option to consider. This reflects in reverse Katsiaounis' argument, since he shows that the right adopted a stronger anti-colonial stance in order to neutralize AKEL.

Legacy

Katsiaounis was a divisive figure, especially in a hyper-nationalized country (owing, in part, to the education system, see Philippou and Varnava 2009) with the writing of modern history dominated by right-wing Greek nationalists who publish very little, if anything, that is peer-reviewed, and what they do publish focuses on highlighting Cypriot Hellenism. In this sense, Katsiaounis was a rare breed. He focused on themes of vital historical significance to the history of Cyprus, not merely points on the mythical script of the Greek nation in Cyprus. In historical order (although not in the order in which he researched these four areas), these were: the British occupation and its impact on the rise of a laboring and middle class; inter-war emigration of the peasant and laboring class to the UK and the links that this diaspora had with the old country; the mass politicization of these classes and the role of their political elites in the anti-colonial movement; and finally, albeit unfinished, the Cyprus conflict and the role of AKEL in Cypriot political life. Katsiaounis belonged to the left and not just any left, but to the AKELlist tradition. On many occasions, he sparked controversy, such as when he spoke about Greek Cypriot war crimes in 1963–1964 and 1974, or when he urged a revision to the history curriculum and textbooks for schools. In this way he was a public historian, opening himself to criticism from various right-wing quarters and never shying from a public stoush.

This is reflected in the comments of Dr. Petros Papapolyviou, an Associate Professor in "Contemporary Greek History" at the University of Cyprus (whose publications assume the form of chronicles/raw information on the history of the "Greeks of Cyprus" (e.g., Papapolyviou 1996, 1997, 1999, 2010), when in his obituary for Katsiaounis he stated:

Fig. 12.1 The historian Rolandos Katsiaounis (*Source* PROMITHEAS Research Institute, Cyprus)

It is not time to assess the human or historical Rolandos Katsiaounis. We had several and intense differences on various issues, but these differences, with the passage of time, did not affect our personal relationship. (Papapolyviou 2014)

I cannot vouch for their relationship, but there is no doubt that their academic differences stemmed from Katsiaounis not being a historian driven by official nationalist historical narratives. Katsiaounis, along with George S. Georghallides (e.g., 1979 and 1985), was one of the few to break this stranglehold on the writing of modern history in Cyprus and was the most important historian of nineteenth and twentieth century Cyprus working and living in the island over the last twenty-five years. Yet for political reasons, he was unable to obtain a position in the history department at the University of Cyprus.

In the same way that Katsiaounis did not mince his words, I have not minced mine either. He was a first-rate historian, passionate about his discipline, and wore his heart (and AKELUist ideology) on his sleeve, sometimes too much. I think he would agree with this statement. Rest in peace Rolandos, we miss you (Fig. 12.1).

Notes

1. I would like to express my thanks to Dr. Nicholas Coureas from the Cyprus Research Centre for his comments on the draft of this essay.
2. Dr. Nicholas Coureas, Cyprus Research Centre, email to author, 13 July 2016.
3. As can be seen, Ioannides sometimes published with his real name and sometimes with his pseudonym for reasons which are not totally clear.

References

Alastos, D. (1944a). *Cyprus*. London: The Committee for Cyprus Affairs.

Alastos, D. (1944b). *Cyprus, Past and Present*. London: The Committee for Cyprus Affairs.

Alastos, D. (1960). *Cyprus Guerrilla: Grivas, Makarios and the British*. London: Heinemann.

Alastos, D. (1964). *Cyprus—What Now? A Short Study*. London: Zeno.

Alastos, D. (1976 [1955]). *Cyprus in History: A Survey of 5,000 Years*. London: Zeno.

Alexander, G. M. (1979). British Policy on the Question of Enosis, 1945–1946. *Kypriakai Spoudai, 79*, 79–94.

Bryant, R. (2004). *Imagining the Modern: The Cultures of Nationalism in Cyprus*. London: I.B. Tauris.

George, V., & Millerson, G. (1967). The Cypriot Community in London. *Race & Class, 8*, 277–292.

Ioannides, E. (1937). *The Case for Cyprus*. London.

Ioannides, E. (1942). *Cyprus—A Rampart*. London: Committee for Cyprus Autonomy, Williams, Lea & CO.

Ioannides, E. (1948). *Cyprus Denied Freedom*. London: Hermes Press for Cyprus Affairs Committee.

Katsiaounis, R. (1992). Οι Ελληνοβρετανικές Σχέσεις, Ο Αντιβασιλέας Δαμασκηνός και η Κύπρος, Οκτώβριος 1944 – Σεπτέμβριος 1945 [Anglo-Greek Relations, Greek Regent Damaskinos and Cyprus, October 1944–September 1945]. *Annual of the Centre for Scientific Research* (Nicosia), pp. 44–514.

Katsiaounis, R. (1996a). Η Κυπριακή Παροικία του Λονδίνου και το Αρχιεπισκοπικό Ζήτημα της Κύπρου, 1928–1936 [The Cyprus Community of London and the Archbishopric Question of Cyprus, 1928–1936]. *Annual of the Centre for Scientific Research* (Nicosia), XXII, pp. 521–556.

Katsiaounis, R. (1996b). *Labour, Society and Politics in Cyprus in the Second Half of the Nineteenth Century*. Nicosia: Cyprus Research Centre.

Katsiaounis, R. (2000a). Τα Πρώτα Βήματα της Επιτροπής Κυπριακής Αυτονομίας [The First Steps of the Commission for the Cypriot Autonomy]. *Annual of the Centre for Scientific Research* (Nicosia), XXVI, pp. 263–287.

Katsiaounis, R. (2000b). *Η Διασκεπτική, 1946–1948: Με Ανασκόπηση της Περιόδου, 1878–1945* [The Consultative Assembly, 1946–1948: With a Survey of the Period, 1878–1945]. Nicosia: Cyprus Research Centre.

Katsiaounis, R. (2007). Cyprus 1931–1959: The Politics of the Anti-colonial Movement. *Annual of the Centre for Scientific Research* (Nicosia), pp. 441–469.

Kelling, G. H. (1988). *British Policy in Cyprus, 1939–1955*. Austin.

Leventis, Y. (2002). *Cyprus: The Struggle for Self-Determination in the 1940s*. Frankfurt: Peter Lang.

Oakley, R. (1987). The Control of Cypriot Migration to Britain Between the Wars. *Immigrants & Minorities*, 6(1), 30–43.

Oakley, R. (1989). Cypriot Migration to Britain Prior to World War II. *Journal of Ethnic and Migration Studies*, 15(3), 509–525.

Papapolyviou, P. (Ed.). (1996). *Εμμανουήλ Μ. Εμμανουήλ, Ημερολόγιον ή Πολεμικαί Σελίδες: Το Ημερολόγιο ενός Κύπριου Εθελοντή του Ελληνοβουλγαρικού Πολέμου του 1913* [Emmanuel M. Emmanuel, Diary or War Pages: The Diary of a Cypriot Volunteer in the Greek-Bulgarian War of 1913]. Thessaloniki: Germanos.

Papapolyviou, P. (1997). *Η Κύπρος και οι Βαλκανικοί Πόλεμοι: Συμβολή στην Ιστορία του Κυπριακού Εθελοντισμού* [Cyprus and the Balkan Wars: Contribution to the History of Cypriot Volunteerism]. Nicosia: Cyprus Research Centre.

Papapolyviou, P. (Ed.). (1999). *Πολεμικά Ημερολόγια, επιστολές και ανταποκρίσεις Κυπρίων εθελοντών από την Ήπειρο και τη Μακεδονία του 1912–1913* [War Diaries, Letters and Responses of Cypriot Volunteers from Epirus and Macedonia 1912–1913]. Nicosia: Cyprus Research Centre.

Papapolyviou, P. (2010). Ο Κυπριακός Εθελοντισμός στους Πολέμους της Ελλάδας, 1866–1945 [Cypriot Volunteerism in the Wars of Greece, 1866–1945]. In A. I. Voskos (Ed.), *Κύπρος: Αγώνες Ελευθερίας στην Ελληνική Ιστορία* [Cyprus: Struggles for Freedom in Greek History] (pp. 204–229). Athens.

Papapolyviou, P. obituary https://papapolyviou.com/2014/07/01/rolandos-katsiaounis-1954-2014/.

Philippou, S., & Varnava, A. (2009). Constructions of Solution(s) to the Cyprus Problem: Exploring Formal Curricula in Greek Cypriot State Schools. In A. Varnava & H. Faustmann (Eds.), *Reunifying Cyprus: The Annan Plan and Beyond* (pp. 194–212). London: I.B. Tauris.

Rappas, A. (2014). *Cyprus in the 1930s: British Colonial Rule and the Roots of the Cyprus Conflict*. London: I.B. Tauris.

Smith, E., & Varnava, A. (2017). Creating a "Suspect Community": Monitoring and Controlling the Cypriot Community in London and Their Immigration to the UK. *English Historical Review, 132*(557), 1149–1181.

Solomos, J., & Woodhams, S. (1995). The Politics of Cypriot Migration to Britain. *Immigrants & Minorities, 14*(3), 231–256.

Stefanidis, I. D. (1999). *Isle of Discord: Nationalism, Imperialism and the Making of the Cyprus Problem*. New York: I.B. Tauris.

Varnava, A. (2009). *British Imperialism in Cyprus, 1878–1915: The Inconsequential Possession*. Manchester: Manchester University Press.

Varnava, A., & Michael, M. N. (Eds.). (2013). *The Archbishops of Cyprus in the Modern Age: The Changing Role of the Archbishop-Ethnarch, Their Identities and Politics*. Newcastle upon Tyne: Cambridge Scholars Publishing.

PART IV

The Local and the Global

Nationalism as Resistance to Colonialism: A Comparative Look at Malta and Cyprus from 1919 to 1940

Iliya Marovich-Old

INTRODUCTION

Nationalism is a political force that often works against imperialism and this was the case for Britain in Malta and Cyprus during the interwar period.[1] In each place nationalism derived from ethnic links to a neighboring nation-state, but the two movements had very different goals. The preservation of aspects of one's culture, and links to a neighboring culture (Italy), was very different to the profound political implications of "union" with another nation-state (Greece). They were also compromised; they had weaknesses the British could exploit.

Malta and Cyprus were, during the interwar period, both a part of the British Empire but each had links to continental Europe. Malta had a close geographic and cultural proximity to Italy, while Cyprus had a majority "Greek Cypriot" population. Nationalism in both places was active and central to resistance to British colonialism. In both cases, this leads to episodes of violence and constitutional suspension.

I. Marovich-Old (✉)
Flinders University, Adelaide, SA, Australia

© The Author(s) 2018
T. Kyritsi and N. Christofis (eds.), *Cypriot Nationalisms in Context*,
https://doi.org/10.1007/978-3-319-97804-8_13

This chapter will examine both what was common and what was distinct between Maltese nationalism and Greek Cypriot nationalism. In Malta nationalists were in favor of *Italianita*, a Maltese identity that embraced Italian language and culture but was not crassly irredentist (in this context meaning union of Malta with Italy). This was opposed by a combination of pro-British "constitutionalists" and the labor movement. In Cyprus a strong and perennial Greek Cypriot *enosis* (a policy of union with Greece) nationalism movement was opposed by both the British and the Turkish Cypriot minority. The policy of *enosis* left no place for a significant Turkish Cypriot minority. In both Malta and Cyprus nationalism was an elite concern, and at times of economic stress, these nationalist elites were able to co-opt working class and rural discontent and direct it toward their own ends. The British suppression of nationalism in both places was swift but different. Maltese nationalist agitation was met with compromise and constitutional change whereas in Cyprus, Greek Cypriot nationalism was met with authoritarianism and the abandonment of the local constitution. This in turn led to different outcomes. Political development in Cyprus was stunted and fixated on *enosis*, while in Malta colonial politics was allowed to continue and evolve.

Two upheavals, one in Malta in 1930 and another in Cyprus in 1931 were prime examples of the violence and unrest that resulted when nationalist movements were able to harness mass concerns and direct their energies against British colonial power. These two events can be contrasted in that one was violent and one was not. Perhaps, more importantly, the value of each colony resulted in differing responses from British colonial authorities. The first event was the failed election and constitutional suspension which occurred in Malta in 1930. In that year a controversial and pro-British politician Lord Gerald Strickland was engaged in an election campaign when the nationalist aligned Catholic Church in Malta forbade its followers from voting for him or his party. This action resulted in the immediate suspension of both the election and the colony. It was a concrete example of nationalism impacting upon British rule within a valuable colony. It was an event which exposed the trouble, the division and the consequent crisis management of the British. The second event was the burning down of Government House in Cyprus. Governor Sir Ronald Storrs had been in Cyprus since 1926, and by 1931 discontent in the Cypriot population was very high. There were economic problems besetting the island, and those Greek Cypriots calling for *enosis* were becoming increasingly frustrated. In October 1931 around 5000 people marched to Government House in Nicosia, and eventually burnt it down (Gwynn 1934).This in turn sparked a period of violent and general unrest which had to be put down by British troops. Both incidents highlight the trouble that nationalism was causing in the British colonies.

Although historians such as Darwin (1991) and Holland (1985) downplay the role of nationalism in the dissolution of the British Empire, it should not be underestimated as a threat and challenge to British imperial hegemony in the interwar central and eastern Mediterranean. Nationalist movements were crucial to unrest in both Malta and Cyprus. They were a major pre-occupation for the Colonial Office in particular, and they complicated the relationship with Italy, Greece, and Turkey. Nationalism is central to the question of imperial control in general and in the Mediterranean in particular. It was, as Burton suggests, more constant and troublesome than is always acknowledged (Burton 2015). To effectively "manage" its colonies the British government had to control these movements either through force or political maneuvering. Although it used force in Malta in 1919, by 1930 Britain was able to manage the challenge of Maltese "Italian" nationalism through political and constitutional means. The political and legal maneuvering was made possible by the broad divide in Maltese society.

Prior to an exploration of the events on the ground in the Mediterranean Colonies, it is useful to examine in more detail the nature of nationalism itself. There are difficulties in achieving a global definition of nationalism, but in the case of Malta and Cyprus the nature of the nationalisms concerned is in fact easily identifiable. They were in the nature of ethnic subnationalisms, that is not the nationalism of the state but the nationalism of groups within the state. The goals of the subnationalism in Cyprus and Malta were less than achieving their own independent nation-state status. In each place, they were elite rather than general concerns, and these movements were most successful when they were able to co-opt issues that appealed to the broader base. The distinction between civic and ethnic nationalism is particularly relevant to Malta and Cyprus. Civic nationalism is associated with the "west", places such as Britain and France. It is based on common political values within a society. Ethnic nationalism is the "assertion of a collective identity centered on a myth of common biological descent" and the term includes movements based on cultural characteristics; that is linguistic, religious and folkloric (Roshwald 2002). In Cyprus and Malta, it was clearly an ethnic nationalism which dominated rather than civic, albeit these ethnic nationalisms was championed by an elite in both places, and ignored a large Turkish minority in Cyprus.

The sting in the tale of this categorization is the assertion by Roshwald (2002) that ethnic nationalism is seen as conducive to intolerant, chauvinistic and authoritarian forms of government. With relation to Cyprus, Loizides (2007) suggests that "ethnic nationalism" was a form of identity formation. As Loizides suggests this was an exclusionary form of nationalism that was imbricated with Greek symbols and practices which immediately excluded the Turkish Cypriot community. The "politicized forms of Greek Nationalism", he argues, "resulted from resentment of British colonialism" (Loizides 2007). This point is supported by others such as Varnava (2009) who argue that British rule sought to impose its own vision of Cyprus upon the island and in so doing brought division to a previously integrated society. With regard to Malta, Frendo (1992) says specifically that Britain attacked the Italian element of Maltese cultural identity through the use of language. They did this because the Italian language was the linguistic-cultural characteristic central to Maltese ethnic nationalism.

Roshwald (2002) also suggests that sociopolitical elites co-opted nationalist themes to legitimize their hold on power. This is true both of Malta and Cyprus. In Cyprus, the Orthodox Church had a privileged position under the Ottoman "millet" system, which was lost when the British came into power. Rappas (2014) notes that the Orthodox Church adopted *enosis* in a bid to maintain this position after being marginalized by the British. By taking this approach the Church was able to support from its community and resist the emasculating effects of the new governing structure. In Malta, the elite were able to harness general economic discontent and direct it toward the British and the pro-British Constitutional Party. This anti-colonial aspect of nationalism has been the subject of a great deal of writing particularly for those concerned with imperial decline.

According to scholars dealing with the history and the decline of the British Empire, colonial rule relied upon the cooperation or acquiescence of the ruled. One perspective, which is known as the peripheral theory, suggests that it was the independence movements of the periphery rather than the problems of the ruling metropoles that consisted the main cause of decolonization. This theory suggests a nationalist or anti-colonial narrative as regards the decline of the empire. According to this approach, the British empire was disrupted by the "nationalism of its subjects, who were mobilized against colonial rule *en masse* and whose opposition made it unworkable" (Darwin 1991). The peripheral theory emphasizes the role of local nationalist political elites at the site of colonialism led by figures such as Kwame Nkrumah in Ghana, Archbishop Makarios III in Cyprus and Enrico Mizzi in Malta.

While this theory is problematic with respect to some sites of decolonization it was an important part of colonial resistance in the British Mediterranean. Nationalists in Malta mobilized around the totemic issue of language. They believed Italian culture and language were an essential element of Maltese identity which should be preserved. Although the language issue was an expression of Maltese Italian nationalism it was, Claudia Baldoli (2008) argues, a pre-occupation of a "bourgeois culture, not shared by the majority of the population, which spoke Maltese and not Italian" and was linked to the liberal nationalism of the Italian *Risorgimento*. Those opposing the Nationalists, the pro-British Maltese, were supporters of Anglicization of Malta and the adoption of the English and Maltese languages to the exclusion of Italian.

Like Cyprus, Malta had a significant division in their society; it was not based on ethnicity, but rather on political and cultural lines. Despite being of the same class the political and economic elite of Malta both resisted and collaborated. One group was mainly concerned with business and commerce, spoke English and mixed socially with British aristocracy. The other was intellectual and religious, spoke Italian and supported the Maltese nationalists (Baldoli 2008). British administrators were able to exploit this fissure in Maltese politics. This situation can be contrasted to Cyprus where there were individuals or even groups who co-operated or collaborated with the British but no major political party committed to furthering British interests.[2] The Turkish Cypriots, for instance, were often in opposition to the Greek Cypriots and voted with the British but they were by no means blindly loyal to British interests. In both places, British administrators exploited these divisions but also became embroiled in local disputes. In Cyprus the key issue for elites, including the Orthodox Church was *enosis*.

Support for *enosis* emerged gradually at the elite level after Britain gained control of Cyprus in 1878. It was assisted in part by the British imposition of "modernist principles – civil and secular institutions and ethnic and racial identification" which "created space for Hellenic nationalists to spread the topological dream of Hellenism" (Varnava 2009).

Enosis was promoted by urban economic elites who had the ability to influence the Greek Cypriot peasantry.[3] It was not a mass movement, but one imposed from above. It can be categorized as a skewed form of nationalism, a Hellenic nationalism rather than an indigenous Cypriot one (Varnava 2009). The strength of this movement within Greek Cypriot elite circles generated distrust among British administrators who responded by carefully balancing the limited power they gave to Cypriots. McHenry (1987) suggests that the inner circle of the movement came from the Church reacting to the loss of its power, the literate urban elite asserting their identity, and school teachers who acted as cultural gate-keepers. These touchstone issues of language in Malta and enosis in Cyprus were present in the two events considered in this chapter.

MALTA—THE PASTORAL LETTER AND THE FAILED ELECTION

The suspension of the constitution in 1930 did not represent a sharp decline in the ability of the British to suppress such challenges to their authority but it did show the enduring support of Maltese elites for the nationalist cause. Malta is often perceived by scholars as one of the more successful colonies but it too had a strong undercurrent of nationalist discontent.

Malta had been part of the British Empire since 1800. It was a "fortress colony" which was the home of the British Mediterranean Fleet. Malta's economy was tied to British military spending and the island always retained great strategic importance for the British. In 1830, Count Camilo Sciberras and George Mitrovich set up the *Comitato Generale Maltese* and successfully petitioned for a Council of Government (a limited form of self-government) which was introduced in 1835.

Although subject to constant change and reform, these self-government mechanisms continued and during the interwar period in Malta, there were three main political parties. The first of these was the Nationalist Party. They were the successors the early nationalist politicians which had pushed for more self-government from the early nineteenth century. Fortunato Mizzi, founder of the Maltese *Partito Nazionale* or Nationalist Party[4] in the late nineteenth century and his son Enrico Mizzi led the Nationalist Party during the interwar period.

The second major party in Malta was the pro-British Constitutional Party formed in 1921 and led by Lord Strickland, a man of Anglo-Maltese heritage. He had been operating in Maltese politics for some time and his party pursued positions consistent with his being in the British Conservative Party, his desire for the Anglization of Malta, his *anti-italianita* leanings, and his antagonism toward Italy (Frendo 1979). The third party was the Maltese Labour Party which emerged from the trade union movement, particularly those operating in the dockyards (Dobie 1967). The new Labor Party, formed in 1921 and led by William Savona, contested the elections under the new constitution (Briguglio 2010). Its policies were pro-British and included a commitment to English as the future official language of Malta (Frendo 1979). The dockyards and naval spending produced many jobs and created a strong labor movement in Malta. The Labor Party policies made for a natural alignment with the Constitutional Party and an antipathy to the Nationalist Party.

In the 1920s, the political situation in Malta settled into a two-sided affair, with a coalition of the Constitutionalist and Labor, opposing the Nationalist Party. The Constitutionalist Party did not achieve government until 1927 when the coalition defeated Nationalist Party led by Enrico Mizzi (Frendo 1979; Holland 2012). This alignment of the Labor party against a pro-Italian party is hardly surprising given the hostility of Italian Fascism toward organized labor. This electoral victory also began a period of "unprecedented internecine political violence" (Frendo 1995). The win may have appeared to be a positive for British administrators but in actual fact the divisive, polemical style of the Constitutional Party made it less amenable to stable government than the Nationalist Party.

The Nationalist Party was pro-Italian language, in favor of Maltese autonomy, anti-imperialist and pro-Church. Their form of nationalism is often referred to as *italianita*. It was not a crass Italian irredentist movement but a culturally based movement focusing on issues such as language, education, and culture. In Malta, nationalism was a product of firstly the geographic and historical link to Italy (especially through language) and secondly a common religion (Frendo 1998). The Maltese cultural elites had an attachment to language that was in part rooted in their professions such as lawyers, academics, and priests. Italian was the language of work for them, they had a privileged position in the establishment, and maintained a conservative position when it came to change.

The Nationalist Party of the interwar period had the misfortune to coincide with the rise of assertive fascism (Frendo 2012). Indeed, Italian Fascism colored all aspects of nationalism, colonial resistance and colonial control in Malta at this time. The presence of Fascist Italy was counterproductive to Maltese nationalists seeking to limit de-Italianization. The nationalists had to contend with Italian commentators who "readily mistook *italianita* for an irredentist programme" and portrayed the Maltese as "Italians under the British flag" who yearned for Italian annexation (Frendo 1992).

Strickland was able to make great political capital out of the situation as he sought to associate Mizzi and the Nationalists with the more extreme politics of Fascist Italy. He was a confrontational politician and he clashed with the strongest cultural institution in Malta, the Catholic Church.

The Catholic Church had tended to cooperate with the British in Malta, so long as the administration respected their hierarchy, religious beliefs and practices (Frendo 2012). This lack of irredentist sentiment in the Church was due in part to the running dispute between the Holy See and the Italian government, which was not resolved until the Lateran Treaties of 1929 between Pope Pious XI and Mussolini (Knee 1990).

In 1928, however, two members of the clergy sitting in nominated seats in the Senate chose to vote with the opposition (the Nationalist Party) against the Strickland Government's appropriation bill (Askwith 1932). The Catholic Church through these clergies had effectively intervened in Maltese politics. This angered Strickland and began a period of antagonism between him and the Church. It was in this atmosphere that an Italian national, Father Felice Romolo Carta, tried to impose a temporal (i.e., not spiritual) penalty on a wayward Monk, Father Guido Micallef, by sending him to Italy (Anderson 1929). Micallef had been drinking and returning to his accommodation late at night in a "breach of monastic discipline" (Askwith 1932). Strickland's Government, believing that the Church was targeting a constitutionalist, responded by attempting to prosecute and deport Father Carta (Act No. 111 of 1924). In August 1929, Mussolini involved himself personally in the matter. He instructed Antonio Bordonaro (Ambassador to London) to express Italy's concern over Strickland. Mussolini had no real ambitions to annex Malta at that time, but he was very willing to provoke Britain and to exacerbate internal tension.

In September, a series of letters were exchanged between the Church and the Maltese Government where the Church tried to claim a right of *Privilegium Fori* (Privilege of the Forum—a right for a priest to be tried before a Canon Court) for Father Carta, a claim strongly rejected by the Maltese Government (Galea 1929). Strickland believed that there was collusion between the Pope and the Duce (Kent 1981). The Foreign Office became involved due to the international aspect of the dispute and it led a more aggressive position under Permanent Under-Secretary Robert Vansittart (Fenech 2013). Vansittart was determined to appease Italy but to maintain a strong line elsewhere, and this included a firm position against the actions of the confident, post-Lateran and legally separate, Holy See.

The international context above this local dispute was of course the building international tension which intensified in the 1930s. Decisions about Malta in the interwar period were often influenced or compromised by geopolitical considerations and this is an important background to Maltese interwar politics.

The Strickland-led Constitutional Party government of Malta had aligned with the British, and the Nationalist Party had aligned itself with the Catholic Church. The political situation in Malta became more intense as the electoral campaign began (Dobie 1967). Then, on 1 May 1930 the Catholic Archbishop of Malta, Dom Maurus Caruana, and the Bishop of Gozo, Monsignor Michael Gonzi, with Vatican approval, took the dramatic step of issuing a highly political pastoral letter. After a long preamble the letter came to the point:

> You may not, without committing a grave sin, vote for Lord Strickland and his candidates, or for all those even of other parties, who in the past have helped and supported him in his fights against the rights and the discipline of the Church, or who propose to help and support him in the coming elections. (Gonzi 1930)

This was followed up by a threat to withhold the Sacraments to those who refused to obey these instructions.

Governor Du Cane wrote that he was

> strongly of the opinion that the issue of the Pastoral Letter makes a free election impossible, and that it discloses pretensions on the part of the Church which cannot be tolerated, as they amount to undue influence in an aggravated form. (Passfield 1930b)

Maltese domestic affairs had reached a point where the British again felt they needed to reassert control. This was a direct result of the political schism between the constitutionalists and nationalists. Nationalist agitation had in effect disrupted British colonial rule in Malta.

Both the Maltese Constitution and the election were suspended on 3 May 1930 by the promulgation of an ordinance by Du Cane. No military power was needed, but rather the tried and true legal mechanisms were again employed (Malta had already been subject to a series of constitutional suspensions in the twentieth century).

In a telegram to London, Du Cane predicted that if an election were held within a few weeks the Constitutional party would be wiped out and:

> the influence of pro-Italians would be increased to an extent that might become a potential danger to security of the fortress. From many sources I hear that the Fascist Government is behind this trouble …The result of the recent Naval Disarmament Conference, however, has no doubt shifted the naval strategic centre of gravity to the Mediterranean thus enhancing the importance of Malta as a naval base. (Passfield 1930a)

Du Cane had the broader picture in mind, but he was exaggerating the direct interference of the Fascists. The actions of the Catholic Church occurred in line with the general political atmosphere, and with its general Maltese nationalist and *italianita* sympathies.

A Royal Commission led by high profile industrial arbitrator Lord Askwith[5] into the suspension of the Constitution began in April 1931 (Askwith 1932). In February 1932, it reported that the Maltese constitution had not worked well, but the Commissioners were of the opinion that a new election should be held and Parliamentary Government restored (Askwith 1932).

Although the Commission was in favor of limited self-government and had both protected the Nationalists and been tough on Strickland, it was not all good news for the Nationalists. The Commission:

> expressed strongly the view that in the interests of the Maltese and of education in Malta a change should be made in the curriculum of the elementary schools in order to make English the only extra language to be taught in addition to the Maltese vernacular. (Cunliffe-Lister, Askwith 1932)

This was an attack on the core Nationalist issue and created conditions for the next crisis. Malta did not suffer the level of repression seen in

Cyprus, but the British still pushed their agenda on key cultural issues forcefully. The Commission's findings were enacted in the Letters Patent of May 1932 which effectively reinstated the diarchy or dual government model. As foreshadowed the Letters Patent included language provisions that specifically limited the teaching of Italian to secondary school.[6]

In line with the Commission's recommendations, a new election was called in 1932, which the Nationalists won comfortably. Led by Sir Ugo Mifsud and Dr. Enrico Mizzi, future Minister of Education, the party campaigned on a platform of return to *pari passu*, the system of teaching both English and Italian in schools at both elementary and secondary level (Frendo 2012).[7] They were in effect politically committed to a course of action that was in breach of the Letters Patent. Defense of the Italian language was for the Nationalists a core part of their defense of *italianita* and the culture of Malta. The impasse over language led to the dismissal of the Nationalist government (Frendo 2012) and the suspension of the constitution in November 1933 (Dobie 1967).

Considering the language issue more generally, it is asserted by historians such as Henry Frendo that the whole language policy was "driven by Anglicization at the expense of Italian—with Maltese mainly as a ruse" (Frendo 2012). This is a correct interpretation; the British concern for an autochthonous language was far secondary to their desire to reduce Italian influence.

The "pastoral letter dispute" demonstrated the significant influence of the Catholic Church in Malta, acting with Italian Government support. It also demonstrated the way in which colonial nationalism worked against British Imperialism. The constant disruption, anxiety, and unrest had to be met with adaptation and change. In Malta the disruption was political rather than violent and the solution was constitutional change rather the broad political repression. The following year in Cyprus, more dramatic events were met with a more severe response. In 1931, Cyprus endured a colony-wide outbreak of violence and dissent, which provoked a sharp change in British rule.

Cyprus—The Violence and Repression of 1931

In 1931, Cyprus was governed by Britain's representative, Governor Storrs, who had been in charge of the colony since 1926. By 1931, he was growing increasingly frustrated by his inability to suppress the resilient and perennial Greek Cypriot demands for *enosis*.

His mismanagement of the colony, its people, and its finances reached a head in late 1931. By this time both the Cypriot Legislative Council (a mechanism for limited self-government) and the Colonial Office were unhappy with Storrs' management of the budget and the *enosis* movement was reaching its interwar zenith. Large rallies were being held around Cyprus and on 21 October 1931 some three to five thousand people gathered in Ledra Street in the center of the capital Nicosia (Morgan 2010). After listening to impassioned pro-*enosis* speeches, the crowd, aware that Storrs was going on leave, proceeded to Government House, a building three kilometers south of Ledra Street (Gwynn 1934).

A small, and ultimately inadequate, force of five mounted and eight-foot police were sent out to guard the entrance to Government House. They were stoned by the crowd which reached the front door of the building. At 9 p.m. cars were burnt, windows were broken by stones and at approximately eleven pm the police, following guidelines, attempted a baton charge which failed (Freeman 1933). Concerted attempts were then made by the crowd to light the building. The police followed procedure and shouted a final warning before firing a volley of shots into the crowd, at which time the crowd fled (Storrs 1931c). One of the protesters subsequently died from his wounds (Storrs 1931d). Despite the shooting, the fire had taken hold of the wooden structure and Government House and Storrs's possessions were lost as the building burnt to the ground (Storrs 1931a). This event was followed by widespread violence across Cyprus and military suppression of dissent.

Cyprus, like Malta, endured its own "sham responsible parliament".[8] On 30 November 1882, a new constitution had been introduced allowing for a Legislative Council made up of eighteen members, of whom six were appointed British Officials and twelve (a majority) were elected, nine by Christians and three by Muslims (Holland and Markides 2006). The ethnic division in the Council roughly translated to that on the island, which was 73.9% Greek Cypriot, and 24.4% Turkish Cypriot (Office and Barry 1884). Although this did not happen immediately the implication of the numbers was that the Greek Cypriot representatives could be stymied by the Turkish Cypriot representatives voting with the British. George Hill in his seminal four volume *History of Cyprus*, using paternalistic language, remarked that Cyprus had acquired a "toy parliament" and that this toy "as so often happens, was to be a great nuisance to the giver" (Hill 2010). The Legislative Council continued up until 1931.

The strict limitation on self-government contributed to stultification of local politics, a fixation upon the messiah of *enosis* among elites and a broad anger among the working and rural classes that in a climate of economic privation could be harnessed by that elite. The events of 1931 saw a rocking back on to an authoritarian mode of government which lacked moral legitimacy, a deficiency that was papered over by military resources. Interwar Cyprus was a site of constant nationalist agitation and insufficient spending.

The difficulty the British had in dealing with the internal dissent and Greek Cypriot nationalism in Cyprus is typified by Governor Sir Ronald Storrs, whose talent and ambition came up against the deep problems in Cyprus resulting in career-limiting failure. A key turning point was the general outbreak of violence sparked by the burning down of Government House in 1931. Rappas (2008) suggests that the desire on the part of the British to show strength in the face of fascism manifested itself not in direct confrontation, which was counter to appeasement policy, but by tightening its rule in Cyprus, an "authoritarian turn". The broad and sustained repression after this event kept Cyprus firmly under British control, but it had long-term consequences and damaged the legitimacy of their rule. The extent of the authoritarian turn in Cyprus is what distinguishes it from Malta.

On 22 October 1931, Storrs, who had escaped harm, telegraphed the Colonial Secretary, James Henry Thomas, to inform him that a:

> Large procession led by three Greek Elected Members of the Council demonstrated for 3 ½ hours last night Wednesday before Government House, threw stones threat (sic) kept police at bay with missiles and finally set fire to Government House which was burnt to the ground. (1931c)

Tabitha Morgan (2010) suggests that the British colonial government and the British community were stunned, that "cocooned by privilege they were detached from the social and political tension within Cypriot society and for the most part ignorant of the extent of economic deprivation". This played into the hands of the Greek Cypriot nationalists, which the British also failed to realize. British administrators of the Empire were on the defensive, Burton (2015) argues more generally that empire was "undefended or underdefended, against the sheer possibility" of dissent and disruption. This blindness she contends can be attributed to "orientalism or racism or whatever sets of belief that account for the incapacity of will or self-governing deficits empire builders only too willingly attributed to those they attempted to colonize". The immediate solution to unrest and the path to restoration of power was violence. The telegram sent by Storrs asked for military support to bolster the permanent garrison, which consisted of only three officers and 123 men (Morgan 2010). Additional troops came from Egypt (Georghallides 1985). On 22 October, six Victoria aircraft each carrying 20 infantry left Heliopolis for Cyprus (Headquarters) and three cruisers and two destroyers were also dispatched (Cunliffe-Lister 1931).

The burning down of Government House was symbolic, but was just one part of a broader outbreak of dissent and unrest. There was unrest in up to one-third of all villages in Cyprus and in Limassol the Commissioner's House was burnt down (Georghallides 1985). The violence and the protests were a result not only of agitation for *enosis* but also of the general political climate. This was depression-era economic privation blended with colonial subnationalism. Britain lost control of the situation in Cyprus and had to resort to military aid to power.

By 27 October, the towns had been pacified, but the disturbances in the rural areas continued until the first week of November (Freeman 1933). The Cypriot Legislative Council was abolished on 12 November and severe political repression and police state tactics, not acceptable within Britain itself, were used. Storrs (1931b) implemented a range of measures including prohibiting the carrying of arms, holding of assemblies, banning Greek flags and the ringing of church bells and a collective fine of £35,000. He ordered the censoring of telegrams, reading and stopping letters and prevented Greek newspapers sympathetic to *enosis* from being imported to the island. In addition to this, there were "several thousand arrests, trials and convictions" (Brendon 2007; Morgan 2010). As a result of the disturbances, the Cypriot Court system tried 3359 people, of whom 2606 were convicted (Georghallides 1985). Storrs began immediately arresting and deporting "ringleaders" including the Bishop of Kitium (Nicodemos), elected Members of Council, Theodotou, Haji-Pavlou and Dionysios Kykkotis, Chief Priest of the Phaneromeni Church in Nicosia (Storrs 1931e). Bishop Makarios of Kyrenia was arrested in the early morning of the 26th making for a total of ten deportations (Freeman 1933).

Storrs (1999) wrote to his friend George Lloyd on December 1931 and described the "numberless tributes" he had received for his handling of the crisis and his opinion that his "stock is not unenhanced" in the eyes of the government. This perception was not accurate; despite the initial support of Thomas, Storrs was "broken and his career shattered" (Morgan 2010).

Colonial Secretary Sir Philip Cunliffe-Lister[9] oversaw the suspension of the Cypriot Constitution in November, and all powers to make laws were granted to the governor (Cunliffe-Lister). The elected members were bitterly upset about the changes and Storrs' handling of the matter in particular. Politician Phidias Kyriakides, for example, wrote in his resignation letter (from the Legislative Council) that

> had I hated England and desired the humiliation and collapse of the British Empire I would have wished for this only – to see England entrusting the administration of the vast British Empire to fifty Storrs' in order that I might see it crumbling to ruins from the very morrow. (Kyriakides 1931)

After the riots, anxious British administrators watched local politics very closely. On 2 December 1932, the acting governor of Cyprus, H. Henniker-Heaton, appraised the General Officer Commander of the British Troops in Egypt and the Colonial Secretary Cunliffe-Lister of the political situation in Cyprus. He noted that the nationalists were mostly quiet, and that the people were tired of political agitation as they realized that the unrest was an expensive failure, that notables were inclined to cooperate "when cooperation does not conflict with other interests" and that *enosis* was "scotched not killed". Henniker-Heaton noted that:

> Political unrest is keenest in the towns. The villager wants political quiet so that he can devote himself to earning a livelihood. In the towns and larger villages there is a body of unemployed, rapscallions, criminals, and excitable school boys, irresponsible persons with little or nothing to lose, among whom disturbances might be created by malevolent persons which might easily become serious. (Henniker-Heaton 1932)

This supports the argument that the general unrest in the Mediterranean colonies was motivated in part by economic distress. The violence in Cyprus took place in 1931, when the Depression was in full swing (Stubbs 1933).

The riots "marked a profound transformation in British attitude to Cypriot culture" and from that point the administration championed an inclusive pan-Cypriot nationalism as distinct from Greek Cypriot nationalism (Morgan 2010). This was not a new approach but one that had developed since the 1915 offer of Cyprus to Greece. In Malta, a move to champion a distinct Maltese identity, over a Maltese identity which incorporated Italian culture, was based on the Maltese language but in Cyprus it was based on the spurious archaeological concept of an "eteo-Cypriot", a distinct ethnic group (Given 1998).

The October 1931 events were ultimately seen by many in the British government as a positive. It was the excuse they needed to dispense with the old constitution (Storrs 1999).

Dawe wrote in a private letter that:

> we shall at last have that reform of the constitution which I have been attempting for over 3 years... We shall be able to abolish that incessant and seditious waving of the Greek flag as indeed might have been done better and easier by my first predecessor, Lord Wolseley, in 1878 or again on the Annexation of the island in 1914 or lastly when it was proclaimed a Crown Colony in 1925. (Storrs 1999)

As Rappas (2014) suggests "the October 1931 revolt constituted an auspicious event as it enabled the removal of the last obstacles in the colonial state's expansion, promoting at the same time the role of colonial administrators". For years the old constitution had left the British in the undesirable position of relying upon the Turkish Cypriot voting bloc in the Legislative Council, always anxious that their measures might be blocked.

The shift to a long-term authoritarian system did not occur in the strategically important, fortress colony of Malta where, despite a series of constitutional crises, the British government doggedly persisted in introducing new constitutions and new systems of government.

Conclusion

The events of 1930 and 1931 described above demonstrate the way in which nationalist internal dissent shaped the nature of the British Empire as the authorities' deployed violence and law to subdue and control colonial populations.

The complicating factor for Cyprus was the ethnic divide on the island and the two "home" countries, namely Greece to the Greek Cypriots and Turkey to the Turkish Cypriots, which had an affinity with and provided support to those ethnic communities. This divide was exacerbated by early British rule. Nationalistic feeling in the majority Greek Cypriot community was skewed to *enosis*. It was not Cypriot but Hellenic, it ignored at least 20% of the population (Turkish Cypriots) and it was divisive rather than inclusive. It fell afoul of the pitfalls of ethnic nationalism described above. During the interwar years the situation in the colony deteriorated, and the British administration regressed from a position of providing some local representation to a period of authoritarian and repressive rule.

In Malta, the nationalist movement also created difficulty for the British as it grappled with failed constitutional processes, the intervention of the Vatican and the need for appeasement of Italian Fascism. Maltese resistance in 1930 was not violent as it was in Cyprus. The Maltese employed powerful cultural institutions and amalgamated support around totemic issues such as language. In Malta, a clear political divide existed between pro-British Constitutionalists and supporters of *italianita*, an elite movement which supported the Italian characteristics of Maltese culture. In Cyprus, Greek Cypriot supporters of *enosis* completely excluded the significant Turkish Cypriot minority of the island.

This chapter has looked at the considerable challenge that nationalism presented to the operation of the British Empire in Malta and Cyprus. Constant unrest, dissent, and challenge were met with multiple reforms and changes in administration. The British government was willing to deploy a series of constitutional schemes to limit internal dissent but was also very willing to take the authoritarian turn when challenged. The response from Britain in each case was adapted to local conditions and considerations. In Malta, Britain was willing to use violence, but always granted legal reform whereas in Cyprus they made a much greater turn toward repression and authoritarianism. This was due to Malta's strategic importance and due to the more violent nature of Cypriot resistance, a source of embarrassment to British authorities.

British administrators in both places got their "hands dirty" in local politics, fighting to maintain their rule and the legitimacy of their position. When seriously challenged they deployed short-term violence and followed it with long-term constitutional change. The British sought calm hegemony, but what they had was a turbulent empire constantly challenged by nationalist thought and activism. The nationalist challenge to colonial rule should not be underestimated or too easily dismissed.

NOTES

1. This chapter utilizes primary source documents obtained from the British National Archives. The referencing in this chapter will use the following acronyms to identify British Government departments: Colonial Office (CO), Foreign Office (FO), Foreign and Commonwealth Office (FCO) and War Office (WO).
2. Members of the Advisory Council set up under Strickland were seen as collaborators. Collaboration was viewed very negatively by some in British colonies. In Cyprus the assassination of Antonios Triantafyllides, a lawyer, politician and member of the advisory council is attributed to this coopera-tion. For further information see FCO 141/2497: Cyprus: assassination of Antonios Triantafyllides.
3. *Enosis* was offered as the solution to poverty and other problems which the British administration had not been able to alleviate (see Varnava 2009).
4. Kent writes that Fortunato Mizzi linked Italian, Maltese culture (and social order) and Catholicism all together. This was a powerful combination, a "potent social ideology" which was to "unite the professional classes and the lower clergy in the political arena in the following years" (Kent 1981).
5. Askwith, George Ranken, Baron Askwith (1861–1942) was an industrial arbitrator and civil servant who was raised to the peerage for his work as the governments leader arbitrator prior to WW1.
6. Letters Patent (from the Latin *potente* or "open") is a type of legal doc-ument issued by a monarch or other person in authority that grants an office, right, property or monopoly or authorizes something to be done. See Seed (1992).
7. Maltese had been used in the school system predominantly at primary school level.
8. According to A.J. Dawe an official with the Colonial Office, Josiah Wedgwood, a Member of Parliament, had described the Cypriot Legislative Council as a "sham responsible parliament" (Ashton et al. 1996).
9. Cunliffe Lister was an active Colonial Secretary, who travelled in the Middle East and visited Cyprus and Palestine specifically (Robbins 2004).

REFERENCES

Anderson, E. G. t. M. (1929). *Letter Regarding Deportation of Priests.*
Ashton, S. R., Stockwell, S. E., & Studies, U. o. L. I. o. C. (1996). *Imperial Policy and Colonial Practice, 1925–1945: Metropolitan Reorganisation, Defence and International Relations, Political Change and Constitutional Reform.* H.M. Stationery Office.

Askwith, G. R. (1932). *Report [of The] Malta Royal Commission, 1931: Presented by the Secretary of State for the Colonies to Parliament by Command of His Majesty, January, 1932.* H.M. Stationery Office.

Baldoli, C. (2008). The 'Northern Dominator' and the Mare Nostrum: Fascist Italy's 'Cultural War' in Malta. *Modern Italy, 13,* 5.

Brendon, P. (2007). *The Decline and Fall of the British Empire, 1781–1997.* London: Jonathan Cape.

Briguglio, M. (2010). Malta's Labour Party and the Politics of Hegemony. *Socialism and Democracy, 24,* 213–226.

Burton, A. (2015). *The Trouble with Empire: Challenges to Modern British Imperialism.* Oxford: Oxford University Press.

Cunliffe-Lister 'Malta (Government's Decision)', 2 March 1932, cc 1089-91, (United Kingdom).

Cunliffe-Lister 'Cyprus', 12 November 1931, cc 254-6 54, (United Kingdom).

Darwin, J. (1991). *The End of the British Empire: The Historical Debate.* Oxford, UK and Cambridge, MA: B. Blackwell.

Dobie, E. (1967). *Malta's Road to Independence.* Norman: University of Oklahoma Press.

Fenech, D. (2013). How Malta Lost Self-Government, 1930–1933. In E. Buttigieg & K. F. Joan Abela (Eds.), *Proceedings of History Week 2011.* Midsea Books.

Freeman, C. H. A. (1933). The Rebellion in Cyprus 1931. *Army Quarterly, XXV,* 268–280.

Frendo, H. (1979). *Party Politics in a Fortress Colony: The Maltese Experience.* Valletta: Midsea Books.

Frendo, H. (1992). Italy and Britain in Maltese Colonial Nationalism. *History of European Ideas, 15,* 733–739.

Frendo, H. (1995). Britain's European Mediterranean: Language, Religion and Politics in Lord Strickland's Malta (1927–1930). *History of European Ideas, 21,* 47–65.

Frendo, H. (1998). The Naughty European Twins of Empire: The Constitutional Breakdown in Malta and Cyprus 1930–1933. *The European Legacy, 3,* 45–52.

Frendo, H. (2012). *Europe and Empire: Culture, Politics and Identity in Malta and the Mediterranean (1912–1946).* Santa Venera: Midsea Books.

Galea, A. (1929). Correspondence with the Ecclesisatical Authorities Regarding the Claim of the Clergy to the *Privilegium Fori.*

Georghallides, G. S. (1985). *Cyprus and the Governorship of Sir Ronald Storrs: The Causes of the 1931 Crisis.* Nicosia: Zavallis Press.

Given, M. (1998). Inventing the Eteocypriots: Imperialist Archaeology and the Manipulation of Ethnic Identity. *Journal of Mediterranean Archaeology, 11*(3), 3–29.

Gonzi, A. C. a. B. (1930). Joint Pastoral of the Bishops (Translation). P1010212 ed.

Gwynn, C. W. (1934). *Imperial Policing.* London: Macmillan.

Headquarters, R. A. F. M. E. Secret Telegram Re Airlift of Troops.

Henniker-Heaton, H. (1932). Letter Regarding Political Situation Reports from Cyprus.

Hill, G. F. (2010). *A History of Cyprus.* Cambridge, UK: Cambridge University Press.

Holland, R. F. (1985). *European Decolonization 1918–1981: An Introductory Survey.* Houndsmills, Basingstoke, Hampshire: Macmillan.

Holland, R. F. (2012). *Blue-Water Empire: The British in the Mediterranean Since 1800.* London: Allen Lane.

Holland, R. F., & Markides, D. W. (2006). *The British and the Hellenes: Struggles for Mastery in the Eastern Mediterranean 1850–1960.* Oxford and New York: Oxford University Press.

Kent, P. C. (1981). *The Pope and the Duce: The International Impact of the Lateran Agreements.* London: Palgrave Macmillan.

Knee, S. E. (1990). The Strange Alliance: Mussolini, Pope Pius XI, and the Lateran Treaty. *Mediterranean Historical Review, 5*(2), 183–206.

Kyriakides, P. I. (1931). Letter to Storrs.

Loizides, N. G. (2007). Ethnic Nationalism and Adaptation in Cyprus. *International Studies Perspectives, 8,* 172–189.

McHenry, J. A. (1987). *The Uneasy Partnership on Cyprus, 1919–1939: The Political and Diplomatic Interaction Between Great Britain, Turkey, and the Turkish Cypriot Community.* New York: Garland Pub.

Morgan, T. (2010). *Sweet and Bitter Island: A History of the British in Cyprus.* London: I. B. Tauris.

Office, G.-B. C., & Barry, F. W. (1884). *Report on the Census of Cyprus, 1881.*

Passfield, D. C. t. (1930a). Telegram Regarding Suspension of Constitution.

Passfield, D. C. t. (1930b). Telegram Regarding Pastoral Letter.

Rappas, A. (2008). The Elusive Polity: Imagining and Contesting Colonial Authority in Cyprus During the 1930s. *Journal of Modern Greek Studies, 26*(2), 363–397.

Rappas, A. (2014). *Cyprus in the 1930s: British Colonial Rule and the Roots of the Cyprus Conflict.* London: I. B. Tauris.

Robbins, K. (2004). Philip Cunliffe-Lister, First Earl of Swinton (1884–1972). In H. C. G. Matthew & B. H. Harrison (Eds.), *Oxford Dictionary of National Biography* (Online ed.). Oxford: Oxford University Press.

Roshwald, A. (2002). *Ethnic Nationalism and the Fall of Empires: Central Europe, the Middle East and Russia, 1914–23.* London: Taylor & Francis.

Seed, P. (1992). Taking Possession and Reading Texts: Establishing the Authority of Overseas Empires. *The William and Mary Quarterly, 49*(2), 183–209.

Storrs, S. R. (1931a). Secret Despatch Regarding Riot.

Storrs, S. R. (1931b). Letter to Colonial Secretary Re Censorship.

Storrs, S. R. (1931c). Telegram from Storrs to Colonial Secretary.

Storrs, S. R. (1931d). Telegram from Storrs to Colonial Secretary.

Storrs, S. R. (1931e). Telgram from Storrs to Colonial Secretary re deportations.

Storrs, S. R. (1999). *RE: Middle East Politics and Diplomacy, 1904–1950 the Papers of Sir Ronald Storrs (1881–1956) from Pembroke College*. Cambridge.

Stubbs, R. E. (1933). Digest of Information Received from the Commissioners on the Political Situation in Their Respective Districts During the Month of March 1933.

Varnava, A. (2009). *British Imperialism in Cyprus, 1878–1915: The Inconsequential Possession*. Manchester: Manchester University Press.

CHAPTER 14

Encountering Imperialism and Colonialism: The Greek and Turkish Left in Cyprus

Nikos Christofis

INTRODUCTION

The Cyprus Question is often rightfully described as a confrontation between two nationalisms on Cyprus, Greek Cypriot and Turkish Cypriot nationalism. These, of course, were forms of Greek nationalism and Turkish nationalism, respectively (e.g., Carpentier 2017; Altay 2005; Anagnostopoulou 2004; Kızılyürek 2002). As an issue that holds nationalism at its core, and carries national connotations, the Cyprus Question has assumed to this day a central place in the political agendas of all parties involved in Cyprus. The literature on Cyprus and the dynamics of nationalism that were deployed in the island, although extensive (see, Christofis 2018), has yet to systematically analyze the politics of the "Motherland" Left parties on the issue.[1] The anti-communist frenzy during the Cold War, but also afterward, made it impossible for the "voice of the Left" to be heard without being thought of as non-patriotic, or even, anti-national (Christofis 2015). Recent studies that focus on the Left (Katsourides 2014; Alecou 2015) deal almost exclusively with the Cypriot Left, namely

N. Christofis (✉)
Center for Turkish Studies and School of History and Civilization,
Shaanxi Normal University, Xi'an, China

© The Author(s) 2018
T. Kyritsi and N. Christofis (eds.), *Cypriot Nationalisms in Context*,
https://doi.org/10.1007/978-3-319-97804-8_14

283

the Communist Party of Cyprus (Κομμουνιστικό Κόμμα Κύπρου, CPC), later renamed the Progressive Party of Working People (Ανορθωτικό Κόμμα Εργαζόμενου Λαού, AKEL). As a result, the political agenda and strategy, as well as discourses and practices of the Greek and Turkish left-wing parties over Cyprus, remain very much understudied.

The present chapter does not focus on the Cyprus Question per se or the politics surrounding it. Instead, it contributes to filling the afore-mentioned gap in the literature in the history of Cyprus by exploring the ways that the Greek and Turkish left-wing parties attempted to play an active role in the politics of their respective countries in the early Cold War through the politics of anti-imperialism and anti-colonialism. Specifically, the chapter focuses on the legal representatives of the Left: in Greece, the United Democratic Left (Ενιαία Δημοκρατική Αριστερά, EDA); and in Turkey, the Workers' Party of Turkey (Türkiye İşçi Partisi, TİP). Both parties were active during a period in which leftist move-ments were under increasing pressure as a result of the Cold War, but also one in which the global anti-colonial movement was reaching its apex during the long 1960s (Palieraki in this volume).

Within the context of the period, the Cyprus Question acquired importance in the parties' political programs and agendas as it was regarded as a key anti-colonial movement at the time. It deployed as well to counter the dominant ideological narratives of the contempo-rary Greek and Turkish political establishments. It did so by contribut-ing to the overthrow of British colonialism and by challenging Western interests, namely British and American imperialism, and by linking these to local collaborators seen as abetting Greek and Turkish depend-ence on the Western powers. In that respect, Cyprus was used as a "safe ground" to do national politics,[2] while allowing the left-wing parties to foreground their core political principles, namely anti-imperialism and anti-colonialism.

A BRIEF NOTE ON THE DEFINITION OF TERMS

More often than not, imperialism and colonialism tend to be used inter-changeably, as analogs of Western economic, political and cultural dom-ination over underdeveloped geographical areas. However, their use often confuses more than it clarifies (Saccarelli and Varadarajan 2015). Avoiding extended theoretical endeavors, empire as a concept, at least in this chapter, follows Howe's (2002) definition of it as "a large political body which rules over territories outside its original political borders"; one that has a core territory, and "whose inhabitants usually continue to form the dominant ethnic or national group in the entire system—and extensive periphery of dominated areas" (p. 14).

Imperialism, on the other hand, refers to the actual process by which empires "formulate various strategies and deploy multiple tactics, techniques, or modalities—sometimes unstated or unofficial—to realize their policies and extend or sustain themselves" (Go 2013, p. 7). In other words, imperialism means that an imperial state annexes foreign land, subordinates the local population and declares official control over it, either by military conquest or non-military subjugation.[3] Contrary to indirect rule, which does not involve official colonization, direct colonial rule moves to radically alter indigenous structures of a society, such as replacing indigenous rulers with foreign ones, puts an end, or limits its capacity to operate freely, while, it takes over the entire operation of the state (Osterhammel 1999; Stoler et al. 2007, p. 10). Drawing on Marxist–Leninist/dependency theory, Coates (2014) emphasizes the element of exploitation, which works to the disadvantage of the periphery (p. 41), specifically, of core state citizens' exploitation of peripheral state subjects. The abrupt robbing of the colonized society's historical line of development, the external manipulation and, eventually, transformation of the dominated society according to the needs and interests of the colonial rulers, as well as the "'ideological formation' of the colonized," leaves the periphery subservient to the core (Motyl 1999, p. 124).

Both colonialism and imperialism, then, involve forms of subjugation and exploitation of one people over another, and as such, from a Marxist perspective, anti-colonialism and anti-imperialism have always formed part of the more general struggle against the system of global capitalism. Largely due to the inspiration of Marxist–Leninist ideas, the term *imperialism* is commonly used in the literature to refer to the particularly ruthless colonial practices used by Europeans in the late nineteenth and early twentieth centuries (LaMonica 2014). Young's (2001) careful articulation on the distinction between Marxist analyses of colonialism and imperialism sets the context to our analysis. As he notes, "[from] an anti-colonial perspective, ... Marxism formed part of the particular struggle against colonialism and could be combined with and adapted to other resources, in particular nationalism" (pp. 111–112).

From Nairn (1981) to Schwarzmantel (1991) and other scholars who have dealt with the issue, it becomes clear that there is "no straight line from Marxism to the nation and nationalism; nor any specifically Marxist theory of the nation and nationalism as distinct from later Marxists providing valuable insights, theoretical and political, for grappling with these modern developments" (Breuilly 1985, pp. 74–75; Vanaik 2018). What has been noted throughout the past two centuries is that "both despite and because of the contradictory nature of the philosophical assumptions of nationalism and Marxism, the former has played a central role throughout the history of the latter" (Connor 1984, p. 6; also, Nimni 1994; Munck 1986). Decolonization and the subsequent emergence of the Third World[4] as a political category implied a geographical shift in the axis of socialism from the West to the Third World. According to Lenin (2010), imperialism provides the vessel of legitimization for all national struggles for liberation that he predicted would follow in the colonial or semi-colonial world. Nationalism in the periphery, which is intensified with capitalist expansion, turns into "an anti-capitalist force, as the national movements in the non-European colonies emerge as a response to the exploitation of the colonial people by the European capitalist powers" (Avineri 1991, p. 645). As such, nationalism became a national attribute in the Third World, while, the nationalism of oppressed national minorities acquired a democratic and progressive content, reminiscent of the Marxian motto that "a nation cannot be free if it oppresses other nations" (Lenin 1974, p. 149). In the Third World, "nationalism is identified with socialism, the peasantry with the proletariat, anti-imperialism with anti-capitalism, until all the distinctions … are cast overboard in favor of a simple dichotomy: Western imperialism versus the starving masses of the Third World" (Ehrenreich 1983, p. 1). Thus, the nationalism of the periphery is transformed into an anti-capitalist, anti-imperialist, and anti-colonial force. Finally, as Osterhammel (1999) rightly argues, "imperialism implies not only *colonial* politics, but *international* politics for which colonies are not just ends in themselves, but also pawns in global power games" (p. 21).

THE GREEK AND TURKISH "MOTHERLAND" LEFT

Although neither country ever experienced official colonialism,[5] both the Greek and Turkish Left considered their respective countries as dependent, having been effectively "semi-colonized" by the great powers that exploited them, politically and economically. Within this context, Cyprus, a society which actually did experience direct colonialism, and carried national links with the two "Motherlands" provided a "contentious" issue (Tilly and Tarrow 2015), on which both ideology and political strategy would meet for the Left.

THE UNITED DEMOCRATIC LEFT (EDA)

The Greek Civil War (1946–1949) between the bourgeois right-wing forces and the Left ended with a country shattered—economically, politically and socially. The communists—outlawed after 1947—found themselves isolated especially after the imposition of the state of *Ethnikofrosyni* (loyalty to the nation), the dominant ideology of the Right, whose goal was to permanently exclude all leftist groups from the circle of power, and to prevent them from making political inroads to influence the ideological convictions (*fronima*) of the Greek people (Katiforis 1975, p. 33; also, Christofis 2017, pp. 211–212). *Ethnikofrosyni*, already evident during the interwar years, acquired new meaning from the 1940s onwards as an ideological process and as a practice, the most important element of which was its strong anti-communism, and its attachment to "national ideals," including post-war irredentist claims (Stefanidis 2007, p. 29; Bournazos 2009; Elefantis 2003).

Within this political environment, the EDA made its appearance on the Greek political scene as the only legal representative of the Left until 1967. It took shape initially, as a coalition of parties and personalities representing both the outlawed KKE and the democratic elements of Greek society. The party's core ideological program and principles were succinctly defined as *National Democratic Change*, where "change" referred to the close alliance between the labor force and the peasant class (EDA 1953, pp. 76–77), and the country's patriotic forces (EDA 1961b). Concomitantly, the EDA called for a "struggle to open the road for democratic rejuvenation" (EDA 1961a, p. 5). According to the party, its program would help Greece counter the policy of "national betrayal" that was being carried out by the Greek bourgeoisie in its support for foreign interests at the expense of the country. In short, as the party chairman, Ioannis Pasalidis, emphasized, the EDA was not demanding a socialist transformation but a change in direction which had as its grounding a "national, anti-imperialist and democratic inspiration" (*Avgi* 1956a). Although the party professed to achieve its goals through a "non-socialist" transformation of the country, this was rather a strategic political move. Considering the Cold War context and especially the fact that Greece had just emerged from a civil war, the EDA wanted to avoid being tarred with the non-patriotic/anti-national brush. This strategic play had a direct impact on the party's internationalist sensibilities since every mention of internationalism was a direct reference to the Soviet Union. The "nation," or nationalism, for the EDA, was both a goal and a means to an end (i.e., socialist transformation).

Against this background, the EDA had to counter and ultimately discredit the right-wing hegemony in defining the content and bound-aries of the nation and thus re-integrate itself into that category by proving its own patriotism in the hostile anti-communist environment of the time. In 1957, Norman Armour, head of an American *Special Committee to Study the Foreign Aid Program*, stated in a report that the Cyprus Question is the issue that the political stability of Greece depends on (*Avgi* 1957; also Lamprinou 2017, p. 365). That was true also for the EDA whose ideological principles, mainly anti-imperialism/anti-colonialism, and political strategy were to be deployed in the national issue of Cyprus.

THE EDA AND CYPRUS

From 1949, when the Greek Cypriots attempted to internationalize what would later come to be called the Cyprus Question at the UN, the issue affected all political parties and developments in Greece, becom-ing eventually the issue that would define the "national interest" vis-à-vis those who work against it. At the same time, the dynamic emergence of anti-colonial movements in the Third World was causing problems to anyone in the NATO camp that would support decolonization in the interior of their countries. Within this context, the Cyprus Question becomes the main issue that would destabilize the Western-oriented Greek foreign policy and allow the regrouped Left to find a way to affect domestic politics. Interestingly, as Stefanidis (2007) argues, this process took place through the prism of a Greek irredentism encapsulated in the demand for *enosis*.

For the Greek Left the opportunity the Cyprus crisis presented was a "godsend," affording it the chance to shake off the accusation of "high-treason" levelled against it by demanding the unconditional ces-sion of Cyprus to Greece and the termination of the Western presence in the island (Stefanidis 2007, p. 91). Furthermore, "stressing its anti-British and anti-colonialist aspect, it could project the *Enosis* struggle as a confirmation of the communist-led resistance and its 'anti-imperialist' aftermath during the 1940s" (Stefanidis 2007, p. 91).

Right from start, the EDA presented the Cyprus Question as an anti-colonial movement. Pasalidis stated before the Greek Parliament that: "the People [of Cyprus are] inspired by the successes and the example of other colonial Peoples, who shook off slavery and from the belief in the just liberation struggle" (*CQGP* 1997b, p. 156). For the EDA, the anti-colonial, and anti-imperialist, character of the Cyprus Question combined with the undisputed issue of *enosis*, which "everybody acknowledges [... bore] a moral and historical rationale of freedom based on the notion of self-determination of the people" (*CQGP* 1997a, p. 40), provided the legitimization the party needed in terms of the dominant narrative of the period, that of national fulfillment (*CQGP* 1997b, p. 30).

The British, in an attempt to counter the EOKA struggle in Cyprus that was launched in April 1955 invited Greece and Turkey, but not the representatives of the island, in London to discuss, among other issues, the situation in Cyprus. The invitation was seen by the EDA as "a British imperialist maneuver" to retain strategic advantage, at the same time advancing the position of local "collaborators" and "the chauvinist Turks" on board to prolong colonial practices on the island (EDA 1959, p. 11). The pogrom against the Rum population of Istanbul in the *6–7 September Events*, just a few days after the London meeting failed saw the EDA call for an immediate and permanent termination of relations with Turkey and its imperialist and colonial allies, the British (Trikkas 2009, p. 309).

At the same time, however, the EDA, as well as the AKEL in Cyprus, disagreed with the methods adopted by the EOKA. The bombing attacks carried out in particular sat poorly with the EDA's anti-colonial stance and opposition to "individual terrorism"; the party argued that "acts of violence cannot in any way promote the national struggle. The people of Cyprus must work for its fighting unity and be ready to undertake all kinds of struggle in order for its sacred desires to be satisfied" (Christofis 2015, p. 101). The bombings also drew a negative reaction from Washington, which urged against a repeated Greek recourse to the UN, urging at the same time that the center parties refrain from any partnership with the EDA. The EDA, for its part, strongly criticized the American intervention and its "anti-Greek actions," and also took the opportunity to attack Lord Radcliffe's proposals for a new constitution on the island, which the party argued ignored "the demand of our [i.e., Greek] Cypriot brothers for self-determination." This situation proved to the EDA that "the Cyprus Question cannot be solved according to the desires of the Greek people within the context of the 'Holy Alliance' of imperialist–colonizers" (EDA 1957, pp. 9–10).

The Suez crisis in 1956 added further grist to the mill. Already in 1955, Nasser had assured the Greek government that Egypt would support Greece in its dispute with Turkey over Cyprus (Hatzivassiliou 1989). Egypt's support opened the way for the Greek bourgeois press to criticize Britain, also in relation to Cyprus, but with the hope that the US would come and save the day (*Kathimerini* 1956). For the EDA, however, the situation was presenting a different reality, as it was disclosing the real intention of imperialism and the inability of the Greek government to handle the situation. "The Cyprus Question, just like the nationalization of the Suez Canal and the devastation of the colonial positions in Egypt," the party argued, can be solved as "the prestige of the imperialist powers was never so low, weakened by the continuous blows of the hereto slaves" (*EDAA*, box 34). Furthermore, the party, in a statement to the Arab countries, noted that "the Cyprus Question can be solved [only] under the condition that it will be incorporated in the anti-colonial struggle" (*EDAA*, box 34). Both the Suez crisis and the anti-colonial struggle in Algeria underlined the party's optimism "for peaceful co-existence of countries with different social systems," despite the constant attempts by the "British colonizers ... to bend the Cypriots over time" (*Avgi* 1956b). In that context, the EDA also blamed the Greek government for its inability to exercise pressure for a demilitarized Cyprus and for assisting foreign interests as it committed itself to discuss the issue in NATO. For the EDA, this policy indicated only that the island was destined to be used as a "military base against the anti-colonial struggle itself" (EDA 1957, p. 24).

The escalation of violent incidents on Cyprus in 1958/59 and the intensive diplomatic efforts at the time paved the way for the Zurich conference in February 1959, where negotiations between Greece and Turkey led to the signing of the London–Zurich Agreements. Although the agreements were presented in Greece, and Turkey, as a success, the EDA fiercely criticized the government's policy and characterized them as "diabolical," as they would create "complications to the constitutional status of Cyprus" and the future of Greece.

What is more, the party argued that the foreign Greek and Turkish military presence in the island, as well as the bases represented a "collective occupation" of the island (*CQGP* 1997c, p. 23). The London–Zurich Agreements disclosed, at the same time, the EDA's internationalist perspective and what kind of solution the party was aspiring to achieve for the island.

Although the image of the "chauvinist Turk" served as a leitmotif in many speeches, statements, and articles in leftist publications, following the London–Zurich Agreements the negative image of the "other" Turk became even more pronounced. In a booklet published by the EDA regarding the agreements, it was argued that "[the agreements were] prolonging colonial slavery [and] adulterated the pure anti-colonial character of the Cypriot struggle" by leveling up the Turkish state as one of the guarantor powers (EDA 1959, pp. 18–19).

In the case of the national ideology of the EDA, which was framed around "resisting Hellenism" (Christofis 2017), the collective national identity was defined negatively; that is to say against others. As Hobsbawm (1996) noted, "collective identities are based not on what their members have in common—they may have very little in common except not being the 'Others'" (p. 40). In the case of EDA—and the Greek Left generally, for that matter—the constant negative references to Turkish Cypriots constituted a lack of, or a distorted, recognition of their community. For the Greek Left, the Turkish Cypriots were gaining substance and visibility as part of the anti-colonial struggle only to the degree that the Turkish Cypriots were accepting of the prospect of the "self-determination—*enosis*" line.

On the one hand, the self-determination of the Cypriot people, the EDA argued, should be based on a united mass struggle in cooperation with the Turkish minority which also had an interest in freeing itself from the British yoke. Yet on the other, the Turkish Cypriots were treated not as a self-conscious group, but rather as a pawn of the imperialist powers, Great Britain and Turkey. In other words, for the EDA, the Turkish Cypriots had but two options: (1) identify with the imperialist interests of the British and the Turks, or; (2) side in favor of *enosis* (*EDAA*, box 372). It becomes obvious that the Turkish Cypriots are stripped off of their rights, they are treated as a "subaltern" group that can define its own future. Interestingly, although the protection of the Turkish Cypriot minority rights should be protected, this again, should be based on *enosis*:

We officially say that the proclamation and the application of the most rig-
orous and unrestricted respect for the rights of the Turkish minority not
only do not contradict but help the case of self-determination. This patriotic demand has nothing to do with it or it has to be disturbed because it
is being damaged by chauvinistic changes. Never national-liberation struggles should degenerate into the oppression of minorities. But that is something else. First of all, [we have to deal with] the self-determination of the
majority and then the respect of the minority. (*EDAA*, box 478)

On the other hand, the Turkish government was presented as "inso-
lently imperialist." For example, the events in Erenköy/Kokkina in
August 1964 were portrayed as an outcome of Turkish subservience to
the NATO alliance and the latter's efforts to destabilize the situation in
Cyprus. In that case, the claim made by the party was that "the NATO
allies [were] willing to intervene ... as long as, from that point onwards,
they were allowed to do [in Cyprus] what they want to do, ... reminding [Greeks] that what the Turks did could happen again." Imperialism
was presented as a conspiracy against Cyprus, Greece and all Middle
Eastern and independent countries generally. By striking Cyprus, the
argument went, the imperialists sought "to numb the morale of liberation movements. They want to establish an offensive military base facing the 'worrying' voices of the Afro-Asian shores" (Diamantopoulos
1964, p. 3). Additionally, the party did not refrain from drawing par-
allels with other cases. It argued, for example, Malta could expect the
same fate as Cyprus, given that "until recently its independence was
strongly opposed" but in light of the loss of bases in Libya and Cyprus,
"this is the only way NATO could establish base and control the Middle
East" (Odysseos 1964b). In that way, the imperialists were seen as moving to shore up the neo-colonial system. This was also the case in the
"American bloody intervention in Congo, the insolent aggressiveness
against Vietnam and Laos, and the frenzied quest for bases in the Indian
Ocean" (Odysseos 1964b).

Within this EDA narrative, the countries of the Third World were
cast as the true bastions of freedom and independence, a role which
was upgraded after the mid-1960s because of the shift in Soviet policy.
The Soviet Union's shift toward Turkey was confirmed in *Izvestiya* in
January 1965 when Soviet Foreign Minister, Andrei A. Gromyko stated
that the two Cypriot "national communities... may choose a federal
form of government" (Christofis 2015, pp. 146–149), an unacceptable

position for the EDA also. The Soviet Union, however, continued to be presented as the only steadfast champion of their national struggles for liberation, as indeed it was in the case of Cyprus. The promises of the Russian leader to "guarantee the independence and integrity of Cyprus," and the fact that the Soviet Union exhorted Great Britain to withdraw its troops and warned Turkey to stop offensives on the island, were advanced as evidence of Soviet support for Greece, Cyprus, and the independent countries more generally. And a declaration was made to the effect of: "The efforts the NATO coalition is making to intervene in the domestic matters of the Cypriot Republic are very dangerous for peace in the Mediterranean, as well as for world peace" (Odysseos 1964a).[6] The reaction of the imperialist powers to the murderous bombardments that took place on the island disclosed the goals the former were hoping to achieve and alarmed the Arab world, which realized through the Cyprus struggle the jeopardy they were also in. Cyprus was therefore identified as part of the greater Middle Eastern crisis and was linked with the politics of the wider Mediterranean region. It was argued that by placing the Cyprus Question within its "proper" regional (i.e., Middle Eastern and Mediterranean) framework, Greece would understand why "a solution that would "nuclearize" and make the island a NATO base, and thus help the imperialist powers fulfill their goal of oppressing people who are rising up in revolt, is not acceptable to the socialist world and independent countries" (Odysseos 1965).

THE WORKERS' PARTY OF TURKEY (TİP)

Cold War realities and Turkey's joining the NATO alliance essentially reflected the country's deeper Western vocation, as was envisioned and dictated by Kemalist circles and Mustafa Kemal himself. As in the Greek case, the Turkish state adopted anti-communism and transmuted it into a key element of state ideology, appropriating at the same time those Cold War elements that it deemed necessary to secure both national unity and the Western orientation of and identification with the nation (Christofis 2015).

After decades of illegality, the Left managed to organize itself through the Workers' Party of Turkey (TİP) in February 1961. The party was founded by a group of trade unionists under the liberalizing conditions brought about by the 1961 Turkish constitution, which allowed leftist parties to form and publications with Marxist content to publish, as long as they distanced themselves from communism. A year later the leadership of the party was assigned to Mehmet Ali Aybar, a well-respected lawyer, known for his socialist and democratic ideas. This change in leadership allowed the party to expand its reach geographically develop a more coherent socialist program and increase its public profile. The party's expansion and ideological articulation coincided with the relative peace in Cyprus during the first years of the island's independence. This allowed the party also to devote its energy to domestic issues, since foreign policy issues at the time failed to attract much more than passing attention (Hale 2000, p. 133).

The party's fundamental difference from the other leftist groups that formed around the same period was its belief that the attaining of power should be achieved through democratic elections and not through a violent class uprising, as well as its commitment to constitutional and parliamentary politics (Ünsal 2002, pp. 139, 143–145).[7] The political program of the party, ratified during its first congress in 1964, was described as a "non-capitalist path to development" (TİP 1964, p. 64), as in other Third World countries, with the aim of making sure that Turkey would become free, through a "planned, etatist, mixed economy" (Boran 1970).

Contrary to its Greek counterpart, whose aim was to strip *Ethnikofrosyni* from its anti-communism and right-wing content, in the Turkish case, the "official" ideology of the state, Kemalism, named after Mustafa Kemal (later Atatürk) was not only embraced, but, as any other party in Turkey since the 1960s, which claimed "the founding father as 'one of them'" (Zürcher 2012, p. 134), was interpreted according to its own political agenda, namely anti-imperialism.

Indeed, the party framed its anti-imperialism through the prism of Kemalism, something that offered a ready source of legitimacy but also highlighted the Left's complex relationship with Kemalism. The origins of this relationship, however, date to the period of the Turkish War of Independence (Kurtuluş Savaşı, 1919–1922). The *realpolitik* of the time led Mustafa Kemal and his circle to maintain friendly relations with the Bolshevik administration in exchange for Soviet support in the war (Christofis 2019), while the communist rhetoric adopted by Mustafa Kemal himself from time to time, and the support provided by the Third International to the national liberation struggle of Anatolia, confused the Turkish communists who found Kemalism to be progressive and anti-imperialist. By the 1960s, the Turkish Left found itself almost instinctively gravitating toward Kemalist rather than Marxist values resulting in a "leftist worldview comprised of a Kemalist core and a Marxist exterior" (Koçak 2013, p. 68). In other words, Kemalism was an embedded element of the Left's political strategy for legitimization, as well as nationalism. "In our Turkey," Aybar argued, "Atatürkist nationalism, apart from protecting the existence of the Turkish nation and keeping it on the path of survival, has shed light on the awakening and liberation of all oppressed nations in the world" (1963, p. 9).

The anti-imperialism of the Turkish Left came to be identified with an independent Turkish foreign policy, having as one of its main point of references the Cyprus Question (Christofis 2015). In contrast to its Greek counterpart, which clearly courted and received Soviet support, for the TİP an independent foreign policy meant equal distance from both the Soviet Union and the US. Following the example of the Third World and Latin America (Ünsal 2003, pp. 247–252), the TİP associated anti-imperialism, among other things, with nationalism, the latter being, according to Aybar (1963) "the ideological expression of our [Turkish] people against the foreign yoke, against imperialism and capitalism. [Nationalism] is resolutely attached to the idea of independence" (p. 9).

THE TİP AND CYPRUS

From the beginning, the TİP openly criticized the Turkish government for its pro-American and pro-NATO foreign policy alliance, a criticism which escalated when the Cuban missile crisis broke out, and demonstrated the "continuity in Turkish cooperation with the United States" (Harris 1972, p. 91). The 1963/64 crisis in Cyprus provided the opportunity the party needed to elaborate and popularize its own position on foreign policy issues, and specifically, on Cyprus. As Aybar argued, "beneath the Cyprus Question lie the interests of imperialism," something left Turkey unable "to pursue an independent foreign policy" (Aybar 1968, p. 322).

As the crisis of 1963/64 broke out, Niyazi Ağırnaslı, one of the TİP's two parliamentary representatives, expressed the party's concerns about the "Turkish Cypriot brothers" (*soydaş*), who needed to find a viable solution to live along the Greek Cypriots and prevent *enosis* from taking it root again. He also stressed that "[Turkish] dominant rights, independence and national dignity, stop at its [Turkey's] borders" (Salman 2004a, p. 54). This final point is of importance here since it directly references the Kemalist policy that was born in the 1919 National Pact, whereby irredentist claims were explicitly abandoned. This was an attempt by the TİP to burnish its Kemalist credentials and present itself as the true representative and continuation of the legacy of Mustafa Kemal.

Indeed, not long after the party published its first account on Cyprus. The article argued that the British were using the Turkish Cypriots to counter the EOKA struggle, with London thus forcing the Turkish government "to take part and make Cyprus a [Turkish] national issue" (*Sosyal Adalet* 1964, pp. 42–44). The same position was expressed in May in a more elaborative form in the party's meeting in Bursa. The main aim of the British, it was argued in Bursa, was "the preservation of their [imperialist] military bases for its own security purposes and to control the Middle East." The most important aspect of Aybar's speech, however, is the fact that he counters the already dominant national thesis on Cyprus. "The Cyprus Question was nonexistent for Turkey until 1955," when the EOKA struggle was launched and presented difficulties for the British, while the Turkish Cypriots were presented as lackeys to the British, never standing up to defend their rights and always collaborating with the colonialists against the Greek Cypriots, who resisted and manifested against the British. These developments led "Cyprus to primarily become an important military base for England since the latter left the Suez Canal," where the political interests of Britain in the Middle East, and in particular oil, could be readily controlled from Cyprus (*NVP*, box 4, folder 122).

Turkish threats to intervene imminently in Cyprus due to the prolonging of the crisis received a harsh answer in the infamous Johnson letter, in which the American president warned the Turkish government not to take any military action against Cyprus. The letter was crystal clear: failure to comply would automatically mean the retraction of any US assistance in the case of a Soviet attack. The American response created a new reality for the Turkish political parties and society triggering a wave of anti-American protests. It was the first time since the Second World War that Turkish and American strategic interests had diverged and thus the first time Turkey's alliance with the West was called into serious question. On the other hand, for the Left, the letter confirmed its fears, that America's initial reluctance was *prima facie* evidence that the US did not want to help Turkey.

For the Left, the American involvement showed that Turkey was fully dependent on foreign capital and had fallen into the trap of Anglo-Saxon imperialism. The adoption of a "multi-faceted" foreign policy by the Turkish government following the Johnson Letter was a kind of acknowledgment by the latter of how far it had been drawn away from Kemalist foreign-policy principles (*KSP*, folder 558). Within this critical juncture and the political developments that played out in the international arena, the TİP argued that "the Cyprus Question turned against Turkey and the Turkish community in Cyprus because of the English and American imperialists' support to their Greek allies" (Salman 2004a, p. 105). Turkey's *déjà vu* situation was explained by Behice Boran, one of the leading figures and later second chairman of the party, as Greece was acting as it had "forty-seven years ago," and:

> [H]ad come to be a pawn of Anglo-Saxon imperialism. On a smaller scale, it had also come to serve the imperialist policy of *Megali Idea*, supported by Anglo-Saxon imperialism. (Boran 1967, p. 10)

The increased popularity of the party and its entrance in the National Assembly with fifteen MPs in the elections of 1965 gave the party an opportunity to call for a common anti-imperialist front among "all the socialists and Atatürkists to unite their power for an independent foreign policy" (*KSP*, folder 551). Similarly, during the general congress held in the city of Malatya in 1966, it was decided that Turkey's primary agenda was to reach full independence by turning back to the foreign policy of Atatürk's Turkey during the National Liberation Struggle (TİP 1966).

The national liberation war was portrayed by the TİP as the historical basis of its understanding of national independence. In the party's narration of that period, those years were depicted as ones of national awakening for the people living within the borders of the National Pact. In Aybar's words:

> Forty-four years after the completion of the first one, we must begin a second National Liberation Struggle [...]. We are determined in the struggle until such time as the last American soldier has left our country. (*KSP*, box 610, folder 1)

Atatürk's nationalism was the battle-standard against Western imperialism and colonialism, and the American and British involvement in

Cyprus through the Johnson Letter and the Acheson Plan in Cyprus, made the people realize this. "The Cyprus Question," a party report notes, "is the most tangible, the most scrutable and sensitive issue of the anti-imperialist struggle and the Second National Liberation movement for the masses and the public opinion." "The Cyprus Question is the point of reference," the party report continues, "and of highest importance for the anti-imperialist struggle" (*KSP*, box 558). The issue of Cyprus, in other words, was presented as the continuation of the Turkish War of Independence, where the anti-imperialist and anti-colonialist spirit and principles of Mustafa Kemal would at last be fulfilled.

It is worth noting, however, that on the election of a significant number of MPs in the National Assembly in 1965, the party began to deviate from its initial position on the issue. The complexity of the Cyprus Question played no small part in that shift. The party had to reckon with three aspects of the issue that called its commitment to non-intervention into serious question: (1) the need to ensure and safeguard the rights and interests of the Turkish community; (2) the need to protect the national security of Turkey because through Cyprus imperialists could control the Mediterranean and the Middle East; and (3) the fact that the Cyprus Question was part of a broader anti-imperialist struggle—i.e., the anti-American struggle as the USA was at the forefront of contemporary imperialism (Boran 1967, p. 10). These three factors led the party to reevaluate the situation and conclude that Turkey's policy could not be limited to Turkey's borders, and therefore, it was "a duty" to "take up arms" and protect the country (Salman 2004b, p. 275).

Although the party still believed in a demilitarized, independent, federal Cyprus, "the duty to take up arms" was rationalized by the party ideologues on the grounds of the undisputed right of the Turkish people to "define its own fate" was being denied by imperialism and its domestic collaborator. This issue was also raised by the party in the National Assembly in 1967 (*TİP Haberleri* 1967) and saw the party eventually come around to endorsing military intervention in an independent state recognized by the UN. Therefore, Cyprus could not return to its rightful owner (i.e., Turkey), and the same stands also on the "double *enosis*—partition" solution which would be blocked by the Greek and Anglo-Saxon imperialists.

The collaborationist, imperialist image of Greece and Cyprus helped the TİP to make its arguments stronger. The process of "otherization," as in the Greek case, has a dual utility. First, it allowed a casting of the

Greeks, as they had been in the Turkish War of Independence, as imperialist collaborators now acting at the expense both of the Turkish Cypriot community and of Turkey more generally. Second, it allowed the party to burnish its nationalist credentials. Within this context, we notice an emphasis in the discourse of the party leadership against Archbishop Makarios, the political and religious leader of the Greek Cypriots and first President of the Republic in 1960.

The persistent attempt to deconstruct Makarios and prove his lack of legitimacy as Turkey's collocutor in the negotiations on the issue, involved also the Third World countries and their support. Makarios has managed to receive the support and assurances of the independent leaders regarding Cyprus, a support which, according to the TİP leadership was unfounded, since the Greek Cypriot leader skillfully played out the "national liberating card," without mentioning that the entire Greek Cypriot cause was "was tied to Enosis" (Salman 2004a, p. 149). Therefore, Makarios was a "de facto" leader and it should not be recognized by the UN or Turkey itself, as collocutor (Aybar 1967).[8] Disclosing Makarios' "double game of Enosis" to the Third World countries (Salman 2004c, p. 77) would be the only way to attract support for Turkey. As the argument went, it would "not be possible for us (Turks) to sustain sound relations and win them (Third World countries) over as long as they see us that way and as long as they believe that we are only by their side just because we want their support on Cyprus" (Salman 2004c, p. 77).

CONCLUSION

This chapter has dealt with the problematic relationship between Marxism and nationalism through the Greek and Turkish cases and their stance on the Cyprus Question. As a confrontation of diverse nationalisms the "national" issue of Cyprus provides a terrain where the complex relationship of Marxism and nationalism can be tested.

Although always foregrounding a consistent anti-imperialism/anti-colonialism, the Left aimed to fulfill the interests of the respective national centers. The goal of the Left was not to acquire national independence for Cyprus (i.e., an independent nation-state). Self-determination for the EDA meant, ultimately, the *enosis* of the island with the Greek Motherland, a rather contradictory anti-colonial position since the Greek party did not fight for the independence of Cyprus, but rather a transitory stage to *enosis*. In the Turkish case, it meant that national independence was the necessary solution since *Taksim* (partition) and accession to Turkey, the so-called "double enosis," were opposed. Within the political context of the period, and the dominant ideologies it had to compete with, it seems that the Left also could not escape from an anachronistic irredentism that saw Cyprus as an extension of the respective motherlands. The image of the national unity, the quest of the national interests and national fulfillment proved to be substantially effective for parties that sought legitimization within the Cold War. In the attempt to present the Left also as patriotic, and gain credentials and popularity by presenting itself as the vanguard of the whole nation, it came to adopt similar ideological tools (i.e., references to the glorious past, image of the negative "other,"), to those of the dominant ideologies, filtered of course, through an anti-imperialist and anti-colonial framework. What becomes evident through the Cyprus case though, is that socialism was subordinated to national ends, placing the anti-imperialist values of socialism at the service of the particularistic irredentist values of nationalism, and not that of an anti-colonial nationalism.

Notes

1. Only recently has scholarship started to focus on the issue in a systematic manner. For example, see Christofis (2015), Antoniou (2015), Güvenç (2008), and Korkmazhan (2017). The Turkish Cypriot Left has not been systematically studied yet at all.
2. Another aspect focusing on the collective memory processes and discourses of the two parties has been published elsewhere (Christofis 2017, pp. 208–227).
3. This depends on *how* political influence is exercised, separating *formal/colonial rule* (direct) from *informal/quasi-colonial control* (indirect) (Go 2013, pp. 9–10; Osterhammel 1999, p. 20).
4. Although the present author acknowledges that "The three worlds configuration was a product of Eurocentric mappings of the world to deal with the postcolonial situation that emerged after World War II" (Dirlik 2004), and that a better term perhaps would be "Tri-continental", uniting, under the same symbolic anti-imperialist umbrella Asia, Africa and Latin America, "Third World" will be used throughout the chapter however, because it was used during the period under study.
5. Turkey has never been colonized and, except in the immediate aftermath of World War I (1918–1922), has never been threatened by any Western country (Bozarslan 2008).

6. The Soviet Union in Greece is presented as the supporter of the Greek cause of self-determination, both symbolically and practically. In the Turkish case, the TİP keeps equal distance both from the US, for ideological reasons, and from the Soviet Union, for practical reasons.

7. The other groups included the intellectuals who gathered around the review *Yön* (*Direction*) and a group led by Mihri Belli. They emerged out of ideological disagreements concerning the method of attaining power used by the TİP, the *Milli Demokratik Devrim* (National Democratic Revolution, MDD).

8. *Yön* argued that the UN Security Council chose Makarios as collocutor on 4 March 1964, therefore, the party's argument is not valid.

REFERENCES

Alecou, A. (2015). *Communism and Nationalism in Postwar Cyprus, 1945–1955: Politics and Ideologies Under British Rule.* Basingstoke: Palgrave.

Altay, N. (2005). *Nationalism Amongst the Turks of Cyprus: The Frist Wave.* Oulou: University of Oulu.

Anagnostopoulou, S. (2004). *Turkish Modernization: Islam and Turkish Cypriots in the Mazy Path of Kemalism.* Athens: Vivliorama.

Antoniou, A. (2015). *Ελληνική Αριστερά και Κυπριακό Ζήτημα στη Δεκαετία του 1950* [The Greek Left and the Cyprus Question during the 1950s]. Ph.D. dissertation, University of Thessaly, Volos.

Avineri, S. (1991). Marxism and Nationalism. *Journal of Contemporary History, 26*(3/4), 635–657.

Aybar, M. A. (1963). Hurriyet ve Demokrasimizin Temeli Anayasa. *Sosyal Adalet, 11,* 8–9.

Aybar, M. A. (1967). Kıbrıs'taki Acı Gerçekler. TİP'in Görüşünü Doğruladı. *TİP Haberleri, 2,* 9.

Aybar, M. A. (1968). *Bağımsızlık, Demokrasi, Sosyalizm.* Istanbul: Gerçek Yayınevi.

Boran, B. (1967). Antiemperyalist Mücadelede Öncü, İşçi Sınıfın Partisidir. *TİP Haberleri, 3,* 10.

Boran, B. (1970). *Türkiye ve Sosyalizm Sorunlari.* Istanbul: Gun Yayinlari.

Bozarslan, H. (2008). Turkey: Postcolonial Discourse in a Non-colonised State. In P. Poddar, R. S. Patke, & L. Jensen (Eds.), *A Historical Companion to Postcolonial Literatures: Continental Europe and Its Empires* (pp. 423–427). Edinburgh: Edinburgh University Press.

Bournazos, S. (2009). Το Κράτος των Εθνικοφρόνων: Αντι-Κομμουνιστικός Λόγος και Πρακτική [The State of the Ethnikofrones: Anti-communist Discourse and Practice]. In C. Chajiiosif (Ed.), *Ιστορία της Ελλάδας του 20ού Αιώνα. Ανασυγκρότηση, Εμφύλιος, Παλινόρθωση, 1945–1952* [History of the Twentieth Century Greece: Reformation, Civil War, Restoration, 1945–1952] (pp. 9–49). Athens: Vivliorama.

Breuilly, J. (1985). Reflections on Nationalism. *Philosophy of the Social Sciences*, *15*, 65–75.

Carpentier, N. (2017). *The Discursive-Material Knot: Cyprus in Conflict and Community Media Participation*. Frankfurt am Main: Peter Lang.

Christofis, N. (2015). *From Socialism via Anti-imperialism to Nationalism: EDA-TIP: Socialist Contest Over Cyprus*. Ph.D. dissertation, Leiden University, Leiden.

Christofis, N. (2017). Collective and Counter-Memory: The 'Invention of Resistance' in the Rhetoric of the Greek and Turkish Left, 1951–71. In L. Karakatsanis & N. Papadogiannis (Eds.), *The Politics of Culture in Turkey, Greece & Cyprus: Performing the Left Since the Sixties* (pp. 208–227). London: Routledge.

Christofis, N. (2018). Politics and Nationalism in Cyprus. In P. James (Ed.), *International Relations: Oxford Bibliographies*. New York: Oxford University Press.

Christofis, N. (2019). War, Revolution, and Diplomacy: The October Revolution of 1917 and the Turkish Anatolian Resistance Movement, 1919–1922. In D. Stamatopoulos (Ed.), *European Revolutions and the Ottoman Balkans: War, Nationalism and Empire from Napoleon to the Bolsheviks*. London and New York: I. B. Tauris (forthcoming).

Coates, D. (2014). *America in the Shadow of Empires*. Basingstoke: Palgrave.

Connor, W. (1984). *The National Question in Marxist–Leninist Theory and Strategy*. Princeton, NJ: Princeton University Press.

Diamantopoulos, A. (1964). Cyprus in the Centre of Conspiracy. *Helliniki Aristera*, *13*, 3–6.

Dirlik, A. (2004). Spectres of the Third World: Global Modernity and the End of the Three Worlds. *Third World Quarterly*, *25*(1), 131–148.

Ehrenreich, J. H. (1983). Socialism, Nationalism and Capitalist Development. *Review of Radical Political Economics*, *15*(1), 1–42.

Elefantis, A. (2003). *Μας Πήραν την Αθήνα... Ξαναδιαβάζοντας Μερικές Πτυχές της Ιστορίας, 1941–1950* [They Took Athens from Us... Rereading Some Aspects of History, 1941–1950]. Athens: Vivliorama.

Go, J. (2013). *Patterns of Empire: The British and American Empires, 1688 to the Present*. Cambridge: Cambridge University Press.

Güvenç, S. Ç. (2008). *Solun Merceğinden Dış Politika İkili Anlaşmalardan Kıbrıs'a TİP Deneyimi, 1960–1970*. Ankara: Daktylos.

Hale, W. (2000). *Turkish Foreign Policy, 1774–2000*. London and Portland: Frank Cass.

Harris, G. S. (1972). *Troubled Alliance: Turkish American Problems in Historical Perspective, 1945–1971*. Stanford, CA: Hoover Policy Studies.

Hatzivassiliou, E. (1989). The Suez Crisis, Cyprus and Greek Foreign Policy, 1956: A View from the British Archives. *Balkan Studies*, *30*(1), 107–129.

Hobsbawm, E. (1996). Identity Politics and the Left. *New Left Review*, *I*(217), 38–47.

Howe, S. (2002). *Empire: A Very Short Introduction*. Oxford: Oxford University Press.

Katiforis, G. (1975). *Η Νομοθεσία των Βαρβάρων* [The Legislature of the Barbarians: Essays]. Athens: Themelio.

Katsourides, Y. (2014). *The History of the Communist Party in Cyprus: Colonialism, Class and the Cypriot Left*. London: I.B. Tauris.

Κıbrıs. (1964). *Sosyal Adalet, 17*(4), 42–44.

Kızılyürek, N. (2002). *Milliyetçilik Kıskacında Kıbrıs*. Istanbul: İletişim.

Koçak, C. (2013). Kemalist Nationalism's Murky Waters. In R. Kastoryano (Ed.), *Turkey Between Nationalism and Globalization*. London and New York: Routledge.

Korkmazhan, A. (2017). *Türkiye Solunun Kıbrıs Çımazı, 1950–1980*. Nicosia: Self-Publication.

Lamprinou, K. (2017). *ΕΔΑ, 1956–1967: Πολιτική και Ιδεολογία* [EDA, 1956–1967: Politics and Ideology]. Athens: Polis.

LaMonica, C. (2014). Colonialism. *Oxford Bibliographies*. https://doi.org/10.1093/OBO/9780199743292-0008.

Lenin, V. I. (1974). *Collected Works* (Vol. 22). Moscow: Progress Publishers.

Lenin, V. (2010). *Imperialism: The Highest Stage of Capitalism*. London: Penguin Books.

Motyl, A. (1999). *Revolutions, Nations, Empires: Conceptual Limits and Theoretical Possibilities*. Columbia: Columbia University Press.

Munck, R. (1986). *The Difficult Dialogue: Marxism and Nationalism*. London: Zed Books.

Nairn, T. (1981). *The Break-Up of Britain* (2nd ed.). London and New York: Verso.

Nimni, E. (1994). *Marxism and Nationalism: Theoretical Origins of a Political Crisis*. London: Pluto Press.

Odysseos, Ch. (1964a). Cyprus, USSR and Imperialism. *Helliniki Aristera, 14*, 79–80.

Odysseos, Ch. (1964b). Cyprus in the Plan of Imperialist Counter-Attack. *Helliniki Aristera, 16*, 79–88.

Odysseos, Ch. (1965). The Middle Eastern Crisis and Cyprus. *Helliniki Aristera, 21–22*, 79–89.

Osterhammel, J. (1999). *Colonialism* (S. Frisch, Trans.). Princeton, NJ: Markus Wiener.

Saccarelli, E., & Varadarajan, L. (2015). *Imperialism: Past and Present*. Oxford: Oxford University Press.

Schwarzmantel, J. (1991). *Socialism and the Idea of the Nation*. London: Harvester Wheatsheaf.

Stefanidis, I. D. (2007). *Stirring the Greek Nation: Political Culture, Irredentism and Anti-Americanism in Post-war Greece, 1945–1967*. Aldershot: Ashgate.

Stoler, A. L., McGranahan, C., & Purdue, P. C. (2007). *Imperial Formations*. Santa Fe, NM: School for Advanced Research Press.

Tilly, C., & Tarrow, S. (2015). *Contentious Politics* (2nd ed.). Oxford: Oxford University Press.

TİP Haberleri. (1967). Kıbrıs İle İlgili İki Bildiri, *2*, 14–15.

Trikkas, T. (2009). *ΕΔΑ, 1951–1967: Το Νέο Πρόσωπο της Αριστεράς* [EDA, 1951–1967: The New Face of the Left]. Athens: Themelio.

Ünsal, A. (2002). *Umuttan Yalnızlığa: Türkiye İşçi Partisi (1961–1971)*. Istanbul: Tarih Vakfı Yurt Yayınları.

Ünsal, A. (2003). TİP'in Ulusal Bagımsızlık Anlayışı. In G. Vassaf (Ed.), *Mehmet Ali Aybar Sempozyumları, 1997–2002* (pp. 247–252). Istanbul: Tarih Vakfı Yayınları.

Vanaik, A. (2018). *Marxism and Nationalism*. Online: https://www.versobooks.com/blogs/3578-marxism-and-nationalism.

Young, R. J. C. (2001). *Postcolonialism: An Historical Introduction*. Oxford: Wiley-Blackwell.

Zürcher, E. J. (2012). In the Name of the Father, the Teacher, the Hero: The Atatürk Personality Cult in Turkey. In V. Ibrahim & M. Wunsch (Eds.), *Political Leadership, Nations and Charisma* (pp. 129–142). Abingdon: Routledge.

Primary Sources

EDA Archives (*EDAA*), ASKI (Contemporary Social History Archives).

Kemal Sülker Papers (*KSP*), IISG (International Institute of Social History).

Nebil Varuy Papers (*NVP*), TÜSTAV (Türkiye Sosyal Tarih Araştırma Vakfı).

Printed Primary Sources

CQGP. (1997). *Το Κυπριακό στη Βουλή των Ελλήνων* [The Cyprus Question in the Greek Parliament] (Vols. a, b, c). Athens: Greek Parliament, Directorate of Scientific Studies.

Salman, T. (2004). *TİP Parlamento'da* (Vols. a, b, c). Istanbul: TÜSTAV.

EDA. (1953). *Πρακτικά της ΕΔΑ* [Statutes of EDA]. Athens: EDA.

EDA. (1957). *Η Πολιτική της ΕΔΑ. Επίσημα Κείμενα (Αποφάσεις – Ανακοινώσεις – Δηλώσεις – Αγορεύσεις βουλευτών της από 18.6.1956 μέχρι 30.11.1956)* [The Policy of the EDA. Official Documents (Decisions—Announcements—Statements—MP Talks from 18.6.1956–30.11.1956)]. Athens: EDA.

EDA. (1959). *Το Κυπριακό Πρόβλημα και οι Συμφωνίες Ζυρίχης και Λονδίνου* [The Cyprus Question and the London and Zürich Agreements]. Athens: EDA.

EDA. (1961a). *Πρόγραμμα της ΕΔΑ* [Programme of the EDA]. Athens: EDA.
EDA. (1961b). *Πρόγραμμα Πατριωτικής Συνεργασίας* [Program of Patriotic Alliance]. Athens: EDA.
TİP. (1964). *TİP Programı*. Istanbul: Istanbul Maatbası.
TİP. (1966). *Türkiye İşçi Partisi II. Büyük Kongresi Alınan Kararlar ve Yapılan Seçimlerin Sonuçları*. Istanbul: Istanbul Maatbası.

Newspapers

Avgi 4/12/1956a, 23/12/1956b, 7/03/1957.
Kathimerini 31/10/1956.

CHAPTER 15

Patriots and Internationalists: The Greek Left, the Cyprus Question, and Latin America

Eugenia Palieraki

INTRODUCTION

On October 1, 2016, in the self-organized social space of Lambidona (Athens), took place the event "Chile, Cyprus, Copper."[1] Following the tradition of Galeano's *Open veins of Latin America*, this event aimed to explore the unknown connections between Cyprus and Chile, from copper to poetry, the US multinationals' interest in the exploitation of copper-induced military coups and Human Rights violations in both countries. But cultural links were also revealed; the organizers referred to the hidden connections between the Chilean singer-songwriter Victor Jara and the Greek Cypriot poet Doros Loizou, as well as the Nobel

The publication of this paper was made possible thanks to the generous support of the Seeger Center for Hellenic Studies at Princeton University. I owe a special thanks to Cyrus Schayegh and to this volume's editors for their insightful reading of this paper.

E. Palieraki (✉)
University of Cergy-Pontoise, Cergy-Pontoise, France

© The Author(s) 2018
T. Kyritsi and N. Christofis (eds.), *Cypriot Nationalisms in Context*,
https://doi.org/10.1007/978-3-319-97804-8_15

Prize-winning Pablo Neruda and the Turkish Cypriot poet Neşe Yaşın. Unexpectedly, the members of the social space of Lambidona became aware of these rather surprising connexions while attending an event on the Cuban Revolution. Thus, Chile and Cyprus found themselves connected through Cuba at an Athenian event! No matter how surprising it may appear now, all these countries were actually connected in the past, although these connections have fallen into oblivion—at least as far as the younger generations are concerned. It is precisely these forgotten connections that I intend to explore in this chapter.

Oblivion can be linked to more than one phenomenon, including collective memory, no matter how overgeneralizing and thus problematic this notion may be. In the eyes of the Greek collective memory, the recent Cypriot history is a national drama, the last and unfortunate chapter of Greek irredentism (Bruneau 2002; Peckham 2001; Sivignon 2005). The Greek nationalist narrative tends not only to isolate Cyprus' history from its wider regional context, but also to victimize Greek Cypriots in such a way as to deny them agency.[2] What I propose here is rather a reversal of our historical gaze: instead of analyzing Cyprus' post-war history as a mere consequence or as an extension of Greek politics, I aim to demonstrate that the Cypriot history of the 1950s to the 1970s is key to the understanding of Greek history in the same period.[3]

As stated before, to a few—though meaningful—exceptions, the younger generations both in Greece and in the Republic of Cyprus have been oblivious of these chapters in Cypriot history that are foreign to the Greek nationalist narrative as far as they are related to other countries or regions. Indeed, when post-war Cypriot history is viewed in a broader context, it is again as a pawn and/or as a victim of the colonial or imperialist powers—Britain or the USA, and in some cases, the USSR (Attalides 1979; Bölükbaşı 1988; Johnson 2000; Mallinson 2005; Stergiou 2007; to a lesser extent, Hatzivassiliou 2005). According to this narrative, the Archbishop Makarios, Cyprus' first president from 1960 to 1974—year of the Turkish invasion and partition of the island—and again from 1974 till his death in 1977, was mostly the superpowers' prisoner, struggling to liberate Cyprus from Goliath(s)' grip and failing to do so. The alliances that Makarios formed with the Afro-Asian Peoples' Solidarity Organization (AAPSO) and the Non-Aligned countries could only be viewed as an attempt to stand up to the British and the USA. Makarios is supposed to have instrumentalized the Non-Aligned countries and have used them as a counterweight to colonial Britain and the

Cold War superpowers (Attalides 1979). Without desiring to downplay here the harmful consequences of the foreign powers' policy in Cyprus, I acknowledge the need to stress Cyprus' agency as well. Notwithstanding Makarios' initial conservative ideological stance, the fact that Cyprus considered itself as part of the Third World[4] and formed alliances with Third World countries was of great importance to the Cypriot political scene and had also a strong impact on the Greek one.

Thus, this essay focuses on the Non-Aligned and Third World politics of Cyprus during the 1950s–1970s, as well as on their impact on the Greek political landscape. My choice of concentrating on Cyprus' relations with a particular segment of the Third World, namely Latin America, is doubly justified: firstly, Latin America is, along with the Arab countries, the part of the Third World that Cyprus was most connected with. Secondly, Latin America is worthy to observe when examining how political experiences that initially seemed (and effectively were, at least from a geographical viewpoint) extremely remote, got translated into a "political grammar" familiar to the Greeks, because of the Cypriot experience. I will thus argue that one of the main effects of Cypriot Third World policy was the "globalization" of the Greek political scene, which—until Cyprus' independence in 1960—was either nation-centered or torn between East and West.

While commonly not included in the Third World, during the "Long Sixties," both Makarios' Cyprus and the Greek Left identified with this label. Indeed, the belated and limited independence of Cyprus, the constant presence of the British ex-colonial power on its soil, the intervention of other foreign powers, but also the non-aligned policy of Archbishop Makarios (nicknamed the "Castro of the Mediterranean") between 1960 and 1974, firmly integrated the island into the nascent "Third World." As for Greece, the April 1967 coup and the establishment of a military regime, viewed by the resistance organizations as having been instituted through direct US intervention, brought those organizations closer to the anti-imperialist and anti-"neo-colonialist" stance of the "Third World" (Voglis 2011).

AN ENTANGLED THIRD WORLD

Before moving forward, it is necessary to specify the theoretical debates with which this essay engages. Since the early 2000s, research on post-war history has undoubtedly been marked by the rise of global history, as well as by the growing interest in the "Long Sixties" (Marwick 2005; Dubinsky 2009). These historiographical trends are intertwined: as "transnational moment of change" (Horn and Kenney 2004), the "Long Sixties" are particularly well suited to the global history approach. However, a substantial part of recent scholarship on the "Long Sixties" tended toward an overgeneralizing view and paid little attention to the local translations of the transnational dynamics. Moreover, most of these studies are limited to Western Europe and the USA (for example, Klimke 2011; Fink 1998).

This essay is both inspired by and critically positioned toward the aforementioned historiographical trends. More precisely, it relates to three distinct, though interconnected, historiographical fields: firstly, global and entangled history; secondly, the New Cold War history (NCWH) and its emphasis on the role played by Third World countries during the post-war period. Finally, the project approaches the political and cultural history of Greece and Cyprus in the "Long sixties" from a more global perspective.

The main epistemological contributions made by global and entangled history, referred to as "relational approaches" (Sachsenmaier 2006; Werner and Zimmermann 2003; Subrahmanyam 1997; Saunier 2004), are the questioning of Western, nation-centered visions and the emphasis on the links that tie different geographical and cultural areas together. My research is fully aligned with the above-mentioned premises. However, "relational approaches" to twentieth century history have mostly focused on questions of social or cultural history and paid little attention to the political field.

In this sense, political science offers a solid theoretical basis for approaching political topics from a transnational perspective (see, for instance, Bertrams and Kott 2008; Boncourt 2013; Rioufreyt 2013). However, not only the majority of transnational approaches on politics showed limited interest in regions other than Western Europe and the USA, but they have almost exclusively focused on international institutions and neglected historical actors such as nation-states or non-institutionalized agency. Thus, this essay—with its focus on both informal transnational activism and on "peripheral" regions and nation-states—addresses key issues absent from previous "relational approaches."

The renewal of the history of the "Long Sixties" owes a great deal not only to "relational approaches" but also to NCWH (Westad 2000, 2007; McMahon 2013; Hahn and Heiss 2000). Although the NCWH is not a homogeneous historical trend, its scholars share some basic premises: an emphasis on agency; the acceptance of the relevance of state ideology, which cannot be summarized as a mere defense of economic interests; and the recognition of the vital role played by regions other than the "First" and the "Second" worlds. Understandably, the last premise has produced a renewed interest in the Third World.

However, NCWH often continues to look at the Third World through a "Cold War lens" (Connelly 2000), that is, exclusively through its relations with the US and/or USSR. Some essays have tried to compensate this (Parker 2013; Pitman and Stafford 2009), but they are not sufficiently supported by archival evidence. Some other publications—mostly chapters on very specific topics in edited volumes—do not offer a real synthesis. Moreover, these publications pay little attention to the connections between the geographical and cultural areas of the Third World (see, for example, Christiansen and Scarlett 2013). Therefore, in order to understand how the Third World, this new "universe of practice and autonomous meaning" (Mathieu 2007), emerged, it is necessary to examine what brings together regions that were mutual strangers in cultural and political terms before the 1950s.

As it also highlights the ideological, organizational and human relations between Latin America, Greece and Cyprus during the Cold War period, this essay aims to contribute to the current debate on the meaning, content and material reality of the Third World, beyond its relations to the USA and USSR.

When one engages with past and current research on the Greek and Cypriot Long Sixties, relational approaches are of great help to the understanding of the Greek case. Until recently, the history of the Greek dictatorship (1967–1974) and the democratic transition (*Metapolitefsi*) has mostly been studied through a national or comparative approach, even though this trend is about to change (Kornetis 2015; Voglis 2011; Gildea et al. 2013). On the other hand, the 1960–1974 period in Cyprus has mostly been studied through a global lens. However, as I have already mentioned, the emphasis has been on the role played by the ex-colonial and Cold War foreign powers. As a result, the domestic agency—Makarios' role, but also that of the Cypriot communist Progressive Party of the Working People (*Ανορθωτικό Κόμμα Εργαζόμενου Λαού*, AKEL) and the Cypriot Social-democracy, the United Democratic Union of Centre (*Ενιαία Δημοκρατική Ένωση Κέντρου*, EDEK)—has been underestimated. In the same way, Cyprus'

Third World policy and networks have not been thoroughly studied, despite the fact that they were—at least temporarily—a serious counterweight to Cold War dynamics.

From a different angle, we can see that the Greek Left's and Cyprus' Non-Aligned and Third World policy was both an "intermediary" and a "mediator" (on both notions see Rioufreyt 2013). Cyprus was an intermediary, in the sense that it established the link between other parties that had no previous contact with each other. I will thus concentrate first on how Cyprus was a major player in creating links between Latin America and Greece.

The notion of "mediator/mediation" refers to the changes that ideas or agents undergo when passing from one context to another. Mediation is a process of translation. Here, I will break down the idea of translation into its two distinct, though interrelated, facets. In the second section, I will explore mediation in terms of metaphor or comparison. Taking Latin America as an example, I will look at how the Greek Left used Cyprus in order to better grasp distant and inexplicable processes and realities, and conversely, at how the Greek Left used Latin America in order to understand Cyprus' colonial situation. Indeed, whereas at the end of the nineteenth century, Cyprus was perceived as an important part of the unredeemed Hellenism—though soon to be liberated and reunited with Greece—in the late 1950s, when Cyprus actually gained independence, the historical experience of more than seventy years of British colonization had distanced Cypriots from Greeks and vice versa.[5] In the 1960s, Cyprus was, to most Greeks, a transformed—and sometimes hardly recognizable—self. This duality—identification and distance—made Cyprus an ideal mediator: sufficiently close to be trusted and distant enough to introduce new and surprising realities.

In the third and final section, I will approach mediation as a process of change and will look into Cypriot politics as a vector of a dramatic transformation in the way the Greek Left perceived both itself and the world in which it acted (also Christofis, this volume). The narrative of this essay will not be linear. Rather, I will propose an essayistic approach on how the Greek Left redefined its relation to the Greek nation and to world politics through the "Cyprus Question."

Both in the Greek and the Cypriot case, I will mostly focus on the non-communist or dissident communist Left. In the case of Greece, I will mainly examine the history of the 1960s Third-Worldist Left in search for revolutionary alternatives to the Soviet model. In the case of Cyprus, I will discuss the role of EDEK, even though AKEL was historically, numerically and socially much more representative of modern Cypriot society (Alecou 2015; Katsourides 2014). But as Kyriakos Markides states:

> Although EDEK's following was small – only two of its candidates were elected in the 1970 parliamentary elections – its influence in Cypriot affairs was considerable, due to the dynamism of Lyssarides and his deputies. EDEK was important... It was instrumental in helping Makarios maintain good relations with Third World countries... Lyssarides was the strongest supporter among the non-communist groups of Makarios' policy of neutrality in international affairs. As private physician to Makarios, he must have exerted influence in matters of international policy ... (Markides 1977, p. 67)

The focus on the non-communist Left does not aim to downplay the Communist parties' role either in Cyprus or in Greece. But, quite logically, a study that wishes to look beyond the politics of the Cold War superpowers must examine, first and foremost, political organizations non-aligned with the USA or the USSR. Moreover, the "Long sixties" ideological renewal that I also wish to briefly address comes from the non-communist or dissident communist Left.

THE CYPRIOT HUB: THIRD-WORLDISM AND ANTI-COLONIAL REVOLUTION

The Non-Aligned policy of Cyprus has either been insufficiently studied or analyzed in terms of manipulation and *realpolitik*. According to the latter interpretation, the Greek Cypriots had no other solution but to form strategic alliances with the USSR or Third World countries, because of the Western powers' and Greece's betrayal. In other words, according to the predominant view, this policy was a necessity rather than a choice and thus the Western identity of Greek Cypriots should not be called into question (Makrides 1977; Attalides 1979; Bölükbaşı 1988; Mallinson 2005; Mayes 1981). Instead, I argue here that the Non-Aligned policy of Makarios did not only stem from a pragmatic calculation of global power relations, but also from a conscious political stance, very similar to the international policy of Egypt in the 1950s–1960s or Algeria in the 1960s–1970s.

Indeed, the Non-Aligned orientation in Makarios' international policy was felt since 1955, at the very beginning of the armed revolt in Cyprus and at the time of the emergence of Non-Alignment. During the 1950s and 1960s, Makarios did not miss a single major Third World appointment: the 1955 Bandung Conference that initiated Afro-Asian Solidarity and Non-Alignment (Mayes 1981, p. 64); the 1961 founding Conference of Non-Alignment at Belgrade (Mayes 1981, p. 158); the 1964, Afro-Asian Solidarity Conference in Algiers, a city that was at that time a major hub for revolutionary and Third World national liberation movements (Byrne 2016).

This last Conference had a wide impact on the Greek Left-wing parties, particularly the ones critical to the USSR that were also more aware of Non-Aligned policy, for two reasons: first, because of the Conference's official statement condemning the 1959 Zurich–London Agreement and the 1960 Cypriot constitution, a statement that gave global visibility to the Cyprus Question; secondly, because of the decision—backed by Cyprus—to include Latin America to the AAPSO and to create a Tri-Continental Conference.[6] The fact that Latin America joined the AAPSO and the subsequent expansion of the group's influence on the United Nations were viewed as an evolution that should favor the countries with pending international issues, including Cyprus.

Finally, in 1967, Cyprus replaced Tanzania in its role of hosting the eighth Council Session of the AAPSO, so that the organization's tenth anniversary would be celebrated in Nicosia (AAPSO 1967). These international meetings, conferences, and festivals were of great importance. Not only did they provide an opportunity for encounters of activists and political leaders, but they also offered the participants a unique opportunity to discover the host country and its political and social changes. In the words of EDEK's founder and also chairman of the eighth Council of the AAPSO, Vassos Lyssarides:

> The presence of such a big number of observers from the Tri-Continental Secretariat and guests from progressive organizations and from socialist countries signifies the wide resounding of our meetings and the broad solidarity of the progressive world. (AAPSO 1967, p. 95)

Lyssarides is a truly Tri-Continental figure. Member of the EOKA—the 1950s nationalist and anti-communist Greek Cypriot guerrilla—he was the personal doctor and a close collaborator of Makarios until the latter's death in 1977. He opposed the 1959 Zurich–London agreements, stating that it would not allow Cyprus a complete and permanent access to independence. In 1969, he founded EDEK, a member of the Socialist International. Married to Barbara Cornwall, an American journalist linked to the Mozambican FRELIMO and to Amílcar Cabral's PAIGC (Cornwall 1972),[7] Lyssarides was also closely related to Arafat's Fatah and to Fidel Castro's Cuba.

The 1967 AAPSO Council Session in Cyprus, attended by four Cubans in their capacity of members of the Tri-continental Conference's Executive Committee (AAPSO 1967, p. 189) strengthened Lyssarides' relationship to Cuba. The Tri-continental Conference—a key meeting for the Third World countries—had taken place a year earlier in the Havana (Faligot 2013). The first member of the Cuban delegation was Osmany Cienfuegos, brother of Camilo Cienfuegos, a major leader of the Cuban Revolution, who had died some months after the victory of the Revolution in a plane crash. Osmany was also a member of the Cuban Communist Party and the Secretary General of the Organization of Solidarity with the People of Asia, Africa and Latin America (OSPAAAL), founded at the 1966 Havana Conference. The second member of the Cuban mission was the intelligence agent Domingo Amuchastegui. The third one, extremely important, was Gabriel Molina, journalist and correspondent in Africa for the Cuban Press Agency *Prensa Latina*. Molina was closely linked to Ben Bella and to the Cuban Ambassador in Algiers, Jorge Serguera, as well as to all the African and Asian national liberation movements present in the North-African capital surnamed "Mecca of Revolution" (Serguera 1997). Both Cienfuegos and Molina were major intermediaries to African and Middle-Eastern leaders and to Latin American Left-Wing parties. The fourth member of the Cuban mission was Silvio Rivera, Ambassador in Cairo. Before Algiers, Cairo was the main pivotal point of encounter and collaboration between national liberation movements of the three continents. Also, Makarios was closely linked to Nasser (Mayes 1981, pp. 66, 237). In addition to the Cuban connection, in the early 1970s, both Makarios and Lyssarides established links with the Popular Unity in Chile.

All the aforementioned connections between Makarios, EDEK and the Latin American Left are also related to the Greek Left. First of all, the Greek Left's interest in the Third World was rooted in the "Cyprus Question." In the early 1960s, the first Left-wing publication with detailed analyses on the Third World and its national liberation movements was the *Bulletin of the Friends of New countries* (*Deltio ton Filon Neon Choron*, FNC). The Bulletin was founded in 1964 with the aim to address the "Cyprus Question":

> Our Bulletin comes into existence in a period when our nation is facing strong hardships: we are referring to the Cyprus question... Cyprus is a part of Greece which struggles to free itself from the colonial web... This is exactly what brings us closer to the peoples of Asia, Africa and Latin America who struggle for their liberation from enslavement and from the imperialists' and the colonialists' control... The Friends of the New Countries set the general goal of contributing to the Greek people's struggle by studying, disseminating and making the best of the experience that the New Countries have gained in their struggles, in their successes and achievements. (Kinisi Antiapoikiakis Allilegguis, January 1964a, p. 1)

This group, created by ex-Communists with Maoist sympathies and by Trotskyists, was the first to generate in Greece a political culture on the Third World through its publications, as well as its cultural center, where seminars and debates, film screenings and exhibits took place (Personal interview with Giorgos Hadjopoulos, 26 August 2016, Athens).

Cyprus also became an intermediary between Greece and Latin America in a very concrete and direct way. After the 1967 military coup in Greece, Vassos Lyssarides developed strong links with the Panhellenic Liberation Movement (*Πανελλήνιο Απελευθερωτικό Κίνημα*, PAK) and its main founder Andreas Papandreou, who is also the future founder of the Panhellenic Socialist Movement (*Πανελλήνιο Σοσιαλιστικό Κίνημα*, PASOK) and Greek Prime Minister (1981–1989; 1993–1997). He thus played a major role in establishing contacts between, Papandreou, PAK and the Latin American Left (mainly, Cuba, Mexico, Chile and the Nicaraguan Sandinistas),[8] but also with the Palestinian liberation movement.

Furthermore, after the 1974 invasion, which also resulted in the overthrow of the Greek military dictatorship, Cyprus' Tri-continental connections "relocated" in Athens. During the first years of the *Metapolitefsi*, Athens, together with Madrid and Rome, became the new Mediterranean hubs for transnational solidarity. But in the case of Athens, it was the Cypriot—and mostly EDEK—transnational networks, which allowed the Greek Left to develop such a global outreach. In 1976, an International Conference of Solidarity with Cyprus, which was at the same time a Conference on Palestine and Lebanon

(AAPSO 1967), was organized in Athens. In 1975, a major international Conference of Solidarity with Chile was also organized in Athens.[9] Those networks—that Cyprus acquired thanks to its implication in the Non-Aligned and Tri-continental Movements—were bequeathed to the Greek New Left, and mostly to the Greek socialists, among which Antonis Tritsis played a key role.

CYPRUS AND THE POWER OF METAPHOR IN POLITICS

During the 1960s and the 1970s, the Greek Left-wing press systematically compared the Cypriot political situation with that of other Third World countries. Drawing a parallel between Cyprus and other Third World countries had various meanings and purposes. First of all, Cyprus' anti-colonial struggle had to be explained to the Greeks of the mainland because it was too different from their own experience. Furthermore, Cyprus' colonial history and anti-colonial fight seemed to impinge upon Greece's identification with the West. Indeed, Cyprus called into question the Western-centered Greek identity, with which even the left-wing activists identified until the 1960s.[10]

This is how Latin America came into play. Latin America shared with Greece a "hybrid" identity, both Western and peripheral. It gained its independence from the Spanish and Portuguese Empire in the early nineteenth century, that is at the same time when Greece won its independence from the Ottoman Empire. Both were still viewed as economically underdeveloped and politically dependent on great regional and world powers. In other words, the independence gained in the nineteenth century was not viewed as true and real: both Latin America and Greece were closer to the countries undergoing a decolonization process; they had to fight for their true independence, which did not consist only in formal and political autonomy, but would also include a process of social and economic emancipation. The comparison with Latin America allowed the Greek Left to assimilate and comprehend the colonial dimension of Cyprus' history, by viewing its own identity as a neo-colonial one:

Cypriots are not a sister nation, they are the Greek nation. Our country has not finished with the conquerors just yet. Hellenism, both in Cyprus and in the rest of Greece, has the obligation to complete the national liberation struggle and the colonialists must be driven out of this patch of earth. However, the Greek peoples' struggle against imperialism,

> colonialism and neo-colonialism is bigger than that. The political and economic dependence of Greece as a state [...] threatens our economic, political, social and spiritual national existence. (*Kinisi Antiapoikiakis Allilegguis*, January 1964a, p. 1)

During the 1960s, Cyprus was systematically compared to Cuba. What Cyprus was to Greece, Cuba was to Latin America: a territory having gained its independence well after the others, not to say a very limited independence. Cyprus' Zurich–London Agreement and Constitution were equivalent to Cuba's Platt Amendment.[11]

And therein lies another facet of the power of metaphor in politics. In a historical period marked by radical changes and uncertainty, as were the "Long Sixties," referring to positive examples, stories with a happy ending, gave hope and the optimism necessary to political action and militancy. Cuba, but also Egypt and Algeria, and later on Vietnam—to cite the most obvious examples—stood up to the great powers and won. These countries had been able to take advantage of the great powers' weaknesses and competition, as a means to securing their independence and self-determination. They were highly appealing role models for both Cyprus and Greece.

Furthermore, just like Cuba became the main driver of Latin America's revolution, Cyprus—thanks to its insularity[12]—was supposed to play the same role for Greece. Insularity was, indeed, considered by a part of the Greek Left as a feature that exacerbated structural weaknesses, and therefore, an ideal trigger for revolution. Cyprus' liminal state[13] was an intermediate stage between colonial submission and true independence. Thus, during the 1960s, the tendencies of the Greek Left, which would later be called "Patriotic Left," considered *enosis* (the union between Greece and Cyprus) as a means to generate a revolutionary outburst in Greece:

> The only real solution to the Cyprus Question is the anti-colonialist and anti-imperialist union between Cyprus and Greece. This is the only national path, the only one at the service of the Greek peoples. (*Kinisi Antiapoikiakis Allilegguis*, May–June 1964b, p. 5)

In the 1960s, the Greek and Cypriot communist Left and the political center had abandoned the project of *enosis*. The main political sector still advocating *enosis* was the Right-wing ultra-nationalists, both in Greece and in Cyprus. Interestingly enough, the "Patriotic Left" struggled for that same goal, but saw in irredentism the possibility for social and political revolution.

Even though it was numerically marginal, the "Patriotic Left," inspired the Third World national liberation movements and had decisive influence over the other left-wing trends and parties. During the 1970s, even the communist Left—that initially had a very limited sympathy for Third World political experiences—started referring to Latin America. In 1974—a year marked by the Greek junta's intervention in Cyprus, the subsequent invasion of the island by the Turkish Army, and the island's partition, which led to the fall of the Greek dictatorship—the communist Left started comparing Cyprus not to Cuba anymore, but to Chile. Solidarity with Cyprus was also solidarity with Chile. In the communist discourse, Makarios was a local version of Salvador Allende, overthrown by military and US intervention in the name of the geostrategic interests of the latter (KNE 1974).

This comparison also conveyed a strong political message. Since the 1930s, the Greek communists were constantly accused of being enemies of the nation. Thanks to their solidarity with Cyprus and with Chile, they could at last present themselves as anti-imperialists and at the same time, as protectors of the national community, on a par with the Right-wing nationalists, now discredited by the Cyprus tragedy. Thanks to Cyprus, the communists' commitment to the national cause was presented as the unifying and central thread of recent Greek history, from Resistance to Nazism, to the solidarity with Cyprus or the opposition to a military junta manipulated by the US.

As in the case of the "Patriotic Left," the Greek redefined their attachment to the nation with an identity built around global revolutionary references. It is true that the revolutionary dimension is less immediately obvious in the case of the Greek communists, who viewed revolution in the Third World not as an armed struggle, but rather in terms of an economic process for gaining auto-sufficiency and state control over natural and human resources. Nevertheless, though it was understood in economic terms, the Third World revolution imagined by the communist Left of the 1970s was a patriotic and at the same time a transnational revolution.

INTERNATIONALISTS AND PATRIOTS: THE (TRANS)
NATIONALIZATION OF MILITANT SUBJECTIVITIES IN POST-WAR
GREECE

Cyprus triggered a twofold process in the Greek Left parties: a major identification with the national cause and a process of transnationalization of militant subjectivities through an increasing connection with national liberation movements of the Third World. As the Movement of Anti-colonial Solidarity—Friends of the New Countries put it:

> The struggle of our people for national independence is organically unified with the struggles of all the oppressed people. We will draw upon examples from the experience of the international movement of national and social liberation [to apply them] to the Greek reality. (*Kinisi Antiapoikiakis Allilegguis*, May–June 1964b, p. 1)

Emotions played a key role in the building of a sense of belonging to the Third World political community (on emotions in politics see Deluermoz et al. 2013; Traïni 2009). Indeed, Third-Worldism was not so much based on a common ideological affiliation (in the sense of rationally defined). It was rather founded upon a history—to a large extent, an invented one—of common suffering, struggles and redemption, which led to the replacement of rationalized "Western" ideological affinities by emotional ones. In the words of Vassos Lyssarides:

> Friends: The people of Cyprus shed blood to break the colonial chains. We are now absolutely determined to fight and die till the last man, but not yield one inch of our soil to the foreign aggressors. This is our duty to our people, but this is also our duty to all the peoples of the world that are still fighting for complete independence and self-determination. (AAPSO 1967, pp. 112–113)

During the 1960s, this process was less obvious in the case of the communist Left, whose own political and ideological references were both determinant and reluctant to novelty. However, the communist dissidents with Maoist sympathies, the Trotskyists, and the social democrats were much more inclined, since the beginning, to this new framing of political identities.

This last section will focus on an essay written by Nikos Psyroukis, under the pen name of Nikitatos, and published in 1965. My claim is that this essay provided the basis for the Greek Third-Worldist thought and had a decisive impact on all left-wing parties, from the revolutionary Left to the social democracy and Papandreou's PASOK. Psyroukis was the main founder of the Movement of Anti-colonial Solidarity— FNC. His personal story was the embodiment of the principles that the Movement FNC stood for. Psyroukis' father was originally from Ottoman Asia Minor, but left his homeland to participate in the Balkan Wars. While still a soldier, he was sent to Ukraine, where he joined the Communist Party. After Ukraine, he was led to Egypt, where after World War I he settled in Ismailia, got married and worked as a typographer. This is where Nikos Psyroukis was born in 1926, while Egypt was still under heavy British influence despite the concession of formal independence in 1922. In the 1940s, Psyroukis became an activist of the anti-British struggle. He left Egypt to avoid being arrested and traveled to Eastern Europe. In 1956, after studying history in Prague, he went back to Egypt and worked for *O Paroikos*, the newspaper of the Communist Egyptiotes.[14] In 1957, he worked for the AAPSO Conference in Cairo. In the early 1960s, he abandoned Egypt and settled in Athens, where he created the FNC (1963), in order to promote Cyprus' independence and its union with Greece.

Cyprus was an obsession for Psyroukis since the 1950s: he followed closely its struggle for independence from the British. He was also profoundly impressed by Makarios' attachment to the Afro-Asian solidarity and to Third World struggles. Getting closer to the national liberation movements, Psyroukis moved away from the Greek Communist Party. He abandoned it in 1963 while, at the same time, he created the FNC (Meletopoulos and Goranitis 1998).

In his essay "The Cyprus Question: our most acute national problem" (1965), Psyroukis not only provides a detailed analysis of the Cyprus Question and its role for Greek politics; he also proposes an overview of the notions of nation and nationalism from the nineteenth century to the 1960s. Interestingly, Psyroukis' historical account does not aim to provide a linear narrative, nor does he consider the Western nation-state as a worldwide model, achieved with delay by other regions of the world. On the contrary, he argues that History's main positive feature is movement and capacity for change:

> Some or many people's minds might be static, but social change is never static. (Psyroukis 1965, p. 6)

Therefore, Third World nationalism should be viewed as a state-of-the-art rather than as a delayed and deficient version of Western nationalism. Its two main advantages are its social-centered/popular facet and its global outlook. According to Psyroukis, since the 1940s European Resistance to Nazism, nationalism had ceased to be bourgeois and turned into a mass, working-class ideology. In the post-war years, nationalism had become, on the global scale, the ideology of the dominated and the oppressed. Cyprus was part of both phenomena: the national liberation struggle in Cyprus was the continuation and radicalization of the Greek national struggle during WWII; it was also an integral part of the anti-colonial Third World struggle. Thus, since the very beginning of his analysis, Psyroukis makes the connection between the national and the global scale:

> Nowadays [...] a fighter of the national liberation struggle is at the same time an internationalist. (Psyroukis 1965, p. 6)

But this connection between Cyprus, Greece and the Third World is also made through what constitutes, according to Psyroukis, a nation:

> Ethnogenesis starts in Greece with Pelasgians and Cretans. [...] Ethnogenesis is a very complex phenomenon. It does not only take place in the economic sphere. The underlying consciousness of a community of birthplace, of the linguistic unity, of a community of psyche, all these reflect the sub-layers and the super-layers of a nation. (1965, pp. 12–13)

Using the territory, the language and the psyche in order to define a nation is certainly a conception that remains close to nineteenth century romantic nationalism. But in the particular case of the *Enosis* of Greece and Cyprus that Psyroukis stood for, a case that he included in the context of Third World Liberation movements, all the elements presented here had, at the time, different implications. Psyroukis embraced the theory of continuity of the Greek nation from the Prehistoric period until the modern times, a theory mainly followed by Greek Right-wing nationalists. His reference to Pelasgians and Cretans added another element: the Greek national space exceeded the Modern Greek states' frontiers to include Asia Minor and Cyprus. It was an updated *Great Idea*

(Megali Idea), the Greek version of irredentism. In his version of it, the Mediterranean shores and the insular space were central. But what is even more interesting and surprising is that Psyroukis claimed at the same time that:

> For insular Greeks, territory always had a linguistic meaning. The Greeks have always viewed territorial unity as a linguistic unity. (1965, p. 13)

More than frontiers and a static national space, Psyroukis seems to understand the nation as a moving and breathing organism. For Psyroukis, the nation is above all language. The territory is language. A nation's main physical manifestation is language. He includes mobility into the notion of nation and does not wish to identify the nation with determined and static borders.

Moreover, the linguistic unit has a special meaning in the Third World context: it brings "Hellenism" closer to the "*grands ensembles*" (Shepard 2012), that is other projects of regional integration based on common language, identity, history and culture, such as Pan-Arabism and Latin-Americanism. Even though there is no direct link between them, Psyroukis' idea is not very far from what Houari Boumediene, head of the Algerian state from 1965 to 1978, had in mind in 1968–1969, when he proposed the creation of an anti-imperialist Mediterranean alliance.

As for his reference to psyche, Psyroukis clearly turns against Western rationality. But he does more than that: he goes on to say that in the case of Cyprus, the psyche or "psychology" is clearly anti-colonial. In other words, the emotional structure of Cyprus and by extension Greece brings them closer to the Asian, African and Latin American countries than to the West.

***

By associating the "Cyprus Question" with Third World nationalism, the Friends of the New Countries and Psyroukis initiated a trend that other left-wing organizations in Greece pursued and enhanced. Indeed, in the discourse of the Left parties, Cyprus embodied at the same time the claim to self-determination and a much broader fight, the Third World's struggle for true liberation and independence. In political discourse, Cyprus was constantly connected to other national causes: to Cuba in the 1960s, to Chile in 1973–1975, but also to Palestine and Lebanon in the mid-1970s. The "Cyprus Question" thus became part of a new militant script, of a Third World political culture built upon national causes (i.e., Cypriot cause, Palestinian cause, Chilean cause) going global.

NOTES

1. Koinoniko Kentro Virona. (2016). *Chili, Kypros, Chalkos: poiimata kai tragoudia gia tis dyo chores.* [Online]. Available from: https://www.facebook.com/events/656985597811673 [Accessed on 25 October 2016].
2. It goes without saying that this narrative also conceals the pre-1974 ethnic and religious diversity of the Cypriot society. However, I will not be able to address here in detail the role of the Cypriot Turks, since their participation in the political movements that I analyse was marginal.
3. This, of course, does not imply that the Greek state's policy on the Cyprus Question did not have a direct responsibility for the island's political crises in the 1960s and the 1970s, and ultimately for its partition.
4. Third World is, without a doubt, an ideological and political construct. But as Christiansen and Scarlett note: "Although the term Third World may be outmoded today—replaced by the vague (and equally questionable) Global South—we stand by its value as a historical idea of vital importance during the Cold War. Discarding the term would be to erase a historical situation that did indeed play a central role in the global protest movement of the 1960s" (Christiansen and Scarlett 2013, p. 3).
5. For a brief historical overview of Cyprus' Modern history see Blanc (2013) and Sakellaropoulos (2017).
6. Kinisi Antiapoikiakis Allilegguis. (1964). I sindiaskepsi tou Symvouliou Afrikanoasiatikis Allilegguis [The Afroasian Solidarity Conference]. *Deltio ton Filon Neon Choron*, 3, April, p. 10.
7. The Mozambican Liberation Front (FRELIMO - Frente de Libertação de Moçambique), founded in 1962, was the main organization fighting for the independence of Mozambique, a Portuguese colony. From the 1975 independence onwards, FRELIMO remains the main Mozambican political party. The African Party for the Independence of Guinea and Cape Verde (PAIGC - Partido Africano da Independência da Guiné e Cabo Verde) is a Pan-Africanist and anti-colonialist party founded by Amílcar Cabral.
8. See Princeton University. Library. Dept. of Rare Books and Special Collections. 1987: Report of the visit of William Hupper and Carlos Zarruck to Greece. Sergio Ramírez Papers. Series 3. Political Archive 3A. Ramirez's Political Activities (cont.) Box 62a Folder 8.
9. *Avgi* (1975). Leuteria sti Chili! [Freedom for Chile!]. 14 November, p. 1.

10. Rappas gives an account of the origins of the disconnection between the Christian Orthodox Cypriot identity and Western identity in the colonial period (2014, pp. 15–16).
11. See for instance, the speech of Vassos Lyssarides in AAPSO (1967, pp. 109–110). In 1901, the Platt Amendment was annexed to the first Cuban Constitution, allowing the US to politically and/or military intervene in Cuba. In the same context, two years later, the first Cuban President, Tomás Estrada Palma allotted a territory to the US in Guantanamo bay, where the famous military base was installed.
12. On the notion of insularity see Hadjikyriacou, A. (2014).
13. On Victor Turner's notion of liminality and its use for political anthropology see Thomassen (2012).
14. Egyptiotes are the Greeks settled in Egypt.

REFERENCES

Afro-Asian Peoples' Solidarity Organization—AAPSO. (1967). *The VIIIth Council Session of the Afro-Asian Peoples' Solidarity Organization: Nicosia-Cyprus, 13–17 February 1967.* Cairo: The Permanent Secretariat of the Afro-Asian Peoples' Solidarity Organization.

Alecou, A. (2015). Shaping Identities: The Cypriot Left and the Communist Party of Greece in the 1940s. *Journal of Historical Sociology, 6*(1), 1–22.

Attalides, M. (1979). *Cyprus. Nationalism and International Politics.* New York: St. Martin's Press.

Bertrams, K., & Kott, S. (2008). Actions sociales transnationales. *Genèses, 71*(2), 2–3.

Blanc, P. (2013). Chypre: un triple enjeu pour la Turquie. *Hérodote, 148*(1), 83–102.

Bölükbaşı, S. (1988). *The Superpowers and the Third World: Turkish-American Relations and Cyprus.* Lanham: University Press of America.

Boncourt, T. (2013). Acteurs multipositionnés et fabrique du transnational. La création du European Consortium for Political Research. *Critique internationale, 59*(2), 17–32.

Bruneau, M. (2002). Hellénisme, Hellinismos: nation sans territoire ou idéologie? *Géocarrefour, 77*(4), 319–328.

Byrne, J. (2016). *Mecca of Revolution: Algeria, Decolonization, and the Third World Order.* New York: Oxford University Press.

Christiansen, S., & Scarlett, Z. (Eds.). (2013). *The Third World in the Global 1960s.* New York: Berghahn Books.

Connelly, M. (2000). Taking off the Cold War Lens: Visions of North-South Conflict During the Algerian War for Independence. *The American Historical Review, 105*(3), 739–769.

Cornwall, B. (1972). *The Bush Rebels: A Personal Accounts of Black Revolt in Africa*. New York: Rinehart and Winston.

Deluermoz, Q., Fureix, E., Mazurel, H., & Oualdi, M. (2013). Ecrire l'histoire des émotions: de l'objet à la catégorie d'analyse. *Revue d'histoire du XIXe siècle, 47,* 155–189.

Dubinsky, K., et al. (Eds.). (2009). *New World Coming: The Sixties and the Shaping of Global Consciousness.* Toronto: Between the Lines.

Faligot, R. (2013). *Tricontinentale: Quand Che Guevara, Ben Barka, Cabral, Castro et Hô Chi Minh préparaient la révolution mondiale: 1964–1968.* Paris: La Découverte.

Fink, C., Gassert, P., & Junker, D. (Eds.). (1998). *1968: The World Transformed.* Washington: Cambridge University Press.

Gildea, R., Mark, J., & Warring, A. (Eds.). (2013). *Europe's 1968: Voices of Revolt.* Oxford: Oxford University Press.

Hadjikyriacou, A. (2014). Local Intermediaries and Insular Space in Late-Eighteenth Century Cyprus. *Journal of Ottoman Studies, 44,* 427–456.

Hadjopoulos, G. (Personal communication, 26 August 2016, Athens).

Hahn, P. L., & Heiss, M. A. (Eds.). (2000). *Empire and Revolution: The United States and the Third World Since 1945.* Columbus: Ohio State University Press.

Hatzivassiliou, E. (2005). Cyprus at the Crossroads, 1959–63. *European History Quarterly, 35*(4), 523–540.

Horn, G. R., & Kenney, P. (2004). *Transnational Moments of Change: Europe 1945, 1968, 1989.* Manham: Rowman & Littlefield.

Johnson, E. (2000). Britain and the Cyprus Problem at the United Nations, 1954–58. *The Journal of Imperial and Commonwealth History, 28*(3), 113–130.

Katsourides, Y. (2014). *History of the Communist Party in Cyprus: Colonialism, Class and the Cypriot Left.* London: I.B. Tauris.

Kinisi Antiapoikiakis Allilegguis. (1964a, January). *Deltio ton Filon Neon Choron* [Bulletin of the Friends of the New Countries], 1.

Kinisi Antiapoikiakis Allilegguis. (1964b, May–June). *Deltio ton Filon Neon Choron* [Bulletin of the Friends of the New Countries], 4.

Klimke, M., et al. (Eds.). (2011). *Between Prague Spring and French May. Opposition and Revolt in Europe, 1960–1980.* New York: Berghahn Books.

KNE [Communist Youth of Greece]. (1974, September 12). Chili: Antiimperialistikos Agonas. Analisi Gegonoton [Chile: Antiimperialist struggle. An analysis of events]. *Thourios,* p. 7.

Kornetis, K. (2015). "Cuban Europe"? Greek and Iberian tiersmondisme in the "Long 1960s". *Journal of Contemporary History, 50*(3), 486–515.

Mallinson, B. (2005). *Cyprus: A Modern History.* New York: I.B. Tauris.

Markides, K. (1977). *The Rise and Fall of the Cyprus Republic*. New Haven: Yale University Press.

Marwick, A. (2005). The Cultural Revolution of the Long Sixties: Voices of Reaction, Protest, and Permeation. *The International History Review, 27*(4), 780–806.

Mathieu, L. (2007). L'espace des mouvements sociaux. *Politix, 77*(1), 131–151.

Mayes, S. (1981). *Makarios: A Biography*. London: Macmillan.

McMahon, R. J. (Ed.). (2013). *The Cold War in the Third World*. New York: Oxford University Press.

Meletopoulos, M., & Goranitis, G. (1998). Συνέντευξη με τον Νίκο Ψυρούκη [Interview with Nikos Psyroukis]. *Nea Koinoniologia, 26*, 6–17.

Nasser, G. (1955). *Philosophy of the Revolution*. Cairo: Dar al-Maaref.

Parker, J. C. (2013). Decolonization, the Cold War, and the Post-Columbian Era. In R. J. McMahon (Ed.), *The Cold War in the Third World* (pp. 124–138). New York: Oxford University Press.

Peckham, S. (2001). *National Histories, Natural States: Nationalism and the Politics of Place in Greece*. London and New York: I.B. Tauris.

Pitman, T., & Stafford, A. (2009). Introduction: Transatlanticism and Tricontinentalism. *Journal of Transatlantic Studies, 7*(3), 197–207.

Psyroukis, N. ["E. Nikitatos"]. (1965, January). Το Κυπριακό: Το Οξύτερο Εθνικό μας Πρόβλημα [The Cyprus Question: Our Most Acute National Problem]. *Bulletin of the Friends of the New Countries, 1*, 5–29.

Rappas, A. (2014). *Cyprus in the 1930s: British Colonial Rule and the Roots of the Cyprus Conflict*. London and New York: I.B. Tauris.

Rioufreyt, T. (2013). Les passeurs de la "troisième voie". Intermédiaires et médiateurs dans la circulation transnationale des idées. *Critique internationale, 59*(2), 33–46.

Sachsenmaier, D. (2006). Global History and Critiques of Western Perspectives. *Comparative Education, 42*(3), 451–470.

Sakellaropoulos, S. (2017). *Ο Κυπριακός Κοινωνικός Σχηματισμός (1191–2004). Από τη Συγκρότηση στη Διχοτόμηση*. Athens: Topos.

Saunier, P. Y. (2004). Circulations, connexions et espaces transnationaux. *Genèses, 4*(57), 110–126.

Serguera Riverí, J. (1997). *Caminos del Che: datos inéditos de su vida*. Mexico: Plaza y Valdés.

Sivignon, M. (2005). La Grèce devant l'adhésion de la Turquie. *Hérodote, 118*(3), 82–106.

Shepard, T. (2012). À l'heure des 'grands ensembles' et de la guerre d'Algérie. L''État-nation' en question. *Monde(s), 1*(1), 113–134.

Stergiou, A. (2007). Soviet Policy Toward Cyprus. *The Cyprus Review, 19*(2), 83–106.

Subrahmanyam, S. (1997). Connected Histories: Toward a Reconfiguration of Early Modern Eurasia. In V. B. Lieberman (Ed.), *Beyond Binary Histories: Re-imagining Eurasia to c. 1830* (pp. 289–315). Ann Arbor: University of Michigan Press.

Thomassen, B. (2012). Notes Towards an Anthropology of Political Revolutions. *Comparative Studies in Society and History, 54*(3), 679–706.

Traïni, C. (2009). *Emotions... Mobilisation!*. Paris: Presses de Sciences Po.

Voglis, P. (2011). 'The Junta Came to Power by the Force of Arms, and Will Only Go by Force of Arms'. Political Violence and the Voice of the Opposition to the Military Dictatorship in Greece, 1967–74. *Cultural and Social History, 8*(4), 551–568.

Werner, M., & Zimmermann, B. (2003). Penser l'histoire croisée: entre empirie et réflexivité. *Annales. Histoire, Sciences Sociales, 58*(1), 7–36.

Westad, O. A. (2007). *The Global Cold War*. Cambridge: Cambridge University Press.

Westad, O. A. (Ed.). (2000). *Reviewing the Cold War: Approaches, Interpretations, Theory*. London and Portland: Frank Cass.

INDEX

© The Editor(s) (if applicable) and The Author(s) 2018
T. Kyritsi and N. Christofis (eds.), *Cypriot Nationalisms in Context*,
https://doi.org/10.1007/978-3-319-97804-8

Printed by Printforce, the Netherlands